Must Read:
Rediscovering
American
Bestsellers

Must Read: Rediscovering American Bestsellers

From *Charlotte Temple* to *The Da Vinci Code*

Edited by

Sarah Churchwell and Thomas Ruys Smith

continuum

Continuum International Publishing Group
A Bloomsbury company

50 Bedford Square   80 Maiden Lane
London   New York
WC1B 3DP   NY 10038

www.continuumbooks.com

Part of the research for this book was supported by the British Academy,
which made a small research grant to Sarah Churchwell for research
into "What Americans Like: Popular Narratives and Mythography
in the American 21st Century".

A version of chapter 15 originally appeared in *The Journal of Popular
Culture* 44.5 (2011): 1085-1101. The editors are grateful to Wiley-Blackwell
for permission to republish.

ISBN: HB: 978-1-4411-5068-4
PB: 978-1-4411-6216-8

Library of Congress Cataloging-in-Publication Data
Must read: rediscovering American bestsellers from Charlotte Temple to
The Da Vinci code / edited by Sarah Churchwell and Thomas Ruys Smith.
p. cm.
Includes bibliographical references and index.
ISBN 978-1-4411-6216-8 (pbk. : alk. paper) – ISBN 978-1-4411-5068-4
(hardcover : alk. paper) 1. Best sellers–United States–History. 2. American
fiction–History and criticism. 3. Popular literature–United States–History and
criticism. 4. Books and reading–United States–History. I. Churchwell, Sarah
Bartlett, 1970– II. Smith, Thomas Ruys, 1979–
PS374.B45M87 2012
813.009–dc23

2012021064

Typeset by Deanta Global Publishing Services, Chennai, India
Printed and bound in the United States of America

CONTENTS

1

Introduction

Sarah Churchwell and Thomas Ruys Smith

Must read

Over the last three or four decades, academic and critical interest in popular culture has exploded, but this explosion has produced (as explosions will) scattershot, unpredictable, and disconnected flare-ups of concentration and flashes of enthusiasm. In terms of American popular literature, a few clusters of intellectual inquiry can be identified: first, surveys of the history of the bestseller, which broadly chart the kinds of books that have interested the American public over the centuries, without necessarily engaging closely with the texts in question. There has also been a constellation of influential books focused more narrowly on the popular writing (usually novels) of a particular historical era, with less breadth of chronological coverage but more depth of textual analysis. More recent are what we might call theoretical inquiries into the production and meanings of popular writing (again usually reduced to fiction), and its relation to cultural value, especially in the contemporary moment. There has also been an upsurge of interest in the category of "middlebrow fiction," which may or may not be bestselling. And finally, there have been essay collections focusing on individual "blockbuster" bestsellers, reading milestone publications more or less in isolation from other blockbusters.

Within all of this activity, however, there has never been a comprehensive critical monograph that offers close readings of individual bestsellers in the United States across its four centuries of existence, and no comprehensive survey of bestselling texts has been published in more than half a century. This collection seeks partially to redress that omission, by considering—and reconsidering—a variety of influential and under-examined popular works in American cultural history within a comparative and developmental context. *Must Read: Rediscovering the American Bestseller* examines a range of American bestsellers across the centuries, reading these books as both individual texts and in relationship with one another.

This seems a vital moment for such a consideration of the evolution of popular taste(s). As Jim Collins has recently argued in *Bring on the Books for Everybody: How Literary Culture Became Popular Culture*, we are living in a moment marked by a particularly "robust popular literary culture," driven by, among other forces, "the ubiquity and velocity of delivery systems in the form of superstores and online book sales" and "the increasing synergy among publishing, film, television and Internet industries." The contemporary literary scene is, therefore, Collins concludes, "a complicated mix of technology and taste, of culture and commerce."[1] And yet, as the essays in this collection amply demonstrate, such a formula might be applied to any period over the last 200 years. To understand what popular literature means, we still need to gain a more rounded understanding of what it has meant.

To begin, we need to ask what constitutes an "American bestseller" in the first place. We have chosen the term "bestseller" because it continues to be used by the publishing industry and the broad reading public, and is in fact more heuristically neutral than some of the more common scholarly rubrics, such as "popular" or "mass" "literature." Each of these words could be said to beg the questions it is supposedly answering: which books count as "literature" and which don't? What is the difference between the "popular" and the "mass"? All of these terms come accompanied by decades of complex scholarly argument about popular culture in an industrial-capitalist age. They also carry with them entrenched cultural biases, as scholars such as Lawrence W. Levine have influentially argued:

> We have found it difficult to study popular culture seriously, not primarily because of the restraints of our respective disciplines—which are indeed far more open to the uses of popular culture than we have allowed ourselves to believe—but because of the inhibitions inculcated in us by the society we inhabit. From an early age, we have been taught that whatever else this stuff is, it isn't art and it isn't serious and it doesn't lend itself to critical analysis.[2]

Levine's assertions are no less true today than they were nearly 20 years ago, and we take them to offer a useful description of the continued denigration not only of popular culture per se, but also still, within certain academic communities, of scholarly engagement with popular literature, a resistance deeply embedded in discourses of cultural value. For self-appointed guardians of "high culture," this resistance circles around the ominous charge of "dumbing down": the "easier" the text, the less academically respectable some scholars continue to deem it, as the modernist exaltation of the difficult proves a particularly tenacious and dogged academic value. Alternatively, those viewing themselves as hostile to "high culture" may still resist various forms of "low culture" as being politically suspect and artistically inauthentic, and contest the meanings of "mass culture" or "the popular." These ideological positions are as persistent as they are familiar, and they continue to shape and define a great deal of academic engagement with popular literature, as do other assumptions about literary value (including the perennial question, "But is it any good?").

Levine also points the way to a solution, however: borrowing from him we might suggest a distinction between works that are widely accessible and works that are widely accessed. By definition, such popular culture is mass culture, as it is mass-produced and mass-disseminated. But, as Levine points out, not all mass culture is popular, although it is the case in an industrial society that most popular culture (in the sense of being well-liked and widely accessed, rather than in the sense of being grassroots folk culture) is also mass culture. Thus, the term "bestseller," despite its many problems, removes us from this value-laden, inconsistent, arbitrary, and confusing terminology, with its vexations about whether the texts we are discussing "belong" to the masses, the people, the folk, the author, the academy, or hegemonic industrial-capitalism. The bestseller becomes a comparatively neutral (although still intransigently problematic) indicator of a text that is, historically speaking, prima facie "popular," in every sense of the word, in an industrial age of mass production.

But this is not to ignore the semantic and definitional vagaries surrounding the term "bestseller." Some of the impediments to establishing what does and does not constitute a bestseller are dealt with by Sarah Garland in our first chapter, "Missing Numbers: The Partial History of the Bestseller"; however, it should still be useful to offer some clarification here. In the main, this volume addresses texts whose sales to a high enough portion of the reading public place them self-evidently in the category of a bestseller, texts whose massive popularity made them contemporary cultural, and sometimes historical, phenomena. (The term "American" in truth proves no less problematic than "bestseller," but it will be used more forgivingly. We use "American" conventionally to refer to the readers and authors of the United States; it remains for other volumes to consider the popular literature and markets of the Hispanophone Americas and Canada.)

The essays in this collection thus enter into an ongoing debate about the value of popular literature—or, at least, the types of popular literature that have often been met with scholarly suspicion, if not outright dismissal. As Pierre Bourdieu put it, "Intellectuals and artists always look suspiciously—though not without a certain fascination—at dazzlingly successful works and authors, sometimes to the extent of seeing worldly failure as a guarantee of salvation in the hereafter."[3] New Critical antagonism toward popular fiction still seems to hold sway, and its roots run deep, back to books like Q.D. Leavis' still-influential 1932 analysis of bestsellers, *Fiction and the Reading Public*, which likened a taste for popular fiction to a "drug habit" that blocks "genuine feeling and responsible thinking by creating cheap mechanical responses and by throwing their weight on the side of social, national, and herd prejudices."[4]

A postwar bestseller boom helped to question this kind of cultural snobbery toward the tastes of the "herd," and precipitated the appearance of two groundbreaking studies of the American bestseller: Frank Luther Mott's *Golden Multitudes* (1947) and James D. Hart's *The Popular Book: A History of America's Literary Taste* (1950). As Mott argued, explicitly attacking the assumptions made by critics like Leavis: "Only the cynic and the heedless can disregard popular literature. Here the sociologist finds material for his inquiries into the mores, the social historian sees the signposts of the development of a people, and students of government observe popular movements at work."[5] Sociologists and historians aside, the work of pioneering critics like Mott and Hart failed to inspire systematic critical attention to bestselling texts. After the first generation of significant critical trailblazing into noncanonical American literature by such important scholars as Jane Tompkins, Lawrence Levine, Cathy N. Davidson, and Michael Davitt Bell, the history of American popular fiction continued to be addressed in a largely ad hoc way in individual journal articles and book chapters or as individual case studies in the battleground of the long (and increasingly Pyrrhic) "culture wars."

Indeed, what critical attention individual American bestsellers have received over the last few decades has almost exclusively focused on a handful of the greatest blockbusters, books whose historical impact was sufficient to overcome qualms about their literary significance or aesthetic quality: *The Last of the Mohicans*, *Uncle Tom's Cabin*, and *Gone with the Wind*, have all accrued significant scholarship, including monographs and edited collections devoted to understanding their place in American literary history. This volume seeks, by contrast, to return more critically neglected but historically popular texts to the frame. Such decisions are necessarily relative: *Charlotte Temple* and *Peyton Place*, for example, have by no means been critically ignored, but neither do they have volumes of scholarship devoted to them in the manner of *The Last of the Mohicans* or *Gone with the Wind*, nor is their significance uncontested. By the same token, we have also excluded from consideration those "classic" books whose perennial global popularity demonstrably correlates with their elevated position in the orthodox literary canon, such as *Huckleberry Finn* or *The Great Gatsby*.

Our effort, therefore, has been to maintain historical coverage of representative texts, but not to fall back on simply focusing yet again on the same three or four texts that so often seem to stand in synecdochally for a more or less monolithic view of "the American bestseller" or "popular fiction" as a fixed and legible category. In short, our purpose is to consider only those texts that have attracted millions of readers—and yet have still, in the main, eluded significant academic attention, the critically "neglected" bestseller. It remains important to note that all of this is certainly not to diminish the important critical precedents for the type of engagements on display in these essays. Indeed, an ars poetica for this volume might be found in Jane Tompkins' 1986 assertion that "it is morally and politically objectionable, and intellectually obtuse, to have contempt for literary works that appeal to millions of people simply *because* they are popular."[6] That popularity is our starting point.

A brief history of reading bestsellers in America

A survey of America's reading habits over the last 400 years reveals, against a backdrop of flux and churn in the production and consumption of books, a remarkable sense of continuity in the ways in which bestselling texts have functioned in American life. At almost all points, bestsellers have served as a perennial battleground in the theater of war that is popular culture, driving discussions about literary value and the landscape of the literary marketplace, and animating moral panics throughout the ages. Moreover, they have served as a site of profound tension, both between authors whose works sell and those who do not, and between consumers and arbiters of taste—what historian Jill Lepore has described as the "democracy of readers . . . against an aristocracy of critics."[7] Exactly what the term "bestseller" signifies might have changed—the term wasn't even coined until 1889, by the *Kansas Times & Star,* while reliable accounts of sales remain fugitive well into the twentieth century—but the values attached to and imposed on the idea of popular reading habits have remained strikingly similar.[8]

From the start, Americans have been, relatively speaking, a nation of readers. E. Jennifer Monagahan's recent summary of the body of research into literacy rates in the colonies reveals that "for the literacy of white men, the colonial period is a dazzling success story. Despite a slump after the founding generation, by the time of the American Revolution, the literacy of white men in New England had reached nearly universal levels, with that of the other colonies close behind. The signature literacy of white women, in contrast, lagged behind that of men throughout the entire colonial period even while it, too, gradually improved."[9] Of course, the driving force behind such literacy rates was the centrality of the Bible—that definitive bestseller—in colonial life. They were a product, in Harvey Graff's words, of "the Puritan stress on the importance of individual access to the Book and the Word . . . Literacy was a universal prerequisite to spiritual preparation."[10]

Yet, even in the colonies, a rich body of popular literature—much of it secular—circulated widely alongside more spiritually edifying fare. What were all of those early American readers reading? Victor Neuberg has traced the contours of what constituted popular reading in colonial America: "almanacs, broadsides, newspapers, medical handbooks, letter writers, and practical manuals of all kinds . . . schoolbooks, devotional works, and chapbooks."[11] Though such ephemeral texts have largely disappeared, both physically and from discussions of American popular literature, the volume of trade associated with them could be quite remarkable. In the 1660s, for example, "as many as four hundred thousand almanacs were sold in a year"—to a national population of approximately 100,000, in an era before universal literacy.[12] And in point of fact, such texts might truly be considered the first home-grown American bestsellers throughout the seventeenth and eighteenth centuries. As Leon Jackson has highlighted, for example, Noah Webster's *American Spelling Book*, "the best-selling textbook of early national and antebellum America," sold "in excess of ten million copies" between 1783 and 1829, providing Webster with a steady income while he worked on his dictionary.[13] Such nonfiction bestsellers have retained a significant prominence in the American literary marketplace.

Chapbooks, arguably the most literary texts circulating in colonial America, and the most obvious precursor of the majority of the bestsellers that are featured in this volume, were a different story. The fact that chapbooks were "a major element of popular literature" in colonial America, as they were in Britain, might alter our sense of the young New World as a place entirely dominated by Puritan antiliterary prejudice, and destitute of literary amusement.[14] As Neuberg describes, chapbooks, cheaply produced and distributed, offered readers a vibrant cornucopia of delights: "songs, riddles, jokes, anecdotes of pirates and highwaymen . . . tales of giants, monsters, and fairies, many of them residue of an oral peasant culture rooted in a long-distant past . . . abridged versions of the romances of knights and maidens . . . versions of *Robinson Crusoe* and *Moll Flanders*."[15] Though the fugitive nature of these texts makes it difficult to reconstruct the impact of individual titles in the literary marketplace, Neuberg highlights the fact that, at his death in 1664, publisher Charles Tias "left ninety thousand chapbooks in stock," and notes that a chapbook like *The Famous History of Whittington and His Cat* went through "no fewer than nineteen editions . . . published in America between 1770 and 1818."[16]

However, as the titles and subject matter of these chapbooks suggest, by far the majority of them were imported to the colonies from England, at least until the Revolution. Here, we can see the first glimpses of what Cathy N. Davidson has summarized as "the omnipresence of European fiction" in the American literary marketplace, and its apparently negative implications for the development of a national literature—and, indeed, native bestsellers.[17] But—as it is throughout American cultural history—that transatlantic relationship was an ambiguous one. On the one hand, it was certainly true, as Neuberg writes, that the "fairly restricted market in the colonies for literary products" meant that the "considerable risk" of publishing made it "much easier, and more profitable to the trade in both countries, to import books from England."[18] As such, this was a story that became increasingly important for British booksellers. According to James Raven's calculations, by 1770, "more books were exported annually from England to the American colonies than to Europe and the rest of the world combined."[19] The "Americanness" of American bestsellers is by no means fixed or transparent.

Nevertheless, some noteworthy American texts did achieve national and international prominence in the Colonial Era. The significance of a text like Mary Rowlandson's *Captivity & Restoration* (1682) lies not just in its status as a bestseller among American readers, but in its popular success back in the Old World. As Richard Slotkin has described, Rowlandson's text "found immediate favour in both America and Europe" and "went through numerous American and English editions during the course of the seventeenth and eighteenth centuries."[20] Indeed, so influential and far-reaching was the popularity of this American bestseller that Nancy Armstrong and Leonard Tennenhouse are willing to contend "that Rowlandson's style of narration . . . provided the basis for the English novel" when it began to take shape early in the eighteenth century.[21]

Of course, it was precisely this literary development that would bring about profound changes in the reading habits of Americans—and, indeed, the conception of the bestseller more widely. Perhaps unsurprisingly, the majority of "best sellers" across America's history has been novels; it is clear that there is an intimate relationship between the literary dominance of the novel and the very concept of the bestseller. Both were the products of cultural, social, and industrial changes that transformed the West over the course of the last three centuries, including rising literacy rates, drives toward universal education, processes of industrial mass production and dissemination, the rise of the middle class, and the gradual inclusion of previously subaltern citizens, including women and African Americans, into the ranks of readers and authors.

In his dissection of the rise of the novel in Britain, William Warner notes that "by the 1720s, novels comprised one of the most high-profile, fashionable, and dynamic segments of the market."[22] By the middle of the eighteenth century, the British conversation about novels had largely shifted from an assessment of the medium shaped by "the old Puritan condemnation of stories of lies" to a debate about "what kind of novel should be read, and what kind should be written."[23] And in 1785, Clara Reeve could look back to 1750 and marvel at the way that novels "did but now begin to increase upon us . . . ten years more multiplied them tenfold." Though finding many novels worthy of praise, Reeve also had reasons to lament that proliferation of popular literature, voicing a suspicion of such texts that would persist (and, indeed, still persists): "Every work of merit produced a swarm of imitators, till they became a public evil, and the institution of the Circulating libraries, conveyed them in the cheapest manner to every bodies hand . . . young people are allowed to subscribe to them, and to read indiscriminately all they contain; and thus both food and poison are conveyed to the young mind together."[24]

While the transformation of reading habits took slightly longer to foment in America, when they did, driven by similar social forces like the circulating library, the effects were equally profound. The extraordinary literary revolution that took place in America alongside the other revolutions of the late eighteenth century was vividly highlighted by Royall Tyler in the Preface to *The Algerine Captive*, published in 1797 (and itself, if not quite a bestseller, then at least popular enough to be serialized and reprinted in Britain):

> One of the first observations the author of the following sheets made upon his return to his native country, after an absence of seven years, was the extreme avidity with which books of mere amusement were purchased and perused by all ranks of his countrymen . . . In our inland towns of consequence, social libraries had been instituted, composed of books designed to amuse rather than to instruct; and country booksellers, fostering the new-born taste of the people, had filled the whole land with modern travels, and novels almost as incredible.[25]

Support for Tyler's observations can be found in James Raven's conclusion that the 1790s were marked by a "great increase in American editions of British novels" and a significant reduction in the lag between British and American editions.[26] This was, in part, a result of the post-Revolution refashioning of copyright law that did away with international restrictions on intellectual property and opened the field for American publishers to reprint British texts at will. Though this state of affairs is often seen as one of the key impediments to the growth of American literature, it also ensured the proliferation of American readers. As William St Clair has concluded, "In America, all recent British writing came quickly and it came cheap . . . Americans of the romantic period had easier access to the literature being written in Great Britain than most of their contemporaries across the ocean."[27] Alongside such developments in copyright and the profession of authorship, the significance of a single bestseller should not be underestimated. Susanna Rowson's profoundly transatlantic *Charlotte Temple*—published in Britain in 1791, reprinted in Philadelphia by Mathew Carey in 1794, written by a woman born in England who moved to America at 15—was such a signal success in the literary marketplace that, as Davidson describes, it was quite simply "a novel that, more than any other, signalled a new era in the history of the book in America."[28]

While Royall Tyler, undoubtedly speaking for many, broadly welcomed these changes in American literary culture—what he saw as an exchange of "sober stories and practical pieties" for "the haunted houses and hobgoblins of Mrs. Ratcliffe"—his optimism did not come without certain telling, and common, caveats. He lamented the fact that "while so many books are vended, they are not of our own manufacture." Second, echoing Reeve while adding a nationalist twist to her concerns, he worried that the American reader is "insensibly taught to admire the levity, and often the vices, of the parent country. While the fancy is enchanted, the heart is corrupted."[29] By no coincidence, such misgivings about the novel were particularly directed at women, and especially at young women. Over the course of the next century, an entire critical literature of sermons, conduct books, and jeremiads appeared on both sides of the Atlantic, warning against the "seductive" dangers of the novel for susceptible "young ladies," including the novel's promotion of "morbid appetites," "sickly sensibility," "erroneous views of life," "evil passions," time-wasting, and the loss of piety and self-control. By 1841, American Harvey Newcomb was instructing young women in his guides to "good Christian character": "If you wish to become weak-headed, nervous, and good for nothing, read novels."[30] As America entered a new era of bestsellers, these fears and misgivings would linger.

A useful guide to what constituted an American bestseller in the Early Republic—that crucible period for the development and popularization of American literature—can be gleaned from Earl Bradsher's 1912 biography of publisher Mathew Carey. As Tyler's 1797 survey of the literary scene suggested, Bradsher confirms "that Mrs. Radcliffe and her school were very popular in America"—especially *Mysteries of Udolpho* (1794). But according to Bradsher, it was certain bestsellers, now forgotten, that were of particular note: Jane Porter's *The Scottish Chiefs* (1810), for example, was subject to an "immense and enduring vogue." As for what Bradsher "should be inclined to regard as the most popular British novel in America before Scott," that accolade he awarded to Regina Maria Roche's *The Children of the Abbey* (1796).[31]

Then, there was Walter Scott himself. Looking back on the genesis of Scott's extraordinary popularity in 1833, a year after his death, the *North American Review* reminisced about the epochal significance of the publication of his first novel in 1814: "When Waverley appeared, men beheld it with as much perplexity, as the out-break of a revolution; the more prudent held their peace, and waited to see what might come of it; the critics were in sad straits, having nothing wherewithal to measure it ... but the public, without asking their opinion, gave decisive judgment in its favor"—until "the tide of favor" had "swelled ... to a torrent."[32] The desire for Scott's books among American readers—like their counterparts in the Old World—was undeniably profound. In St Clair's judgment, "In histories of American reading, or in any attempt to assess how far cultural formation and mentalities were influenced by reading, he must be regarded as one of the most influential authors."[33] In 1818, an American correspondent confirmed to Maria Edgeworth, herself a sometime bestseller in the United States, that Scott's novels "have excited as much enthusiasm in America as in Europe," noting particularly, "Boats are now actually on the lookout for 'Rob Roy,' all here are so impatient to get the first sight of it."[34] Moreover, the fierce rivalry that developed between publishers to bring the first pirated edition of the new Scott to the American market had a clear effect on the nation's book buyers. As Frank Luther Mott concluded, "competition had an exciting effect on the public, and it made immediate best sellers possible." It was a business model that would last "until well past the midcentury mark," and the same kind of popular excitement would soon surround the arrival of new works by authors like Dickens and Bulwer.[35] As Bradsher put it, "From Waverley in 1814, to *The Mystery of Edwin Drood*, 1870, the year that did not produce at least one highly popular British novel was a barren period."[36]

It is an established irony that as much as Scott's popularity helped to foster a new climate for bestsellers in America, the cheap, pirated editions of his work made it more difficult for American authors to establish their own foothold in the literary marketplace. But here, too, there are transatlantic nuances to consider. Scott had a profound effect on the generation of bestselling American novelists who emerged in his wake, and not just as influence and example, but in concrete terms. Even a brief perusal of Scott's novels demonstrates his abiding fascination with the United States and his openness to American writers. Particularly telling is his engagement with the works of Washington Irving. Scott developed a fondness for Irving's writing after reading his *History of New York* (1809)—what Mott describes as "a great success," though "not perhaps an immediate best seller."[37] Accordingly, in 1820, when the British publication of Irving's *Sketch Book* was threatened by the bankruptcy of Irving's publisher, he turned to Scott for help. Scott's "favourable representation" persuaded John Murray to publish the *Sketch Book*, and the fate of a bona fide, seminal American bestseller, on both sides of the Atlantic, was secured.[38]

Scott had an equally influential, if less amiable, relationship with James Fenimore Cooper, who modeled himself on Scott when publishing *Precaution*, his first novel (a comedy of manners written in frank of imitation of Jane Austen) in 1820. Cooper wrote to his publisher Andrew Goodrich that he wanted his novel to emulate "the style of the Philadelphia edition of *Ivanhoe*"—Scott's latest, just published.[39] As Wayne Franklin describes, Cooper also adviced Goodrich that he "should avoid any suggestion that *Precaution* was an '*original*' American work," and tacitly foster the sense that he was "republishing a British work" in order to appeal "to the Anglophile tendencies of the native marketplace."[40] While such promotional tactics failed to establish *Precaution* itself as a bestseller, it did establish Cooper's canny presence in the literary marketplace and pave the way for the bestselling texts that he would soon produce, including *The Last of the Mohicans* (1826).

Many British writers were no less interested in American readers than they were in American writers. Lord Byron wrote excitedly in 1813 at the prospect of being "redde on the banks of the Ohio!," "To be popular in a rising and far country has a kind of *posthumous feel*."[41] And the vogue for American texts was hardly restricted to the literary elite. By 1825, Mary Tyler, Royall Tyler's wife, could marvel at the "rage . . . for American literature," on both sides of the Atlantic.[42] Clarence Gohdes has concluded that authors like Irving and Cooper "were as well known during the eighteen twenties and thirties as most of their British contemporaries," and that, in turn, their popularity "was a mere trickle to that which was to come."[43] With no little irony, it was once again the vicissitudes of international copyright law that helped to ensure American authors' bestseller status in the Old World. As St Clair highlights, after the Copyright Act of 1842, "American books and magazine were among the few sources of texts which could be printed to be sold cheaply in Britain . . . shops which sprang up near the new railway stations, it was noticed, were filled with offshore piracies of American books"—to the point that some commentators "feared that their own national identity was being undermined."[44] Copyright would continue to be associated with a proprietary sense of national identity for another century and more.

The extraordinary growth in the nineteenth century domestic consumption of American novels can be traced through some telling statistics. As Richard Teichgraeber outlines, "During the 1820s 128 American novels were published, almost forty more than had been published in the previous 50 years, and five times the number published during the previous decade—and yet more than double that number appeared in the 1830s; and the total more than doubles again in the 1840s, to nearly eight hundred."[45] The book boom of the 1850s marked a new era in the history of the American bestseller—a phenomenon clearly visible to contemporary commentators. Addressing the Association of New York Publishers in 1855, George Putnam declaimed to his colleagues, "20 years ago who *imagined* editions of 100,000 or 75,000, or 30,000, or even the now common number of 10,000?"[46] In December 1857, when a financial panic appeared poised to put an end to the publishing boom, George William Curtis could look back wistfully at the moment when "every book of every publisher was in the twenty-sixth thousand, and the unparalleled demand was increasing at an unprecedented rate; when presses were working night and day; when, owing to the extraordinary demand, the issue of the first edition must be postponed from Saturday to Thursday; when not more than fifty thousand copies could be furnished in three days; when the public must have patience, and would finally be supplied."[47]

On its own, the cultural phenomenon of *Uncle Tom's Cabin* (1852)—"for an immense number of people," Henry James recollected, "much less a book than a state of vision, of feeling and of consciousness"—would guarantee the era a unique place in the genealogy of bestselling American texts.[48] But for all that, there are still uncertainties about the exact topography of the bestselling landscape at this crucible moment. As Ronald Zboray has noted, the "easy equation of technological innovation in printing"— steam-driven presses, stereotyping and electrotyping, the changes in distribution brought on by the transport revolution—"and the dramatic growth of the antebellum reading public" is too pat.[49]

After all, throughout the antebellum years, most books, "even most paperbacks," and certainly most American books, "remained too expensive for working-class people."[50] The antebellum bestseller explosion was driven by urban, middle-class readers; the era of mass market book consumption had not yet arrived in full force.

Similarly in need of a corrective is the abiding sense of binary divisions in the antebellum literary marketplace—between, particularly, men and women, and high culture and low culture. Nathaniel Hawthorne's now proverbial dismissal of the "d—d mob of scribbling women" that he perceived to have taken over "the public taste" erected an apparent division between the "trash" produced by popular female writers and the literature of neglected male writers.[51] But as Lucy Freibert and Barbara White have highlighted, while female authors might have written extraordinarily popular bestsellers, in overall terms, "men outnumbered women on the best-seller list three to one."[52] And, as writers like Lawrence Levine and David Reynolds have argued, the idea of a distinct split between American Renaissance figures like Nathaniel Hawthorne and popular literary culture is a fallacious one. In the words of Levine, "in the nineteenth century, especially in the first half, Americans . . . shared a public culture less hierarchically organised, less fragmented into relatively rigid adjectival boxes than their descendants were to experience a century later."[53] Indeed, Hawthorne's correspondence suggests a familiarity with the work of plenty of "scribbling women"—writers like Grace Greenwood and Julia Ward Howe, not to mention a pointed admiration for a real bestseller like Fanny Fern.[54] Conversely, Michael Davitt Bell also highlights the fact that "Hawthorne . . . published much of his early work in giftbooks and ladies' magazines." Indeed throughout his career, Hawthorne's readers would have been "the same people (or a subset of the same people)" who read bestselling authors like Susan Warner or Maria Cummins.[55]

At least one truism about popular writing in the 1850s remains eminently clear: in that decade, the American bestseller carved out an unassailable place for itself in the literary marketplace. In 1896, the *London Illustrated News* would declare:

> Perhaps the most entirely popular books in prose and poetry which have been read by the masses of the English people during the last fifty years have come to us from America – the poems

of Longfellow and "Uncle Tom's Cabin" . . . Certain it is that Longfellow's sales in this country have far exceeded those of any of our own poets.[56]

By the end of the nineteenth century, though, the shifting literary landscape meant that the tensions revealed in Hawthorne's outburst against popular women writers became sharpened. In the antebellum years, as Nina Baym outlines, "Reviewers of the time assumed that without the seal of popular approval a novel could not be put forward as a great work of art . . . though popularity was by no means in itself the test of artistic merit, one could never assume the opposite: that popularity implied poor art."[57] In the late nineteenth century, the rise of realism and the simultaneous arrival of what James described in 1898 as "literature for the billion" meant that such assumptions would be increasingly overturned.[58] As the *Hour* put it in 1883, "The increase in the number of books published in the United States . . . is the most significant fact in the history of printed literature."[59] The era was marked by what Nancy Bentley has described as a new "explosion in print and in book buying."[60] Supported again by technological change—linotype, cheap paper— print culture finally became "not only voluminous but remarkably cheap," and debate once again raged over its significance.[61] Unlike the expansion of books and readers in the antebellum era, the fin de siècle seems to have been marked out by a fracturing of reading communities. As Bentley notes, the burgeoning audiences for popular writing constituted, on some levels, a "readership for whom elite authors were largely outsiders."[62]

An examination of what constituted popular reading at the end of the nineteenth century both supports and troubles the sense that this was a moment when distinctions between high and low literary culture became more meaningful. While Mark Twain and Stephen Crane produced books that sold well, the definitive popular bestseller of the era was Lew Wallace's religious epic *Ben-Hur* (1880), which, at the time of Mott's calculations, ranked "among the top half-dozen best sellers by American authors."[63] But even that picture of popular reading can be further destabilized by emerging archives and newly available data. "What Middletown Read" is an online database built from the lending records of the Muncie, Indiana Public Library from 1891 to 1902.[64] This archive of every book borrowed by every lender in a representative Midwestern town reveals a surprisingly unfamiliar literary landscape. Horatio Alger's books—the most popular author among the Muncie library patrons—were borrowed 9320 times across the decade. The works of other forgotten series authors like Charles Fosdick, Martha Finley, and William T. Adams dominate the list of most borrowed authors, and each run into the thousands. As for the most borrowed book, that accolade went to Louisa May Alcott's *Under the Lilacs*, first published in 1878. However, the records of individual patrons also demonstrate the ways in which such bald statistics always blur the distinct stories of individual readers. We can see, for example, that the Arthur Case who borrowed *Under the Lilacs* on May 23rd 1901 also borrowed George Eliot's *Adam Bede* and William Cullen Bryant's translation of the *Iliad*—not to mention Howell's *The Minister's Charge*. To misquote Raymond Williams, there are in fact no mass readers; there are only ways of seeing people as mass readers.

Nonetheless, now-familiar literary hierarchies became only more culturally fixed in the early years of the twentieth century. As Lisa Botshon and Meredith Goldsmith have illuminated, that story was complicated in the 1920s by the rise of a further stratification driven by the popular "middlebrow fiction that was, in fact, consumed by a majority of readers"—a field dominated by critically neglected "women writers of diverse class, ethnic and racial backgrounds" like Edna Ferber, Anita Loos, and Edith Hull.[65] To that category, one might also add a self-help book like Emily Post's *Etiquette* (1922) which has remained a persistent bestseller ever since and also helped to define the era for millions of readers. F. Scott Fitzgerald's rationale for the relative commercial failure of *The Great Gatsby* in 1925— "the book contains no important woman character and women controll [*sic*] the fiction market at present"—has become almost as emblematic of modernism's ambivalent relationship to the feminized popular as Hawthorne's antebellum complaints.[66] But perhaps less familiar is the knowledge that canonical literary figures like Ernest Hemingway and John Steinbeck, and indeed Fitzgerald himself, "reached huge audiences"—or tried to reach them—through mass market book-selling innovations like the Book-of-the-Month Club. As James West reveals, even Eugene O' Neill "sold some 97,315 copies" of his collection *Nine Plays* through such channels.[67]

As the twentieth century progressed, popular literature found itself challenged—and also sustained—by new forms of mass culture, especially cinema and television. Evan Brier notes that at mid-century, "mass culture exerted itself powerfully on American novels, shifting the cultural and economic space they occupied as surely as television did to movies, magazines and newspapers."[68] At the same moment, elite attacks on mass culture, popular literature included, became more barbed. Dwight Macdonald's *Against the American Grain: Essays on the Effects of Mass Culture* (1962), for example, could note of the "reading matter" of the Book-of-the-Month Club, for example, "the best that can be said is that it could be worse."[69] But there is some irony, as Brier highlights, to the fact that, while cultural commentators expressed "alarm over the fate of both reading in general and high literature in particular . . ., more books than ever before were produced and sold to a growing population of educated consumers."[70] Or as Peter Swirski has highlighted, "More than half of all the books ever published came out after the first hydrogen bomb; more than half of all wordsmiths who ever put pen to paper did so after the birth of TV . . . The number of new titles released each year in the United States more than quadrupled between 1950 and 1991."[71] Bestselling books negotiated their way through this marketplace as they had done at least since the early nineteenth century, working in new productive synergy with the other cultural forms that also threatened their extinction.

The novel that most bears out this observation remains the most famous blockbuster of the twentieth century. Before the early twenty-first century was marked by such epoch-defining books as J. K. Rowling's Harry Potter books and Dan Brown's global bestseller *The Da Vinci Code,* it was Margaret Mitchell's *Gone with the Wind*—and the symbiotic relationship between the 1936 book and the 1939 film—that set records which still stand today. The number one bestseller of 1936 and 1937, selling a million copies in the first six months of publication alone, *Gone with the Wind* would go on to sell more copies than any other novel in the history of the United States to date. Within a year it had sold almost 2 million copies and won the Pulitzer Prize for fiction; but as Ellen Firsching Brown and John Wiley Jr. have shown, it was also "developed, marketed and groomed for success." And once again, transformations in copyright law were inextricable from the story of the book's popularity: "Mitchell changed the course of international copyright law through her struggle to

maintain control over the *GWTW* literary rights, . . . fend[ing] off
unauthorized editions of her book around the globe, [and] calling
attention to the inadequacy of copyright protection for American
writers."[72] The novel's popularity was reinforced by the commercial
and critical triumph that was David O. Selznick's 1939 Hollywood
adaptation. The film version catapulted *Gone with the Wind* back
to the top of the bestseller list, where it vied at the end of the decade
for preeminence against the other great parable of Depression-era
America, *The Grapes of Wrath*—another book whose place at the
top of the US bestseller list in 1939–40 owed much to its Hollywood
adaptation that same year. *Gone with the Wind* was just as
successful internationally as it was domestically; by December 1936,
it had reached the top of the British bestseller list, and eventually
Mitchell would declare that "everybody except the Chinese and the
Albanians" were trying to purchase rights to publish the novel.[73] In
its first 50 years, *Gone with the Wind* would go on to sell 25 million
copies in 27 languages, and returned to the bestseller lists in 1986
(thanks to a special anniversary edition), and again in 1991, when
its authorized sequel, *Scarlett*, finally appeared—and itself shot to
the top of the bestseller list. Film and TV adaptations, VHS and
then DVD collectors' editions, marketing and publicity campaigns,
the machinery of media and reception, reprints, reissues, sequels
both "authorized" and "unauthorized," copyright, translation,
and international rights: all of these processes and machineries are
cranking behind the scenes to elevate "blockbusters" like *Gone
with the Wind* (or, indeed, the Harry Potter books) above the status
of mere "bestseller" and into the ranks of cultural phenomena.

As James West explained back in 1988, even before the revolutions
of e-publishing were on the horizon, throughout the history of
book-making and book-selling "the pressure of technology, exerted
through new and better mass-production methods, has periodically
forced manufacturers to address larger markets . . . and each time
an old guard has mounted a vigorous campaign to defeat, or at
least weaken, the pressure of the mass market."[74] Over the last
century and a half, those books that have become bestsellers have
been propelled there by a publishing industry whose practices
have, in many ways, altered little since the nineteenth century.
In the last decades of the twentieth century, the book superstore,
an institution represented most iconically by the now bankrupt
Borders chain, rose to prominence against a chorus of complaints,

not least from independent booksellers. In Laura Miller's words, in terms of dismissal not dissimilar to those leveled at the bestsellers on their shelves, "detractors . . . scoffed that the superstores were better at promoting coffee drinking than an interest in ideas and the intellect."[75]

As the experience of Borders attests, those institutions are themselves in the process of falling beneath the market pressures brought on by the unstoppable rise of internet booksellers (Amazon.com most notably), the dominance of the Kindle and its cognate devices, and the extraordinary availability of out-of-copyright works through distributors like, but not limited to, Google Books. But even in this apparently democratized age of accessibility where, in Jim Collins' terms, book reading has (again?) become "an exuberantly social activity, whether it be in the form of actual books clubs, television book clubs, Internet chat rooms," and the divisions between hierarchies of culture have apparently been deconstructed beyond repair, some of the old anxieties about the meaning of bestselling texts stubbornly abide.[76] Jonathan Franzen's famous discomfort with being included in Oprah Winfrey's book club, or Pulitzer Prize winner Jennifer Egan's dismissal of contemporary bestsellers like Sophie Kinsella's *The Princess Diaries* (2000) as "derivative, banal stuff," suggest that old debates about the degradation of literary popularity are very much alive and kicking, even as their controversy highlights shifting cultural norms.[77] Whatever form the bestseller takes in the future, however it is produced, marketed, distributed, and consumed, and whatever anxieties continue to coalesce around it and its readers, there seems little doubt that there will always be some books that we all simply must read.

Rediscovering the bestseller

From this long history of popular reading, then, we have sought to identify a range of texts that might have a claim to warrant continued, or renewed, critical attention. Some of our chapters feature definitive bestselling texts; others seek to trouble our understanding of what a bestseller looks like; but, ranging over times and contexts, all are joined in the attempt to turn again to some of the books that have been the most read, but not the most studied.

As the above suggests, it would clearly be quixotic, not to mention futile, to attempt to be exhaustive in this volume's coverage. A truly comprehensive account of American bestsellers through the ages, as we have tried to show, would need to take into account an extraordinary array of texts, starting with the Bible and working through broadsides, chapbooks, sermons, religious and political treatises, philosophy, Shakespeare, British novelists including Richardson, Defoe, Scott, and Dickens, yellow-backs, dime novels, pulp fiction, genre fiction, cookbooks, advice manuals, children's books, and the so-called mass market paperbacks whose sales are anecdotally colossal in aggregate but statistically elusive (for reasons addressed by Sarah Garland in our first essay; an example might be L. Ron Hubbard's *Dianetics*). The texts under consideration in this volume, therefore, have all been selected as representative books that suggest larger stories about the complex and contested meanings of the bestseller. Taken as a whole, they present a different picture of the development of American literature from that found in the orthodox canon.

Though Susanna Rowson's *Charlotte Temple* (1794) begins the collection, it is dominated by bestsellers that were written, published, distributed, and read in an industrial age, from an antebellum sensation like Timothy Shay Arthur's *Ten Nights in a Bar-Room* (1854), through an early twentieth-century smash like E. M. Hull's *The Sheik* (1919), up to popular twenty-first-century blockbusters like Dan Brown's *The Da Vinci Code*, Khaled Hosseini's *The Kite Runner* (2003), and the romances of Nicholas Sparks. That said, to limit the scope of this volume entirely to novels would be reductive and misrepresentative. As such, in a few significant and emblematic instances, chapters are dedicated to texts that challenge definitions of what constitutes a bestseller. These texts also aid in demarcating some of the boundaries of the task at hand—influential instruction manuals like Emily Post's *Etiquette* (1922), for example, or Edward Everett Hale's perennially popular short story, "The Man Without A Country," (1863) test prevailing assumptions about the market dominance of long narrative fiction in Anglo-American culture.

The approaches taken by the contributors to this volume vary considerably, though most are based around historicized readings of these neglected texts within their cultural contexts, and in relation to the wider critical issues surrounding bestsellers. Framed against the background of the marketplace, authors and readers engage in the complex conversations surrounding bestselling books. These conversations return persistently to questions of the mechanisms of authorship (celebrity, branding, publicity, reputation); of publishing (editing, marketing, advertising, distributing); of reading (habits of reading, dissemination, adaptation, longevity); and of cultural value (the politics of high and low, canonicity, pleasure, escapism).

Each chapter explores a different aspect of the bestseller puzzle, but mosaic patterns also emerge from these small building blocks of national identity and an emergent American modernity. Consistent themes appear, including the evolution of normative identities; religion; sentimentality; violence; erotics; nation-building; cosmopolitanism; consumer capitalism; landscapes; dreams and fantasies; and nightmares and prohibitions, to name just some of the shared preoccupations of these immensely popular books. In short, these texts and their audiences contain multitudes.

The history of American bestsellers cannot properly begin without a careful consideration, however definitionally incomplete, of the problematics of "bestseller" as a heuristic term. Sarah Garland's "Missing Numbers: The Partial History of the Bestseller" traces some of the problems in attempting to use the term "bestseller" as an objective, quantifiable way of calibrating the popularity or commercial success of individual books. Garland begins with the relativity, partiality, and contingency of the term "bestseller" itself, before considering some of the difficulties in measuring, evaluating, and identifying bestsellers (and all this before one even begins the task of interrogating or establishing the "literary" or aesthetic value of a text). Reminding us that "it's not just fiction which takes on the task of telling us how to live," Garland argues that "the history of American 'bestsellers' as told by the bestsellers lists is not so much a history of stock-taking and accounting as a history of discourse— of comment, interpretation and opinion . . . the lists themselves represent multiple tastes, multiple purchases, overlapping and diverging American patterns of consumption." Bestseller lists always come to us "already read," as Garland points out: "they represent books that have been consumed and statistics that come to us interpreted."

If the meaning of American bestsellers is contested, so is the proper starting point of any historical enquiry or genealogy. In order to ascertain when America begins reading bestsellers, we need to ascertain when America begins. Because of the elasticity of the meanings of "America" across its history—pre-Colombian settlements and populations; the European colonies of the sixteenth and seventeenth centuries; the original thirteen colonies of the revolutionary United States; the ever-expanding boundaries of the United States through the nineteenth and into the twentieth century; late twentieth and early twenty-first century broadening of the concept of Americas beyond the territory, history, or peoples of the United States, to a more inclusively conceived Atlantic culture— what makes the first American bestseller American is as difficult to establish as what makes it a bestseller.

If the story of American bestsellers might be said, in one sense, properly to begin with the story of America, then *Charlotte Temple* becomes a persuasive place to open that story. Susanna Rowson's 1794 *Charlotte: A Tale of Truth* was not just a bestselling book about America that thrilled audiences on both sides of the Atlantic in the early years of the American republic; it was also a story that recognizably dramatized the family romance of the American Revolution itself, as Cathy N. Davidson has influentially argued.[78] A novel defined by rebellion and loyalism, and by anxieties about origins, begins our genealogy: *Charlotte Temple* is one of the first bestsellers to contest and establish the meanings of America itself in relation to the Mother Country it has just abandoned. Gideon Mailer's "The History of *Charlotte Temple* as an American Bestseller" returns "Rowson's debt to evangelical revivalism" to our understanding of *Charlotte Temple*, arguing that "its ultimately forgiving message" helped ensure its popularity: "its appeal to private and familial social codes assumed a universal aesthetic sensibility, whose moral aspect could also transcend social divisions."

Sixty years later, one of the most popular writers in America was another woman who wrote tales of sensation and sensibility, a woman whose career spanned four decades across the middle of the nineteenth century, including the famous "book boom" of the antebellum years. Rachel Ihara points out that what scholarly attention Mrs E. D. E. N. Southworth has received has focused almost exclusively on one novel, *The Hidden Hand*, and suggests instead that Southworth was "defined less by her ability to produce a major best-selling novel than by her capacity to maintain a large and loyal audience" across nearly half a century, by means of a strategic deployment of the mechanisms of periodical publication. Ihara argues that Mrs Southworth's success was partly dependent upon an emergent authorial identity that we would now call a "brand." Although Southworth has been dismissed as a careless or lazy writer, Ihara suggests that the demands of serial fiction took precedence over concerns for unity of characterization or originality of plot: "tolerance for fragmentation, multiplicity, and contradiction . . . were at the heart of Southworth's aesthetic." Hsuan L. Hsu similarly suggests that form is central to understanding Edward Everett Hale's 1863 "The Man Without A Country," as that form adapted and evolved over Hale's career. Resisting the easy and common temptation of reading Hale's cautionary tale as "a transparent patriotic parable," Hsu argues instead that the evolving story "reframed its nationalist object lesson to suit the increasingly expansionist outlook of American readers," a frame that properly must take in emergent nationalist sentiment during the antebellum years, as well as postbellum "U.S. nation building, imperialism, and the denationalization of racialized subjects throughout the nineteenth century."

Timothy Shay Arthur's *Ten Nights in a Bar-Room* was another profoundly popular cautionary tale; it was also one of the most familiar texts of nineteenth-century American popular culture. William Gleason reconsiders *Ten Nights* within the context of its original illustrations and their references to the iconography and visual economy of the temperance movement. The recognition that the representational strategies of *Ten Nights* make it "as significant a visual artefact as it is a literary one" also enables a reevaluation of the novel's narrator and his "photographic" ways of seeing. Arguably a text situated on the cusp between the conduct and guidance manuals of the long nineteenth century and the "self-help" and "advice" books of the long twentieth century, *Ten Nights* draws on the shifting tactics of a temperance movement as it transitions from "sensational approaches" to "legalistic" ones, and may have helped open the door to the psychological methods of twentieth-century advice manuals.

As the nineteenth century draws to a close, James Russell returns our attention to the most popular novel in American history until *Gone with the Wind* in 1936, a novel that reportedly outsold in aggregate even *Uncle Tom's Cabin*, Lew Wallace's *Ben-Hur*. Russell reads *Ben-Hur* as a conversion narrative that used emergent marketing methods to encourage its audience to believe the novel itself could be a vehicle for readers' conversion to a good Christian life.

Russell situates *Ben-Hur* within a genealogy of mainstream fictions that have "sought to close the gap between the beliefs of American Christians and the pleasures of popular entertainment." Russell thus reminds us of the importance of conversion narratives—and not just a broader notion of redemption—to a specifically American notion of popular culture. Conversion narratives constitute not just an ideology but also an aesthetic, America's preeminent, perdurable model for individual transfiguration, community formation, and nation-building, and they continue to permeate all aspects of its popular culture.

If commonsense holds that bestsellers are in the business of wish-fulfillment, J. Michelle Coghlan considers the "curious" pressure of renunciation in Edgar Rice Burrough's *Tarzan of the Apes*, and "not simply because so many books that have gone on to become American bestsellers refuse us the ending we most wanted." It has become axiomatic that *Tarzan* is the compensatory, racialized fantasy of a white man as "lord of the jungle," but this reading fails to take sufficient account, Coghlan suggests, of *Tarzan's* "vectors of desire." Instead of privileging Tarzan's desires, Coghlan argues for reading the novel's interracial anxieties within the context of "queer exchanges of desire" and situates this sexual economy within the historical context of contemporary anxiety about "white slavery" as the racialized female sex trade. Sarah Garland's "Ornamentalism: Desire, Disavowal and Displacement in E.M. Hull's *The Sheik*" also considers Americans' attraction to exoticism and the way another favorite American form was adapted by the changing discourses and meanings of empire. Reading the supertext of Hull's novel as both captivity narrative and formula romance, Garland argues that both "the luxurious orientalist *mise en scene* and the captivity plot" of *The Sheik* provide loci "where patriarchally legitimized forms are rearranged, subverted, re-enforced or sidelined by women." Suggesting that the novel's tactical orientalism works both as an ornament and as a screen for displacement, Garland finds that these strategies enable Hull "to provide a happy ending that fits with both the erotics of property under patriarchy and the class logic of imperialism."

The perils and pleasures of ornamentalism and materialism emerge as an increasing preoccupation of American popular culture as the twentieth century gathers pace. Although the pressure of ostensibly nonfiction forms—conversion narrative, temperance literature, captivity narrative, national histories—is felt throughout this collection, Grace Lees-Maffei's consideration of Emily Post's *Etiquette*, first published in 1922, is our only chapter devoted solely to the question of popular nonfiction in general and advice literature in particular. Lees-Maffei considers how the evolution of *Etiquette* across the near-century of its existence offers "a useful tool in calibrating the changing nature of the American dream." If popular novels have often adopted or adapted nonfiction forms, Lees-Maffei suggests the ways in which this "pre-eminent example of American advice literature" borrows novelistic techniques and can itself be read as a peculiar type of serial fiction. Reading *Etiquette* in this way reveals an America that views itself as "theoretically classless—or at least largely homogenized into a self-identified and broadly defined middle class," but in fact "is practically well-versed in reading subtle delineations of class codes from mien, gesture, expression and behavior, as well as dress, accessories and possessions." Ardis Cameron's reading of *Peyton Place* might suggest that Grace Metalious's bestselling novel could be seen as offering advice directly opposed to Emily Post's protean, evolving social guidance: Metalious's transgressive subjects were so popular because they defied the taboos that Emily Post carefully calibrates and reinforces. Cameron reads both the figure of Metalious, America's "unnerving 'authoress,'" and her "sexsational bestseller," through a reception history of the letters and memories of Metalious's readers in the conformist, neo-Victorian 1950s. For Cameron, Metalious "authorized" the nation to speak the unspoken: "incest, oral sex, divorce, adultery, homosexuality, social inequality and the bitter unfairness of female desire" were licensed by the "excitable speech" of *Peyton Place*. In his consideration of Mario Puzo's *The Godfather,* Evan Brier continues this turn toward audiences and the marketplace, situating Puzo's blockbuster within "the inescapable unpredictability of the marketplace for fiction," an unpredictability only accelerated by the rapid growth of the postwar American publishing industry. For Brier, *The Godfather* is the result of Puzo's "fortunate misreading of the book trade and of his place in it." Instead of transcending the binary distinction between the "literary" and the "popular," Brier argues, *The Godfather* was animated by this foundational distinction and is a product of it.

Sarah Churchwell argues that Nicholas Sparks's bestselling twenty-first-century romances are similarly driven by anxieties about the "literary" and the "popular," anxieties that rapidly become gendered. Offering fantasies of mastery to counter a sense of historical loss by reviving the nineteenth-century novel of sentiment, Sparks's novels emblematize "the recent resurgence of Victorian models of sentimental domestic fiction in mainstream popular romance." This form, Churchwell maintains, "has enabled evangelical writers to smuggle a covert but explicitly Christian agenda into ostensibly secular fiction via the rhetoric of 'choice.'" Instead of the paranoid model of *The Da Vinci Code*, Sparks's romances offer metanoia, or spiritual conversion, a form that melds easily with the sentimental novel's "exaltation of feminine morbidity, and sublimation of erotic desire into religious ecstasy." If Sarah Garland reads *The Sheik* as a novel that begins as captivity narrative and turns into formula romance, Churchwell argues that the romances of Nicholas Sparks seek cultural value *qua* mastery by transforming themselves into conversion narratives. Georgiana Banita's reading of Khaled Hosseini's 2003 *The Kite Runner* brings American history, geopolitical paranoia, and the novel of sentiment together in one global blockbuster. Banita argues that what she terms "the Hosseini aesthetic—an eminently recognizable blend of epic storytelling, sentimentality, and morality tale," is itself symptomatic of an emergent transnational discourse after 9/11, "especially through narratives that recount the 'untold stories' of the regions in which the US is taking a distinct strategic interest." Asking "whether the novel indeed reflects a post-American outlook or merely disguises its deeply American convictions beneath a cosmopolitan façade of travelling identities and fates," Banita argues that this novel is both a "deeply American fable disguised as a transnational text" and a novel that deploys "the transnational paradigm to shed light on Afghanistan's national project and humanitarian crises."

Stephen J. Mexal similarly reads Dan Brown's blockbuster 2003 *The Da Vinci Code* as a response to global anxieties, in this case "a deep and persistent ambivalence about the relationship between fictional narrative and historical subjectivity." The "bestselling bestseller" ever, *The Da Vinci Code*, Mexal argues, "reveals a deep longing, in a global, transnational public, for a coherent master historical narrative." This global public is drawn by "the allure of a single and authoritative narrative of human history," and comes together to "mourn the loss of the authority of the historical master narrative."

If history cannot provide us with a master narrative or foundational authority, it is not the case that continuities and genealogies cannot be identified; our partial history of American bestsellers does not purport (or aspire) to offer mastery, but we hope it may serve. As these chapters demonstrate, bestsellers enunciate national fictive truths; they prescribe and challenge normative identities and values; they offer the consolations of wishful thinking and the inducements of guilty pleasures; they are instruction manuals for self-improvement and conduct books for the improvement of others. They present us with an imaginary national diegesis that resists or even prohibits exegesis, as we are told how to read popular books—and how not to read them. By contrast, *Must Read: Rediscovering the American Bestseller* holds it to be self-evident that these "must-reads" must be read as critically as they are, or once were, read widely.

Bibliography

Armstrong, Nancy and Leonard Tennenhouse. *The Imaginary Puritan: Literature, Intellectual Labor, and the Origins of Personal Life* (Berkeley: University of California Press, 1992).

Baym, Nina. *Novels, Readers, and Reviewers: Responses to Fiction in Antebellum America* (Ithaca: Cornell University Press, 1987).

Bell, Michael Davitt. *Culture, Genre, and Literary Vocation: Selected Essays on American Literature* (Chicago: University of Chicago Press, 2001).

Bentley, Nancy. *Frantic Panoramas: American Literature and Mass Culture, 1870–1920* (Philadelphia: University of Pennsylvania Press, 2009).

Botshon, Lisa and Meredith Goldsmith. "Introduction," in Lisa Botshon and Meredith Goldsmith eds, *Middlebrow Moderns: Popular American Women Writers of the 1920s* (Boston: Northeastern University Press, 2003).

Bourdieu, Pierre. *The Field of Cultural Production* (London: Polity Press, 1993).

Bradsher, Earl L. *Mathew Carey: Editor, Author and Publisher* (New York: The Columbia University Press, 1912).

Brier, Evan. *A Novel Marketplace: Mass Culture, the Book Trade, and Postwar American Fiction* (Philadelphia: University of Pennsylvania Press, 2010).

Brown, Ellen F. and John Wiley, Jr. *Margaret Mitchell's* Gone With the Wind: *A Bestseller's Odyssey from Atlanta to Hollywood* (Lanham, MD: Taylor Trade Publishing, 2011).

Bruccoli, Matthew J., ed. *F. Scott Fitzgerald: A Life in Letters* (New York: Scribner's, 1994).

Collins, Jim. *Bring on the Books for Everybody: How Literary Culture Became Popular Culture* (Durham: Duke University Press, 2010).

Davidson, Cathy N. "The Life and Times of *Charlotte Temple*," in Cathy N. Davidson ed., *Reading in America: Literature & Social History* (Baltimore: Johns Hopkins University Press, 1989), 157–79.

— *Revolution and the Word: The Rise of the Novel in America* (New York: Oxford University Press, 1986).

"Editor's Easy Chair," *Harper's New Monthly Magazine*, 91:16 (December 1857), 129.

Franklin, Wayne. *James Fenimore Cooper: The Early Years* (New Haven: Yale University Press, 2007).

Freibert, Lucy M. and Barbara A. White. *Hidden Hands: An Anthology of American Women Writers, 1790–1870* (New Jersey: Rutgers University Press, 1994).

Gohdes, Clarence. *American Literature in Nineteenth Century England* (Carbondale: Southern Illinois University Press, 1944).

Graff, Harvey J. *The Legacies of Literacy: Continuities and Contradictions in Western Culture and Society* (Bloomington: Indiana University Press, 1991).

Hart, James D. *The Popular Book: A History of America's Literary Taste* (New York: Oxford University Press, 1950).

Irving, Pierre M., ed. *The Life and Letters of Washington Irving* (London: Richard Bentley, 1862), 3 volumes.

Jackson, Leon. *The Business of Letters: Authorial Economies in Antebellum America* (Stanford: Stanford University Press, 2008).

James, Henry. *A Small Boy and Others* (New York: Charles Scribner's Sons, 1913).

— *Literary Criticism, Volume One* (New York: Library of America, 2004).

"Jennifer Egan on Winning the 2011 Pulitzer Prize for Fiction". *Wall Street Journal Speakeasy Blog*, April 18 2011: http://blogs.wsj.com/speakeasy/2011/04/18/jennifer-egan-on-winning-the-2011-pulitzer-prize-for-fiction/.

Leavis, Queenie. *Fiction and the Reading Public* (London: Chatto & Windus, 1939).

Lepore, Jill. "Dickens in Eden," *The New Yorker*, August 29, 2011, 52–61.

Levine, Lawrence. "The Folklore of Industrial Society: Popular Culture and Its Audiences," *American Historical Review*, 97:5 (December 1992), 1369–99.

— *Highbrow / Lowbrow: The Emergence of Cultural Hierarchy in America* (Cambridge: Harvard University Press, 1988).

Macdonald, Dwight. *Masscult and Midcult: Essays Against the American Grain* (New York: New York Review of Books, 2011).

Miller, Laura J. *Reluctant Capitalists: Bookselling and the Culture of Consumption* (Chicago: University of Chicago Press, 2006).

Monaghan, E. Jennifer. *Learning to Read and Write in Colonial America* (Amherst: University of Massachusetts Press, 2005).

Moore, Thomas, ed. *Life and Journals of Lord Byron: With Notices of His Life* (London: John Murray, 1830), 2 volumes.

Mott, Frank Luther. *Golden Multitudes: The Story of Best Sellers in the United States* (New York: Macmillan, 1947).

Myerson, Joel, ed. *Selected Letters of Nathaniel Hawthorne* (Columbus: Ohio State University Press, 2002).

Neuberg, Victor. "Chapbooks in America: Reconstructing the Popular Reading of Early America," in Cathy N. Davidson ed., *Reading in America: Literature & Social History* (Baltimore: Johns Hopkins University Press, 1989), 81–113.

Newcomb, Harvey. *The Young Lady's Guide to the Harmonious Development of Christian Character* (Boston: James B. Dow, 1841).

Oliver, Grace A. *A Study of Maria Edgeworth* (Boston: A. Williams and Company, 1882).

Raven, James. "The Importation of Books in the Eighteenth Century," *A History of the Book in America: Volume 1: The Colonial Book in the Atlantic World* (Chapel Hill: University of North Carolina Press, 2007), 183–98.

— "The Novel Comes of Age," in *The English Novel 1770–1829: A Bibliographical Survey of Prose Fiction Published in the British Isles, Volume 1: 1770–99*, edited by James Raven and Antonia Forster (New York: Oxford University Press, 200), 15–121.

Reeve, Clara. *The Progress of Romance* (Colchester: W. Keymer, 1785), 2 vols.

Reynolds, David S. *Beneath the American Renaissance* (New York: Alfred A. Knopf, 1988).

Rooney, Kathleen. *Reading With Oprah: The Book Club That Changed America* (Fayetteville: University of Arkansas Press, 2005).

"Sir Walter Scott". *North American Review*, 36:79 (April 1833), 289–315.

Slotkin, Richard and James K. Folsom, eds. *So Dreadful a Judgment: Puritan Responses to King Philip's War, 1676–7* (Wesleyan University Press, 1978).

St Clair, William. *The Reading Nation in the Romantic Period* (Cambridge: Cambridge University Press, 2004).

Swirski, Peter. *From Lowbrow to Nobrow* (Montreal: McGill-Queen's University Press, 2005).

Teichgraeber III, Richard F. *Sublime Thoughts / Penny Wisdom: Situating Emerson and Thoreau in the American Market* (Baltimore: Johns Hopkins University Press, 1995).

Tompkins, Jane. *Sensational Designs: The Cultural Work of American Fiction, 1790–1860* (New York: Oxford University Press, 1985).

Tyler, Royall. *The Algerine Captive; or, The Life and Adventures of Doctor Updike Underhill* (Hartford: Peter B. Gleason and Co., 1816).

Wadsworth, Sarah. *In the Company of Books: Literature and Its "Classes" in Nineteenth-Century America* (Amherst: University of Massachusetts Press, 2006).

Warner, William B. *Licensing Entertainment: The Elevation of Novel Reading in Britain, 1684–1750* (Berkeley: University of California Press, 1998).

West III, James L. W. *American Authors and the Literary Marketplace* (Philadelphia: University of Pennsylvania Press, 1988).

"What Middletown Read," http://www.bsu.edu/libraries/wmr/index.php.

Zboray, Ronald J. "Antebellum Reading and the Ironies of Technological Innovation," in Cathy N. Davidson ed., *Reading in America: Literature & Social History* (Baltimore: Johns Hopkins University Press, 1989), 180–200.

Notes

1 Jim Collins, *Bring on the Books for Everybody: How Literary Culture Became Popular Culture* (Durham: Duke University Press, 2010), 7.

2 Lawrence Levine, "The Folklore of Industrial Society: Popular Culture and Its Audiences," *American Historical Review*, 97:5 (December 1992), 1369–99, 1372.

3 Pierre Bourdieu, *The Field of Cultural Production* (London: Polity Press, 1993), 116.

4 Queenie Leavis, *Fiction and the Reading Public* (London: Chatto & Windus, 1939), 7, 73–4.

5 Frank Luther Mott, *Golden Multitudes: The Story of Best Sellers in the United States* (New York: Macmillan, 1947), 5.

6 Jane Tompkins, *Sensational Designs: The Cultural Work of American Fiction, 1790–1860* (New York: Oxford University Press: 1985), xiv.

7 Jill Lepore, "Dickens in Eden," *The New Yorker*, August 29, 2011, 52–61, 54.

8 Received wisdom holds that the *Bookman* first coined the term, in 1895, but according to the *OED*, it was the American Midwest

that deserves the credit—or blame—for transforming high sales into a categorical distinction.

9   E. Jennifer Monaghan, *Learning to Read and Write in Colonial America* (Amherst: University of Massachusetts Press, 2005), 3.

10 Harvey J. Graff, *The Legacies of Literacy: Continuities and Contradictions in Western Culture and Society* (Bloomington: Indiana University Press, 1991), 164.

11 Victor Neuberg, "Chapbooks in America: Reconstructing the Popular Reading of Early America," in Cathy N. Davidson ed., *Reading in America: Literature & Social History* (Baltimore: Johns Hopkins University Press, 1989), 81–113, 83.

12 Neuberg, "Chapbooks," 81.

13 Leon Jackson, *The Business of Letters: Authorial Economies in Antebellum America* (Stanford: Stanford University Press, 2008), 19.

14 Neuberg, "Chapbooks," 81.

15 Neuberg, "Chapbooks," 81.

16 Neuberg, "Chapbooks," 95.

17 Cathy N. Davidson, *Revolution and the Word: The Rise of the Novel in America* (New York: Oxford University Press, 1986), 11.

18 Neuberg, "Chapbooks," 82.

19 James Raven, "The Importation of Books in the Eighteenth Century," *A History of the Book in America: Volume 1: The Colonial Book in the Atlantic World* (Chapel Hill: University of North Carolina Press, 2007), 183–98, 183.

20 Richard Slotkin and James K. Folsom eds, *So Dreadful a Judgment: Puritan Responses to King Philip's War, 1676–77* (Wesleyan University Press, 1978), 301.

21 Nancy Armstrong and Leonard Tennenhouse, *The Imaginary Puritan: Literature, Intellectual Labor, and the Origins of Personal Life* (Berkeley: University of California Press, 1992), n266.

22 William B. Warner, *Licensing Entertainment: The Elevation of Novel Reading in Britain, 1684–1750* (Berkeley: University of California Press, 1998), 6–7.

23 Warner, *Entertainment*, 8.

24 Clara Reeve, *The Progress of Romance* (Colchester: W. Keymer, 1785), 2 vols, 2:7, 77.

25 Royall Tyler, *The Algerine Captive; or, The Life and Adventures of Doctor Updike Underhill* (Hartford: Peter B. Gleason and Co., 1816), v.

26 James Raven, "The Novel Comes of Age," in *The English Novel 1770–1829: A Bibliographical Survey of Prose Fiction Published in the British Isles, Volume 1: 1770–99*, edited by James Raven and Antonia Forster (New York: Oxford University Press, 200), 15–121, 38.

27 William St Clair, *The Reading Nation in the Romantic Period* (Cambridge: Cambridge University Press, 2004), 390, 386.

28 Cathy N. Davidson, "The Life and Times of *Charlotte Temple*," in Cathy N. Davidson ed., *Reading in America: Literature & Social History* (Baltimore: Johns Hopkins University Press, 1989), 157–79, 158.

29 Tyler, *Algerine*, vi.

30 Harvey Newcomb, *The Young Lady's Guide to the Harmonious Development of Christian Character* (Boston: James B. Dow, 1841), 183.

31 Earl L. Bradsher, *Mathew Carey: Editor, Author and Publisher* (New York: The Columbia University Press, 1912), 81–2.

32 "Sir Walter Scott," *North American Review*, 36:79 (April 1833), 289–315, 310.

33 St Clair, *Reading Nation*, 388–9.

34 Grace A. Oliver, *A Study of Maria Edgeworth* (Boston: A. Williams and Company, 1882), 315.

35 Mott, *Golden Multitudes*, 69.

36 Bradsher, *Carey*, 84.

37 Mott, *Golden Multitudes*, 71.

38 Pierre M. Irving ed., *The Life and Letters of Washington Irving* (London: Richard Bentley, 1862), 3 volumes, 1:378.

39 Wayne Franklin, *James Fenimore Cooper: The Early Years* (New Haven: Yale University Press, 2007), 253.

40 Franklin, *Cooper*, 265.

41 Thomas Moore ed., *Life and Journals of Lord Byron: With Notices of His Life* (London: John Murray, 1830), 2 volumes, 1:460.

42 Quoted in Davidson, *Revolution*, 199.

43 Clarence Gohdes, *American Literature in Nineteenth Century England* (Carbondale: Southern Illinois University Press, 1944), 16.

44 St Clair, *Reading*, 393.

45 Richard F. Teichgraeber III, *Sublime Thoughts / Penny Wisdom: Situating Emerson and Thoreau in the American Market* (Baltimore: Johns Hopkins University Press, 1995), 162.

46   Quoted in Ronald J. Zboray, "Antebellum Reading and the Ironies of Technological Innovation," in Cathy N. Davidson ed., *Reading in America: Literature & Social History* (Baltimore: Johns Hopkins University Press, 1989), 180–200, 181.

47   "Editor's Easy Chair," *Harper's New Monthly Magazine*, 91:16 (December 1857), 129.

48   Henry James, *A Small Boy and Others* (New York: Charles Scribner's Sons, 1913), 159.

49   Zboray, "Antebellum Reading," 181.

50   Zboray, "Antebellum Reading," 196.

51   Joel Myerson ed., *Selected Letters of Nathaniel Hawthorne* (Columbus: Ohio State University Press, 2002), xiv.

52   Lucy M. Freibert and Barbara A. White, *Hidden Hands: An Anthology of American Women Writers, 1790–1870* (New Jersey: Rutgers University Press, 1994), xii.

53   Lawrence Levine, *Highbrow / Lowbrow: The Emergence of Cultural Hierarchy in America* (Cambridge: Harvard University Press, 1988), 9. See also David S. Reynolds, *Beneath the American Renaissance* (New York: Alfred A. Knopf, 1988).

54   Myerson, *Letters*, xv.

55   Michael Davitt Bell, *Culture, Genre, and Literary Vocation: Selected Essays on American Literature* (Chicago: University of Chicago Press, 2001), 184.

56   Gohdes, *American Literature*, 101.

57   Nina Baym, *Novels, Readers, and Reviewers: Responses to Fiction in Antebellum America* (Ithaca: Cornell University Press, 1987), 45.

58   Henry James, *Literary Criticism, Volume One* (New York: Library of America, 2004), 653.

59   Quoted in Sarah Wadsworth, *In the Company of Books: Literature and Its "Classes" in Nineteenth-Century America* (Amherst: University of Massachusetts Press, 2006), 115–16.

60   Nancy Bentley, *Frantic Panoramas: American Literature and Mass Culture, 1870–1920* (Philadelphia: University of Pennsylvania Press, 2009), 33.

61   Bentley, *Panoramas*, 34.

62   Bentley, *Panoramas*, 33.

63   Mott, *Golden Multitudes*, 174.

64   "What Middletown Read," http://www.bsu.edu/libraries/wmr/index.php.

65 Lisa Botshon and Meredith Goldsmith, "Introduction," in Lisa Botshon and Meredith Goldsmith eds, *Middlebrow Moderns: Popular American Women Writers of the 1920s* (Boston: Northeastern University Press, 2003), 4.

66 Matthew J. Bruccoli ed., *F. Scott Fitzgerald: A Life in Letters* (New York: Scribner's, 1994) 107.

67 James L. W. West III, *American Authors and the Literary Marketplace* (Philadelphia: University of Pennsylvania Press, 1988), 125–6.

68 Evan Brier, *A Novel Marketplace: Mass Culture, the Book Trade, and Postwar American Fiction* (Philadelphia: University of Pennsylvania Press, 2010), 2.

69 Dwight Macdonald, *Masscult and Midcult: Essays Against the American Grain* (New York: New York Review of Books, 2011), 36.

70 Brier, *Novel*, 7.

71 Peter Swirski, *From Lowbrow to Nobrow* (Montreal: McGill-Queen's University Press, 2005), 20.

72 Ellen F. Brown and John Wiley, Jr., *Margaret Mitchell's* Gone With the Wind*: A Bestseller's Odyssey from Atlanta to Hollywood* (Lanham, MD: Taylor Trade Publishing, 2011), 1.

73 Brown and Wiley, *Margaret Mitchell's* Gone With the Wind, 147.

74 West, *American Authors*,149.

75 Collins, *Books*, 4.

76 Laura J. Miller, *Reluctant Capitalists: Bookselling and the Culture of Consumption* (Chicago: University of Chicago Press, 2006), 4.

77 "Jennifer Egan on Winning the 2011 Pulitzer Prize for Fiction," *Wall Street Journal Speakeasy Blog*, April 18 2011: http://blogs.wsj.com/speakeasy/2011/04/18/jennifer-egan-on-winning-the-2011-pulitzer-prize-for-fiction/. See also Kathleen Rooney, *Reading With Oprah: The Book Club That Changed America* (Fayetteville: University of Arkansas Press, 2005).

78 See Davidson, *Revolution*.

2

Missing numbers: The partial history of the bestseller

Sarah Garland

No documents (from Crevecoeur's Letters to signing
evidence on marriage records) can simply be "read" as if
they were objective, scientific data produced or preserved
as some pure product of a people and the abiding record of
their times. The record always suppresses more than it tells.
Why, we must ask, are certain records kept in the first place?
Why are they saved? The whole process of historiography,
the archive itself, must be subjected to rigorous analysis.
Who is keeping the records and for what purpose?
Who is writing, to whom, and why?[1]

CATHY N. DAVIDSON

Bestsellerism, bestsellerdom, and bestseller lists

On the cover of a new paperback, the term "bestseller" works as a marker of the tried and tested. At the very least, it suggests that this book has been already sold in volume, possibly in expensive hardback editions, and that it's been consumed by enough people to represent a usable purchase. At its most fanciful, the hyperbole of the "best" suggests some kind of intensity of content, the trace of an excessive hope—perhaps that this self-help book will change your life, that this novel will be unputdownable, that this autobiography will reveal the real celebrity, that this diet book will create a new "you." Beyond the dreams hidden in that type of tried and tested guarantee, a bestselling book is also positioned by its publishers and readers as timely, as happening *now*. In his book on popular fiction in the 70s, *Bestsellers*, John Sutherland argues that for both its contemporary readers and to cultural and literary historians, this very ephemerality constitutes the particular value of the bestseller; the bestseller marks its time because it is an "all-or-nothing" achievement, "commonly the book that everyone is reading now, or that no one is reading anymore."[2] Marking a volume of sales is a way of quantifying the more abstract cultural din that surrounds that book's author and plot, its values and attitudes, and its potential for information and entertainment. What we talk about when we talk about bestsellers is popular and commercial culture at its most noisy and dynamic.

The bestseller's connection to cold hard cash, real readers, and royalty payments suggests that its tradition might conceivably constitute one of the most concrete structures of literary studies. However, significant problems arise when we try to correlate the historical flow of this real and obvious cultural activity with actual mathematical volumes of sales. As Sutherland states, "the word 'bestseller' and its derivatives (bestsellerism, bestsellerdom) are not governed by any agreed definitions," and a bestseller can designate an author, a series, or single megaselling book.[3] Generally, what academics and literary critics talk about when (if?) they talk about bestsellers is a certain kind of easy read, an intentionally popular fiction that appears on a bestseller list, despite the fact that in terms of numbers the real American bestsellers are bibles, cookbooks, almanacs, school books, and inspirational and devotional manuals—that it's not just fiction which takes on the task of telling us how to live.

The term "best-seller" (or bestseller) as it is used by the press is, in a sense, always hyperbole. As Frank Mott points out in *Golden Multitudes*, strictly speaking, there is only one bestseller—the Bible—"and all others are only 'better sellers' or 'good sellers.'"[4] Even given the logical impossibilities in the term, the data sampling and grouping necessary to compile a comparative entity like a list represents a series of choices that problematize the term. To call a book a bestseller already indicates that the book has come through a series of decisions about whether to count it. The bestseller represents the highest sales, but, as Mott argues, "the highest in sales where and when? And for how long? The Colossal Department Store's bestseller among Saturday book bargain? Or the world's biggest seller in a round hundred years?," "is a weekly, or even a yearly, leader necessarily entitled to the accolade 'best seller'?."[5] And, I would add—by whose measure? As Eliza Truitt points out, the current weekly American bestseller lists in the *New York Times*, *Washington Post, San Francisco Chronicle, Boston Globe,* and *Los Angeles Times* are valued precisely because of their differences from one another. The Los Angles, Boston, Washington, and San Francisco lists record only regional sales, with the emphasis on the tradition of the state or city, so, for example, the San Francisco list has a certain maverick "predictive value," possibly because it contains a larger proportion of independent booksellers and will often show up literary bestsellers before the New York list.[6] America's independent booksellers have their own chart, the BookSense bestseller list. Her point is that "book industry people don't want a single compilation of what's really selling best throughout the country; they want a variety of lists that break down sales figures in ways beneficial to them"—the partiality of these lists is what makes them valuable to an industry that relies on selling to what is, after all, a relatively small section of the consuming American public. Catch-all charts like the *USA Today* list tell us that many of the biggest selling books in the country are children's books—fine if your object of investigation is the culture at large, less useful if you are looking, as Ken Gelder does in his excellent *Popular Fiction*, at the bestseller as a literary field.[7] As Alice Payne Hackett, compiler of one of the most authoritative historical surveys of the bestseller, puts it, "the term 'best seller' is a relative term."[8]

The relativity and partiality of the designation 'bestseller' is thrown into sharp focus when we look more closely at the differences in the way these lists are compiled. As Laura Miller convincingly demonstrates in "The Bestseller List as Marketing Tool and Historical Fiction," the lists are self-generating, they are both agents and records of sales. Miller tells of the 1983 case where David Blatty sued the *New York Times* because sales of *Legion*, his follow-up to the bestselling *Exorcist*, had not been displayed on their bestseller list until fairly late in the book's sales. Only making number one on the list for one of the four weeks it was eligible had cost him $4 million in royalties and movie rights, Blatty maintained. The Supreme Court ruled that Blatty's suit for intentional interference with sales was a reasonable one, but decided against the author in the end. The *Times* won the case with an argument that maintained that its bestseller list was editorial content—because of its nature as a constructed, inherently incomplete reading of the marketplace, the *Times* bestseller list can, and did, claim First Amendment protection.[9] As Clark Hoyt explains, the *New York Times* rankings don't reflect total US sales, but sales at thousands of outlets which are then statistically weighted by the *Times* to reflect the proportions in the country as a whole in a formula that remains a trade secret. Some booksellers send *The New York Times* their full rankings and others carry on the older tradition that Blatty fell foul of where booksellers filled in figures for the *Times'* preselected lists of watched titles, writing surprise sellers onto the bottom. The *Times* doesn't reveal its sources for fear of strategic buying, and marks bulk bought books with a dagger on the end lists. Books that stay on the list long enough to be classified as "evergreens" are also removed to keep a list "that's lively and churns and affords new authors the opportunity to be recorded" according to Deborah Hoffman, the current editor of the list.[10] The impetus for Hoyt's article was the abrupt removal of the 2008 translation of Elie Weisel's *Night* after 80 weeks on the list while it was still selling; from the point of view of the *Times*, he tells us, the sales were becoming less eligible for the charts because they were coming from the book's movement onto college literature courses as a modern classic and therefore no longer represented popular taste. The history of American "bestsellers" as told by the bestsellers' lists is not so much a history of stock-taking and accounting as a history of discourse—of comment, interpretation, and opinion.

The bestseller lists and figures represent the already read in both senses of the phrase; they represent books that have been consumed and statistics that come to us interpreted.

One unexpected revelation to the more casual reader may be that even now, in an age of standardized selling and huge amounts of digital recording and publishing, there is no complete record of American book sales; even Nielsen's BookScan, the industry's electronic point of sales database (used by *The Wall Street Journal* for its list), is not complete. Although it charts the major American retailers, Amazon, Barnes and Noble, and Borders included, BookScan only covers 75 per cent of the market. And, as we will see in the case of the religious publishers, sales at Walmart are one of BookScan's big omissions, and its coverage of airports is sketchy too. *The New York Times* bestsellers' list is meticulously compiled and aims to be representative—because of the size of its sample and the settlement of the publishing industry it is taken to be the most important of the newspaper lists. Nevertheless it is, like all the other bestseller lists, a carefully mediated interpretation of popular and literary taste. *The New York Times's* power to increase sales generates enough momentum to warrant escalator clauses in writers' contracts, but its cultural authority is not in its capture of statistics but in the reputation of the paper for cutting-edge journalism. The bestseller lists are part of this journalism—they are collected by the same department that conducts the news polls and, like those polls, they are mediated to create a narrative of success and change with a cast of carefully chosen players.[11]

Writing the history of the bestseller

The Times's direct statement that these lists are not empirical but editorial also gets to the heart of the problems of plotting the movements of popular fiction over any period of time. Not the least of these problems is the fact that the mapping of the history of the bestseller as told by its lists necessitates coming to terms with a history of compilation and choice by publishers, journalists, and scholars. The history of serious scholarly engagement with the bestseller begins with Frank Luther Mott's 1947 *Golden Multitudes*, an excellent and very influential study which—surprisingly, given that it is now over 60 years old—still provides most of the information on what was read in English in the American colonies. The current most authoritative work on the history of American bookselling, John Tebbel's monumental *A History of Book Publishing in the United States*, still returns to Mott for the early figures which he based on painstaking scholarship into early American bibliographies, into probates, and into early booksellers' and importers' records. Given the obvious problems of surveying a market and a public 400 years after the event, *Golden Multitudes* does a remarkable job, but Mott's cautions about the gaps in his archives are worth considering in some depth, not only because they have considerable bearing on the kind of analytical work one can and cannot do with these titles, but also because the way he uses bibliographies, adverts, word-of-mouth and author's statements to work around missing industry numbers prefigures the kinds of loose arithmetic that are still necessary to map the field of the bestseller even today.

Sutherland tells us that the very first lists were distrusted by the British bookselling community because of a suspicion not only of "quick, rather than real bestsellers," but also because they felt that the lists would be used to boost figures of a flagging book.[12] Mott too considers American publishers inclined to boast of their successes, and even when he can get to the accounts,

> records are often faulty, or non-existent, even for books published in the last forty or fifty years. Moreover, some books have passed through the hands of several publishing firms, complicating an investigator's problem. And hundreds of publishing companies have sunk beneath the waters of oblivion in the century and a half of active American book publishing, and usually they have carried their records with them down to Davy Jones's locker.[13]

Mott's list does not give a total sales figure because, "in most cases exact figures are completely and hopelessly nonexistent." Mott, like James Hart after him, is looking to write the (for him) 350-year-long history of the popular book in America and so sets his minimum total sales figures for a book against population figures, classifying as a bestseller a book that sells copies equal to or more than one percent of the American population for the beginning of that decade. By this method, he is able to convincingly isolate some of the founding texts of American popular culture while taking into account the exponential rise in settlement—the bar for a bestseller

in 1800, when the population was counted as 5,300,000, needs to be
set far lower than in 1900, when it was 76,000 000, and, of course
in 2000, when the census figures give the population of the United
States as 281,421,906. Mott's figures may even be considerably
understated. Because of the fragmentary nature of his evidence in
the compilation of those lists, the inquiry was not how many copies,
precisely, were sold, but whether enough copies of the book were
sold in the United States to reach his minimum measure.[14]

As Sutherland points out, Mott's method works well for
establishing a relatively stable canon of popular fiction, but it
doesn't give much idea of the kinds of cultural movements marked
by the pace of sales.[15] Twenty years later, in the mid-60s, the
sociologist Robert Escarpit came at a way of refining these patterns
with respect to the speed and volume of sales, drawing graphs that
differentiated books that sell a lot in their first weeks of release
before dropping away without reprinting (fastsellers, he calls them),
books that sell consistently over a period of time (steadysellers)
and bestsellers which, he writes, "represent the most spectacular
type of success, since they combine both sorts of sales–beginning
as fastsellers, they end up as steady sellers."[16] The kinds of cultural
penetration we are looking for to begin to sketch the history of
the bestseller are well described by Escarpit's definition, but even
here the lists are mirrors of the intentions of the compiler; one of
Escarpit's goals in *The Book Revolution* is to give an international
account of the meteoric rise of the paperback edition since its birth
in the early 60s, and so the development of this kind of taxonomy
allows him to account for publishers' decisions to reprint hardback
successes in cheap mass market forms.

Escarpit tells us that sales of a first edition generally begin to
peak after an initial lag which "seldom exceeds three weeks,"
after which his graphs chart two years in the life of a fast, steady,
and bestseller. This turnover points out another of the significant
challenges to writing the history of the bestseller—historians and
journalists work on very different timescales, and while two years
represent ephemerality for the literary and cultural historian, it
remains a remarkable achievement in the realms of bestsellerdom.
Writing the history of the bestseller necessitates a recalibration of
scale for history as it is conventionally written, because a book
that tops the bestseller charts for more than one year is exceptional
indeed, as Sutherland points out in his *Very Short Introduction* to

the bestseller. Indeed, the *Times* list removes books known to the industry as "perennials," precisely to consolidate its function as a gauge of the new. A consideration of the largely uncollated second-hand book market complicates these timescales still further—the latest research in that field suggests that these slow, selective sales might constitute what is being called "the long tail" of reading—those books with historical duration or recurring interest that move outside of mass market control.[17]

Charts and lists are forms that perpetuate their own popularity because they demand we undertake some form of comparison, whether that is within the list itself, or with the previous week's or year's list. The point of these ambitious early lists was to create a way of comparing the movements of popular culture through time and it remains so; even if we take the weekly fluctuations of the *New York Times* list as our focus of interest, we are still looking for trends, differences of opinions, and perhaps confirmations of our own judgments. As the sampling methods get ever more sophisticated, the comparative impulse behind the listing of sales in rank order remains consistent. However, in this sense, the various partialities of all the lists present a real problem for a researcher looking to approach the history of the bestseller quantitatively. In short, all these lists, scholarly and industry alike, are only mathematically consistent when treated in isolation.

Apocalyptic histories

This kind of problem is vividly brought into relief when we attempt to use the numbers we do have to undertake a comparative historical analysis. The first American press was run out of Cambridge, Massachusetts in 1638, and Mott records Michael Wigglesworth's epic apocalyptic poem, "The Day of Doom," (1662) as the first American bestseller, selling at least to 3 per cent of the population of New England in an edition of 1,800 copies. (This kind of information about edition size is a bonus—Mott states that we have a pretty good idea of the average size of American editions, but seldom states what that size is—a researcher would have to go back to Mott's often fragmentary sources for that information.) If we try to compare this account of Armageddon to a late-twentieth-century apocalyptic fiction like Tim Lahaye and Jerry B. Jenkins'

Left Behind series, the problems become apparent. Because of the *Times'* recording methods, the most reliable lists for the twentieth and twenty-first century are generally considered to be those in *Publishers Weekly*, summarized by Alice Payne Hackett and James Burke in *80 Years of Best Sellers, 1895–1975* and thereafter by Daisy Maryles in the *Bowker Annual Library and Book Trade Almanac* and on the *Publisher's Weekly* website. As Hackett points out, the twentieth-century records of the biggest sellers often underplay the phenomenal success of series novels and series novelists because they fail to take into account cumulative sales. Something like Zane Gray's westerns, or Horatio Alger's 120-plus novels, or E. D. E. N Southworth's 50-plus bestsellers (see Rachel Ihara's essay in this collection), or even Agatha Christie's series mysteries—the two billion sales of which, Sutherland tells us, put her in the *Guinness Book of Records* as the world's bestselling author ever—don't register on the lists to the extent they do in culture because the individual books often slip under the radar, especially of the older hardcover-only lists.[18] In the case of La Haye and Jenkins, all the novels charted in both the *Publishers Weekly* lists and the *New York Times* lists, so we do have some usable figures. Even so, analyzing the sales of a single book can only be a gesture toward measuring the cultural penetration of the series as a whole.

Pressing on despite this caveat reveals more problems. The biggest selling book in the *Left Behind* series, *Desecration: Antichrist Takes the Throne*, *Publishers Weekly* records as selling a combined total of 3,573,698 copies in hardback and paperback between the years of 2001 and 2002, even though yearly sales for the series as a whole peaked earlier, in 2000. (The annual totals can be found in the *Bowker Almanac*, the aggregate total is mine). Setting this against a US population of 281,421,906 for 2000, we get a figure of 1.27 per cent to compare with Wigglesworth's 'Day of Doom's' 3 per cent. (Using this method, the modern texts that most closely match Wigglesworth's success would be Grace Metallious's 1956 *Peyton Place* and Dan Brown's 2005 *DaVinci Code*, both covered by this collection, and both of which have sales figures that represent just over 3 per cent of the American population, although even here in the twentieth century, the comparison is not watertight—the *Peyton Place* figures are from research on John Unsworth's excellent University of Illinois bestsellers' website, the *Da Vinci Code* from *Publishers Weekly*). The tally with Mott's minimum of one percent suggests that despite the phenomenal growth in the industry's distribution machinery, a bestseller, interestingly enough, reaches approximately the same proportion of the population, but that in the Colonial period, the penetration of the popular texts may have been even higher than for the kinds of cheap, mass products we think of as characteristically modern. And this does not begin to factor in the types of reading one may find in each period; although religiously oriented books like LaHaye's, Nicholas Sparks's phenomenally successful Christian romances (see Sarah Churchwell's essay in this collection), and Rick Warren's Christian self-help book, *The Purpose Driven Life*, are now being promoted, discussed, and distributed through church communities, in the 17th and 18th centuries a fewer number of books may have been read more intensely, their readers responding to them slowly, meditatively, and over a life time.[19]

Even census figures complicate these calculations. First, there's the vexing question of just who counted as a person in early American censuses. The population figures for the colonial period are problematized by the indefinite status of slaves, women, and indentured servants. As Hart points out in *The Popular Book*, population figures are political, they depend on settling the definition of personhood.[20] The population figure of just under six million used by Mott for the 1800 census does not count the slave population, which made it nearly seven million in reality, and there is no record of whether Native Americans were counted. Second, there's the question of how many copies of Wigglesworth's book were exported or sent as gifts to England; the fact that other early American bestsellers were texts like the English protestant Foxe's *Book of Martyrs* and Isaac Watt's *Divine and Moral Songs for Children* suggests an early start to the transatlantic trade.

On the other end of history, even if we can stand behind twentieth-century census figures, the coverage of the lists is still not directly comparable because *Publishers Weekly* only includes books distributed "through the trade, that is to bookstores and libraries." This means that *Publishers Weekly* misses the massive American book club sales and can't be directly compared to retailers' figures because its statistics are for books "shipped and billed." Crucially, the *Publishers Weekly* charts don't (and can't) take into account the number of units returned unsold to a publisher six months later. A look at the number of reprints of the LaHaye books suggests that returns aren't a huge factor here, but may be in, say, J. K. Rowling's case, where the giant first hardback print runs of the later books were used to generate advertising in the form of news stories. Industry gossip suggests that there were high remainders for Rowling's hardback editions, although the paperback editions remained steady enough sellers to offset this objection. Even so, returns remain an issue when interpreting the *Publishers Weekly* lists, because there's no guarantee (except perhaps a commonsense one about levels of investment) that large "shipped and billed" figures equate to large sales figures. The promotional value of making the bestseller list with a large first printing of a book with dubious predicted sales might be part of an advertising strategy; as their name suggests, the bestseller lists are histories of selling as much as they are histories of buying.

If we want to gauge the percentage of the reading public engaged with a book like 'The Day of Doom' or the *Left Behind* series, then literacy will also be a factor. Literacy figures for present-day America stand at 99 per cent, according to the World Factbook USA, maintained by the CIA, but even here, functional literacy is suspected to be much lower.[21] Literacy figures for colonial America are far fuzzier. As Davidson argues, the general literacy figures for early America are taken by looking back over legal records to see what proportion of the population signed with an X. However, she cites studies that maintain that a high proportion of those signatures recorded were by clerks on behalf of signatories, and reminds us that the literacy of women and slaves was hardly being tracked at all by these methods because their status excluded them from being part of their own legal negotiations. Citing Kenneth A. Lockridge's study, she argues that universal literacy did exist, "but only in John Adams's America—an America that defined itself as New England, elite, urban, white, male."[22] She tells of a large number of early bestsellers where the owners would practice the alphabet on the flyleaves and annotate difficult words over the years, with increasing levels of literacy. These kinds of marks of ownership of a book Davidson reads as a reader's response to a culture where single ownership of a hard-earned item like a book was something special, and the levels of competence needed to negotiate these complex objects were won over the years. In more than one sense, a Colonial bestseller was highly valued—as she writes, "the manufacturing and distribution expenses of the time simply did not allow for book price that the public could generally afford," so that, for example, "a common day laborer in Mass. had to work two days to buy a copy of *Wieland*."[23] Even though a high number of the early colonists were gentle born, setting these expensive seventeenth- and eighteenth-century copies against relatively cheap twentieth century copies considerably vexes any investigation into comparative historical levels of consumption.

There is also strong evidence to suggest that the newspaper lists in our own time underrepresent the popularity of many mass market texts, religious books included. The *New York Times* lists don't poll WalMart, Costco, or specialist bookstores, and BookScan omits the two cut-price stores as well. Even if the levels of consumption are more traceable in the 20th and 21st centuries, the patterns of book consumption are equally, if not more, scattered because of the increased number of outlets. To keep with the example of religious texts, as nonbookstore outlets count for 40 per cent of the sales of many bestselling titles, large sectors of the Red state sales are going uncharted by what are generally Blue state newspapers, according to Rachel Elinsky.[24] (This would also suggest a buried audience for children's books, romance, and genre fiction too, if one takes into consideration their strong showing on the Walmart charts). Elinsky suggests that for religious books, what gets recorded in the secular press are actually the crossover sales, a point absolutely in keeping with Escarpit's point back in the 60s that bestsellers are fundamentally books that have broken out of their target market and secured a readership beyond the original projections that governed the size of the first hardcover printing. John Sutherland's *Bestsellers: A Very Short Introduction* suggests that these sales are not anomalous and gives a list of religious bestsellers through the ages that includes Lew Wallace's 1880 *Ben Hur* (see the essay by James Russell in this collection), Charles M. Sheldon's *In His Steps* (1897), and Lloyd C. Douglas's *The Robe* (1843), but again, he refrains from tying the list to monolithic cultural judgments. The incredible variances in the texture, priorities, and choices about history entailed in making the list mean that we have to accept the realm of bestsellerdom as a significant but dizzyingly uncertain discourse. Despite the fact that archivists work with highly visible commercial objects, the numerous and compound choices made about what sales to record and when to record them hollows out the foundations of any composite structure we attempt to build from these numbers.

Colonial bestsellers

As the relatively low levels of scholarship in the last half century suggests, popular texts in the Colonial period are hardest to track, but difficulties continue into the Revolutionary era and nineteenth century. The many bestselling eighteenth- and nineteenth-century novels that were sold, in the main, by subscription—Mark Twain's are a good example—or given away as 'extras' in the papers don't make the lists, nor do the number of people who may gain access to a single text through Franklin's new subscription libraries. (The current library bestsellers have a 'most borrowed' chart in the form of the *Library Journal's* bestseller list).[25] These library lists are more stable than the newspaper charts in many ways—perennially bestselling authors and books continue to be borrowed in libraries long after their sales drop off the scales). The demographic for the bestseller also changes with the libraries. James Hart argues in *The Popular Book* that in this early period the big three-volume editions of the eighteenth- and nineteenth-century novel were seldom purchased. Instead, they moved through circulation libraries into the hands of the many. He cites a commentator from 1772 who marvels that in America "the common people are on a footing, in point of literature, with the middle ranks of Europe," that "it is scarce possible to conceive the number of readers with which even every little town abounds," and that "for one person of distinction and fortune, there were twenty tradesmen" using circulating libraries.[26]

As the American book market expanded, it continued, even after the colonists had settled down into Independence, to be a decidedly trans-Atlantic industry. The biggest sellers in the American nineteenth century, as Dickens and Walter Scott complained, were English books, ferociously and expertly pirated as soon as they came off the boat at a relatively low cost to the consumer, zero profit for the author, and a high margin for the publisher. Because American texts were protected by copyright from 1783, the pirated British texts were much cheaper and sold much better; American authors like Washington Irving and James Fennimore Cooper found they had to reach across the Atlantic to the more regulated English market to make a profit. Hart gives a telling anecdote about Samuel Johnson who, when condescending to the nascent country with a dismissive "The Americans! What do they know and what do they read," gets his suitably witty answer in terms of high, Europeanized discourse and Johnson's own books: "they read, Sir, *The Rambler*."[27] For scholars, this trans-Atlantic dimension to the eighteenth- and nineteenth-century American intellect raises some serious questions about national identity that still haven't gone away—how American does an American bestseller have to be? The first massive selling novel in America, Susanna Rowson's *Charlotte Temple* (see the essay in this collection by Gideon Mailer), was written by an Englishwoman, and the current bestselling author in American history, J. K. Rowling, is also English. Michael Korda argues that it took the passage of the International Copyright Act in 1891 to create the conditions necessary for the bestseller list; whereas before international copyright publishers were inclined to keep revenues a trade secret because exposing them meant that authors would come asking for royalties, "once copyright protection was instituted and the author's right to receive royalties was recognized, boasting about sales very quickly became a way of boosting sales."[28] The first of these lists was famously the list published by the Bookman in 1895 that brought together books in demand in 16 cities until it was bought out by *Publishers Weekly* in 1912.[29] Nonfiction was added to the lists in 1913.[30]

Harry Potter and the "young adult" bestseller

The implicit categorization of the bestseller as a popular adult fiction is considerably challenged by the record kept by these lists. Writing in 1975, Hackett explained that "today the nonfiction bestsellers outsell the novels by two to one." This ratio remains stable, with the notable exception of J. K. Rowling's books which outsold even adult nonfiction. In a year like 2005, where John Grisham's *The Broker* topped the *Publishers Weekly* adult hardcover list with shipped and billed figures of 1,827,877, and *Natural Cures "They" Don't Want You to Know About* by Kevin Trudeau holds top position on the nonfiction adult hardcover list with 3,724,422 units, *Harry Potter and the Half Blood Prince* shipped and billed for 13,500,000 copies.[31] Even allowing for the smoke and mirrors of advertising, counting, and recording sales, this accounts for an extraordinary degree of cultural penetration—the *Half Blood Prince* alone, by Mott's criteria, reached 4.8 per cent of the total population of America. If we try and scale this down to children's reading and estimate that half these sales were to readers under 18, and that, according to the US Statistics office, 25 per cent of Americans were under 18 at that point in time, we get a figure that suggests that just above 9 per cent of all American children owned a copy of this one Harry Potter novel. These extraordinary sales for young adult novels are not just confined to Rowling. The top 20 for the current *USA Today* list, which brings together mass market paperback, trade paperback, and hardback sales, is dominated by children's and young adult serial fiction.

Paperbacks and platforms

The difference in cultural visibility between these three books also raises interesting questions about the lists. The *New York Times* created a separate children's list in 2000 with the result that J. K. Rowling's dominance of the top of the charts was sidelined in favor of a faster-moving, more obviously adult chart.[32] The cultural worries of the time about the retreat of adults into juvenile reading aren't necessarily anything new. As Clive Bloom suggests, genre fiction in particular has always been considered juvenile and has tapped such large markets because it's always been read by a large proportion of children and young adults.[33] The *Harry Potter* phenomenon reverses the same flow, but what it does make obvious is that the picture painted by the bestseller list of the national imagination is an important part of its content. This is the reason for the sheer number of lists—they represent different, and often warring, interpretations of American culture to different sections of that culture. The kinds of comments made about the *USA Today* list are indicative: "unlike the more prestigious lists," Eliza Truitt writes, tongue-in-cheek, *USAT* doesn't "prune out the lowbrow riffraff," and indeed the stratification of the *New York Times* list works to try and keep discourse moving for the new releases both in the more traditionally canonical literary arena and in the realm of the popular book.[34] Creating a separate list for the cheapest, massive selling trade paperbacks, the editors argue, "gives more emphasis to the literary novels and short-story collections reviewed so often in our pages (and sometimes published only in softcover)," while preserving the trade list as a record of popular interest.[35] The physical differences between the books, as Dixler explains them, mirror exactly the class distinctions at work in the rakish history of the bestseller:

> Mass-market books are designed to fit into the racks set near the checkout counter at supermarkets, drugstores, hospital gift shops and airport newsstands. They are priced affordably so they can be bought on impulse. There are other production differences in binding and paper quality (historically, paperbacks were printed on "pulp" and could fit in the consumer's pocket). The format is often used for genre fiction, science fiction, romance, thrillers and mysteries.[36]

Trade paperbacks, on the other hand, are what most review papers, including the *Times,* focus on, because although the discourse of selling works outside the canon, the discourse of reviewing reworks the canon from the inside. Trade paperbacks are the "novels that reading groups choose and college professors teach," Dixler writes, and "are generally printed on more expensive paper and with sturdier binding." "Because they are more expensive to produce they are higher in price and often (not always) printed in smaller numbers" and "unlike mass-market paperbacks, which are usually sold on racks, trade paperbacks are sold in bookstores ('to the trade') and are shelved with their spines facing out, like hardcovers." "A trade paperback," she writes, "in short, is the book you'd want to be reading if you were sitting at Les Deux Magots and Simone de Beauvoir was looking straight at you."[37] Conversely, I'd add, because of the single-page format of the Kindle, Nook, and Sony Ebook Readers, the downloaded book is the title you can read in public without anyone's knowledge. (The lists are suitably evasive about ebooks—*The New York Times* includes ebooks, but not for all genres, *The Wall Street Journal*, because it uses Nielsen ratings, includes ebooks across the genres, and *Publishers Weekly* does not yet include any electronic texts. Amazon keeps its own counsel, complicating the whole notion of a "bestseller" yet again by giving many of its classic books away for free on the Kindle.) Years ago, the hardback would have been the status symbol of choice, but in recent years, publishers have begun to produce less expensive trade paperback originals with the distinctive rough-cut edges and wraparound flyleaves of hardback books. And with the advent of lightweight digital readers, the medium is now perhaps the message—as regards status symbols, at least. As the class distinctions of the literary canon come under increased scrutiny, every year the stiff boards of the conventionally literary book come closer to resembling the loose leaves of the paperback bestseller.

In his study, Mott found publishers fairly cooperative about providing the numbers, except for a few contemporary publishers who "add to our embarrassments by citing a 'rule of the house' which requires sales figures be kept a close secret," but these early hints that the bestseller lists might be guarded because of their high industrial stakes are significant. Even now, those lists, such as *The Wall Street Journal*, based on the detailed Nielsen BookScan data, are prohibited from publishing unit sales. And, regardless of the completeness of the dataset, we would face the same questions about comparing books released at different times of the year in a single year end figure, whether, at the other end of the scale, a week of very fast but exhaustive sales is enough to make a book culturally significant, or indeed whether, as Blatty v. *The New York Times* suggests, a book needs to already be judged to be culturally significant to make it to the data pool in the first place.

Even if they were based on a mythical total set of records, cultural conclusions drawn from the bestseller lists would still belong to the realm of discourse, analysis, and argument because the lists themselves represent multiple tastes, multiple purchases, and overlapping and diverging American patterns of consumption. "We must guard against two misconceptions," Mott wrote back in 1947 "(a) that there is, at a given time, only one best seller public" and "(b) that anybody can describe, or conceive of, such a thing as a typical best seller."[38] This caution, like many of the early ones in the history of the bestseller, still stands. Jane Tompkins' conception of the popular book as an intervention in culture, or Claud Cockburn's idea that the bestseller provides for lacks and shortfalls in everyday life, or Davidson's emphasis on the popular book as the trace of individual lives and choices, all continue to be viable because they take account of the kinds of subtleties inherent in reading consumed objects. Although the bestseller list charts value in the sense of sales and profits, deducing cultural values from these integers is more of an art than a mathematical science. The history of the bestseller is the history of a discourse that is undeniably partial—in both senses of the word.

Bibliography

Anderson, Chris. *The Long Tail: Why the Future of Business is Selling Less of More*. New York: Hyperion, 2006.

Bloom, Clive. *Bestsellers: Popular Fiction Since 1900*. Basingstoke: Palgrave, 2002.

Bolonik, Kera. 'A List of their Own,' *Salon.com*, August 16th 2000. http://www.salon.com/2000/08/16/bestseller/.

Brown, Candy Gunther. *The Word in the World*. Chapel Hill: UNC Press, 2004.

Davidson, Cathy N. *Revolution and the Word: The Rise of the Novel in America*. New York: Oxford University Press, 1986.

Dixler, Elsa. 'Paperback Row,' *New York Times*. March 16th 2008. http://www.nytimes.com/2008/03/16/books/review/PaperRow-t.htm.

Donadio, Rachel. 'Faith-Based Publishing' *New York Times*, November 28th 2004. http://www.nytimes.com/2004/11/28/books/review/28DONADIO.html.

Dreher, Christopher. 'Random Numbers,' *Salon.com* June 25th 2002. http://dir.salon.com/story/books/feature/2002/06/25/bestsellers.html.

Elinsky, Rachel. 'Religious publishing for the red state consumers and beyond,' *Publishing Research Quarterly*, 21:4. December 6, 2005. 11–29.

Escarpit, Robert. *The Book Revolution*. Paris: UNESCO, 1966.

Gelder, Kenneth. *Popular Fiction: The Logics and Practices of a Literary Field*. London: Routledge, 2004.

Hackett, Alice Payne. *80 Years of Best Sellers, 1895–1975*. New York: R. R. Bowker, 1977.

Hart, James D. *The Popular Book: A History of America's Literary Taste*. New York: Oxford University Press, 1950.

Hoyt, Clark. 'Books for the Ages, if Not for the Best-Seller List,' *New York Times*, October 21st 2007.

Kirkpatrick, David D. 'Shaping Cultural Tastes at Big Retail Chains,' *New York Times*, May 18th 2003.

Korda, Michael. *Making the List: A Cultural History of the American Bestseller, 1900–99*. New York: Barnes & Noble Books, 2001.

Miller, Laura J. 'The Best-Seller List as Marketing Tool and Historical Fiction,' *Book History* 3, 2000. 286–304.

Mott, Frank Luther. *Golden Multitudes: The Story of Best Sellers in the United States*. New York: Bowker, 1960.

Offman, Craig. 'Gray Lady Down,' *Salon.com*, October 14th 1999. http://www.salon.com/books/feature/1999/10/14/nytimes.

Rocha, Sean. What's With All the 'National Best Sellers?' How so many books get to the top of the charts,' *Slate*, October 15th 2004. http://www.slate.com/id/2108296.

Sorensen, Alan T. 'Bestseller Lists and Product Variety,' *The Journal of Industrial Economics*, 55:4. December 2007. 715–38.

Sutherland, John. *Bestsellers: Popular Fiction of the 1970s*. London: Routledge & Kegan Paul, 1981.

Tebbel, John. *A History of Book Publishing in the United States*. New York: Bowker, 1972.

Tompkins, Jane. *Sensational Designs: The Cultural Work of American Fiction, 1790–1860*. New York: Oxford University Press, 1986.

Truitt, Eliza. 'Apocalypse Soon: Bookseller's Biggest Nightmare has Already Come True,' *Slate*, July 30th 2001. http://www.slate.com/id/112530.

Wyatt, Edward. 'Literary Novels Going Straight to Paperback.' *New York Times,* March 22 2006.

Notes

1 Davidson, Cathy N., *Revolution and the Word: The Rise of the Novel in America* (New York: Oxford University Press, 1986) 257.

2 John Sutherland, *Bestsellers: Popular Fiction of the 1970s* (London: Routledge & Kegan Paul, 1981) 11.

3 Sutherland, *Bestsellers*, 5.

4 Frank Luther Mott, *Golden Multitudes: The Story of Best Sellers in the United States* (New York: Bowker, 1960) 7.

5 Mott, *Golden Multitudes*, 6.

6 Eliza Truitt, 'Apocalypse Soon: Booksellers' Biggest Nightmare has Already Come True,' *Slate*, July 30th 2001, http://www.slate.com/id/112530.

7 Ken Gelder, *Popular Fiction*.

8 Alice Payne Hackett, *80 Years of Best Sellers, 1895–1975* (New York: R. R. Bowker, 1977) 3.

9 See Laura J. Miller, 'The Best-Seller List as Marketing Tool and Historical Fiction,' *Book History* 3 (2000) 286–304, and

Michael Korda, *Making the List: A Cultural History of the American Bestseller, 1900–99* (New York: Barnes & Noble Books, 2001) xxii.

10   Clark Hoyt, 'Books for the Ages, if Not for the Best-Seller List,' *New York Times*, October 21st, 2007.

11   See Hoyt, 'Books for the Ages, if Not for the Best-Seller List'.

12   Sutherland, *Bestsellers*, 15.

13   Mott, *Golden Multitudes*, 9.

14   Mott, *Golden Multitudes*, 9.

15   Sutherland, *Bestsellers*, 6.

16   Robert Escarpit, *The Book Revolution* (Paris: UNESCO, 1966) 116.

17   The most authoritative list for secondhand books is the chart compiled by the world's largest secondhand book network, ABE books, available on their website, http://www.abebooks.com.

18   Sutherland, *Bestsellers*, 36.

19   See Davidson, *Revolution and the Word*, Chapters 1–4 for a detailed investigation into how books were read in the early republic.

20   James D. Hart, *The Popular Book: A History of America's Literary Taste* (New York: Oxford University Press, 1950) 8.

21   World Factbook USA, https://www.cia.gov/library/publications/the-world-factbook/.

22   Davidson, *Revolution and the Word*, 56.

23   Davidson, *Revolution and the Word*, 24; 25.

24   See Kirkpatrick for the WalMart figures.

25   See www.libraryjournal.com.

26   Hart, *The Popular Book*, 24; 25.

27   Hart, *The Popular Book*, 30.

28   Korda, Making the List, xvii.

29   Laura J. Miller, 'The Best-Seller List as Marketing Tool and Historical Fiction'; Hackett, 3.

30   Hackett, *80 Years of Best Sellers*, 4.

31   Hackett, *80 Years of Best Sellers*, 4.

32   See Kera Bolonik, 'A List of their Own,' *Salon.com*, August 16th, 2000, http://www.salon.com/2000/08/16/bestseller/.

33   Clive Bloom, *Bestsellers: Popular Fiction Since 1900* (Basingstoke: Palgrave, 2002) 4.

34 See Ken Gelder's *Popular Fiction: The Logics and Practices of a Literary Field* for a reading that emphasizes the qualitative, as well as quantitative differences between popular and canonical fiction.

35 Elsa Dixler, 'Paperback Row,' *New York Times*. March 16th 2008. http://www.nytimes.com/2008/03/16/books/review/PaperRow-t.htm.

36 Dixler, 'Paperback Row.'

37 Dixler, 'Paperback Row.'

38 Mott, *Golden Multitudes*, 4.

3

The history of *Charlotte Temple* as an American bestseller

Gideon Mailer

From 1875 to 1920, a number of New York newspapers devoted several articles to potential "evidence" relating to the previous existence of a young woman and the man who betrayed her. Their names were Charlotte Temple and Lieutenant Montraville. Public interest in their past lives had increased steadily since 1850, when a tombstone had been anonymously erected in the graveyard of New York's Trinity Church. The name "Charlotte Temple" was engraved on the granite, surrounded by nothing more than unetched space. On August 29, 1875, the *Sunday New York Times* recounted local suspicions that a "medal plate" engraved with the name "Charlotte Stanley" had been "stolen" from the same graveyard. Charlotte Stanley was thought by some to be the real Charlotte Temple because the tombstone was erected when the churchyard was under renovation, and supposedly "replaced" the stolen medal plate.[1] In 1876, a librarian at the New York Historical Society claimed that "while erecting the present church the engine room was over it, the rumor was that the plate had been removed at that time. The foreman of stone cutting carved the name [Charlotte Temple]."[2] In the same year, a journalist for *The Sun* interviewed a church officer who claimed that his wife had known a "Mrs. Freeborn."

Freeborn had apparently provided refuge for Charlotte after she was abandoned by two of her betrayers, "Montraville and La Rue." Charlotte had died in her home, in a semi-clandestine state.[3] A French gardener at Trinity Church remembered that "an old English woman used to come here every day or two, whenever the weather was fine. She was well dressed in black always. She was a lady, not a common woman. She would stand a long time by the grave just so . . . Some people about her said she was Charlotte Temple's daughter or her granddaughter, but I don't believe it."[4] Francis W. Halsey cited a letter to the *New York Post* written by a man whose office overlooked the graveyard:

> The first tears I ever saw in the eyes of a grown person were shed for her. In that churchyard are graves of heroes, philosophers, and martyrs, whose names are familiar to the youngest scholar, and whose memory is dear to the wisest and best. Their graves, though marked by imposing monuments, win but a glance of curiosity, while the turf over Charlotte Temple is kept fresh by falling tears.[5]

A mysterious tomb to Charlotte Temple, in a graveyard surrounded by office-workers, was "kept fresh by falling tears."

But there was no real Charlotte Temple. She was a fictional character created in a 1791 novel by Susanna Rowson, an English-born writer, poet, and educator, who had moved as a young girl to Massachusetts in 1767, returned to England in relative poverty in 1778, and finally resettled in America in 1793.[6] Still, Rowson portrayed her most famous work as a "Tale of Truth." Its preface requested that her "fair readers" consider it as "not merely the effusion of Fancy, but as a reality."[7] Elizabeth Barnes has suggested that Rowson's attempt to harness the "power of representation" allowed the "reality" of her fictional character to be "proven not by historical record but by affective response." Sympathies could be "exploited, manufactured, even mass-marketed, but readers nonetheless experience them as personal and, in that sense, real."[8] Thus, the real grave of a fictional character received far more visitors than the neighboring graves of such illustrious men as Alexander Hamilton and Robert Fulton.[9] Hundreds of visitors continued to make a pilgrimage to it for 100 years. Thousands more bought and read the book, which became "America's first best-seller"—the highest selling American novel prior to the publication of Uncle Tom's Cabin.[10]

From its initial 1794 American edition, published by Matthew Carey in Philadelphia, *Charlotte Temple* (originally titled *Charlotte: A Tale of Truth*) was continually re-published after its first large print run, which ran to around 1000 copies.[11] In an 1812 letter to Rowson, her publisher rejoiced at the novel's two-decade-long success:

> Charlotte Temple is by far the most popular & in my opinion the most useful novel ever published in this country & probably not inferior to any published in England ... [its sales] exceed those of any of the most celebrated novels that ever appeared in England. I think the number disposed of must far exceed 50,000 copies; & the sale still continues ... I have an edition in press of 3000, which I shall sell at 50 or 60 ½ cents each.[12]

Despite having written such a "useful" text, like most novelists in America before 1820, Rowson was never able to support herself solely by writing: she was "breadwinner for herself, her husband, his sister, his sister's children, his illegitimate son, and two adopted children of her own" and managed financially in part because of her prodigious output as "a novelist, poet, playwright, essayist, songwriter, and anthologist."[13] Still, Cathy Davidson estimates that more than 40,000 copies of Rowson's most famous novel were sold by 1812.[14] Throughout the nineteenth century, *Charlotte Temple* appealed to more than just "the young and thoughtless of the fair sex" whom Rowson had originally sought to address.[15] In his 1870 biography of Rowson, Elias Nason stressed the novel's long-standing popularity among people of all descriptions:

> It has stolen its way alike into the study of the divine and into the workshop of the mechanic; into the parlor of the accomplished lady and the bedchamber of her waiting-maid; into the log-hut on the extreme border of modern civilization and into the forecastle of the whale ship on the long ocean. It has been read by the grey-bearded professor after his 'divine Plato' ... [and] by the school girl stealthfully in her seat at school.[16]

Whether read by gray-bearded Platonists or stealthy schoolgirls, *Charlotte Temple* had appeared in more than 200 editions by 1930.[17] Charlotte's plight appears to have become something of an obsession not only for white middle-class women, but also for "husbands," "lawyer[s]," "divines," "brothers," "sisters," "young black women," "factory girls," "accomplished lad[ies]," "maids[s]," "farmers," "grandmothers[s]," "grandsons," and settlers of the "Western prairies."[18]

How should we understand the popularity of Rowson's novel in the decades after its first American publication? Did its "truth" appeal to differing individual identities or to common social norms? If the former, how could a representation of subjective isolation maintain a bestselling appeal? If the latter, how could a didactic reflection of communal values arouse such an emotional response among individual readers?

Whether appealing to a mass of subjective perceptions or to objectively defined morality, *Charlotte Temple* pricked the conscience of more American than British readers, despite its publication two years earlier on the eastern side of the Atlantic. Selling the novel for between 50 cents and a dollar (depending partly on the bindings), Matthew Carey made sure to remind readers in the first page of the book that Rowson was now "of Philadelphia." William Lane, on the other hand, did not include *Charlotte Temple* in his 1798 prospectus of the most popular works from *Minerva Press*, nor was it ever reprinted in England before 1819.[19] Thus, any examination of *Charlotte Temple's* bestselling status should address a further question: how and why did the American context for Rowson's publication and reception differ so greatly from that of Britain's?

Charlotte Temple: Conservative or radical sensibility?

Reporting back on his 1819 journey through America, Henry Bradshaw Fearon reflected the jaundiced views of many British commentators on American literary culture, when he claimed:

> The reading of Americans . . . is English; there being few native writers, and but a small number of these who possess the respect of even their own country men. Our novels and poetry, not

excepting those which proceed from the Minerva Press, meet with an immediate reprint, and constitute practically the entire American library . . . Notwithstanding this voluntary national dependence, there are, perhaps, no people, not even excepting the French, who are so vain as the Americans.[20]

Fearon observed, with a hint of smugness, that Americans could only mimic or reprint English letters, "not excepting those which proceed from the Minerva Press." How true was his observation? Did *Charlotte Temple's* bestselling popularity simply reflect the continuing provincial anxieties of American readers, writers, and publishers, and their struggle to maintain coherence against the British benchmark? Matthew Carey's edition of *Charlotte, a Tale of Truth* was indeed an accurate reprint of the original English version which had been published by William Lane's *Minerva Press*. Until "well into the nineteenth century, American publishers pirated popular British novels with great frequency, and often works of American authorship were passed off as English novels and even as Lane novels."[21] That Lane's less-than-highbrow publishing output and methods were adopted in the new American republic would seem to support Fearon's contention that indigenous originality was cast off at the expense of popular emulation.

On the surface, at least, America's first bestseller did incorporate a classic—even hackneyed—sentimental plot: seduction, deceit, melodrama, and intense emotionalism all appear. Charlotte is born in England and educated at a female boarding school. She is seduced by Montraville, a serving lieutenant in the British army. Despite his promise to marry her once they arrive on American soil, Charlotte equivocates. It is ambiguous as to whether her ocean transport takes place according to her own will or as an act of coercion by La Rue and Montraville. It is presumed in the text that Charlotte loses her virginity sometime on that voyage. She is eventually abandoned by Montraville, and his male friend, Belcour. She is left to die in madness and childbirth by a man who instead marries a wealthy woman and absconds to fight in the Revolutionary War.

The first 'modern' generation of American literary scholarship came uncomfortably close to Fearon's damning judgment of early-national publishing history. According to Francis Matthiessen and then Leslie Fiedler, the popularity of novels such as *Charlotte Temple* owed much to the reception of bad English literary habits in America, practices which had long since waned on the eastern side of the Atlantic. An underdeveloped literary culture encouraged maudlin sentimentalism and crudely moralistic warnings against seduction. Where aesthetic sensibilities had not sufficiently developed, a text's popularity could only derive from its cheap evocation of common and uneducated emotions, and prurient morality. As Fiedler argued in 1960, it "is not enough however simply to say that Sentimentalism triumphed everywhere in our fiction; it must also be added that it proved almost everywhere a blight, a universal influence which was also a universal calamity." And chief among the "third rate sentimentalists" responsible for this "calamity" was Susanna Rowson.[22] In such an analysis, the popularity of *Charlotte Temple* many decades after its first publication owed much to the continued naiveté and hunger for trite sentimentalism among its readership.[23] British literary culture had moved on by the end of the eighteenth century, achieving a critical maturity which emotional American readers continued to lack, not yet having enjoyed their own literary "renaissance."

While refraining from restricting Rowson's entry into the American literary canon (*pace* Fiedler), a later generation of scholars have damned her novels as conservative morality tales. *Charlotte Temple*'s popularity was somehow "permitted" by elites because its underlying message corresponded with the values promoted by male-orientated political, educational, and religious establishments. The novel's sentimentalism, according to this critique, harnessed a binary division between public and private forms of discernment, as it found its way into the private homes of women who were constrained by the gilded cage of "republican wifehood." Educated American men keenly adopted "moral sense" theories whose philosophical emphasis on private speculation and prerational discernment justified the "civic" importance of feminine domesticity.[24] These theories were popularized by "the Sentimental formula" which, according to Herbert Ross Brown's seminal definition, "was a simple equation resting upon a belief in the spontaneous goodness and benevolence of man's original instincts," and which was

> informed throughout with a moral purpose to which all other elements were subordinated. Into its capacious framework were poured the stock characters and situations dear to popular

storytellers of every generation. The final solution was neatly reserved for the last chapter where the punishment was made to fit the crime, and the reward to equal the virtue. To achieve it, authors subjected the long arm of coincidence to the rack of expediency where it was stretched and fractured to suit every need of the plot. The reader, meanwhile, was made to cry- and to wait. As a 'true-feeler,' he was expected to match pang for pang, and sigh for sigh with the persecuted victim; he was mercifully roasted over the slow firers of suspense . . .[25]

Certain fundamental moral codes could be discerned "aesthetically" rather than rationally, a good act uncontrollably perceived as "beautiful" just as a flower was innately perceived as pleasant. More sensitive to their sentiments and sensuality, women were able to harness their aesthetic and prerational form of ethical discernment. They were to cultivate the sensory development of their male relations, who would then enter the public sphere, able to act "benevolently." Women's own role in the public sphere was diminished at the expense of their private familial and civic function.[26]

Several more recent scholars have adopted Herbert Ross Brown's tacitly disparaging definition of sentimentalism. They argue that Rowson's popularity contributed to the reimposition of moral standards whose first philosophical principles lay in the maintenance of social order and patriarchal control. The association between *Charlotte Temple* and didactic moral philosophy affirmed wedded sexuality, in contrast to Charlotte's tragic extramarital fate.[27] The evocation of the need to harness a common ethical sense warned against seduction and promoted "a form of 'self-governance' by which [the new American woman] check[ed] both sexual desire and the desire for [public] social eminence.[28] Female readers could sympathize with the plight of *Charlotte Temple*'s seduced protagonist without necessarily condoning the actions that led to her fall.[29] According to this analysis, Rowson's novel achieved bestselling popularity as a 'sham sermon to hold change at bay, mere imitations of older British forms."[30] It was one of many "not very subtle warnings to young women without dowries that their value lay in their virginity; [that] if they would be sought after on the marriage market, they must keep that commodity intact. The sentimental tale of seduction thus has been seen as an instrument of bourgeois respectability and middle-class conformity."[31] *Charlotte Temple* was apparently one of many novels which depicted "the family as a model for the nation, [and] demonstrated the ways in which it has become an instrument of social control."[32] The "limitations on women's expression" were "encoded within . . . sentimental culture."[33] "Sentimentality" was a "cultural fantasy which organize[d] social obligations along segregated and idealized gender lines" and offered "a socializing moral force."[34]

These conservative interpretations of *Charlotte Temple's* popular reception, however, risk overlooking a more radical gendered dimension in Rowson's work: if moral norms were discerned "aesthetically" and universally, then innate judgment logically remained after a transgression, sexual or otherwise. Thus, in addition to its genteel associations, the novel appealed to women of a more "liminal social and sexual status" because of its ultimately forgiving message: Charlotte's loss of chastity did not deny her eventual entry into familial domesticity and her assumption of its private moral code. The leveling possibilities of sensory moral perception, therefore, may also explain the popularity of Rowson's most famous work. Its appeal to private and familial social codes assumed a universal aesthetic sensibility, whose moral aspect could also transcend social divisions and particular sexual circumstances.[35]

The affliction of Rowson's female protagonist may even have offered a contemporary critique, mirroring the fate of women who continued to lack political agency in the early American republic despite their innate moral capabilities. They were unable to act according to their ethical sense because their words and deeds were deemed inferior to those of men: their bodies were defined as "sensual" according to the word's sexual rather than moral sense.[36] These implications explain why male civic leaders often lamented the popularity of female sentimentalism during the 1790s and 1800s. An 1802 edition of the *New England Quarterly* reprinted a 1797 article from England, which denounced "Novel Reading, a Cause of Female Depravity." The subjective fictional world of sentimental novels apparently destroyed the natural order and bond between women, their parents, and the wider community.[37] Would anxious men have issued such denunciations had they believed that novels such as *Charlotte Temple* aided the quest for social and moral stability? How do we square general fears by the male establishment with the received view that American sentimentalism during the early national period was a conservative and stabilizing force?

Charlotte Temple's subsequent publishing history may offer one explanation. Perhaps the novel rose in popularity during the first half of the nineteenth century precisely because American printers marketed its text in a way that assuaged initial anxieties about female authored and predominantly female-read works.[38] Matthew Carey followed the first American edition of Rowson's work with many subsequent editions, and several re-titled versions after 1797 referred to the "truth" (read morality) of the tale. By 1802, *The History of Charlotte Temple* had been published by John Babcock of Hartford, Connecticut, and by William W. Morse of New Haven, Connecticut. Peter Stewart published another Philadelphia edition, while others were printed in Alexandria, Virginia, and in New York City.[39] That a number of these subsequent editions were marketed to children demonstrated a popular awareness that the novel was inflected with moral pedagogy rather than salacious sentimentalism. In 1811, Samuel Avery even produced a "toy book" *Charlotte Temple*, at 13 × 7 cm. Appended to it was a large advertisement which pointed out that Avery also published "school books, bibles, and testaments" as well as "a great variety of juvenile books, which he intends to sell, (wholesale and retail) as cheap as can be purchased in the United States."[40] Rowson's novel was also marketed as a genteel gift, with editions in the 1850s which were set in gold-signed Morocco leather. "Story paper versions" of the narrative later "masqueraded as newspapers" to take advantage of the low postal rates accorded to the post-Revolutionary press and circumvent high distribution costs.[41] All these new versions gave the novel a quotidian legitimacy, allaying earlier fears that sentimental "art" led to female corruption.

Charlotte Temple and the popular evangelical narrative

So far we have considered whether and how moral sense reasoning contributed to *Charlotte Temple's* emerging popularity in America, either as a conservative or radical force. Such an analysis, however, risks privileging the perceived importance of common sensibility in the novel's composition and reception. Readers shed tears at Charlotte's "grave" because they believed they shared her affliction. Yet, shared affliction did not necessarily denote universal moral discernment. In Charlotte's plight and in her readers' response, aroused passions could indicate the individual's unintelligibility to other beings: crying on her own, suffering from her own subjective affliction, aroused by a confusing vision of another person's separate passions and agonies. During the early-national era, the "democratization of American Christianity" popularized this precept, particularly among women. American evangelicalism offered an alternative to moral sense reasoning.[42] But therein lay a paradox and a certain commonality: perceptual isolation was the only human response which readers shared objectively. Rowson's continual reference to Charlotte's oscillation between "muteness" and "hysterical engrossment," and her communication through bodily movements rather than words, were all redolent of revivalist religious narratives.[43] The realization of universal ethical subjectivity necessarily evoked fear, even terror. Nonetheless, evangelicalism counseled that common comfort, provided by divine grace, would flow as a gift to any individual who acknowledged the fallibility of their own unregenerate moral perception.[44]

Let us examine more closely, then, Rowson's debt to evangelical thought and its potential contribution to *Charlotte Temple's* immediate popularity. Charlotte begins the novel "Pure and innocent by nature."[45] Yet, the narrator exclaims early on: "But alas! Poor Charlotte, she knew not the deceitfulness of her own heart or she would have avoided the trial of her stability." Charlotte continually suffers from and laments her subjective perceptual stance. "I am afraid I ought not," she constantly repeats to herself during the novel. "Alas! My torn heart!," she exclaims before she leaves her family with Montraville and La Rue. "How shall I act?" Rowson often addresses her readers as "volatile," suggesting their unpredictable emotionalism rather than common sensibility. Yet while Charlotte becomes ever more "tremblingly alive" to her own isolated perceptions, she initially fails to transmute this realization onto the behavior of others.[46] She believes that the words of other individuals correspond to their objective definition and so is easily seduced and deceived.

Charlotte's later recognition that her friend La Rue has misled and betrayed her marks her growing confusion, and her eventual demise. Seemingly alone in the world, she begs La Rue (now Mrs Crayton) for charity, only for her former friend to claim not "to know" Charlotte. "[N]ot know me," cried Charlotte, rushing into the room,. . . "not know me, not remember the ruined Charlotte Temple, who, but for you, perhaps might still have been innocent, still have been happy. Oh! La Rue, this is beyond every thing I could have believed possible."[47] La Rue's hysteria is put on: "Take her away," said Mrs. Crayton, "she will really frighten me into hysterics; take her away I say this instant." Charlotte's is real, and uncontrolled: "I can at least die here," said Charlotte, "I feel I cannot long survive this dreadful conflict. Father of mercy, here let me finish my existence." Her agonizing sensations overpowered her, and she fell senseless on the floor.[48]

In a letter to her mother toward the end of the novel, written after the period of confusion, a "guilty, but repentant" Charlotte Temple describes her cruel seduction and betrayal by Montraville, and the agony of her separation from her mother, "like the separation of the soul and body." She yearns: "Oh could I but receive your blessing and forgiveness before I died, it would smooth my passage to the peaceful grave, and be a blessed foretaste of a happy eternity. I beseech you, curse me not . . . but let a tear of pity and pardon fall to the memory of your lost Charlotte."[49] Evangelical narratives had always stressed the necessary separation between "soul and body" that followed feverish passion, and which provided eventual serenity alongside the reception of grace at conversion.[50] The "kneeling figure of Charlotte" remained in "her affecting situation." According to the narrator, such a pious vision would naturally "affect" a response in those who witnessed it, "even a Stoic." On the surface, however, Crayton appears unmoved by Charlotte's uncontrolled performance. But this response is only a corrupt mask, for Charlotte's confusion and volatility reminds Crayton of her *own* identity's subjective nature: "don't let me ever see her [Charlotte] again. I declare she has flurried me so, I shan't be myself again this fortnight."[51] Crayton refuses to concede the inevitability of her own sensory confusion, which had been made apparent in her encounter with Charlotte's specific affliction. In a bid to maintain her "own self," Crayton deliberately avoided arousing further—and thereby acknowledging—her personal "flurries." Here, the reader encounters a subtle but powerful vision of human corruption: a failure to recognize the universality of individual perceptual subjectivity.

Rowson, as the narrator, "blushes" while recounting the corruption of Belcour, another of Charlotte's betrayers: "Belcour's visits became less frequent; he forgot the solemn charge given him by Montraville; he even forgot the money entrusted to his care; and, the burning blush of indignation and shame tinges my cheek while I write it, this disgrace to humanity and manhood at length forgot even the injured Charlotte; and, attracted by the blooming health of a farmer's daughter . . . left the unhappy girl to sink unnoticed to the grave." Belcour's behavior reminds the narrator of her own individual frailty, a blush of her *own* shame. He is unable to have such a reaction, but Charlotte, Rowson, and presumably her readers, can.[52] When Charlotte attempts to describe her betrayal in writing, a "burning blush of shame die[s] her cheeks" red.[53] This distinguishes her from betrayers such as Belcour and La Rue. According to the narrator, "certain I am that when once a woman has stifled the sense of shame in her own bosom . . . she grows hardened in guilt."[54] It is the refusal of charity from *another* being which makes Charlotte "tremblingly alive" to her "own treacherous heart."[55] From early on in the novel, Charlotte continually worries that she has failed the biblical injunction to honor her parents. But she does not yet have the wherewithal—or the tragic experience—to ascribe her comprehension of personal sin onto other beings, each equally subjective, corrupted, and fallible. As readers, until this later point, we are made to "dwell in the kind of anxious self-doubt that Charlotte found so painful."[56]

In contrast to Crayton's feigned self-control, Charlotte's oscillation between silent melancholia and frenzied confusion finally transforms into more predictable prayer: ". . . I have but one care—my poor infant! Father of mercy," continued she, raising her eyes, "of thy infinite goodness, grant that the sins of the parent be not be visited on the unoffending child. May those who taught me to despise thy laws be forgiven; lay not my offences to their charge, I beseech thee; and oh! Shower the choicest of thy blessings on those whose pity has soothed the afflicted heart, and made easy even the bed of pain and sickness."[57] She was "exhausted by the fervent address to the throne of mercy, and though her lips still moved her voice became inarticulate: she lay for some time as it were in a doze."[58] The novel's narrator assumes the role of an evangelical communicator, highlighting and elucidating the oral and physical signs of Charlotte's revival. In her final moments, a "beam of joy," like the "streams of light" that are Christ's love, crosses Charlotte's face: "her countenance was serenely composed," she raised her eyes to heaven and then closed them for ever.[59] Having demonstrated her submission to the "throne of mercy," Charlotte asks for her child, who is brought to her, after which "she put it in her father's arms. "Protect her," said she, "and bless your dying."[60]

Assuming that she would be female, Rowson suggests that a reader of her narrative might now cast her eyes toward the final resting place of one of her own "frail sister[s] of morality": "Shame bows her to the earth, remorse tears her distracted mind, and guilt, poverty, and disease close the dreadful scene." Interrupting this ideal vision, the narrator then evokes a more sanctimonious "finger of contempt" who might think it appropriate to point out to "some passing daughters of youthful mirth, the humble bed where lies this frail sister."[61] Such an "uncharitable and insensate wretch" believed in her objective and superior judgment of Charlotte's affliction. Rowson rebukes those who would use the novel as a simple tool of education and warning: "Oh no! had she a heart of sensibility, she will stop, and thus address the unhappy victim of folly—'Thou had'st thy faults, but sure thy sufferings have expiated them: thy errors brought thee to an early grave; but though wert a fellow—creature—thou hast been unhappy—then be those errors forgotten."[62] The digression ends: "For ever honoured be the sacred drop of humanity; the angel of mercy shall record its source, and the soul from whence it sprang shall be immortal."[63] Thus, Rowson avoided framing her novel as a cautionary tale in the mode of conservative sensibility. She defines a more subtle representation of the dangers of human affliction and presents an alternative possibility: the acknowledgment of an individual's subjective stance as a state shared by all people, revealed and mitigated by an influx of grace. It is not surprising, then, that Matthew Carey increasingly sought to market Rowson's novel alongside published evangelical tracts. In his editions of *Charlotte Temple*, he only included reviews that focused on Charlotte's status as a "saintly martyr."[64] Significantly, none of the novel's British publishers included statements in their subsequent editions. Carey copied the public exoneration of a "fallen woman" and placed it under the heading

"Of Charlotte, the Reviewers have given the following character."[65] The message of universal affliction and potential regeneration was more marketable on the western side of the Atlantic.

At the end of the novel, Mr. Temple, Charlotte's father, meets Montraville. He refrains from vengeance or rancour, despite his daughter's death: "if thou wert the seducer of my child, thy own reflexions be thy punishment. I wrest not the power from the hand of omnipotence." The novel returns to London, where Charlotte's parents and her new daughter Lucy meet a ruined La Rue. Mr. Temple "could not behold her in this distress without some emotions of pity." As she dies in a hospital, La Rue is "a striking example that vice, however prosperous in the beginning, in the end leads only to misery and shame."[66] Her inability to feel her own shame—unlike Charlotte and even the novel's narrator—maintains her alienation in fictional death: readers do not feel for her, paradoxically, because she has not acknowledged her own perceptual isolation. Conversely, Charlotte's continual ability to feel indignity—her acknowledgment of her "own treacherous heart"—places her in a sentimental community even after her demise. In her fictional death, Charlotte had a continued life in the cult that developed around her mysterious "grave." Rowson's debt to evangelical revivalism in her narrative technique, dually terrifying and comforting as it was, accounted for *Charlotte Temple's* immediate and continued popularity during the first half of the nineteenth century—above and beyond alternative readings which centered on its supposed delineation of common sensibility, conservative or otherwise.

Bibliography

Barnes, E. *States of Sympathy: Seduction and Democracy in the America Novel.* New York: Columbia University Press, 1997.

Blakey, D. *The Minerva Press 1790–1820.* Oxford: Oxford University Press, 1939.

Davidson, C. *The Revolution and the Word.* New York: Oxford University Press, 1986.

Evans, G. "Rakes, Coquettes, and Republican Patriarchs: Class, Gender, and Nation in Early American Sentimental Fiction," *Canadian Review of American Studies* 25, 1995.

Fiedler, L. *Love and Death in the American Novel.* New York: Stein and Day, 1966.

Fliegelman, J. *Prodigals and Pilgrims: The American Revolution against Patriarchal Authority, 1750–1800.* New York: Cambridge University Press, 1982.

Green, J. *Mathew Carey: Publisher and Patriot.* Philadelphia: James N. Green, Library Company of Philadelphia, 1985.

Gustafson, T. *Representative Words: Politics, Literature, and the American Language, 1776–1865.* Cambridge: Cambridge University Press, 1992.

Hatch, N. *The Democratization of American Christianity.* New Haven: Yale University Press, 1991.

Rowson, S. *Charlotte, a Tale of Truth*, Philadelphia: Matthew Carey, 1794.

— *Charlotte Temple and Lucy Temple.* ed. Ann Douglas, New York: Penguin, 1991.

Rust, M. *Prodigal Daughters: Susanna Rowson's Early American Women.* Chapel Hill, NC: University of North Carolina Press, 2008.

Samuels, S. "The Family, the State, and the Novel in the Early Republic," *American Quarterly* 38(1986): 381–95.

Stern, J. A. *The Plight of Feeling: Sympathy and Dissent in the Early American Novel.* Chicago: University of Chicago Press, 1997.

Notes

1 J. Barnitz Bacon, "Reminiscences of New York in Olden Time," *The New York Sunday Times*, August 29, 1875.

2 William Crommelin, "Letter to William Kelby," July 8, 1876, *New York Historical Society*.

3 "Poor Charlotte Temple," *The Sun*, June 25, 1876.

4 Ibid.

5 *New York Post*, liii, cited in Elizabeth Barnes, *States of Sympathy: Seduction and Democracy in the America Novel* (New York: Columbia University Press, 1997), 62.

6 For biographical details of Rowson, see Marion Rust, *Prodigal Daughters: Susanna Rowson's Early American Women* (Chapel Hill, NC: University of North Carolina Press, 2008), introduction.

7 Susanna Rowson, *Charlotte Temple and Lucy Temple*, ed. Ann Douglas (New York: Penguin, 1991), 5.

8 Barnes, *States of Sympathy*, 61–2.

9 "H.S.B," "Letter to New York Evening Post," September 12, 1903; and "Charlotte Temple's Grave," *New York Daily Tribune*, June 8, 1900.

10 Julia A. Stern, *The Plight of Feeling: Sympathy and Dissent in the Early American Novel* (Chicago: University of Chicago Press, 1997), 10, 35.

11 Cathy Davidson, *The Revolution and the Word* (New York: Oxford University Press, 1986), 7. Rowson's publisher, Matthew Carey, was a 'former Irish revolutionary turned American Democrat and a champion of social causes ranging from equal taxation to improved wages for exploited government seamstresses who were forced to live in poor conditions. Having published several Irish nationalist newspapers, Carey immigrated to America in 1784, where Marquis de Lafayette lent the twenty-four year old immigrant four hundred dollars to set up his printing operation.' See Mathew Carey, *Cursory Reflexions on the System of Taxation, Established in the City of Philadelphia; With a Brief Sketch of Its Unequal and Unjust Operation*, (Philadelphia, 1803); *Wages of Female Labour*, (Philadelphia, 1829); and his *Address to the Wealthy of the Land, Ladies as Well as Gentlemen, on the Character, Conduct, Situation, and Prospect, of Those Whose Sole Dependence for Subsistence, is on the Labour of Their Hands*, (Philadelphia, 1831). For studies of Carey's life, see Earl Bradsher, *Mathew Carey: Editor, Author, and Publisher* (New York, 1912); James Green, *Mathew Carey: Publisher and Patriot*, (Philadelphia, 1985).

12 Carey, cited in Bradsher, *Matthew Carey*, 50.

13 Cathy Davidson, "Ideology and Genre: The Rise of the Novel in America." Fourth Annual James Russell Wiggins Lecture in the History of the Book in American Culture, Worcester, Mass: American Antiquarian Society, 1987. Reprinted in the *Proceedings of the American Antiquarian Society*, 96 (Oct. 1986), 300.

14 Cathy Davidson, *The Revolution and the Word*, 17.

15 Rowson, *Charlotte Temple*, 5.

16 Elias Nason, *A Memoir of Mrs. Susanna Rowson, with Elegant and Illustrative Extracts from Her Writings in Prose and Poetry*, (Albany, NY: 1870) 50' Cathy Davidson, Introduction to Susanna Rowson, *Charlotte Temple*, (Oxford University Press, 1986) xii, xiii.

17 Robert Vail, "Susanna Haswell Rowson, the Author of Charlotte Temple: A Bibliographical Study." *American Antiquarian Society Proceedings*. n.s. v. 42 (1933): 47–160.

18 Cathy Davidson, *Charlotte Temple*, xii–xiii.

19 See Dorothy Blakey, *The Minerva Press 1790–1820*, (Oxford University Press, 1939), appendix 4 (n.p.).

20 Henry Bradshaw Fearon, *Sketches of America. A Narrative of a Journey of Five Thousand Miles Through the Eastern and Western States of America*, (London, 1818), 365–8.

21 Cathy Davidson, "Ideology and Genre," 301.

22 Francis O. Matthiessen, *American Renaissance: art and expression in the age of Emerson and Whitman* (New York: Oxford University Press, 1941); Leslie Fiedler, *Love and Death in the American Novel* (New York: Stein and Day, 1966), 75, 83.

23 See John Frederick, "Hawthorn's 'Scribbling Women'" *The New England Quarterly*, 48.2 (Jun., 1975): 231–40.

24 On the association between Scottish moral sense reasoning and sentimental emotionalism and sympathy, see Rosemarie Zagarri, "Morals, Manners, and the Republican Mother," *American Quarterly* 44.2 (1992): 192–215.

25 Herbert Ross Brown, *The Sentimental Novel in America, 1789–1860* (Durham, N. C., 1940), 44, 176.

26 Jan Lewis "The Republican Wife: Virtue and Seduction in the Early Republic," *William and Mary Quarterly* 44, (1987), 715; Rosemarie Zagarri "Morals, Manners, and the Republican Mother," *American Quarterly* 44.2 (1992), 192–205.

27 On the growing association between "low class" and sexual freedom, see Clare A. Lyons, *Sex among the Rabble: An Intimate History of Gender & Power in the Age of Revolution, Philadelphia, 1730–1830* (Chapel Hill: University of North Carolina Press, 2006), 15, 65, 242–6, 264, 279–80, 288, 295, and 333.

28 See G. Evans, "Rakes, Coquettes, and Republican Patriarchs: Class, Gender, and Nation in Early American Sentimental Fiction," *Canadian Review of American Studies* 25 (1995), 42; Jeffrey Rubin-Dorsky, "The Early American Novel" in E. Elliot and C. Davidson eds, *The Columbia history of the American novel* (New York: Columbia University Press, 1991), 15; Shirley Samuels "The Family, the State, and the Novel in the Early Republic," *American Quarterly* (1986): 386; Thomas Gustafson, *Representative Words: Politics, Literature, and the American Language, 1776–1865*, (Cambridge: Cambridge University Press, 1992), 37; Jean Pfaelzer *Parlor Radical: Rebecca Harding Davis and the Origins of American Social Realism* (Pittsburgh: University of Pittsburg Press, 1996), 86.

29 Ibid. Such a benevolent response in the reception of sentimental novels of seduction 'could point to what passed for philosophical justification' in the writings of the 'Scottish Enlightenment.'

30 Jeffrey Rubin-Dorsky, "The Early American Novel," in Emory Elliot and Cathy Davidson, eds, *The Columbia history of the American novel* (New York: Columbia University Press, 1991), 15.

31 Jan Lewis, 'The Republican Wife," 715.

32 Shirley Samuels, "The Family, the State, and the Novel in the Early Republic," *American Quarterly* (1986): 386, 387.

33 Gustafson, *Representative Words*, 37.

34 Pfaelzer, *Parlor Radical*, 86.

35 Ibid., 65–6 See also Jay Fliegelman, *Prodigals and Pilgrims: The American Revolution against Patriarchal Authority, 1750–1800* (New York: Cambridge University Press, 1982); Melvin Yazawa, *From Colonies to Commonwealth: Familial Ideology and the Beginnings of the American Republic* (Baltimore: John Hopkins Press, 1985), 87–110.

36 See D. Nelson "Women and Gender in the State of Sympathy," *Feminist Studies* 28.1 (2002): 175; Julia A. Stern, *The Plight of Feeling: Sympathy and Dissent in the Early American Novel* (Chicago: University of Chicago Press, 1997), 9.

37 "Novel Reading, A Cause of Female Depravity" *New England Quarterly* 1 (1802): 172–4. This article was originally published in the British *Monthly Mirror* in November 1797.

38 Marion Rust claims that 'Charlotte Temple may be unique among early American sentimental novels in its avoidance of sexually charged language' and points out that 'William Hill Brown's *The Power of Sympathy* (1798), for example, capitalizes the word "seduction" in the dedication to its 1789 edition. See Marion Rust, "What's wrong with Charlotte Temple?" *William and Mary Quarterly*, 60.1 (2003), footnote 8. See also "letter5" in Hannah W. Foster, *The Coquette* (New York, 1986), 8, 12; Brown, *The Power of Sympathy*, ed. William S. Kable (Columbus, Ohio, 1969).

39 Davidson, "Ideology and Genre," 298.

40 American Antiquarian Society copy of Samuel Avery's 1811 (Boston) edition, cited in Davidson, "Ideology and Genre."

41 Ibid.

42 See Nathan Hatch, *The Democratization of American Christianity* (New Haven, Yale University Press, 1991).

43 Rowson's writing was germane to the period of revivalism which marked the first decades of the nineteenth century. See Dorothy A. Mays, *Women in Early America: Struggle, Survival and Freedom in the New World* (Santa Barbara, CA: ABC Clio, 2004), 167–7.

44 See Jonathan Edwards *A narrative of many surprising conversions in Northampton and vicinity*, 1736, (Worcester, Moses W. Grout: 1832), 200.

45 Rowson, *Charlotte Temple*, 27.

46 Ibid., 38.

47 Ibid., 119.

48 Ibid., 120.

49 Ibid.

50 Edwards, 'Some Thoughts Concerning the Present Revival of Religion in New England' (1743), cited in Joseph Tracy, *The Great Awakening: A History of the Revival of Religion in the time of Edwards and Whitefield* (Boston: Tappan & Tennent, 1842), 228; Edwards, 'Geniuses of the work illustrated by examples, particularly in the case of one individual,' in *Thoughts on the New England Revival*, 52.

51 Rowson, *Charlotte Temple*, 125.

52 See Karen Halttunen, "Humanitarianism and the Pornography of Pain in Anglo-American Culture," *American Historical Review*, 100 (1995): 317.

53 Rowson, *Charlotte Temple*, 80.

54 Ibid., 32.

55 Ibid., 47.

56 Rust, "What's wrong with Charlotte Temple?."

57 Rowson, *Charlotte Temple*, 126.

58 Ibid.

59 Ibid., 127.

60 Ibid.

61 Ibid., 67.

62 Ibid.

63 Ibid.

64 *Critical Review*, 2d ser. 1, (1791): 468–9.

65 Susanna Rowson, *Charlotte, a Tale of Truth*, (Philadelphia, 1794). The review is affixed to the verso of the front flyleaf.

66 Rowson, *Charlotte Temple*, 117–20.

4

"Like beads strung together": E. D. E. N. Southworth and the aesthetics of popular serial fiction

Rachel Ihara

Emma Dorothy Eliza Nevitte Southworth (who signed her novels E. D. E. N. Southworth) was more than a bestselling author; she was one of the most prolific and popular fiction writers of the latter half of the nineteenth century. Upon her death in 1899, the *New York Times* identified Southworth as "the most voluminous producer of fiction in the literary history of this country."[1] Six decades later, in his pioneering study of American bestsellers, Frank Luther Mott called Southworth "the most popular authoress in the annals of American publishing," naming three novels all-time bestsellers, by virtue of their having been read by at least one percent of the US population at the time they were written, and including three titles among the "better sellers" of their day.[2] Yet another study of popular American fiction credits two additional Southworth novels with having sold "without question" a million copies or more.[3]

Yet despite this impressive publication record, it was not until the 1980s that literary critics began to see Southworth's work as an important part of American literary history. Almost without exception, recent critical attention has centered on *The Hidden Hand*, which was reissued by Rutgers University Press in 1988. Dubbed by one critic "Southworth's only readable novel," *The Hidden Hand* is certainly a compelling tale with much to interest contemporary readers and critics, who see the novel's adventuresome, cross-dressing heroine as evidence of Southworth's incipient feminism.[4] Yet, without denying the novel's appeal, I would argue that to focus primarily on this single text is to miss something central to this popular author's literary career, which was defined less by her ability to produce a major bestselling novel than by her capacity to maintain a large and loyal audience for a prodigious stream of serialized fiction, from 1848, when Southworth's first novel appeared in the pages of the *National Era*, until 1886, when her final serial ran in the *New York Ledger*. At one point, the *New York Ledger*, which published many of Southworth's serial novels, boasted a readership of "one-eighth of the population of the United States."[5] This and the fact that serial novels often appeared in more than one periodical at a time and sometimes ran more than once, suggest that more readers encountered Southworth's novels as installments published over time than as bound books.

This essay thus offers a shift in perspective, one that pulls back from a focus on *The Hidden Hand* and takes seriously the question of what it meant for an author to have a serial novel running for nearly four decades. This distinction, between book publication and serialization, is by no means superficial. Although we are accustomed to think of bestsellers in terms of book sales, the widespread nineteenth-century practice of serializing popular novels, either prior to or in lieu of book publication, raises some important questions for any larger analysis of American bestsellers. To what extent is the experience of reading shaped by encountering a novel as installments released over time? And in what ways does serial publication affect composition, the author's understanding of genre, and our own sense of the novel as a cultural artifact?

Due, in part, to an increased scholarly interest in periodical publishing history, these questions have received some critical attention in recent years, with most book-length treatments of serialization focusing primarily on the effects of serial reading.

For instance, in their coauthored analysis of the Victorian serial, Michael Lund and Linda Hughes challenge the notion that serial novels exhibit shared formal characteristics, arguing instead that the determining feature of the serial novel is its capacity to extend the reading experience over time, resulting in the construction of a unique "community of readers."[6] Jennifer Hayward makes a similar argument about the social implications of serial reading, rejecting the idea that all serials share "distinctive and much derided tropes."[7] And, in *Social Stories: The Magazine Novel in Nineteenth-Century America* Patricia Okker considers the phenomenon of serialization within a US context, ultimately arguing that the nineteenth-century magazine novel played a key role in uniting an emerging and heterogeneous nation.[8]

While these works consider serial fiction writ large, other scholars zero in on specific serial texts in order to demonstrate the interplay, sometimes subtle and sometimes more overt, between works of serial fiction and the textual and visual materials that compose the newspaper or magazine in which the work appears. This approach is evident in Christopher Looby's essay on Southworth in which he identifies a number of connections between *The Hidden Hand* and the stories and articles surrounding it, which he sees as evidence of Southworth's ability to "[exploit] the immediate paratextual environment of the *New York Ledger* to her distinct advantage."[9] For instance, Southworth's decision to send some of her characters off to fight in the Mexican American War makes considerably more sense when we recognize the newspaper's frequent attention to this war as the novel was appearing in installments.

Although Looby's careful analysis of *The Hidden Hand* in its periodical context serves to establish the importance of serialization to a fuller understanding of Southworth's best-known novel, I would like to suggest that a broader view of her fiction also yields important insights into Southworth's creative engagement with serial publication. This requires some attempt to take stock of Southworth's prodigious fictional output, no small task given the complexity of her publication practices.[10] Not only is it difficult to access all of the periodicals in which her serial novels appeared, almost all of the novels that were published originally in serial form were repackaged and re-titled, frequently in multiple volumes. Pirated versions were sold in England, sometimes with the locations and character names silently altered, and advertisements for Southworth's works point to additional titles that seem to have vanished from libraries and bookstores.

Still, the very challenges inherent in investigating Southworth serve as a reminder of what makes her a special case. It was, after all, her intense productivity that kept her before the public eye for so many years. It was not merely that she wrote one bestselling book, but that she was able to turn out one compelling serial novel after another for nearly four decades. Consequently, Southworth's popularity must be understood as inextricably bound to her ongoing relationship with periodical publication, from her earliest contributions to the *National Era* to her many decades of work for the *Ledger*. It was in periodicals that Southworth emerged as a fiction writer and developed as a novelist. It was her lifelong engagement with serial publication that gave the novels form and informed Southworth's understanding of the possibilities inherent in popular serial fiction. And it was her ability to craft novels uniquely suited to serial reading that enabled her to maintain a loyal following decade after decade.

Developing a serial style

As was true for many nineteenth-century women writers, Southworth's transition from short fiction to long fiction occurred in the periodical press. Much like her friend and contemporary Harriet Beecher Stowe, whose early fiction also appeared in the *National Era*, Southworth began writing short stories and sketches before moving on to longer stories in multiple installments, and then to full-length novels. Indeed, both authors seem to have conceived of their first novels as extended versions of their earlier short fiction. According to one account, Stowe began *Uncle Tom's Cabin* without expecting it to last more than three or four installments.[11] Southworth recalled her own evolution as a novelist in similar terms, noting in an 1890 interview in *Book News*, that she began one "without knowing [she] could write a novel."[12]

If publication in periodicals facilitated the transition to novel writing, it also helps to explain the episodic form of many serial novels, which, when encountered as discrete volumes, can appear uneven and fragmented. For instance, Southworth's first novel, *Retribution*, consists of extended sections of dialogue, chatty narration, and chapters composed entirely of letters. Back stories, digressions, and subplots are constantly threatening to take over what is ostensibly the main focus, the story of a timid orphan named Hester Grey. This feature of Southworth's fiction, her reliance on the episode as a structuring device, is characteristic of her other novels as well and merits more attention than it generally receives. Although critics like Peter Brooks have emphasized serial fiction's capacity to create suspense through "cliffhanger" endings, making the serial novel an exemplar of "commercialized literature" in "an era of triumphant capitalism," I would argue that the episodic structure of Southworth's popular serials is just as important.[13] This is not to say that Southworth ignored the possibilities inherent in the temporal breaks between installments. Many installments do end with a classic "cliffhanger," and some even make explicit reference to the necessity of delayed gratification, as when Capitola complains, in one weekly installment of *The Hidden Hand*, that it was "awful to go to bed over such a horrible mystery."[14] However, if it made sense to string readers along through the creation of suspense between temporal divisions, it was equally important to offer readers some self-contained installments and set pieces that could be enjoyed on their own merit.

Southworth herself was clearly conscious of her reliance on installment breaks as a means of structuring her fiction, frankly describing her approach to fiction writing in terms that emphasized the construction and arrangement of parts. As she affirmed in an interview with *Book News*, *The Hidden Hand* was actually an amalgam of various stories and events she had heard of or read about. Capitola's "adventure with Black Donald was taken from a somewhat similar adventure, in which figured a woman of Maryland and a colored ruffian who, in 1812, was the terror of the neighborhood," Southworth recalled; "The court-martial, its causes and scenes, occurred during the Mexican war." "All these separate incidents . . .," she explained, "were like beads; I strung them together."[15]

Southworth uses this image of a string of beads to refer to a single novel, but analysis of the novels as an oeuvre suggests that the metaphor is equally appropriate to her work as a whole. For, if *The Hidden Hand* was constructed out of a series of incidents, this principle of composition also functions on a macro level given Southworth's practice of reshuffling plots and characters to produce a virtually endless supply of popular fiction. Repetition of various fictive elements not only allowed Southworth to write at a breakneck pace but also encouraged a reading of the novels as episodes in an ongoing saga. Thus, while there is a persistent tendency to think of individual novels as discrete entities, it may be more useful to understand Southworth's novels as composing an elaborate fictive system in which repeating episodes and recurring character types echo and comment on one another, resulting in an aesthetic and thematic uniformity that was a recognizable part of the Southworth "brand."

Places, people, and plots

One of the most obvious ways that Southworth established a sense of continuity and familiarity from one novel to the next was to return again and again to a few locations, most frequently, the picturesque Blue Ridge Mountains of Virginia and Maryland.[16] Three early novels, *The Mother in Law* (1849–50), *Shannondale* (1850), and *The Outcast* (1850–51), evoke this mountain setting, which is predictably described as "beautiful," "savage," and "sublime." *The Hidden Hand* opens with a similar scene of "one of the loneliest and wildest of the mountain regions of Virginia."[17] Indeed, this location appears often enough that in *The Hallow Eve Mystery* (1869) Southworth's narrator excuses herself from launching into a complete description of yet another such scene. "It was one of those fearful passes so frequently to be found in the Allegheny Mountains, and which I have described so frequently that I may be excused from describing this," Southworth's narrator remarks.[18]

While the settings establish a sense of connection between Southworth's novels, recurring character types also remind readers they have returned to the same fictive universe. The figure of Capitola is a prime example, for despite her reputation an exceptional figure in nineteenth-century American literature, she is hardly the author's only spunky, gender-bending female character. In serial novels published both before and after the *Hidden Hand*, Southworth imagines female characters that bear a striking resemblance to Capitola: charming tomboys who are no less attractive for failing to meet conventional standards of ladylike behavior. In *Shannondale*, for instance, Southworth introduces readers to Harriet, who is known as "Harry" and, like Capitola, is referred to as a "mad cap." "Harry Joy looked like a saucy—a very saucy boy, and nothing else," Southworth's narrator notes (anticipating Capitola's flirtation with cross-dressing).[19] In *The Curse of Clifton* (1852), Zuleime Clifton bears more than a passing resemblance to Southworth's better-known heroine, with her "glittering black hair and sparkling black eyes" and her love of "fun and frolic."[20] *The Hallow Eve Mystery* (1869) presents readers with two female characters who compete to fill Cap's shoes: Sybil Berners, a "black-haired, bright-eyed" beauty who is "full of fire, spirit, and self-will" and denounces "all weak and whimpering women"; and Gentiliska Dubury, a dark-haired gypsy girl who displays Capitola's penchant for slang terms like "bosh" and "you bet" and has little patience for pathetic "lovesick women."[21] In *Between Two Fires* (1871–72), Electra shares Capitola's upbringing, having been raised in the slums of New York City. And in *Gloria, or Married in a Rage* (1877), a character named Philippa, goes by Phil, dreams of fighting, and insists upon riding the most dangerous horses and hunting the fiercest game.[22] As Michele Ann Abate has observed, other Southworth characters that exhibit tomboy traits include Garnet Seabright of *The Discarded Daughter* (1852), Helen Wildman of *Vivia; or, The Secret of Power* (1857), and Lionne Delaforet and Kate Kyte of *The Fatal Marriage* (1863).[23]

If these figures resemble the better-known Capitola in terms of appearance and high spirits, others share her heroic tendencies. While Sybil and Gentiliska, like Cap, are quick to offer assistance to the weaker members of their own sex, Britomarte of *Britomarte the Man-Hater* (1865–66) and Gertrude Lion of *The Mother-in-Law* (1849–50) assume heroic roles traditionally reserved for men. Britomarte Conyers adopts Cap's cross-dressing strategy to enlist in the army, fighting in battles in the American Civil War and eventually rising to the rank of captain. The six-foot-tall Gertrude Lion, who is referred to as "the Gerfalcon" and likened to an Amazon, saves a rather frail and foppish young man from a carriage accident, fends off would-be slave catchers, and, in the final scene, storms into a church to disrupt a wedding ceremony and denounce the novel's villain. Nor is Gertrude compelled to suffer for her deviance from traditional feminine behavior. When a bailiff accuses Gertrude of "[defying] all the laws of delicacy proper to your sex," Gertrude is nonplussed and ready with a sassy comeback.[24] When Gertrude falls for the young man named Frobisher, whom she has rescued, she too is granted a happy marriage. "Some women want a master," Southworth's narrator remarks evenly, "and some men need a mistress. Frobisher was one of the latter."[25]

Although it is tempting to focus solely on these feisty, bold, and heroic heroines, other character types occur nearly as often, suggesting a consistent and strategic approach to character construction. Major Warfield, Capitola's irritable benefactor in *The Hidden Hand*, Aaron Rockharrt in *For Woman's Love* (1884), and Squire Darling of *Shannondale* are all blustering, crotchety old men who are used to having their way and quick to fly into a rage when they are defied.[26] Traverse Rocke and Herbert Greyson, the two candidates for male lead in The *Hidden Hand*, are not only virtually indistinguishable, they also bear a striking likeness to the title character of *Ishmael*, another sensitive young man raised in poverty by a single woman. Marah Rocke and Clara Day of *The Hidden Hand* are but two in a long list of fair female victims that includes Winnifred Darling of *Shannondale*, Louise Armstrong of *The Mother-in-Law*, the Countess of Hurstmonceux of *Self-Made*, and Desolee Dubois of *David Lindsay* (the sequel to *Gloria*). And one must not forget Southworth's beautiful, scheming seductresses, among them Rosa Blondelle of *The Hallow Eve Mystery*, Mrs. Clifton of *The Curse of Clifton*, Juliette of *Retribution*, Sina Hinton of *Shannondale*, Mrs. Grey of *Between Two Fires*, and Rose Flowers of *For Women's Love*.

Such resemblances among characters from one novel to the next could easily be seen as a stylistic weakness. And some of Southworth's contemporary critics did complain that her characterization was "incomplete, unformed, contradictory, and altogether in proof of haste."[27] Yet, the sheer number of stock characters within Southworth's repertoire, and her constant rearrangement of these character types, saves her novels from redundancy: similar characters may appear in one novel after another but never in precisely the same formation or with the same emphasis accorded to a given type. *The Hidden Hand*, for instance, has a "tom-boy" but no seductress, while *The Hallow Eve Mystery* is notably lacking in exemplary upstanding young men.

Nor is Southworth's characterization as fixed as her reliance on type would suggest. In fact, the same character is occasionally called upon to play two different roles in the course of a single novel.

Rose Flowers, of *For Woman's Love*, is initially introduced as a gold-digging siren, but she reemerges as an object of sympathy midway into the novel. Having succeeded in her scheme to seduce a wealthy older man, Rose then assumes the role of the unfortunate, powerless young bride, languishes for a while, and dies. In *The Hallow Eve Mystery*, Rosa Blondelle undergoes a different transformation. Initially introduced as a sympathetic victim, yet another of Southworth's helpless blonds, by Chapter 10 Rosa, has reemerged as one of the novel's chief villains, a vain coquette who thinks nothing of seducing her benefactor's husband. The other characters in *The Hallow Eve Mystery* change over the course of the novel as well. The shy and noble Mr. Berner of the opening chapters is virtually indistinguishable from the thoughtless, straying husband of the middle section of the novel. Sybil, the feisty, strong-willed heroine of the first part of the novel bears little resemblance to the subdued and passive victim of the latter section. The villain of the novel, Mr. Blondelle, like other Southworth rogues, is guilty of dastardly crimes against womankind but also capable of chivalrous selflessness when it serves the plot. And in the oddest example of inconsistent characterization, a relatively minor character in *Self-Made* named Jem Morris is initially introduced as a free "mulatto" who speaks in strained dialect, but by the end of the serial has reemerged as someone with no racial markers whose speech is not markedly different from that of Ishmael and his aunt.

What such transformations reveal, I would argue, is not so much carelessness as a pragmatic responsive to the conditions of serial publication. Southworth may have relied on stock figures as a sort of shorthand that allowed readers to manage a large cast and to assimilate new characters easily, but sustaining interest from one week to the next took precedence over consistent characterization. Given this understanding of the serial novel's essential function—to supply ongoing entertainment and keep story paper readers coming back for more—it was more important that a character should suit the immediate circumstances of the story or subplot currently underway than exhibit strict continuity or logical development over time. If the new scene called for a helpless female victim, Southworth was willing to make the necessary adjustment. If a character's racially marked language no longer suited the circumstances, Southworth would quietly drop the dialect in favor of standard speech.

Those who read the novels in book form, including Southworth's reviewers, may have noticed these incongruities, but the reader encountering the novels doled out in weekly portions over many months was less likely to focus on such inconsistencies. Instead, readers following Southworth's serial novels from week to week would have been caught up in a barrage of dramatic episodes and proliferating subplots. Not surprisingly, these plots, like Southworth's characters, show a marked tendency to repeat. Thus, several of Southworth's novels include stories of the devastating consequences of secret marriages. *Self-Raised* begins with a long preamble in which a poor woman agrees to marry her wealthy landlord in secret, resulting in bigamy since there happens to be a first wife. Similarly, in *The Brothers*, Lady Linlithgow is obliged to give up a child conceived in a secret marriage to a husband who has been falsely reported to be dead. Not only do these cases involve clandestine unions, they also turn upon inaccurate reports of deaths, another common plot twist in Southworth's fiction. In *Gloria*, the heroine realizes her love for David Lindsay only after she receives the inaccurate news that he has been killed in a fire, whereas, in *For Woman's Love*, Corona Haught reads in the papers that her estranged husband has died in an Indian massacre, upon which she determines to carry on his missionary work on her own.

If inaccurate news of death does not disrupt the happiness of a married couple, jealousy, in response to real or imagined infidelity, does. At least three of Southworth's novels include a significant section in which a marriage is threatened by a single woman living with newly married couple, although the woman may set out to seduce the husband, as Juliette does in *Retribution*, or may be unconscious of the effect she is having upon the inconstant husband, like Rosalia in *The Deserted Wife*. In *The Hidden Hand*, Major Warfield denounces his unacknowledged wife Marah Rocke when he finds Captain Le Noir half-undressed in her bedroom and assumes she is having an affair, a situation that is echoed in two incidents in *Self-Made* whereby both Berenice Hurstmonceux and Claudia are trapped in elaborate setups to "prove" their infidelity.

These stories of marital discord are interwoven with more blatant criminal activities, often involving misleading evidence. In *The Hallow Eve Mystery*, for instance, everything suggests that Sybil Berner has murdered her rival Rosa Blondelle: she is found holding a bloody dagger and standing over the dead girl. When the heroine disappears from *Astrea*, all evidence points to her new husband's guilt, including the fact that the Colonel's clothing is covered in blood. And in *Between Two Fires*, Victor Hartman is convinced of his own guilt when he wakes up from a drunken spree to be told that he has killed his former employer. In the first two instances, the crimes are actually perpetrated by shadowy criminal organizations acting on the orders of "well-born" villains. The pirates who capture Astrea and sell her into slavery are employed by a scheming younger brother who is trying to rob her of her inheritance, a situation that recalls Gabriel Le Noir's plot to defraud his brother's family of their inheritance in *The Hidden Hand*, as well as his reliance on common outlaws like Black Donald to perform his dirty work.

As with the repetition of certain character types and settings, the return to similar situations from one novel to the next could be seen as an aesthetic flaw. Still, I would like to suggest that Southworth skillfully managed this repetition of settings, plots, and characters in productive and interesting ways. The exigencies of serialization may have encouraged Southworth to fall back on old formulas, to pack her novels full of familiar stories, and to neglect larger issues of unity and consistent characterization, but she was able to maintain a sense of novelty from year to year by continually varying the arrangement, order, and emphasis of her fictive elements. To use her own metaphor, if characters and situations were "beads," then she was a master jeweler, continuously trying out new combinations to produce new effects. Plots and subplots may echo those of other novels, but no two novels are alike in their unique combination of elements, nor in the emphasis accorded a particular plotline and set of characters. Thus, *The Hidden Hand* features a scheming younger brother and a band of bandits, but no domestic love triangle; a secret marriage, an estranged couple, and a lost heiress, but no instances of mistaken identity. *The Hallow Eve Mystery* begins with a mismatched union between a wealthy heiress and a poor lawyer, before moving on to the story of an abandoned wife, and then shifting to a narrative of a domestic love triangle, events that are followed by a false accusation of murder, a kidnapping by a band of outlaws, and a final court hearing that results in exoneration. None of these situations is unique in and of itself. Other Southworth women are subjected to abuse and neglect by their husbands; other heroines lose their husbands' affections to unscrupulous seductresses; other characters are falsely accused of murder; other novels feature bands of outlaws and include court scenes in which a convicted murderer is exonerated. However, no other novel can boast this particular combination of events in just this order.

Reading serially and the implications of Southworth's serial style

Southworth's fragmented episodic narratives clearly served her well, enabling her to turn out some 40 pages of fiction every month and to satisfy readers' ongoing demands for serial novels that were both new and familiar. One reviewer commended her for writing "numerous works of considerable length and absorbing interest," while another noted that "No one ever read a chapter of one of her works without wishing to read the whole . . ."[28] A critic might express skepticism about the quality of Southworth's novels while recognizing her capacity to maintain "movement," to "[arrest] the attention and [keep] her reader to her pages, until she dismisses him at the end."[29] Even Southworth's most vehement detractors seem to have been susceptible to her appeal. One was unable to abandon *The Deserted Wife*, admitting "[f]or ourselves, we should not have gone further than the Introduction . . . had not our attention been especially directed to the latter portions."[30] A negative review of *The Mother-in-Law* grudgingly concludes that Southworth's "plots are generally, with the exception of the last half of every volume, good," sounding more like a disappointed reader than a disapproving reviewer.[31]

Part of this tension between critical censure and readerly absorption seems to have stemmed from considerations of the novels as discrete works rather than ongoing serialized narrative. Evidently, most readers of Southworth's texts in serial form found little cause for complaint. The editor of the *Ledger* encouraged Southworth to write as much as she saw fit, reassured her when she worried that a work was beginning to drag, and offered her increasingly attractive contracts.[32] As the *Ledger's* circulation continued to rise throughout the 1860s and 1870s, Southworth's serial novels were consistently featured on the front page.

This success in the story papers, I would suggest, had much to do with Southworth's acute awareness of the advantages inherent in serial reading, her ability to take advantage of the unique possibilities inherent in publication by installment. Although her novels would go on to sell as books, prior serial publication was just as important to the goal of acquiring and sustaining a mass audience. After all, one of the distinct advantages of the serial novel was that readers could be sustained over time. Readers of the *New York Ledger* did not have to worry about being "dismissed at the end," since, as editors were quick to reassure readers, a new "even better" novel was likely to pick up immediately after the current one came to a close. The episodic nature of Southworth's novels, moreover, made even the novels' resolutions feel provisional. Even though the vast majority of the novels end happily (supposedly deceased husband reappear, long-lost heiresses reclaim their rightful fortunes, falsely accused men and women are exonerated, and children are reunited with their parents), the sheer number of twists and turns along the way from beginning to end preclude real closure. Readers would have seen enough marriages gone awry to be skeptical of the double or triple weddings that conclude many of the novels and aware that it would only take another scheming villain, charming coquette, or forbidden romance to start the whole drama rolling again.

Patterns of characterization across novels also foster a reading of each new serial as part of a broader narrative tapestry. For Southworth's most loyal readers, the reappearance of character types from one novel to the next encourages a sense of familiarity, the impression of being in the same fictive universe. Southworth reinforced this pattern by having some characters appear in more than one novel. The reappearance of Ishmael Worth and Jem Morris, two characters from *Self-Made*, in *The Hallow Eve Mystery*, rewards Southworth's readers with a flash of recognition, just as references to a lawyer named Berner in both *Self-Made* and in *Victor's Triumph* suggest that this minor character is none other than Sybil's lawyer husband Lyon Berner of *The Hallow Eve Mystery*. Such repetition is not necessarily unique to Southworth; nonetheless, it encourages an intertextual reading of the novels, setting up resonances between novels, particularly for those following Southworth's periodical fiction year after year.

More important, perhaps, the reappearance of characters and the repetition of types serves as a reminder that a given character's location at the center (or at the periphery) of a novel is essentially arbitrary. Just as narrative attention may shift in the course of a single novel—as the author follows one set of characters and then moves on to others, picks up one plotline and drops another— Southworth's serial fiction as a whole may be read as an ongoing narrative characterized by constant shifts in focus. In a single novel, the "main" character is typically at the center of only a portion of the novel. *Retribution's* Hester Grey is introduced as the heroine, but the novel doesn't end when she dies in the eighth chapter; Ishmael, the ostensible hero of *Self-Made*, does not make an appearance until the 15th chapter; even Capitola is absent from over a third of the novel in which she plays such a memorable part. A similar principle underlies the novels as a whole. Ishmael's story merits its own novel, but with a slight shift of perspective, he becomes merely a bit player, a star lawyer, who makes a brief courtroom appearance. Capitola may be the heroine of *The Hidden Hand*, but her fictional doubles are often relegated to the sidelines.

The implications of this understanding of fiction are actually quite profound, as Southworth was well aware. One offhanded comment by the narrator of *The Hallow Eve Mystery* is particularly telling. In relaying a bit of back story delivered by a minor character, Southworth's narrator is compelled to exclaim, "Ah what a volume might be written on that tragedy; but let it pass!"[33] It is a mere narrative aside; however, the implication is clearly that each narrative thread, however incidental, might have been spun out to form a narrative of its own, each subplot could easily have assumed a larger part in a new "novel" yet to come, each minor character might yet take center stage at a later date or in a different novel.

Some critics have noted that this type of multiplicity is a common feature of popular literature. In his work on popular fiction, John G. Cawelti identifies melodrama's failure to follow a single protagonist as typical of the genre, and that, in contrast, "melodrama typically makes us intersect imaginatively with many lives."[34] Peter Brooks makes a similar point in his discussion of Wilkie Collins, whom he sees as a master of serial plotting. Focusing on *The Woman in White*, which appeared in weekly installments in Dickens's *All the Year Round*, Brooks proposes that "Collins's representation of readers and writers constantly scribbling and constantly reading one another . . . suggests an image of the popular serial novel as a prelapsarian age of unlimited storytelling and unlimited consumption of story."[35]

Southworth would surely insist that this feature of her fictional world merely reflected reality, which she saw as abounding in dramatic incident. Southworth's novels may be replete with stories—Harriet Beecher Stowe once told her that she had enough incidents in a single novel "to supply a half dozen novels"—but this was simply because the world itself was full of equally shocking, dramatic, and sordid events.[36] This understanding of the world as brimming with stories is reflected in the characters' relationships to narrative: characters in Southworth's novels are constantly telling one another tales, reading reports in the papers, recalling neighborhood gossip, and writing and reading letters—exchanges that are implicitly linked to novel-reading.

But this notion of the world as made up of such stories is affirmed more explicitly by Southworth's narrators, who continually remind her readers that specific incidents are true or "drawn from life" and that characters are modeled after real-world types. One of Southworth's favorite methods for relating a given episode's basis in fact is to simply attach a footnote denoting the relevant section as "a fact!" At other times, the connection is between the fictional character and a real world "type." "We every one of us know, or know *of*, Mr. Horace Blondelle," remarks the narrator of *The Hallow Eve Mystery*; "There are scores of him scattered about the great hotels of all the large cities in Europe and America."[37] Even the extraordinary story of Ishmael's struggle "out of the depths of poverty, shame, and ignorance, to competence, honor, and distinction," Southworth insists, is one that "may be repeated again in the person of the obscurest boy that reads these lines."[38]

Of course, it was common enough for authors to insist that a given work of fiction was founded in fact. In his study of popular literature, James D. Hart points out that many early American novels claimed to be based on actual events.[39] Such an attitude toward fiction, which Southworth embraces wholeheartedly, encouraged readers to see, not only serial fiction, but also their own lives as full of excitement and drama; to imagine themselves as the spunky heroine, the suffering victim, or both at different points in time; to recognize their acquaintances as manifestations of the sinister seducer or scheming seductresses; to see dramatic possibility everywhere. It was a conception of fiction that justified the novel's reliance on the sensational episode and satiated the reader's demand for incident but also one that encouraged a renewed interest in the daily struggles and triumphs of actual lived experience.

Southworth also seems to have been conscious of the negative implications of such an approach to narrative, the potential for chaos and inconsistency to overwhelm novels of numerous dramatic incidents, repeated character types and plots, and resonances across episodes and between novels. In one striking narrative digression in *Shannondale*, Southworth's narrator remarks on the importance of names. "There is a spell, a charm, a talisman in a name," she asserts, explaining: "If you want to make a girl a flirt, call her 'Fanny,'" But, she continues:

> [i]f you want to make her anything and everything in turn, and nothing long—a medley of inconsistencies—a chaos of contraries, give her a long string of names, and I warrant you she will cook you up a sermon or a satire, preach orthodoxy with Isaac Taylor, or skepticism with Shelley; be a nun or a bacchante through life, and [have] no individuality, no self, NO UNITY.[40]

The narrator's observation here is doubly ironic: first, because it is, of course, the author who is responsible for bestowing the name "Fanny" (and there are a number of "flirts" by this name in Southworth's novels), but also given E. D. E. N. Southworth's undeniably long string of names.

Thus, in this relatively early novel, Southworth already appears to be quite conscious of a "flaw" in her chosen literary aesthetic, a feature of her serial fiction that was also at the heart of her success. Just as her adopted pen name strings together her many names to form one acronym, the various episodes and character types are reshuffled and pulled together under a single title, resulting in an uneasy tension between part and whole, an understandable structure for work published initially in parts. Some contemporary reviewers of Southworth's novels in book form may have complained about inconsistencies in characterization and careless plotting, whereas contemporary critics tend to impose order on her texts by focusing on a novel's treatment of a single social or political issue. However, in tracing the history of "best-selling" American fiction, it is important not to lose sight of the tolerance for fragmentation, multiplicity, and contradiction that were at the heart of Southworth's aesthetic in her long and productive career as a popular serial author.

Bibliography

Abate, Michele Ann. "Launching a Gender B(l)acklash: E. D. E. N. Southworth's *The Hidden Hand* and the Emergence of (Racialized) White Tomboyism." *Children's Literature Association Quarterly* 31.1 (2006): 40–64.

Brooks, Peter. *Design and Intention in Narrative.* New York: Alfred A. Knopf, 1984.

Cawelti, John. *Adventure, Mystery, and Romance: Formula Stories as Art and Popular Culture.* Chicago: University of Chicago Press, 1976.

Habegger, Alfred. "A Well Hidden Hand." *NOVEL: A Forum on Fiction* 14 (1981): 197–212.

Hackett, Alice Payne and James Henry Burke. *80 Years of Best Sellers, 1895–1975.* New York, London: R. K. Bowker, 1977.

Hart, James D. *The Popular Book: A History of America's Literary Taste.* New York: Oxford University Press, 1950.

Hart, John S. *Female Prose Writers of America*, 5th edition. Philadelphia: E. H. Butler & Co., 1866.

Hayward, Jennifer. *Consuming Pleasures: Active Audiences and Serial Fictions from Dickens to Soap Opera.* Lexington: University Press of Kentucky, 1997.

Kelley, Mary. *Private Woman, Public Stage: Literary Domesticity in Nineteenth-Century America.* New York: Oxford University Press, 1984.

Looby, Christopher. "Southworth and Seriality: 'The Hidden Hand' in the New York Ledger." *Nineteenth-Century Literature* 59 (2004): 179–211.

Lund, Michael and Linda K. Hughes. *The Victorian Serial.* Charlottesville: University Press of Virginia, 1991.

Mott, Frank Luther. *Golden Multitudes: The Story of Best-Sellers in the United States.* New York: R. R. Bowker, 1960. First published 1947 by Macmillan Co.

"Mrs. E. D. E. N. Southworth," *Book News* (November 1890): 66–7.

"Mrs. Southworth is Dead," *New York Times*, July 1, 1899.

Mullane, Janet and Robert Thomas Wilson, eds. "Emma Dorothy Eliza Nevitte Southworth, 1819–1999." *Nineteenth Century Literature.* Vol. 26. Detroit, New York, London: Gale Research Inc., 1990. 429–44.

Naranjo-Hueble, Linda. "The Road to Perdition: E. D. E. N. Southworth and the Critics." *American Periodicals* 16 (2006): 124–50.

Okker, Patricia. *Social Stories: The Magazine Novel in Nineteenth-Century America.* Charlottesville: University of Virginia Press, 2003.

Papashvily, Helen Waite. *All the Happy Endings: A Study of the Domestic Novel in America, the Women Who Wrote it, the Women Who Read it, in the Nineteenth Century.* 1956. New York: Kennikat Press, 1972.

"A Pioneer Editor," *Atlantic Monthly* 17 (1866): 743–51.

Salzer, Kenneth. "Call Her Ishmael: E. D. E. N. Southworth, Robert Bonner, and the 'Experiment' of *Self-Made*." *Popular Nineteenth-Century American Women Writers and the Literary Marketplace.* Eds, Earl Yarington and Mary De Jong. Newcastle, UK: Cambridge Scholars Publishing, 2007.

Southworth, E. D. E. N. *Cruel as the Grave*. Philadelphia, PA: T. B. Peterson & Brothers, 1871.

—. *The Curse of Clifton: A Tale of Expiation and Redemption.* Philadelphia, PA: A. Hart, LATE Carey & Hart, 1852.

—*Gloria; or, Married in a Rage*. New York: R. Bonner's Sons, 1891.

—. *The Hidden Hand; or, Capitola the Madcap*. New Brunswick, NJ: Rutger's University Press, 1988. First published 1888.

—. *The Mother-in-Law; or, The Isle of Rays*. New York: D. Appleton & Company, 1851.

—. *Self Raised; or, From the Depths*. Chicago: W. B. Conkey Company, 1904. First published 1876.

—. *Shannondale*. Philadelphia, PA: D. Appleton & Company, 1850.

—. *Tried for her Life*. Philadelphia, PA: T.B. Peterson & Brothers, 1871.

Notes

1   "Mrs. Southworth is Dead," *New York Times*, July 1, 1899.

2   Frank Luther Mott, *Golden Multitudes: The Story of Best-Sellers in the United States* (1947, repr. New York: R. R. Bowker, 1960).

3   Alice Payne Hackett and James Henry Burke, *80 Years of Best Sellers, 1895–1975* (New York: R. R. Bowker, 1977), 221.

4   Alfred Habegger, "A Well Hidden Hand," *NOVEL: A Forum on Fiction* 14 (Spring 1981): 209.

5   [Robert Bonner], "The Newspaper," *The New York Ledger* 14.50, 1859, quoted in Christopher Looby, "Southworth and Seriality: *The Hidden Hand* in the *New York Ledger*," *Nineteenth-Century Literature* 59 (2004): 196. Mary Kelley places the *Ledger's* circulation at 180,000 in 1855 and claims that it eventually reached 350,000. *Private Woman, Public Stage: Literary Domesticity in Nineteenth-Century America* (New York: Oxford University Press, 1984), 4.

6   Michael Lund and Linda K. Hughes, *The Victorian Serial* (Charlottesville: University Press of Virginia, 1991), 10.

7   Jennifer Hayward, *Consuming Pleasures: Active Audiences and Serial Fictions from Dickens to Soap Opera* (Lexington: University Press of Kentucky, 1997), 4.

8   Patricia Okker, *Social Stories: The Magazine Novel in Nineteenth-Century America* (Charlottesville: University of Virginia Press, 2003).

9   Looby, "Southworth and Seriality," 183. Looby adopts this term from Gérard Genette's *Paratexts: Thresholds of Interpretations* (1997).

10 Information about the number of novels Southworth wrote varies. One profile claimed that she had written "forty-four bound volumes and twenty-three serials, making a total of sixty-seven," a figure that overlooks the republication of serials in book form. "Mrs. E. D. E. N. Southworth," *Book News* (November 1890): 66. Helen Waite Papashvily sets the figure at forty-six. *All the Happy Endings* (1956; repr. New York: Kennikat Press, 1972).

11 "A Pioneer Editor," *Atlantic Monthly* 17 (1866): 748.

12 "Mrs. E. D. E. N. Southworth," *Book News* (November 1890): 67.

13 Peter Brooks, *Design and Intention in Narrative* (New York: Alfred A. Knopf, 1984), 143.

14 E. D. E. N. Southworth. *The Hidden Hand; or, Capitola the Madcap.* (New Brunswick, NJ: Rutger's University Press, 1988), 77.

15 "Mrs. E. D. E. N. Southworth," *Book News*, 67.

16 There are some exceptions to this general pattern. In *Self-Made*, the heroine marries a viscount who takes her to a lonely Scottish castle, *The Brothers* takes place in Scotland, and the *Trail of the Serpent* is partly set Australia.

17 *The Hidden Hand*, 7.

18 When *The Hallow Eve Mystery* was published in book form, it appeared in two volumes, *Cruel as the Grave* and *Tried for Her Life*. I am citing from the first volume. *Cruel as the Grave* (Philadelphia, PA: T. B. Peterson & Brothers, 1871), 208.

19 *Shannondale* (Philadelphia, PA: D. Appleton & Company, 1850), 11.

20 *The Curse of Clifton: A Tale of Expiation and Redemption* (Philadelphia, PA: A. Hart, LATE Carey & Hart, 1853), 46, 49.

21 *Cruel as the Grave* (Philadelphia, PA: T. B. Peterson & Brothers, 1871), 14, 18; *Tried for her Life* (Philadelphia, PA: T. B. Peterson & Brothers, 1871), 63.

22 *Gloria; or, Married in a Rage* (New York: R. Bonner's Sons, 1891), 286.

23   Michele Ann Abate, "Launching a Gender B(l)acklash: E. D. E. N. Southworth's The Hidden Hand and the Emergence of (Racialized) White Tomboyism," *Children's Literature Association Quarterly* 31.1 (2006): 47.

24   *The Mother-in-Law; or, The Isle of Rays* (New York: D. Appleton & Company, 1851), 126.

25   *The Mother-in-Law*, 183.

26   Alfred Habegger notes that Ira Warfield "is that familiar type in eighteenth- and nineteenth-century literature—the crusty, good-natured, old-school tyrant." "A Well Hidden Hand," 203.

27   [Unsigned review of *Shannondale*], *Southern Quarterly Review* 3 (April 1851): 566. For an analysis of critical reception, see Linda Naranjo-Huebl, "The Road to Perdition: E. D. E. N. Southworth and the Critics," *American Periodicals* 16 (2006): 124–50.

28   Both reviews are cited in the book edition of *The Curse of Clifton*, which credits *The New York Weekly Dispatch* and the newspaper *Jersey Blue*, respectively.

29   [Unsigned review of *The Lost Heiress*], *Putnam's Monthly Magazine* 4 (December 1854): 670.

30   [Unsigned review of *The Deserted Wife*], *The Southern Literary Messenger* 11 (Nov 1850): 111. For excerpts from other reviews, see Janet Mullane and Robert Thomas Wilson, eds, "Emma Dorothy Eliza Nevitte Southworth, 1819–1999," *Nineteenth Century Literature* 26 (Detroit: Gale Research Inc., 1990), 429–44.

31   It is impossible to be sure that this was the same reviewer since the reviews are all unsigned; however, repeated complaints about French influence suggests that the same individual was responsible for all of the negative *Southern Literary Messenger* reviews. [Unsigned review of *Shannondale*], 128; [Unsigned review of *The Mother-in-Law*], *The Southern Literary Messenger* 17 (June 1851): 390.

32   According to Kenneth Saltzer, Bonner's attitude contrasts with that of the *Saturday Evening Post* editor Henry Peterson, who was more critical of Southworth's fiction. "Call Her Ishmael: E. D. E. N. Southworth, Robert Bonner, and the 'Experiment' of *Self-Made*," in *Popular Nineteenth-Century American Women Writers and the Literary Marketplace*, eds, Earl Yarington and Mary De Jong (Newcastle, UK: Cambridge Scholars Publishing, 2007), 220.

33   *Cruel as the Grave*, 76.

34   John Cawelti, *Adventure, Mystery, and Romance: Formula Stories as Art and Popular Culture* (Chicago: University of Chicago Press, 1976), 45.

35 Brooks, *Design and Intention in Narrative*, 170.
36 Papashvily, *All the Happy Endings*, 114.
37 *Cruel as the Grave*, 61.
38 *Self Raised; or, From the Depths* (Chicago: W. B. Conkey Company, 1904), 311–12.
39 Hart, James D. *The Popular Book: A History of America's Literary Taste* (New York: Oxford University Press, 1950).
40 *Shannondale*, 75–6.

5

Ten Nights in a Bar-Room and the visual culture of temperance

William Gleason

At the peak of the "vast popular movement"[1] of nineteenth-century temperance fiction stands Timothy Shay Arthur's monumental bestseller, *Ten Nights in a Bar-Room, And What I Saw There* (1854). Appearing in the middle of a decade that saw "the biggest boom in American book publishing ever known,"[2] Arthur's graphic tale sold at least 400,000 copies, far surpassing all other temperance texts and making it one of the bestselling novels of the century. Aided by a thriving stage adaption and further popularized in late-century magic lantern shows, *Ten Nights* lived vividly in the American imagination well into the twentieth century, not only staying in print but also finding its way to the silver screen.[3] Critics have often attributed the popularity of *Ten Nights* to its visual power, citing its "lurid waxworks realism" and "titillatingly horrific portrayal" of drink and destruction.[4] And yet we lack a detailed study of the book's use of such images, whether those shaped in prose by Arthur or the ones that literally appeared as frontispieces and illustrations in different versions of the work. When we do look closely at the visual texture of *Ten Nights*—in relation not only to its own publishing and marketing history but also to new forms of visual representation—we gain a clearer understanding of the images themselves and of several important corollary matters. These include the novel's place within the visual culture of the nineteenth-century temperance movement, its multiple and at times overlapping rhetorics of reform, as well as some of its most puzzling narrative quirks. By examining the relays between *Ten Nights* and the visual economy of mid-century temperance prints, engravings, and lithographs; by exploring the effects of the text's specular preoccupations on narrative point of view; by recovering for analysis the images that appeared in different editions of the novel; and finally by showing how seamlessly *Ten Nights* was incorporated into new forms of postbellum visual media, I suggest that the vividness of Arthur's novel indexes not merely a representational strategy but also an important cultural phenomenon. *Ten Nights*, we might say, turns out to be as significant a visual artifact as it is a literary one.

Picturing temperance

By the 1840s, pictorial illustration had become a crucial component of American temperance reform. While vivid verbal imagery had always been a movement staple, and crude illustrations did appear in early temperance broadsides, such as J. W. Barber's 1826 *The Drunkard's Progress, or The Direct Road to Poverty, Wretchedness & Ruin*, the new prominence of the visual culture of temperance was a product of several related developments. These include technological innovation, particularly the rise of commercial lithography; a vigorous market for temperance-themed materials, as membership in temperance organizations soared to more than 1.5 million members; the emergence of what David Reynolds has termed "dark-temperance" narratives, which relied on increasingly graphic descriptions of alcohol's destructive power; and, not least, the decision by the 1836 National Temperance Convention to endorse the use of fiction in the battle against demon rum. The range and sophistication of temperance images grew exponentially by mid-century, helped along by the explosion of illustrated print materials in the United States more generally and in particular by the arrival of what David Morgan aptly calls "the new mass media of illustrated periodicals."[5] In short, in the 1840s and early 1850s, temperance images were everywhere.

These images differed in style and execution according to the media in which they appeared. The lithograph, for example, was a popular format for colorful print series depicting mini-narratives of dissolution and/or redemption. Printmaker Nathaniel Currier produced a number of widely circulating lithograph series, most notably his 1846 reinterpretation of Barber's broadside, *The Drunkard's Progress. From the First Glass to the Grave*, which closes not, as in Barber's sequence, with a home foreclosure, but with a suicide (see Fig. 1). Illustrated temperance newspapers typically featured stark woodcut engravings. And at the high end of the commercial spectrum, one found more lavishly illustrated temperance annuals. These volumes—designed for gift-giving and parlor display—included a range of image formats, from the occasional woodcut, to richly colored lithograph frontispieces to, most distinctively, full-page mezzotint illustrations, a form of intaglio engraving that produces tonally rich images with shades and textures like those found in painting.

FIGURE 1 The Drunkard's Progress. From the First Glass to the Grave. *Lithographed and published by Nathaniel Currier, New York, c.1846. Courtesy Library of Congress Prints and Photographs Division.*

Temperance imagery varied not just by medium but also by rhetorical aim. Some images emphasized the moral and physical benefits of reform. *Son of Temperance*, for example, a lithograph produced by Currier in 1848 at the height of a new middle-class men's movement supporting prohibition, foregrounds the sleek and stylish bearing of its handsome teetotaler (see Fig. 2). Other images

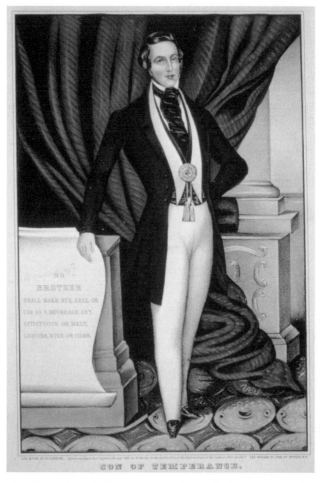

FIGURE 2 Son of Temperance. *Lithographed and published by Nathaniel Currier, New York, c.1848. Courtesy Library of Congress Prints and Photographs Division.*

worked chiefly through sentimental appeals to the sanctity of the temperate home. Many of the richly shaded mezzotint images in the lavish gift books—in contrast to the bright colors of temperance lithographs or the starker lines of woodcuts—fall into this category. Some of the most popular temperance images, on the other hand, eschewed sentiment for sensation, seeking to prompt outrage or horror through the depiction of progressive, unalterable ruin, whether of the drunkard himself (as in Currier's interpretation of *The Drunkard's Progress*) or of an entire family (as in British illustrator George Cruikshank's popular series, *The Bottle*). And although historians of temperance rightly note that the "discourses and strategies" of the movement's main reform efforts changed over time[6]—from the didacticism of the evangelical phase in the 1820s and 1830s, to the sensationalism of the Washingtonian phase in the 1840s, to the legalism of the prohibitionist phase of the 1850s—the images produced by the movement and its allies did not always hew to these strict chronological markers. When *Ten Nights in a Bar-Room* was published in 1854, in other words, virtually all these discourses (indeed more, including what we might call sentimentalism) would not only have been circulating in the visual culture of temperance but would also at times have been blurring, blending, and overlapping.

The visual texture of *Ten Nights*

Timothy Shay Arthur was deeply familiar with the possibilities and permutations of this culture. Not only had Arthur, in a sense, grown up with the movement—he was born in 1809, just a year after the founding of the first temperance society in the United States—by the early 1850s, he had been involved in nearly every genre of temperance publishing. He had, for example, seen his stories appear in mass-market temperance weeklies; he had issued a special illustrated edition of his collected temperance tales; and he had edited several prominent temperance gift annuals. Even the volume that launched his career as a temperance writer, *Six Nights with the Washingtonians* (1842), was reissued in 1848 with eight engravings pirated from Cruikshank's *The Bottle* tipped in as illustrations. And although *Ten Nights in a Bar-Room* was initially published with very few illustrations of its own, it is

nonetheless—as its subtitle, *And What I Saw There*, makes clear—
an intensely visual book.

One striking characteristic of the visual texture of *Ten Nights*
is its variety, a dimension existing criticism has not adequately
captured. Cultural historian Graham Warder comes closest when he
notes that *Ten Nights* is "structurally bifurcated between political
advocacy and emotionally evocative imagery." But Warder does not
quite recognize that even the novel's scenes of political advocacy,
as we shall see, also draw on specific (and evocative) temperance
iconography. Moreover, Warder's characterization of the novel's
narrator as only a detached "spectator" and "voyeur" who "passes
moral judgment but does little else"[7] fails to account for the different
ways of looking—and acting—embodied in Arthur's odd yet crucial
shifts in narrative point of view. Some of those differences are hinted
at in the Publisher's Preface to the novel, which highlights not just
the striking visuality of *Ten Nights* but also some of its different
modes:

> "Ten Nights in a Bar-Room" gives a series of sharply drawn
> sketches of scenes, some of them touching in the extreme,
> and some dark and terrible. Step by step the author traces the
> downward course of the tempting vender and his infatuated
> victims, until both are involved in hopeless ruin. The book is
> marred by no exaggerations, but exhibits the actualities of bar-
> room life, and the consequences flowing therefrom, with a severe
> simplicity, and adherence to truth, that gives to every picture a
> Daguerrean vividness.[8]

This prefatory comment is of course in part an aggressively
defensive marketing gesture, meant to assure readers that although
they are reading a work of fiction, what they are getting is a morally
uplifting picture of "truth"—a common trope in popular fiction
since at least *Charlotte Temple*. But it also provides a road map for
the novel's pictorial strategies, from its "sharply drawn sketches"
(some "touching," some "terrible"), to its display of bar-room
"actualities," to its images of "Daguerrean vividness." While these
are all metaphors for representational realism—highlighting, in
Warder's term, the novel's "hyperreality"—they do not describe the
same ways of picturing "truth."

Let's start with the last phrase: "Daguerrean vividness." Early commentators on Daguerre's new process, perfected in France in the late 1830s and brought to the United States in the early 1840s, were fascinated by the intensity of detail such images could produce as well as the way they seemed to capture the "truth" of a particular moment in time. (Edgar Allan Poe compared their powers to those of "a positively perfect mirror.")[9] In the bar-room scenes of *Ten Nights*, the narrator registers visual details—particularly in regard to faces—as though he were a daguerreotype portraitist. On one level, such attention to faces might seem unremarkable. It is both a common way for someone to become oriented to new persons and surroundings and a storyteller's indispensible tool for helping readers picture the characters in a tale. And yet the narrator of *Ten Nights* scrutinizes faces with an observational intensity that might best be called photographic. Just before sitting down to his first meal at the Sickle and Sheaf, for example, the narrator notices Fanny Slade, the proprietor's wife:

I had not observed her before; and now could not help remarking that she had a flushed, excited countenance, as if she had been over a hot fire, and was both worried and fatigued. And there was, moreover, a peculiar expression of the mouth, never observed in one whose mind is entirely at ease—an expression that once seen is never forgotten. The face stamped itself, instantly, on my memory; and I can even now recall it with almost the original distinction.[10]

This account does more than merely describe Mrs. Slade's face; it fixes its view on a particular detail (the "peculiar expression" of her mouth) and then mimics the popular sense of the way images are recorded on daguerreotype plates: "The face stamped itself, instantly, upon my memory." During the novel, the narrator pauses over nearly every face with this same precision.[11]

In a more literal sense than is usually meant by such metaphors, in the bar scenes of *Ten Nights*, the narrator acts as a human lens, returning to the fictitious Cedarville over a period of 10 years to record new images of the townspeople much as itinerant daguerreotypists often roamed from town to town offering to take portraits of the inhabitants.[12] When the narrator's images are lined up in sequence—from "Night the First" through "Night the Tenth"—they tell their tale of decline one altered face at a time, bringing photographic clarity to the slippery slope iconography of popular mid-century print series like *The Drunkard's Progress* and *The Bottle*. By "Night the Fifth," for example, the "good-natured" face of tavern owner Simon Slade has turned "gross and sensual." By "Night the Eighth," he is little more than a "coarse, bloated, vulgar-looking man." Slade's son Frank's decline is even more precipitous, as the narrator registers his transformation from a "delicate, innocent-looking boy" to a "disgustingly sensual" man.[13] By the end of "Night the Ninth," Frank will have murdered his father, attempted suicide with a pistol (an apt echo of the final frame of Currier's *The Drunkard's Progress*), and been imprisoned in the county jail.

If in these scenes the narrator behaves like a photographer, in other parts of the novel, he acts (and depicts the actions of other characters) in strikingly different ways. Take the scenes set, for example, in the Morgan home—the sentimental rather than the realist heart of the novel—in which young Mary Morgan extracts from her drunkard father Joe the redemptive pledge never to touch another drop of alcohol. In these scenes, the narrator's eye is drawn not to individual portraits but to group tableaux, which he composes with the storytelling eye and the rich tonal textures of a temperance gift-book mezzotint artist or a mid-century genre painter rather than with the "severe simplicity" of a daguerreotypist. These scenes, in other words, correspond more closely to the Preface's "sharply drawn sketches . . ., some of them touching," than to its Daguerrean portraits. In a narrative sense, this shift in mode is quite fitting, for within the logic of the story, the narrator cannot actually have witnessed the scenes inside the Morgan home in the first place, since he never receives an invitation to their house nor follows them out of the tavern. The narrator side-steps this impossibility by simply announcing, "Let us leave the bar-room . . . and look in upon the family of Joe Morgan, and see how it is in the home of the poor inebriate."[14] But if the narrator cannot have "taken" these pictures, as it were, how does he produce them?

I would suggest that the narrator does so through his own vivid imagination, prompted by an image he records in "Night the First" of Mary Morgan entering the tavern to lead her father home.

This strikes me as the significance of the following passage near the end of the first chapter, as the narrator reflects on the events of his first day in the Sickle and Sheaf:

> The picture of [Mary's] mournful little face was ever before me; and I seemed all the while to hear the word "Father," uttered so touchingly, and yet with such a world of childish tenderness. And the man, who would have opposed the most stubborn resistance to his fellow men, had they sought to force him from the room, going passively, almost meekly out, led by that little child—I could not, for a time, turn my thoughts from the image thereof! And then thought bore me to the wretched home, back to which the gentle, loving child had taken her father, and my heart grew faint in me as imagination busied itself with all the misery there.[15]

We are thus meant to understand, I would suggest, that the sentimental images within the Morgan home in "Night the Third" and "Night the Fourth" are produced by the mind's (or heart's) eye rather than with a camera. Within these scenes, moreover, it is imaginative empathy, not photographic exposure, that guides the narrative point of view, which not only shifts from first-person singular to an unusual combination of first-person plural and third-person omniscient but which also lingers sympathetically—in the present tense, no less—over expressive exchanges of glance and touch among two or more characters. Indeed in "Night the Third" and "Night the Fourth," when one character places his or her hand on someone else, the narrative almost always pauses to stage a tableau, as when Fanny Morgan reassures her husband that his promise not to go out at night until Mary is well is his first step to recovery:

> Now [Fanny] comes nearer to them, and says, *as she lets a hand rest on the shoulder of her husband*—
> "You feel better for that promise, already; I know you do."
> *He looks up to her, and smiles faintly.* He does feel better, but is hardly willing to acknowledge it.[16]

If the realist daguerreotype and the sentimental sketch provide the visual textures, respectively, for the ruin and redemption narratives of *Ten Nights*, there are yet other modes at work, with recognizable temperance analogues, for what the Publisher's Preface calls the novel's "dark and terrible" scenes and also for its interludes of political advocacy. The depiction of the latter, for example—which reaches its height in the novel's penultimate scene, where a sober, redeemed Joe Morgan urges his fellow townspeople to prohibit the sale, purchase, and use of alcohol in Cedarville—draws recognizably on the tropes of respectability and legal intervention popularized in such images as Currier's *Son of Temperance* lithograph shown in Fig. 2. Much as in Currier's image, in which the respectable teetotaler stands proudly beside a tablet bearing a membership pledge, Morgan, "well dressed" and "erect," rises to offer four "resolutions"[17] to turn the town completely dry. The novel's "dark and terrible" images, on the other hand—including Mary being struck in the head by Slade with a tumbler; bar-room "tempter" Harvey Green stabbing young Willy Hammond, the judge's son; and Frank Slade murdering his father—are rendered with a melodramatic hyperbole that most strongly mimics the bold lines of temperance weekly woodcuts. The murder of Slade by his son provides a representative example:

> Instantly, the young man, infuriated by drink and evil passions, threw the bottle at his father's head. The dangerous missile fell, crashing upon one of his temples, shivering it into a hundred pieces. A heavy, jarring fall too surely marked the fearful consequences of the blow. When we gathered around the fallen man, and made an effort to lift him from the floor, a thrill of horror went through every heart. A mortal paleness was already on his marred face, and the death-gurgle in his throat! In three minutes from the time the blow was struck, his spirit had gone upward to give an account of the deeds done in his body.
> "Frank Slade! you have murdered your father!"[18]

In this passage, the narrator also steps emphatically out of his role as spectator and voyeur to involve himself directly in the scene: "When *we* gathered around the fallen man, and made an effort to lift him from the floor . . . ."[19] In fact, in the second half of the novel, the narrator increasingly finds himself drawn into the action, in part, it would seem, because of what he has witnessed (or brought to life in his imagination) visit after visit. "Although I had no delegated right of intrusion," he admits in the cataclysmic chapter "Night the Seventh," when he helps a friend of Willy Hammond locate the fallen young man in one of the secret gambling rooms of the Sickle and Sheaf, "my feelings were so much excited in the case, that I went forward, scarcely reflecting on the propriety of doing so."[20] The knock on the door—which the narrator not only witnesses but also enables—explodes in a whirl of violence that ends with Green's fatal knifing of Hammond. Though Green escapes, the narrator eventually discovers him hiding under his own bed. In trying to arrange for his arrest, the narrator then inadvertently triggers the lynch mob that murders Green right before his eyes.

So much for detached observation. The narrator of *Ten Nights* both observes scenes and participates in them, just as he both records images and imagines them. It also seems clear that the novel, far from simply providing "lurid waxworks realism" or a "titillatingly horrific portrayal" of drink and destruction, produces and manipulates specific and resonant images drawn from the full spectrum of the mid-century visual culture of temperance. We might even speculate that this powerful amalgam of images and discourses—collated by an author uniquely familiar with this culture, and appearing just as the representational strategies of the movement were shifting from the evangelical and sensational approaches of the 1830s and 1840s to the more legalistic tactics of the 1850s—had much to do with the phenomenal success of Arthur's novel.

Illustrating Arthur's *Bar-Room*

A brief study of the illustration history of *Ten Nights* supports this view. In its earliest printings, the book was not heavily illustrated, which might seem surprising given the rich visual texture of the novel and the increasing frequency in the 1850s with which popular fiction was published with woodcuts. Even some of Arthur's earlier temperance works, including *The Lost Children, A Temperance Tale* (1848) and *Illustrated Temperance Tales* (1850), had included multiple images. Despite numerous early imprints, however, three years passed before an edition of *Ten Nights* included illustrations besides frontispieces.

Those frontispieces nonetheless tell a great deal about the novel's engagement with the visual culture of temperance. The first edition of *Ten Nights*, a joint imprint by Philadelphia publishers Lippincott, Grambo and Co., and J. W. Bradley, had in fact not one but two frontispieces. Both were executed as woodcuts by engraver William H. Van Ingen and appeared on facing pages. The left frontispiece depicts the crowded interior of the Sickle and Sheaf and in particular the scene from "Night the First" in which Mary comes to the tavern to take her father home (see Fig. 3). The right frontispiece, a faux title page, portrays the outside of the tavern with the novel's title superimposed in rough-hewn lettering over the top half of the image (see Fig. 4). Taken together, the Van Ingen woodcuts suggestively foreground the novel's legal attack on alcohol, a stance affirmed by the opening sentences of the Publisher's Preface: "This new temperance volume, by Mr. Arthur, comes in just at the right time, when the subject of restrictive laws is agitating the whole country, and good and true men everywhere are gathering up their strength for a prolonged and unflinching contest."[21] Van Ingen's images put a particularly poor face on the tavern. In the left frontispiece (Fig. 3), the bar-room appears crowded and dirty, the floorboards irregularly cut. Smoke rises from cigars or is being blown out of someone's mouth, and hand-lettered signs are tacked to the shelving behind the bar. In the right frontispiece (Fig. 4), the outside of the tavern fares little better: the ground cover needs trimming, fowl scavenge in the foreground, and a barrel leans sideways in the lower left corner of the frame. To the reader steeped in the visual culture of temperance, the barren branches on the large tree in the center of the frame would likely have recalled the foreboding imagery of Currier's popular 1849 lithograph, *The Tree of Intemperance* (see Fig. 5). What might at first glance pass for rustic charm, in other words—down to the crooked lettering of the title—carries the unmistakable iconography of the dissolution produced by a society that condones drink.

Roughly a month after this first edition appeared, however, J. W. Bradley issued a new printing of *Ten Nights* with only a single and very different frontispiece: an elaborate copper mezzotint engraving, also of Mary leading her father from the Sickle and Sheaf, by one of the most respected mezzotint artists in the United States, John Sartain (see Fig. 6). I say "new printing" rather than "new edition"

FIGURE 3 *Left frontispiece to T. S. Arthur,* Ten Nights in a Bar-Room, And What I Saw There *(Philadelphia: Lippincott, Grambo and Co., 1854). Woodcut engraving by William H. Van Ingen. Courtesy Sinclair Hamilton Collection, Graphic Arts, Department of Rare Books and Special Collection, Princeton University Library.*

FIGURE 4 *Right frontispiece to T. S. Arthur,* Ten Nights in a Bar-Room, And What I Saw There *(Philadelphia: Lippincott, Grambo and Co., 1854). Woodcut engraving by William H. Van Ingen. Courtesy Sinclair Hamilton Collection, Graphic Arts, Department of Rare Books and Special Collection, Princeton University Library.*

FIGURE 5 The Tree of Intemperance. *Lithographed and published by Nathaniel Currier, New York, 1849. Courtesy Library of Congress Prints and Photographs Division.*

FIGURE 6 *Frontispiece to T. S. Arthur,* Ten Nights in a Bar-Room, And What I Saw There *(Philadelphia: J. W. Bradley, 1854). Drawing by George G. White, mezzotint engraving by John Sartain. Courtesy Sinclair Hamilton Collection, Graphic Arts, Department of Rare Books and Special Collection, Princeton University Library.*

because both versions were printed from the same stereotype plates and thus between the covers differ only in their frontispieces. (All printings of *Ten Nights* would be made from the same plates until Arthur commissioned a new typesetting of the novel in 1882.) Even though Sartain's mezzotint depicts the same scene as Van Ingen's woodcut, the two artists' depictions could not be less similar. While Van Ingen's woodcut emphasizes the sordidness of the Sickle and Sheaf, in Sartain's mezzotint, the tavern is spotless, the patrons neat. A small spittoon stands in the same corner of the frame as in the earlier woodcut but either no one uses it or everyone's aim is perfect, since there is no wayward tobacco juice on the floor. Even the floorboards are in precise alignment. Just as striking are the different delineations of Joe Morgan. In Van Ingen's woodcut, Morgan appears haggard. His hair straggles out from under his decrepit hat; his face is pockmarked; and his bent posture marks not just the act of standing up but also perhaps the unsteadiness of his legs. He appears to be rising in anger, his mouth open as though speaking or about to speak. The scene is tense, and Morgan looks ready to erupt. In Sartain's mezzotint, by contrast, Morgan's clothes, though patched, are neat (a lone pocket turned inside out indicates his poverty), and there are few signs of anger. Morgan's mouth is closed and he turns a backward glance at the patrons—or perhaps at Slade, half-visible in the right background—as if in embarrassment or regret rather than fury. His overall posture indicates submission rather than aggression.

Scholars have never quite understood the relationship between these different frontispieces. Early-book historians were uncertain about which version appeared first, and even one of the most respected mid-twentieth-century catalogs of early American books misidentifies the provenance and purpose of the Sartain mezzotint, suggesting that it depicts a scene from the popular 1858 stage adaptation of the novel and was designed to "replace" the Van Ingen woodcut.[22] Not only did the Sartain mezzotint appear well before the stage adaptation, but both the Van Ingen and Sartain versions were available for sale through the 1850s—and were in fact supplemented by yet a third version in 1857. It seems more sensible to imagine Arthur's publishers designing different versions for different classes of buyers, aiming the more stylish mezzotint at readers with more disposable income. Although this seems more likely—especially since Bradley not only changed the frontispiece but also replaced the plain brown boards of the Lippincott edition with the fancier colored boards and gilt embossing of a gift-book—this hypothesis has its own problem: while Bradley did indeed emphasize the beauty of the mezzotint engraving in advertisements for his new edition, copies of the Sartain version could be had for the same price as the Van Ingen version until at least 1859.[23]

I propose a new way of thinking about these frontispieces: namely, that the simultaneous availability of differently illustrated versions of the book—presenting starkly divergent interpretations of the same scene—reflects different ways Arthur's publishers chose to highlight the multiple temperance rhetorics at work in Arthur's novel. As we saw in the previous section, *Ten Nights* draws its narrative and rhetorical power from a broad range of related yet distinct temperance images and discourses, themselves overlapping in the early 1850s. If Van Ingen's woodcuts accentuate the novel's legal rhetoric, Sartain's mezzotint succinctly captures *Ten Nights'* emotional appeal to the imperiled family bond, epitomized by the Mary/Joe Morgan subplot and reiterated in a whole range of doomed parent-child relationships. (That Joe Morgan will eventually not only survive but also achieve redemption—though at the price of the sacrificial death of his daughter—heightens the tragedy of familial destruction in the novel.) Consider again the two frontispieces, focusing this time on Mary's interaction with her father. Where the uplifted eyes of Van Ingen's Mary express patient concern, Sartain's Mary seems more overwrought, pulling at her father rather than merely supporting him, her body bending with his, her upturned face radiating commingled anxiety and pathos. We have already seen how within the text "that mournful little face" affected the narrator so powerfully he found himself transported, imaginatively, to the Morgan home. I would suggest Arthur and/or Bradley elected to publish a version of the novel with the Sartain mezzotint—particularly with its added caption, "*Father, come Home!*"—to capitalize not simply on Sartain's reputation but also on the book's emotional appeal. That the Sartain frontispiece struck precisely this chord with some readers is confirmed by the reviewer for the *American Courier* who, commenting specifically on the Bradley edition, linked image and text: "One touching passage," noted the review, "supplies the beautiful mezzotint illustration by Sartain."[24]

This of course does not mean readers of one version could not perceive the variety of appeals in the book. Quite the contrary, as evidenced by a review of the Van Ingen edition in the *Metropolitan*, which informed its readers that *Ten Nights*

> is a tale of the 'Uncle Tom' and 'Hot Corn' class,—being intended to subserve the cause of the Maine Liquor Law. Like its prototypes, it contains of course plenty of horrors illustrative of the subject which it takes in hand, and like them, of course, one of the little child-heroines, whom Eva in 'Uncle Tom' made so popular. It may be inferred from this statement that the book is not free from a certain sentimentality which is doing as much harm now as the vice of drinking.[25]

Although the *Metropolitan* is clearly dismayed by Arthur's approach—"We do not approve of the principle of carrying political measures, even of a moral tendency, by the aid of exciting fictions"—these comments testify that one did not need the Sartain mezzotint to sense the "sentimentality" undergirding the novel's potent blend of "horrors" and legal activism.

But this also did not stop Arthur's publishers from trying to find the right images with which to market the book. I would suggest that it was this desire—to find a combination of images and ornamentation that would best represent the novel's multiple temperance discourses and thus appeal to a wider audience—that may have led Bradley, Arthur's most innovative publisher, to produce the image-laden 1857 edition of *Ten Nights*. Recall that Bradley had co-issued the first edition, with the Van Ingen woodcuts, and then reissued a new version with the Sartain mezzotint. In 1857, he decided to reinstall the Van Ingen frontispieces, introduce six new full-page woodcuts within the text, and package the volume once again as a gift-book edition. This new version appeared under the imprint of John E. Potter and Company, but with Bradley, rather than Arthur, listed as the book's copyright holder. The layered visual texture of the Potter/Bradley edition tells a more complicated story about temperance than either the Van Ingen or Sartain versions. The gift-book ornamentation announces the book's middle-class respectability; the Van Ingen frontispieces indict the tavern; and the new illustrations by an engraver named Rea[26]—which were far more sensational than any that had previously appeared—bring to life the novel's darker side while simultaneously exploring a selection of highly emotional scenes and even expressing some of the story's humor.

Where both the Van Ingen and Sartain frontispieces, for example, focus on Mary's tearful appearance in the Sickle and Sheaf on "Night the First," the first new woodcut in the 1857 edition depicts the scene in "Night the Second" when Slade strikes Mary in the head with a tumbler (see Fig. 7). Three of the other six new illustrations depict similarly melodramatic scenes, including the stabbing of Willy Hammond by Harvey Green; Hammond's mother's "long scream of horror" and "lifeless" collapse after seeing his dead body; and the murder of Slade by his son Frank, which like the illustration of Mary being struck by the tumbler depicts the precise moment that the bottle Frank throws shatters on Slade's forehead (see Fig. 8). Another darkly shaded woodcut illustrates a frightening episode from inside the Morgan home, imagining a terrified Joe Morgan in the throes of the DTs (see Fig. 9). Yet another illustration seems designed to dissipate some of the novel's tension by depicting the drunken Sickle and Sheaf patron who shouts "Huzza for the Rummies! That's the Ticket!" during the discussion of the legal attack on alcohol in "Night the Fifth." If the general feel of the 1857 edition, especially in comparison to the Sartain version, is a turn from sentiment toward melodrama—as even the fraught scene in the Morgan home tilts toward horror rather than tears—the addition to the first Van Ingen frontispiece of the heart-rending caption "Come, Father! Won't You Come Home?" is perhaps an attempt to make sure that the emotional appeal was still foregrounded. At any rate, Bradley carefully hedged his bets, continuing to sell the more overtly sentimental Sartain edition for at least several years even as the more visually complex 1857 Potter edition took hold as the version most late nineteenth-century readers would know.[27]

FIGURE 7 *"It's Joe Morgan's Child! He's Killed Her! Good Heavens!"*
From T. S. Arthur, Ten Nights in a Bar-Room, And What I Saw There
(Philadelphia: John E. Potter and Company, 1857). Woodcut engraving,
unsigned, facing page 50. Author's collection.

FIGURE 8 *"There it is now! Jump! Get out of bed, quick! Jump out, Mary! See! It's right over your head!" From T. S. Arthur,* Ten Nights in a Bar-Room, And What I Saw There *(Philadelphia: John E. Potter and Company, 1857). Woodcut engraving by [J.] Rea, facing page 88. Author's collection.*

FIGURE 9 *"Frank Slade! You have murdered your father!" From T. S. Arthur,* Ten Nights in a Bar-Room, And What I Saw There *(Philadelphia: John E. Potter and Company, 1857). Woodcut engraving by J. Rea, facing page 284. Author's collection.*

Conclusion: Visual branding

Within a short time, this is exactly how *Ten Nights* came to be understood by readers and marketed by Arthur's publishers: as a powerful amalgam of temperance discourses and images, at once sensational *and* didactic, sentimental *and* prohibitionist. New advertising copy for the novel stressed this variety in particular detail:

> The sad and terrible history of the "Sickle and Sheaf," and its landlord, Simon Slade, is intensely exciting. Poor Joe Morgan, his noble wife Fanny, and their angelic little Mary, are among the most interesting characters, and the scenes between the daughter and the father, ere her little spirit joins the angels of the resurrection, are so deeply impressive that few men or women can read them without frequently shedding tears. The ruin of Judge Hammond, the death of his son, and the gambler Green's death, are full of the dark and terrible. This work affords some of the most sharply-drawn sketches of scenes and characters to be found in any book in the English language. With Illustrations.[28]

The first sentence nearly says it all: the novel is sad, terrible, and yet "intensely exciting." (And the final sentence is no mere throwaway: "With Illustrations.") There are echoes from the original Publisher's Preface here to be sure—the phrases "dark and terrible" and "sharply-drawn sketches of scenes" are direct quotations—and yet the description of the book is much more specific, invoking scenes and characters, particularly Mary and her father, that were quickly becoming iconic pop culture images. Compared to the 1854 preface, this new sales pitch also places less emphasis on the "truth" of the novel than on the feelings it produces in readers, highlighting *Ten Nights*' emotional rather than factual power and connecting readers to the text not merely as viewers but also as active responders to the book's blend of appeals. While some of these changes suggest that Arthur's publishers were simply taking advantage of the novel's familiarity among mid-century readers, they also reflect its clearer branding as a dynamic mix of temperance images and rhetorics, a branding that the evolution of its early illustrated editions helped both mark and create. After 1860, the illustrating of *Ten Nights* appears to have stabilized, with multiple versions still in circulation but with the 1857 Potter images becoming the new standard. When Arthur himself in 1882 prepared, for the first time, a completely new edition of the novel, he too used the images from the 1857 Potter text.[29]

The debut in 1858 of William W. Pratt's melodramatic stage adaption of *Ten Nights* at the National Theater in Boston surely helped this stabilization. Pratt's play, handbills for which frequently included one or both of Van Ingen's frontispieces, zeroed in on the novel's most iconic, and now most illustrated, moments—Mary's beaning, Morgan's abjection, Slade's murder—while introducing new characters for comic relief as well as a romantic side plot. Pratt's melodrama played all over the country and was a staple of regional theater well into the late century. But if, as some critics have suggested, the play's success helped catapult the novel to its greatest circulation, the reverse is likely also true: the novel's intense visuality, accentuated by the 1857 illustrated Potter edition, made the play not only possible but also inevitable. Nor would Pratt's adaptation be the last time entrepreneurs in collateral fields sought to capitalize on the visual power of Arthur's text. In 1864, poet and songwriter Henry Clay Work, for example, transformed the image of little Mary leading Joe Morgan out of the Sickle and Sheaf from popular frontispiece into popular song; in time, Work's temperance ballad ("Come Home, Father!") was even incorporated into performances of Pratt's play. In the 1880s and 1890s, just as the stage version was finally receding from public view, late-century temperance reformers dramatized their lectures with full-color magic lantern slide shows retelling the story of *Ten Nights*. Many of these lantern slides, not surprisingly—including, for example, the depiction of Frank Slade striking his father dead with a liquor bottle (see Fig. 10)—have clear antecedents in the 1857 Potter illustrations.[30] In the twentieth century, *Ten Nights* would finally be turned into a truly moving picture, being filmed for the screen at least six times during the silent era and again in 1931 after the introduction of sound. Only after the failure of Prohibition, ironically, did Arthur's story threaten to disappear, albeit temporarily, finding its way back to the stage as a musical in 1958 and then as a musical comedy in 1969. Revival performances appear sporadically even today.[31]

So too do contemporary paperback reprints of Arthur's novel, although none has seen fit to include any illustrations except Van Ingen's original woodcuts from the 1854 first printing. This omission merely follows the lead of earlier scholarly editions of the

FIGURE 10 *"In a drunken rage, Frank kills his father." Late nineteenth-century magic lantern slide. From William M. Clark, "Ten Nights in a Bar-Room,"* American Heritage *15.4 (June 1964), 17. Princeton University Library.*

novel, which have typically included either the Van Ingen or Sartain frontispieces but nothing else. In the end, the absence of the full-page illustrations introduced in 1857 robs us not only of some of the texture of Arthur's novel but also of a crucial moment in the cultural history of temperance, as what would become the movement's most popular artifact initially struggled to find the most effective pictorial expression of its rich mixture of images and discourses. Until we have an edition that provides this more complete visual history, we will likely never fully appreciate the ways in which Arthur's images—in words and in pictures—helped *Ten Nights* insinuate itself so deeply into nineteenth and early twentieth-century popular culture.

Bibliography

Arthur, Timothy S. *The Lost Children, A Temperance Tale*. New York: Oliver and Brother, 1848.

—. *Illustrated Temperance Tales*. Philadelphia: J. W. Bradley, 1850.

—. *Six Nights with the Washingtonians: A Series of Original Temperance Tales*. Philadelphia: L. A. Godey and Morton M'Michael, 1842.

—. *Ten Nights in a Bar-Room, And What I Saw There*. Philadelphia: Lippincott, Grambo and Co., 1854.

—. *Ten Nights in a Bar-Room, And What I Saw There*. Philadelphia: J. W. Bradley, 1854.

—. *Ten Nights in a Bar-Room, And What I Saw There*. Philadelphia: John E. Potter and Company, 1857.

—. *Ten Nights in a Bar-Room, And What I Saw There*. Philadelphia: J. W. Bradley, 1858.

—. *Ten Nights in a Bar-Room, And What I Saw There*. Philadelphia: Porter and Coates, 1882.

Barber, John W. *The Drunkard's Progress, or The Direct Road to Poverty, Wretchedness & Ruin*. New Haven, CT, 1826.

Bennett, Whitman. *A Practical Guide to American Book Collecting (1663–1940)*. New York: The Bennett Book Studios, 1941.

Brown, Herbert Ross. *The Sentimental Novel in America, 1789–1860*. Durham, NC: Duke University Press, 1940.

"Catalogue of Valuable and Interesting Works." In T. S. Arthur, *Ten Nights in a Bar-Room, And What I Saw There*. Philadelphia: J. W. Bradley, 1858.

Clark, William M. "Ten Nights in a Bar-Room." *American Heritage* 15, 4 (June 1964): 14–17.

Cruikshank, George. *The Bottle: In Eight Plates*. London: David Bogue, 1847.

Currier, Nathaniel. *The Drunkard's Progress. From the First Glass to the Grave*. New York, c.1846.

—. *Son of Temperance*. New York, c.1848.

—. *The Tree of Intemperance*. New York, 1849.

"Descriptive Catalogue of T. S. Arthur's Popular Works." In T. S. Arthur, *Woman to the Rescue*. Philadelphia: J. M. Stoddart, 1874.

Hamilton, Sinclair. *Early American Book Illustrators and Wood Engravers, 1670–1870*. Princeton: Princeton University Library, 1958.

Lehuu, Isabelle. *Carnival on the Page: Popular Print Media in Antebellum America*. Chapel Hill, NC: University of North Carolina Press, 2000.

Lender, Mark Edward and James Kirby Martin. *Drinking in America: A History*. New York: The Free Press, 1982.

Mavity, Nancy Barr. "Alcoholic Atmosphere Hangs Heavy Over 'The Beautiful and the Damned': F. Scott Fitzgerald Paints Rake's Progress Via Ten Nights in a Barroom to a Doom of Damnation." *San Francisco Chronicle*, March 26, 1922.

Morgan, David. *Protestants and Pictures: Religion, Visual Culture, and the Age of American Mass Production*. New York: Oxford University Press, 1999.

Mott, Frank Luther. *Golden Multitudes: The Story of Best Sellers in the United States*. New York: Macmillan, 1947.

Newhall, Beaumont. *The Daguerreotype in America*, 3rd ed., rev. and enl. New York: Dover, 1976.

Poe, Edgar Allan. "The Daguerreotype." *Alexander's Weekly Messenger* 4, 3 (Jan. 15, 1840), 2.

Pratt, William W. *Ten Nights in a Bar-Room: A Drama in Five Acts*. New York: S. French, 1858.

Review of *Ten Nights in a Bar-Room, And What I Saw There*, by T. S. Arthur. *Metropolitan: A Monthly Magazine Devoted to Religion, Education, Literature, and General Information* 2, 8 (September 1854), 498.

Reynolds, David S. *Beneath the American Renaissance: The Subversive Imagination in the Age of Emerson and Melville*. Cambridge, MA: Harvard University Press, 1989.

Reynolds, David S. and Debra J. Rosenthal. *The Serpent in the Cup: Temperance in American Literature*. Amherst: University of Massachusetts Press, 1997.

Warder, Graham. "Temperance Nostalgia, Market Anxiety, and the Reintegration of Community in T. S. Arthur's *Ten Nights in a Bar-Room*." In *Cultural Change and the Market Revolution in America, 1789–1860*, edited by Scott C. Martin, 217–45. New York: Rowman and Littlefield, 2005.

Welling, William. *Photography in America: The Formative Years, 1839–1900*. Albuquerque, NM: University of New Mexico Press, 1987.

Notes

1   David S. Reynolds and Debra J. Rosenthal, *The Serpent in the Cup: Temperance in American Literature* (Amherst: University of Massachusetts Press, 1997), 6.

2   Frank Luther Mott, *Golden Multitudes: The Story of Best Sellers in the United States* (New York: Macmillan, 1947), 122.

3   In the 1920s, the title of Arthur's novel could still be used as cultural shorthand, as evidenced by a 1922 newspaper review of F. Scott Fitzgerald's latest novel: "Alcoholic Atmosphere Hangs Heavy Over

'The Beautiful and the Damned': F. Scott Fitzgerald Paints Rake's Progress Via Ten Nights in a Barroom to a Doom of Damnation" (Nancy Barr Mavity, *San Francisco Chronicle*, March 26, 1922, 4F).

4 Herbert Ross Brown, *The Sentimental Novel in America, 1789–1860* (Durham, NC: Duke University Press, 1940), 219; David S. Reynolds, *Beneath the American Renaissance: The Subversive Imagination in the Age of Emerson and Melville* (Cambridge, MA: Harvard University Press, 1989), 69.

5 David Morgan, *Protestants and Pictures: Religion, Visual Culture, and the Age of American Mass Production* (New York: Oxford University Press, 1999), 71. On temperance society membership, see Mark Edward Lender and James Kirby Martin, *Drinking in America: A History* (New York: The Free Press, 1982), 68–74. On "dark-temperance" narratives, see Reynolds, *Beneath the American Renaissance*, 59–84. On the 1836 National Temperance Convention, see Brown, *The Sentimental Novel*, 201–3. On mid-century print media, see Isabelle Lehuu, *Carnival on the Page: Popular Print Media in Antebellum America* (Chapel Hill, NC: University of North Carolina Press, 2000).

6 Reynolds and Rosenthal, *The Serpent in the Cup*, 4.

7 Graham Warder, "Temperance Nostalgia, Market Anxiety, and the Reintegration of Community in T. S. Arthur's *Ten Nights in a Bar-Room*" in *Cultural Change and the Market Revolution in America, 1789–1860*, ed. Scott C. Martin (New York: Rowman and Littlefield, 2005), 227.

8 T. S. Arthur, *Ten Nights in a Bar-Room, And What I Saw There* (Philadelphia: Lippincott, Grambo and Co., 1854), 3.

9 Edgar Allan Poe, "The Daguerreotype," *Alexander's Weekly Messenger* 4, 3 (Jan. 15, 1840), 2.

10 Arthur, *Ten Nights* (1854), 16–17.

11 Technically, daguerreotypes are not created by "stamping" images on plates but by subjecting exposed silvered copper plates, presensitized with iodine fumes, to heated mercury vapor. But even Daguerre often described the process as a way of "fixing" images onto plates. See Beaumont Newhall, *The Daguerreotype in America*, 3rd edn. (New York: Dover, 1976), 17.

12 On itinerant daguerreotypists, see William Welling, *Photography in America: The Formative Years, 1839–1900* (Albuquerque, NM: University of New Mexico Press, 1987), 61–2.

13 Arthur, *Ten Nights* (1854), 113, 203, 43, 205.

14 Ibid., 61.

15 Ibid., 33.

16   Ibid., 64; emphases added.

17   Ibid., 237, 239.

18   Ibid., 233–4.

19   Ibid., 165; emphasis added.

20   Ibid., 165.

21   Ibid., 3.

22   Whitman Bennett, *A Practical Guide to American Book Collecting (1663–1940)* (New York: The Bennett Book Studios, 1941), 113.

23   Bradley sold two versions of his Sartain edition, one with a gilt back for 75 cents—the same price as the original Lippincott, Grambo, Van Ingen edition—and one with full gilt edge, back, and sides for $1.00.

24   "Catalogue of Valuable and Interesting Works," 5, advertising supplement to T. S. Arthur, *Ten Nights in a Bar-Room, And What I Saw There* (Philadelphia: J. W. Bradley, 1858).

25   Review of *Ten Nights in a Bar-Room, And What I Saw There*, by T. S. Arthur, *Metropolitan: A Monthly Magazine Devoted to Religion, Education, Literature, and General Information* 2, 8 (September 1854), 498.

26   Rea is likely the J. Rea identified by Sinclair Hamilton as one of the engravers for the 1872 J. M. Stoddart edition of Arthur's *Three Years in a Man-Trap*. See *Early American Book Illustrators and Wood Engravers, 1670–1870* (Princeton: Princeton University Library, 1958), 73.

27   When the copyright on *Ten Nights* expired in the 1890s, publishing houses reissuing Arthur's novel almost always included the 1857 illustrations rather than the Sartain mezzotint.

28   This advertisement is taken from a "Descriptive Catalogue of T. S. Arthur's Popular Works," 27, appended to Arthur's *Woman to the Rescue* (Philadelphia: J. M. Stoddart, 1874), but this description of the novel may have appeared as early as 1860.

29   The 1882 edition includes only one frontispiece, Van Ingen's woodcut of the bar-room exterior. The Van Ingen woodcut of Mary leading her father out of the tavern was repositioned as a full-page illustration facing page 32.

30   On magic lantern slide performances of *Ten Nights*, see William M. Clark, "Ten Nights in a Bar-Room," *American Heritage* 15, 4 (June 1964), 14–17.

31   The Hackmatack Playhouse in Berwick, Maine, for example, revived Pratt's play for their summer 2011 season (http://www.hackmatack. org/hackmatack; accessed 6/21/11).

6

"The Man Without a Country": Treason, expansionism, and the history of a "bestselling" short story

Hsuan L. Hsu

Whether through gift editions, word of mouth, the mass media, or anthologies like *Famous Stories Every Child Should Know* (1907), most children growing up in the United States in the decades after the Civil War would have come across the story of Philip Nolan, who cursed his country once and spent the rest of his life regretting it. After it first appeared in the December 1863 issue of *The Atlantic Monthly*, Edward Everett Hale's short story "The Man Without a Country" quickly became one of the most widely read American short stories of its time: by 1881, Hale alleged that over 90,000 copies had been sold.[1] While sales figures are not available for a short story that frequently circulated in magazines and anthologies, Hale's story certainly shared the popularity and widespread reprinting of many book-length "bestsellers." Since its initial appearance, "The Man Without a Country" has been reprinted, anthologized, and assigned in public schools to instill patriotism, invoked in a

Supreme Court case on birthright citizenship, cited by writers like Mark Twain and Social Gospel leader Josiah Strong, reissued during every major war from 1898 to Vietnam, and adapted for mass media productions (as a play in 1918, an opera in 1937, a number of radio shows during the Cold War, and a made-for-television movie in 1973).[2] Most recently, Hale's story has been referenced by both neoconservative rants condemning Joseph Walker Lindh[3] and progressive authors like Kurt Vonnegut and the historian Linda Kerber, who cites the story as a parable not of patriotism, but of the legal production of "stateless" subjects stripped of citizenship and civil rights. Although "The Man Without a Country" shares themes such as historical events, intense nationalism, and sentimental setpieces with many of the novel-length bestsellers discussed in the present volume, the brevity of Hale's short story made it particularly accessible to magazine subscribers and schoolchildren, and a frequent subject of both authorized and unauthorized reprintings. This essay will situate "The Man Without a Country" within the various contexts of its plot and setting in 1805–7, its composition during the Civil War, and its republications later in the nineteenth century. Hale's historical allusions and subsequent commentaries on the story gradually reframed its nationalist object lesson to suit the increasingly expansionist outlook of American readers, making the character of Philip Nolan an important focal point for reformulating the tangled and often contradictory relations between US nation building, imperialism, and the denationalization of racialized subjects throughout the nineteenth century.

Origins: The Burr Conspiracy and the Vallandigham affair

Hale would have been pleased by his story's ongoing reprintings, reenactments, and appropriations—for he himself had initiated the story's various circulations as a nationalist parable, a pedagogical legend, and a tool of propaganda. A Harvard-educated abolitionist, grandnephew of the martyred spy Nathan Hale (1755–76), nephew of the statesman Edward Everett, and Unitarian pastor at Boston's South Congregational Church, by 1863, Hale had already written tracts endorsing the emigration of antislavery settlers to Kansas and Nebraska and urged his congregants to enlist in the Union Army. "I threw myself into every effort for the national life," he wrote. "So soon as there was any recruiting, I urged on the young men of the congregation their duty to enlist. I said that the moment the enlistment from my church stopped, I should go myself; and I should have done so" ("A Church" 182). Connected to the New England intellectual elite through his Whig father (Nathan Hale, nephew of the Revolutionary hero) and wife (Emily Perkins, a niece of Harriet Beecher Stowe, whom he married in 1852), Hale wrote regularly for such periodicals as *North American Review* and Boston's *Daily Advertiser* (edited by his father); in 1858, he began contributing to *The Atlantic Monthly*. During this time, he had also conducted historical research on topics such as Spanish America, Christopher Columbus, and military history. After the Civil War, Hale would become involved with a series of civic and philanthropic endeavors, ranging from the Freedman's Bureau and the Chautauquas movement to *Lend A Hand: A Journal of Organized Philanthropy* (established in 1886); he later became the chaplain of the Senate in 1903, and his fame as a sort of nineteenth-century public intellectual was recognized by the erection of a memorial statue on Boston Common in 1913, four years after his death. With these connections to writing, preaching, historiography, patriotism, abolition, and public education, Hale was thus ideally poised to influence the public opinion of *The Atlantic*'s readers in 1863.

Specifically, Hale intended "The Man Without a Country" to appear in time to help turn public opinion against Clement L. Vallandigham (1820–71) the exiled Copperhead leader who was running *in absentia* in Ohio's November gubernatorial election.[4] In May 1863, Vallandigham had given a speech denouncing "King Lincoln" for infringing on the Confederate states' rights, and for supporting military regulations that constituted "a bane usurpation of arbitrary power."[5] In a commentary written decades later, Hale explains that

A man named [Clement] Vallandigham . . . was the candidate of the party which opposed the National Government. This Mr. Vallandigham had said that he did not want to belong to a nation which would compel by arms the loyalty of any of its citizens; he did not want to belong to the United States. General Burnside, who was the Union commander-in-chief in the West, with the powers of martial law, sent Mr. Vallandigham, with his compliments, to the rebel commander on the other side of the Ohio. He said that if Mr. Vallandigham did not want to live in the United States, the United States did not want to have him there. ("Introduction," May 5, 1898, 116)

In fact, a military court had sentenced Vallandigham to two years in prison for violating General Burnside's General Order Number 38, which prohibited "the habit of declaring sympathies for the enemy"[6]; and it was Lincoln himself who ordered Hale turned over to the Confederacy, fearing that imprisoning him in the Union would make him a martyr for free speech, antiwar sentiment, and states' rights.[7] Vallandigham's case was closely watched and widely commented on in newspapers, meetings, and Democratic pamphlets.[8] On the night of his arrest, a crowd of Copperheads burned down the office of the Cincinnati Republican newspaper; his supporters challenged Lincoln's suspension of *habeas corpus* or the "writ of liberty," but the Supreme Court refused to hear a martial case; finally, a group of Peace Democrats in Albany published a pamphlet criticizing Lincoln for what they perceived as despotic infringements on individual liberties. The case became so controversial that Lincoln prepared a direct response to his critics, insisting on the military's power to suppress dissent that aims to discourage men from enlisting or accepting the draft: "Must I shoot a simple-minded soldier boy who deserts, while I must not touch a hair of a wily agitator who induces him to desert?" (748). Like Vallandigham's case and Hale's 1863 story, Lincoln's defense of his position enjoyed an exceptionally wide circulation: one scholar estimates that, between 500,000 pamphlet copies and its publication in several major newspapers, over 10,000,000 people read the president's commentary on the Vallandigham case.[9]

　　Hale chooses to address the important political questions raised by this case indirectly—not by creating a contemporary version of Vallandigham but by adopting the techniques of historical fiction. "The Man Without a Country" recounts the treason trial and unusual punishment of Philip Nolan, a fictional coconspirator in Aaron Burr's 1805–7 plot to conquer parts of New Spain. At his court-martial, Nolan bitterly exclaims: "D—n the United States! I wish I may never hear of the United States again!" (*Two Texts* 21) The outraged court sentences him to live out this very wish by spending the rest of his life aboard naval ships, where he is always treated kindly but never allowed to hear another word about the United States. Passengers and fellow crewmen are instructed to omit the United States from their conversations with Nolan, and censors even excise all references to his homeland from the newspapers he reads. To assuage his frustrated and belated patriotism over the years, Nolan occasionally finds ways to serve the naval ships on which he is imprisoned; also, on a regular basis, he ritualistically extrapolates and re-sketches the changing borders of the expanding nation on an old map that he keeps at the foot of his bed. Exiled from America, Nolan paradoxically becomes what Hale refers to as elsewhere as an "exaggerated American," preaching of loyalty to younger officers while fervently imagining not only the admission of new states into the Union, but also its forcible annexation of new territories. When Nolan is on his deathbed, a sailor takes pity on him and "told him the names [of the newly admitted states] in as good order as I could, and he bade me take down his beautiful map and draw them in as best I could with my pencil. He was wild with delight about Texas, told me how his cousin died there; he had marked a gold cross near where he supposed his grave was; and he had guessed at Texas. Then he was delighted as he saw California and Oregon;—that, he said, he had suspected partly, because he had never been permitted to land on that shore. . . . And he drank it in and enjoyed it as I cannot tell you" (*Two Texts* 229, 36). In an emotionally charged scene that would have resonated all the more widely to readers in an era when geography textbooks and accounts of exploring expeditions ranked as bestsellers[10], Nolan imbibes nothing less than the contours of his identity as he watches the boundaries of his expanded nation emerge before his eyes. (Yet, ironically, Hale highlights the imaginary dimensions of this scene of geographical pedagogy by mentioning that Nolan's young instructor thought it best not to mention the present rebellion to the dying patriot: for Texas had seceded from the Union two years earlier and would not strictly have belonged on Nolan's national map.) In dramatizing the folly—and ultimately the impossibility— of rejecting one's country, Hale's story elevates the nation as an object of desire loved all the more in its absence, felt all the more intensely on account of its prohibition. The story's last lines spell out this patriotic object lesson in the epitaph that Nolan, who asks to be buried at sea, composes for a memorial stone to be erected at Fort Adams or Orleans: "He loved his country as no other man has loved her; but no man deserved less at her hands" (*Two Texts* 37). Despite the lingering ambiguity of "less at her hands," this epitaph personifies the United States as a wronged mother or spurned lover, giving bodily and emotional substance to Hale's stated aim of dramatizing the emergence of national sentiment in the antebellum period.[11]

Hale's preliminary research for this historically grounded parable was extensive: he later recalled that "I read first the reports of the Navy Department from 1798, when it was still a branch of the War Department, down to 1861. I did this that I might be sure of local color, that I might never, by any accident, place a vessel in the place where she really was, or name an officer so that a real man could be annoyed" (1898: 9). Originally published under the pseudonym "Captain Frederic Ingham, U. S. N.," the story's multifarious allusions to heroic officers, naval vessels, and locations convinced many readers of Nolan's historical authenticity, despite the obvious impracticability of Nolan's sentence.[12] Hale recounts that Nolan's story was only partially denied by various bureaus of the Navy department when readers wrote with inquiries; moreover, the author's friends and correspondents continued to treat Nolan as a real personage over the years: for example, "[o]ne of the most accurate of my younger friends had noticed Nolan's death in the newspaper, but recollected 'that it was in September, and not in August'" (1895: 6).

But if Hale's references to "real" objects and personages mined the history of the United States for what Van Wyck Brooks calls a "usable past" in a time of national crisis, these embedded historical indices frequently exceeded—and occasionally even contradicted—the author's nationalistic aims. For example, by beginning the story with Ingham stranded at the Mission House on Mackinac Island, Hale does more than identify a key fortification from the War of 1812: he also names a tourist hotel that had been built in 1825 as a mission school for Native Americans, and thus the genocidal strategies of Indian Removal and forced assimilation that played key roles in US nation-building. Hale's repeated references to ships that had served in the Barbary Wars—most notably the *Intrepid*, a captured Tripolitan vessel refitted by the US navy and used to infiltrate enemy positions in 1803–4—invoke both naval heroism and the extranational violence associated with Barbary corsairs or "pirates." Finally, allusions to Liberia and the Marquesas indicate antebellum sites of US imperial influence where a combination of trade, emigration, missionary interventions, and outright conquest denationalized nonwhite communities by eroding their self-determination, creating groups of Americanized noncitizens abroad who were dependent, variously colonized, and to some degree "without a country."[13]

The inappropriateness of these historical sources is echoed in Hale's literary allusions to a range of European texts that counteract the story's nationalist exceptionalism: Ingham's comparison between Shakespeare's Richard III and Thomas Jefferson (undertaking "to break on the wheel all the possible Clarences of the then House of York"), for example, seems to echo Vallandigham's bitter criticisms of "King Lincoln"'s abuse of power; linking Nolan to Robinson Crusoe provides an alternate, British genealogy for the protagonist's individualistic self-reliance; and rumors that Nolan was the "Man in the Iron Mask" associate his form of imprisonment with a notorious emblem of French despotism (*Two Texts* 21, 27). Together, these passing references to imperial and European abuses of power remind us that Hale's narrative—as often as it has been cited as a parable of treason—is only able to make its patriotic point by moving its reader to sympathize deeply with Nolan and to desire his unattainable pardon.

In addition to rendering the narrative ambivalent toward Nolan, these instances of despotism also highlight the peculiar combination of expansionism, nationalism, and treason at play in Aaron Burr's alleged attempt to organize an expedition into Texas, which Hale mobilizes as a historical analogue for Vallandigham's betrayal of the Union. In the summer of 1863, Hale made himself an expert on the so-called Burr Conspiracy, "read[ing], in full, all that I could find of Aaron Burr's two voyages down the Mississippi . . . the three volumes of General Wilkinson's 'Memoirs,' [and] the proceedings of Burr's trial at Richmond" (1898: 10–11). Although neither his 1807 treason trial nor the historical record presented any conclusive evidence about Burr's intentions, Hale's story depicts Burr as a "dashing" traitor who "seduce[d]" willing US soldiers and officers into attempting to establish an independent empire in the Southwest (*Two Texts* 20, 21).[14] Yet, as Joseph Fichtelberg has shown, both the officers involved with Burr's plans and the national audience that followed every detail of the conspiracy participated in a "speculative excess" that defined early national society as one based on risk and enterprise: on this reading, Burr represented a focal point of the self-fashioning, careerism, and disembedded ambitions that comprised a key aspect of post-Revolutionary capitalist culture (498). Burr's early filibustering expedition appealed to so many coconspirators because (allegations of treason aside) its racial and imperial aims derived from notions of Anglo-American and Puritan supremacy that played a key role in the formation of national identity.

Historically, Hale's reference to Burr's expeditions also resonates with over a dozen other extralegal filibustering expeditions, including Francisco de Miranda's 1806 attempt to liberate all Spanish colonies in Latin America[15] and William Walker's repeated forays into Central American countries in the 1850s.[16] These incidents—along with the fact that the United States *had* forcibly "liberated" Texas from Mexico in 1848—suggest that a filibustering expedition like Aaron Burr's would hardly have seemed treasonous in 1863, when both the Union and Confederacy felt that the future of their peculiar customs and modes of production lay in the western territories—and thus in the fruits of aggressive expansionism. As Burr himself reportedly put it when the Republic of Texas was declared in 1836, "I was only thirty years too soon. What was treason in me thirty years ago is patriotism today!" (Parton 319). Similarly, Hale writes that, when Texas was annexed, the officers entrusted with Nolan's detention were at a loss as to "whether they should get hold of Nolan's handsome set of maps and cut Texas out of it,—from the map of the world and the map of Mexico. The United States had been cut out when the atlas was bought for him. But it was voted, rightly enough, that to do this would be virtually to reveal to him what had happened, or, as Harry Cole said, to make him think Old Burr had succeeded" (*Two Texts* 33). These ironic reminders that Burr's once treasonous plans had at least partially been carried out by the United States itself suggest that "The Man Without a Country" is as concerned with empire building as with nationalism, as much a tale of the state's own investments in extraterritorial and extralegal force as it is a parable of treason and redemption.

Reframings: From Napoleon to the War of 1898

Perhaps it is this ambivalence toward the elaborate method of indefinite, extraterritorial detention it represents that led Hale—along with his readers and critics—to revisit the story of Philip Nolan repeatedly in the decades following its initial publication. Soon after its publication, "The Man Without a Country" drew "the grave displeasure of the *Observer* for the reason that it was so well written as to produce a general impression of its actual truth" ("Book Cable" 886). Other commentators, on the other hand, praised precisely this quality of verisimilitude in Hale's execution of historical fiction, and *Every Saturday: A Journal of Choice Reading* boasted that "One might search among the English magazines for the past three years, and not find so excellent a story as 'The Man Without a Country'" ("Foreign Notes" 156). By 1869, *The Universalist Quarterly* was asking, "Who has not read 'The Man Without a Country'[?]" (127). Before long, Hale was regularly introduced as the author of "The Man Without a Country," and the phrase he coined was variously mobilized both to denote traitors—as Elizabeth Stuart Phelps did in an arch review of Henry James's "denationalization"[17]—and, surprisingly, to represent in a positive light a number of such cosmopolitan-minded figures as the Abolitionist Wendell Phillips, the statesman John Hay, foreign missionaries, Heinrich Heine, expatriates in Paris (Roger Baldwin, "The Capital of the Men Without a Country," *Survey* 1 [Aug 1927]), and Christ himself. This divergence in later echoes of Hale's sympathetic, denationalized hero is especially pronounced in instances of US imperialism: for example, the cosmopolitan hero of Richard Harding Davis's *Soldiers of Fortune* (1897), after effectively taking over a Central American republic, muses that "I have worn several uniforms since I was a boy, but never that of my own country" (105); in the same decade, Queen Liliuokalani and the Apache leader Geronimo were among many racialized figures forcibly denationalized and imprisoned by the United States.

Although the story appeared in anthologies, gift books, and elementary school reading lists[18] in the nineteenth century, Hale's story did not attract much critical attention in the nineteenth century, beyond William Dean Howells's remembrance of his "humor, the most inventive and the most fantastic, the sanest, the sweetest, the truest, which had begun to find expression in the Atlantic Monthly" (*Literary Friends and Acquaintance*) and a number of short reviews emphasizing the story's status as a "classic" that had "undoubtedly had a significant influence in keeping northern patriotism at white heat" during the war (*Literary World* 446). However, early twentieth-century critics like Henry Seidel Canby and Albert Bigelow Paine considered it an exemplary short story—the latter ranking it "with the half-dozen great English short stories of the world" (*Mark Twain: A Biography*). Carl Van Doren and Van Wyck Brooks later wrote introductions to gift editions of the book, but even these critics focus on its popularity as a patriotic parable—"a classic that almost everybody knows and that every child has read" (Brooks v). The only existing scholarly edition of Hale's story, published in 2002 by the Naval Institute Press, overemphasizes Hale's interests in naval history while glossing over the story's relevance to questions of discipline (whether through imprisonment or schoolroom pedagogy), imperialism, and transnationalism that have become increasingly central to the field of American literary history.

These issues become increasingly prominent in Hale's own critical reframings of "The Man Without a Country." For, although Hale bemoans his story "passed out of my hands" (5) after it went into print, he attempted to take it in hand in reprints, updated prefaces, author's notes, an 1881 copyright trial ("Literary and Trade Notes"), and the novel-length "sequel," *Philip Nolan's Friends* (1876). (Originally serialized in *Scribner's Monthly*, *Philip Nolan's Friends*—whose melodramatic plot was intended to restore the reputation of the historical Philip Nolan by tracing his adventures along the Texas-Mexican border and his eventual execution as a suspected filibuster by the Mexican government—was nowhere near as popular as "The Man Without a Country.") These reframings of the story struggle to renew its relevance to changing historical situations as the United States moved from national crisis of the Civil War to Reconstruction and continued Indian Wars, from the relatively provincial republic of Burr's era to the overseas imperial conquests of 1898. Among other things, Hale's commentaries tell us that his story was inspired not only by Vallandigham's expulsion from the Union, but also by European precedents like the medieval concept of the "personal captive" and the brief offshore captivity of Napoleon Bonaparte aboard the Bellerophon.[19] They also allude to the *Virginius* affair—in which a ship flying the US flag was captured by the Spanish government in Cuba—and, more generally, to historical transformations that were making the world more "closely united" than ever before in the decades following the Civil War (1905: x).

In the initial stages of the War of 1898, Hale wrote a new introduction to "The Man Without a Country" in the Christian periodical *The Outlook* that glossed over the story's critical attitude toward Burr's expeditions while favoring a familiar racist, imperialist narrative in which white men intervene in the flawed domesticity of racialized subjects:

> as ex-President Harrison said so well the other day, if you see a man abusing his wife or his child, if when you remonstrate with him he does not cease, if he goes on beating his wife or his child you do not wait to send for a sheriff or a police officer, but you take him by force of arms and compel him to behave himself. In this case, this country is in a similar position with regard to the monarchy of Spain. ("Introduction," May 5, 1898, 116)

Nolan's treasonous expansionism of 1807 has mutated into a jingoistic patriotism, as the United States finally fulfills Burr's alleged conspiracy to assume international police powers in simultaneously liberating and acquiring Spain's imperial possessions.[20] Reversing his story's aversion to Burr's scheme, Hale proclaims in 1898 that anyone who speaks out against America's campaign to "rescue" the Spanish empire is "to all purposes 'A Man Without a Country'" (117). Indeed, this redeployment of his original parable seems to have influenced public opinion at least as strongly as Hale had in 1863: "The interest in such matters now is such that the sales of this book in the year of the Spanish War were larger than those of the year after its publication" ("Preface" xxiii). How did Philip Nolan and Aaron Burr's extralegal filibustering scheme—formerly a reason for denationalization and the deprivation of rights—become the model of a vigorous US imperialism? How did anti-imperialists seeking—like George Washington and Thomas Jefferson a century before—to keep clear of "foreign entanglements" come to be denounced as traitors?

Philip Nolan and "The Change of Western Empire"

Philip Nolan's Friends represents a key moment in Hale's rethinking of the phenomenon of extrastate violence that links Nolan's indefinite detention in the 1863 story with the longer development of US imperialism through the nineteenth century. The novel's subtitle—*A Study of the Change of Western Empire*[21]—announces its interest in the nation's large-scale geopolitical transition from settler colonialism to more flexible forms of overseas empire. Hale's preface, however, frames *Philip Nolan's Friends* as an attempt at historical restitution for having unintentionally slandered a real Southern horse-trader named Philip Nolan in his earlier short story. Hale admits to having "unguardedly" appropriated Nolan's name (possibly because of its suggestive echo of the word "alone") and sets out to immortalize the historical Nolan in a thoroughly researched yet wildly romanticized novelization of the events surrounding the alleged filibuster's death at the hands of Spanish soldiers.[22] Whereas "The Man Without a Country" focused almost entirely on the imperialist enthusiasm and patriotic anguish of its antihero, *Philip Nolan's Friends* takes the form of a large-scale historical romance whose plot evokes the geopolitical (if not physical) proximity of Paris, Washington, New Orleans, Mexico City, London, and Madrid during the months surrounding the transfer of the Louisiana territory first from Spain (back) to France and then from France to the United States. In keeping with this world-historical scope, Hale's preface orients this novel in terms of significant geopolitical events such as John Adams's plan to attack and seize Orleans and the Spanish government's violation of its own passports in pursuing and killing Nolan. The concluding paragraphs of the novel even suggest that it was Nolan's courage and resourcefulness that taught the Spanish and Mexicans to fear Anglo-American prowess and superiority— that "It was he who taught them how near was Kentucky to Potosí" (*Two Texts* 348). However, Hale's geographical references once again exceed his patriotic intent here: Potosí, in Bolivia, was home to vast silver mines worked under deadly conditions by native laborers and imported African slaves.[23]

Despite his apotheosis in the novel's concluding scene, Nolan and his fellow filibusters appear only in the novel's running subplot, while its main focus is on Inez, the daughter of a Cuban woman and a New Orleans merchant and planter who hails from New England.[24] Inez is briefly escorted by Nolan and his friends during her westward journey to visit her maternal aunt in the Mexican town of San Antonio, and this entanglement leaves her a virtual prisoner in San Antonio when the Spanish government turns against Nolan and Americans more generally. The latter part of the novel recounts Inez's "rescue" from Spanish territory, followed by the US "rescue" of New Orleans itself as Spain's colonial government mysteriously detains Inez's merchant father, and then releases him when his son Roland returns from Europe, in the nick of time, with a note from Napoleon confirming the sale of Louisiana to the United States. Throughout *Philip Nolan's Friends*, Inez functions as a sort of sentimental counterpart to the figure of the treasonous "man without a country": for although she has never set foot in US territory, Inez disdains her mother country and pines for "what should have been her native air," sobbing at one point that "This poor child is a girl without a country!" (100)

Later, at a moment when the fate of New Orleans seems balanced between Spain, France, the United States, and possibly Britain, Inez revises her earlier plaint: "'I told Capt. Nolan one day,' said Inez, in mock grief, which concealed much real feeling, 'that I was a girl without a country. I seem to be likely to be a girl of three countries, if not of four'" (196). What is the difference between statelessness and being under the protection of unrecognized, unloved states? When a well-meaning British officer claims Inez's father and his servant as British citizens by birth in order to protect him from the abusive Spanish government, they proudly refuse the protection, citing and even producing documentary evidence of their previous renunciation of the British government during the Revolution. *Philip Nolan's Friends* climaxes, then, with dramatic, ritualistic inversions of Nolan's originating renunciation of the United States in "The Man Without a Country." The language of citizenship comes to resemble the language of love: Hale's characters renounce the countries they don't want to claim them, mock grief, and conceal feeling; having too many countries is just as bad as having none; and—like President Harrison's abuse of Filipinos, Cubans, and Puerto Ricans—they long for the United States to rescue and claim them. What makes the United States such a lovable country is the license it gives to cosmopolitanism and cultural mixing: instead of spending his life in international waters, Nolan's cosmopolitanism in this novel takes the form of fluency in Spanish, French, English, and several Indian languages, including their *lingua franca* of pantomimed gestures. Likewise, Hale's erotic subplots reiterate familiar nineteenth-century dynamics of racial assimilation, as the half-Cuban Inez becomes engaged to marry the dead Philip Nolan's "double," a Kentuckian named Harrod; Inez's New England aunt ends up with a gallant Englishman; and "Ma-ry," a Scotch-Irish girl who grew up in Indian captivity, agrees to marry Inez's half-Cuban brother. All these interracial and international erotic alliances take place under the sign of US expansionism in both its territorial and commercial forms, as the sale of Louisiana puts an end to Spanish restrictions on the international merchant community in New Orleans and foreshadows a time when Nolan's heroism "will give [Texas]" to the United States. Transnational and transracial eroticism thus allegorizes the expansion and desirability of unregulated international commerce, the liberation of captive markets by vigorous capitalist impulses.

This narrative emphasis on free markets, hybridity, and development leads Hale to downplay the importance of slavery to Louisiana's economic and social life. Whereas the Civil War context of "The Man Without a Country" motivated a scene in which one of Nolan's host ships rescues and repatriates a group of Africans (the point being that even these socially dead slaves benefited from a concept of homeland unavailable to Nolan), *Philip Nolan's Friends* includes only a handful of happy, serviceable slaves, and never criticizes either Perry's plantation outside the city or the racist rants of Inez's charmingly brutish protector—a New Englander named Ransom whose ravings about "niggers" seem intended to be endearing in a local color kind of way. New Orleans's crucial role as a port[25] stemmed not only from its choice geographical position, but also from the specific forms of wealth that made that geographical position so significant in the first place: Carribean and Southern plantations where sugar, tobacco, cotton, affective goods, and slave children were brutally extracted from enslaved bodies. When Hale represents the annexation of Louisiana as a victory for "the merchants of every nation,"[26] it is important to remember how much of New Orleans's lively international commerce revolved around the sale and exploitation of slaves whose situation of "social death" rendered them another race of men and women without a country (342).[27] The novel does gesture toward the injustices of slavery when the Spanish governor arrests Harrod and Mr. Perry in connection with a suspected slave insurrection connected to San Domingo; but here, too, Hale turns a blind eye to the fact that the US annexation of Louisiana only led to the influx of more West Indian slaves and *gens de couleur* by allowing a freer flow of goods and bodies.

In *Philip Nolan's Friends,* it is primarily the Spanish empire and its various, fractious colonial agents who practice coercion, arbitrarily issuing and violating passports; sentencing Nolan's associates to imprisonment and execution; virtually imprisoning Inez and her party in a "Franciscan and Moorish cage" in San Antonio; and mysteriously kidnapping and detaining Silas Perry and his servant Ransom with the intention to ship them to be tried in Cuba (258). In addition to scenes of coercion and detention that invoke the Spanish Inquisition, the novel includes two miniature captivity narratives: first, the Scotch-Irish girl named "Ma-ry," who is rescued from her Indian captors only to be locked away in a New Orleans convent school, until she is finally rescued (and married) by Inez's brother; second, Nolan's associate and virtual "double," Will Harrod, is captured and "enslaved" by Comanches, and then repeatedly arrested by Spanish guards after he escapes (309–10, 345). Arbitrary imprisonment, martial law, and violations of rights in the name of security—actions enthusiastically affirmed by "The Man Without a Country"—are here projected onto "savage" Indians and the premodern, Catholic agents of the Spanish empire. By contrast with Spain, the United States appears as a welcome guarantor of free trade and the rule of law. Published in a year of bitter Indian Wars and removals, Hale's novel represents the US acquisition of Louisiana in terms of its formal purchase rather than its contested, ongoing conquest.

The "change of Western empire" referred to in the novel's subtitle involves an increasing normalization of US imperial violence, whether through its legitimation by Inez's suffering or through its displacement onto a tyrannical Spanish government. The act of filibustering that led to Burr's treason trial becomes liberating in *Philip Nolan's Friends;* international waters become valued not as spaces of extraterritorial incarceration but rather as spaces of unfettered trade; and conquest paradoxically endows its subjects with a country, rather than depriving them of one. At the end of the novel, Hale's attitude toward extraterritorial expansion has come full circle: Napoleon Bonaparte, whose imperial violence inspired the form of shipboard detention imagined in "The Man Without a Country," reappears as the *deus ex machina* of that story's corrective sequel. *Nolan's Friends* could perhaps just as well be titled *Napoleon's Friends*, since in restoring dignity, patriotism, and competence to the border-crossing figure of Nolan, it also rehabilitates and Americanizes Bonaparte's aspirations for an aggressively enlightened, forcibly liberated empire. Reading "The Man Without a Country" with the sustained dramatization of the Southwestern transnational contact zone presented in its sequel draws attention to the complex entanglements between extralegal force, indefinite detention, and nation building that underlie one of the most popular American short stories—a story that has too often been read as a transparent patriotic parable.

Bibliography

Anonymous. "The Man Without a Country." *The Literary World; a Monthly Review of Current Literature* 19 (Dec 8, 1888): 25.

—. "Book Cable." *The Independent* 17 (Nov 23, 1865): 886.

—. "Foreign Notes." *Every Saturday: A Journal of Choice Reading* 6 (Dec 26, 1868): 156.

—. "If, Yes, and Perhaps" (Review). *The Universalist Quarterly and General Review* 6 (Jan, 1869): 127.

—. "Literary and Trade Notes." *Publishers' Weekly* 19:48 (Apr 2, 1881): 392–3.

—. *The Trial of Hon. Clement L. Vallandigham by a Military Commission.* Cincinnati: Rickey and Carroll, 1863.

Adams, John R. *Edward Everett Hale.* Boston: Twayne, 1977.

Brooks, Van Wyck. "Introduction." In *The Man Without a Country*, v–x. New York: Franklin Watts, Inc. (First Book Edition), 1960.

Curtis, Michael Kent. "Lincoln, Vallandigham, and Anti-War Speech in the Civil War." *William and Mary Bill of Rights Journal* 7 (1998–9): 105–91.

Farber, Daniel. *Lincoln's Constitution.* Chicago: University of Chicago Press, 2003.

Hale, Edward Everett. "Author's Note to Edition of 1897." *The Works of Edward Everett Hale. Library Edition, vol. 1. The Man Without a Country and Other Stories*, 3–19. Cambridge: Little, Brown, & Co., 1898.

—. "Preface to the Birthday Edition." In *The Man Without a Country,* v–xxiv. New York: Outlook, 1902.

—. *Two Texts by Edward Everett Hale: "The Man Without a Country" and* Philip Nolan's Friends. Eds, Hsuan L. Hsu and Susan Kalter. Lanham, MD: Rowman & Littlefield, 2009.

Hyde, Carrie. "Outcast Patriotism: The Dilemma of Negative Instruction in 'The Man Without a Country." *ELH* 77:4 (Winter, 2010) 915–39.

Klement, Frank L. *The Limits of Dissent: Clement L. Vallandigham and the Civil War.* Lexington: University Press of Kentucky, 1998.

Lincoln, Abraham. "The Truth From an Honest Man. The Letter of the President. . . ." In *Union Pamphlets of the Civil War, 1861–65,* 2:739–51. Ed. Freidel, Frank. 2 Vols. Cambridge: Belknap Press, 1967.

McCaleb, Walter. *The Aaron Burr Conspiracy.* New York: Dodd, Mead, 1903.

Meinig, Donald William. *The Shaping of America: A Geographical Perspective on 500 Years of History. Continental America* 1800–67. New Haven: Yale University Press, 1995. 4 vols.

Parton, James. *The Life and Times of Aaron Burr.* New York: Mason Brothers, 1858.

Phelps, Elizabeth Stuart. "The Man Without a Country." *Independent* 32 (May 6, 1880) 1640–1.

Thomson, Janice E. *Mercenaries, Pirates and Sovereigns: State-Building and Extraterritorial Violence in Early Modern Europe.* Princeton: Princeton University Press, 1994.

Van Doren, Carl. "Introduction." In *The Man Without a Country,* vii–x. New York: Limited Editions Club, 1936.

Notes

1   "Literary and Trade Notes." *Publishers' Weekly* 19:48 (Apr 2, 1881): 392–3.

2   *United States v. Wong Kim Ark* (169 US 649 [1898]). Hale reports in 1898 that the story "was copied everywhere without the slightest deference to copyright" ("Author's Note," 13).

3   Cf. Adams's report that a retired Marine Corps officer in 1968 proposed a "Philip Nolan Law" that would recognize deliberate acts of desertion and draft-dodging "as a voluntary and deliberate renunciation of U.S. citizenship punishable" by indefinite exile (qtd Adams 37).

4   The story ended up coming on in December, too late to influence the election, which Vallandingham lost.

5   Quoted in Klement, *Limits of Dissent*, 154.

6   "The habit of declaring sympathies for the enemy will not be allowed in this Department. Persons committing such offenses will be at once arrested. . . . [T]reason, express or implied, will not be tolerated in this Department" (*Trial* 7).

7   Lincoln's order reads, "The President directs that, without delay, you send C. L. Vallandigham, under secure guard, to the headquarters of General Rosecrans, to be put by him beyond our military lines. . ." (qtd. In McPherson, "History of the Rebellion," 162). From Tennessee, Vallandigham went to Canada via Bermuda, & ran unsuccessfully for governor of Ohio *in absentia* from Windsor, Ontario. See Klement and Curtis; also Farber 157–75 on Lincoln's wartime suspension of *habeas corpus* and infringements on the freedom of speech, which drew criticism from Republicans and abolitionists, as well as Vallandigham's Copperhead supporters.

8   "Transcripts of the trial and *habeas* proceeding were published both in the press and as a book. As a result, the words for which Vallandigham was prosecuted and arguments about them reached a large audience" (Curtis 131) & see fn.137. Curtis describes several violent responses to the Vallandigham episodes: "convalescent soldiers seized a group of Vallandigham delegates returning from a state Democratic convention and forced them to kneel and take an oath of allegiance. Other incidents also occurred: 'A butternut [a phrase used for Vallandigham supporters] was hung until almost lifeless, by a crowd of excited citizens . . . for traitorous language'" (188). Despite criticism from all sides, General Burnside continued to impinge upon free expression in Ohio: "As a result of Burnside's orders, an Ohio publisher abandoned publication of a book of Vallandigham's speeches. Burnside showed an interest in finding the plates so that he could prevent printing elsewhere" (188–9).

9   See Curtis 183–4, and 183n.487.

10 See Brückner for a detailed account of the diverse and popular forms geographical education characteristic of the Early Republic.

11 In his 1902 "Preface," Hale provides an extended history of the transition, between 1830 and the 1860s, from sectionalism and ideas of "Separate Sovereignty" (vii) to the growth of the "National idea" (v) that culminated with the Civil War (v–x).

12 "No court-martial can ever have had the right to fix such a penalty. It is hard to believe that any navy could have had the patience and tact to carry it out . . ." (Van Doren vii).

13 For an extended analysis of the ways in which political dispossession underlies Nolan's patriotic lesson, see Hyde.

14 As the prosecution witness Commodore Truxton put it, Burr was accused of "intend[ing] to attack Vera Cruz and Mexico, give liberty to an enslaved world, and establish an independent Government in Mexico" (qtd McCaleb 343). For Hale's own account of his research on Burr, see *Memories* 1: 86–100. In his 1902 "Preface," Hale writes of Burr's intentions in organizing his expeditions that "I double myself if he knew very well what they were" (xvi).

15 In *Nolan's Friends,* Hale mentions that Miranda's schemes had, at one time or another, the support of the US Army, the US president, and, ironically, Aaron Burr's nemesis, Alexander Hamilton; later in the novel, an Englishman suggests that, with his plans to "free Mexico and Cuba and the Spanish main," Miranda was "the South American Washington of the future" (229–30; 286).

16 The popularity of filibusters—which peaked in the years before Walker was captured and executed in in Honduras in 1860—was fueled by factors like Southerners' enthusiasm to expand the reach of slavery, the ideology of "Manifest Destiny," and a federal government weakened by sectionalism. The consolidation of federal power, the deaths of thousands of young men, and the 1860 Homestead Act played significant roles in quelling filibustering after 1865. See Thomson 118–42.

17 Titled "The Man Without a Country," the article reviews James's book on Hawthorne. Phelps writes that "This clever and petted young man has, indeed, become 'A Man without a Country.' By a deterioration subtler, but hardly less sad than that which fastened upon poor Philip Nolan, our fastidious cosmopolitan has been slowly smoothing away the still sturdy and respectable, if a little angular qualities of love and reverence for home" (*Independent* 32 [May 6, 1880] 1640).

18 For example, *The Elementary School Teacher*, a journal published by the University of Chicago, regularly listed "The Man Without a Country" on seventh-grade curricula between 1902 and 1925.

19 Hale reports that, during the Civil War, he had proposed a similar punishment for Jefferson Davis: "No, dear boys, we will not hang him to any tree. We will put him in comfortable quarters on the 'New Hampshire' ship of the line, and we will send him on her serial three-year voyages" (1897: 8).

20 In a footnote hastily added, in 1898, to his "Author's Note To Edition of 1897," Hale directly connects the War of 1898 with the Spanish government's actions against the historical Philip Nolan (of whom I will say more in the second half of this paper) in 1801: "As this sheet passes the press, after the short Spanish war, I think it may

be well to say that the universal contempt of Spain, in the lower Mississippi valley, and the hatred bred in her treachery in 1801 in this Nolan transaction, have shown themselves, bitterly enough, in the determination to administer the well deserved punishment for which Jefferson was too weak. The wheels of the gods grind—when the time comes" (18). Regarding Hale's longstanding interest in the Spanish empire, Adams writes: "Thus Hale's boyhood curiosity, aroused by family letters from Spain, had developed into a permanent interest that had led to his collecting documents and to his ambition, never realized, to write a comprehensive 'History of the Pacific Ocean and its Shores.' The Madrid archives were his special destination in 1882" (11). William Sloane Kennedy reports that "For six years [Hale] was the South American editor of [*The Boston Advertiser*]" (339).

21 Hale's alternative subtitle—*Or, Show Your Passports*—alludes to the Spanish government's violation of its own passports in attempting to arrest Nolan's expedition, as well as to broader issues of international law.

22 For Hale's historical account of the "real" Philip Nolan, see *Memories* 1:65–85. In 1902, Hale gives a slightly different account of the novel's significance, noting "that if any one is curious to know why, from 1801 down, Spain was hated in the Southwestern States of our own Country, he may find one of the causes of such hatred in the story of 'Philip Nolan's Friends'" ("Preface" xxiii).

23 Hale may also have known that Moses Austin had named Potosi, Missouri—where he settled down to mine lead—after the Bolivian city in 1798.

24 Hale also distinguishes *Philip Nolan's Friends* from his other writings by specifically addressing an imagined "young reader of seventeen, who seeks in these pages only the history of her country" (*Two Texts* 275).

25 Cf. Jefferson's insistence that "There is on the globe one single spot, the possessor of which is our natural and habitual enemy. It is New Orleans, through which the produce of three-eighths of our territory must pass to market, and from its fertility it will ere long yield more than half of our whole produce and contain more than half our inhabitants" (qtd in Meinig V2 p. 10).

26 The novel represents Americans in New Orleans primarily in terms of trade interests, so that while the Spanish feared both US invasions and slave insurrections, "The handful of Americans chafed under the unrighteous restriction on the trade for which they lived there" (*Two Texts* 241).

27 Patterns of racial disenfranchisement and exclusion continued into
    the postbellum years when Hale wrote the novel: in the South, race
    riots (like the bloody 1873 riot in Colfax, Louisiana, in which over
    50 blacks were killed), lynchings (the White League was founded
    in 1874 in Louisiana), and chain gangs established the reign of
    Jim Crow; the 1870s also saw the intensification of violence on
    the frontiers (1876 was the year of Little Bighorn, as well as the
    year when the United States ordered all Native Americans into
    reservations).

7

Exhilaration and enlightenment in the biblical bestseller: Lew Wallace's *Ben-Hur, A Tale of the Christ*

James Russell

In 1913, the department store Sears and Roebuck ordered one million copies of General Lew Wallace's *Ben-Hur, A Tale of the Christ*, the largest single order for a work of fiction ever placed.[1] The executives at Sears clearly believed that, 8 years after the death of its author and 33 years after its first publication, their customers were more interested in the adventures of Ben-Hur than in any other single work of fiction ever published, and they were correct. The special edition, priced at 39 cents, sold out within months.[2] The order was a testament to the novel's colossal popular appeal in the United States. In fact, *Ben-Hur, A Tale of the Christ*, was the most commercially successful American novel of the nineteenth century.[3] It outsold and outgrossed anything published by the "great" American authors of the age, from Hawthorne to Melville, and yet the book and its author have slipped into obscurity. *Ben-Hur* is now best known as a 1959 film, directed by William Wyler, starring Charlton Heston, and featuring a spectacular chariot race. However, the lasting renown of MGM's movie is a clear sign of the story's enduring cultural significance. In various forms, *Ben-Hur* enjoyed a privileged position in American popular culture for well over 80 years.

Following the Sears and Roebuck order, *Ben-Hur* became the most popular novel in American history, a position it occupied until the publication of Margaret Mitchell's *Gone with the Wind* in 1936.[4] William Young's 1899 stage adaptation ran for 30 years on Broadway, and was one of the most popular stage productions of the prewar years.[5] With domestic rentals of over \$4 million, MGM's 1925 film adaptation of *Ben-Hur*, directed by Fred Niblo, became the third highest grossing movie ever made (after D.W Griffith's 1915 *The Birth of a Nation* and Rex Ingram's 1921 *The Four Horsemen of the Apocalypse*), a position it occupied for over two decades.[6] In similar fashion, the 1959 version was by far and away the most commercially successful film of the 1950s, generating over \$36 million in rentals, and it remains today the fourteenth highest grossing domestic release of all time.[7] By almost every commercial standard, *Ben-Hur* was, and remains, a staggering success. Although it was never considered great literature, the book connected, sometimes in fairly profound ways, with a vast mass of ordinary readers, and this chapter is an attempt to explain the somewhat unlikely success of Wallace's novel.

Ben-Hur tells the story of a young Jewish nobleman's encounters with Christ in first-century Judea. It is an early entry in a subgenre of novels set at the time of Christ, which use the events of the Bible as backdrop to a fictional narrative that is often, but not exclusively, devotional or evangelical in tone. The first such novel was William Ware's 1841 *Julian, or Scenes in Judea*, and the success of *Ben-Hur* sparked many imitators, including Henry Sienkiewicz's 1895 *Quo Vadis*, Wilson Barret's 1896 play *The Sign of the Cross*, and, later, Lloyd C. Douglas's 1942 *The Robe*. The genre lives on today in the form of books like Jim Crace's 1997 *Quarantine*.

It is particularly telling that a devotional novel, based closely on the events of the Bible, was so successful for so long. *Ben-Hur* spoke directly to the beliefs of millions of ordinary Americans, and as we shall see, the novel has often been said to have appealed to vast swathes of Christian readers who had previously forsworn novel reading. As a result, the Christian content and philosophizing in *Ben-Hur* is particularly worthy of study. In fact, I will argue that with *Ben-Hur*, Wallace sought to offer his readers a moving, philosophically and metaphysically affecting experience, which deployed the thrilling conventions of popular, sensation fiction to a spiritual end. Thus, *Ben-Hur* can be understood as the first in a long line of mainstream fictions which have sought to close the gap between the beliefs of American Christians and the pleasures of popular entertainment. The second half of this chapter interprets the book in precisely these terms, as a devotional, Christian work, but in order to understand *Ben-Hur*, we must know about its origins, and I start by looking at the life of its author, General Lew Wallace.

Lew Wallace and the origins of *Ben-Hur*

Even before he wrote *Ben-Hur*, Lew Wallace was a relatively well-known public figure in nineteenth-century America. He was born in Indiana in 1827, and after a brief period in state politics, he achieved fame during the Civil War as a colonel and then general in the Eleventh Indiana Infantry.[8] In particular, Wallace's valor during the taking of Fort Henry in Tennessee was immortalized in an engraving of the cover *Leslie's Weekly*, and established him as one of the early popular heroes of the Union cause. However, his career took a backward step when his company was integrated into Ulysses S. Grant's larger Army of the Tennessee. In April 1862, Grant's army was caught unprepared by a larger Confederate force at Shiloh, Tennessee.[9] Union forces incurred heavy losses, and Grant heaped blame on Wallace, accusing him of failing to deliver his troops in sufficient time to turn the tide. Wallace, who had been camped some distance away, maintained that he had received conflicting orders from Grant's runners which had impeded his arrival.[10]

Whatever the degree of his culpability in the fiasco at Shiloh, Wallace's good name and reputation vanished virtually over-night, and he had made a powerful enemy, in the form of Ulysses S. Grant. Despite vociferous complaints about what he saw as an unfair character assassination, and repeated attempts to have Shiloh investigated in order to clear his name, Wallace maintained an active role in the army for several more years, but he never escaped the stain on his character associated with Shiloh, and he resigned his military commission in relative disgrace. With little to do after the war, he joined the Republican Party, and settled down to practice law in Crawfordsville, Indiana—essentially, in exile from public life.[11]

Wallace had written occasionally, albeit with little public success, but following his return to Indiana, he seems to have taken solace in writing, which he began to pursue more stridently than before.[12] He published his first novel in 1873, a romantic account of the conquistadors told from the perspective of the Mexican Indians, entitled *The Fair God*. He also began work on a short piece about the birth of Christ. By his own admission, Wallace's interest in the nativity was the product of commercial considerations rather than any spiritual inspiration. His military career was over, he did not enjoy the law, and he had achieved some limited success with *The Fair God*. He began writing about the birth of Christ in an attempt, "to compose a brochure that might be acceptable to Harper Brothers. Seeing the opportunities it afforded for rich illustration, they might be pleased to publish it as a serial in their magazine."[13]

In part, writing offered Wallace an escape from the life of a small town lawyer, but it also provided him with an opportunity to reenter public life without having to rely on the kinds of intermediaries who Wallace felt had betrayed him in the past.[14] Certainly, he was not motivated to write of the time of Christ out of any great need to 'spread the good word." Later he would claim that for much of his life "my attitude with respect to religion was one of absolute indifference."[15] However, his lack of interest in spiritual matters changed when he fell into conversation with the noted public speaker and agnostic Robert G. Ingersoll on a train Indianapolis in 1876. After initially proposing that they speak of spiritual matters, Wallace reported that "I sat spellbound, listening to a medley of argument, eloquence, wit, satire, audacity . . . and a pungent excoriation of believers in God, Christ and Heaven. He surpassed himself, and that is saying a great deal."[16]

Far from being convinced by Ingersoll, Wallace fell into a "confusion of mind not unlike dazement," and he complained that Ingersoll "had made me ashamed of my ignorance: and then—here is the unexpected of the affair—I was aroused for the first time in my life to the importance of religion."[17] Wallace claimed that he was inspired for the first time to "study" the Christian faith. Out of this study, *Ben-Hur* was eventually born. At the same time, Wallace's fortunes began to improve. The presidency of his old enemy, Ulysses S. Grant, ended in disgrace in 1877, and Wallace made a return to public life. He took up the post of State Governor of New Mexico in 1878, which required him to manage the competing requirements of the new territory's ethnically and culturally diverse inhabitants, and deal with bandits such as Billy the Kid. At the same time, Wallace continued work on *Ben-Hur*, which was completed in 1880, a year before Wallace's tenure as State Governor was concluded.

The novel was sold to Harper and Brothers and published to mixed reports. In his summary of contemporary reviews, Shaun Chandler Lighty notes that the *Atlantic Monthly* judged the book "a failure, artistically," and *The Century* described it as "something of an anachronism, nowadays."[18] However, the *New York Times* reviewer took the opposite tack, praising Wallace's "daring . . . startlingly new and distinctive romance," and concluding:

> To those who see no reasonable objection, the book cannot fail to give much pleasure, for it is written not only with considerable power, but with a rare a delicate appreciation of the majesty of the subject with which it presumes to deal.[19]

In spite of the disdain expressed by some literary critics, *Ben-Hur* did connect with a mass audience, although sales of the book were slow at first. Between November 1880 and March 1883, only 16,000 copies were sold, but a combination of positive word-of-mouth, and Harpers' astute marketing efforts, helped to boost sales significantly.[20] Harpers included excerpts from the novel in reading primers aimed at schoolchildren, issued chapters in the form of special Christmas gifts, and repeatedly promoted Wallace and his novel in the pages of their bestselling magazine, *Harper's Weekly*, putting him on the cover in 1886.[21] Throughout 1883, an average of 750 copies were sold per month. By 1886, this had risen to 4500, and by the end of the decade, nearly 400,000 copies had been sold, a figure which this increased to over a million by the end of the 1890s.[22] As we have seen, such astonishing levels of demand were sustained well into the 1910s.

The popular success of *Ben-Hur* transformed Wallace's public status and elevated him to a level of celebrity far beyond anything he had enjoyed before the fiasco of Shiloh. He became a regular fixture on the literary lecture circuit, and he continued to hold public office, acting as US Minister to the Ottoman Empire from 1881–85. He continued to write, finding success with a similar devotional work, *The Boyhood of Christ*, in 1886, and with a much longer novel based on his experiences in Turkey, *The Prince of India*, in 1893. He also wrote a number of biographies and plays, as well as his own autobiography, in years before his death in 1905. However, none of this would achieve the same kind of cultural impact of *Ben-Hur*. Wallace's professed desire to "study" Christ and offer some account of his divine character, had clearly chimed with the broader desires of American readers in the late 1800s. We might reasonably ask why?

Sensation and spirituality in *Ben-Hur*

In part, *Ben-Hur*'s enormous popular success was dependent on its appeal to a sizable demographic of committed Christians who had previously avoided the "frivolous" pleasures of novel reading. According to Robert Detweiler, *Ben Hur* opened "many a nineteenth-century home to novel reading that would have remained otherwise closed for a much longer time."[23] In similar fashion, Lee Scott Theisen has observed, "it is a book which broke down the last prejudices in the American public to the novel and made acceptable to many the stage and then the motion picture."[24] In fact, the widespread acceptance of *Ben-Hur* among Christian readers of all denominations was one notable part of a broader process of liberalization that occurred across all levels of American Christianity in the wake of the Civil War. Strict Calvinistic rules, which forbade any representation of Christ, and discouraged all forms of frivolous behavior, had characterized worship for many American Protestants since the founding of the nation. However, by the end of the nineteenth century, such practices were being challenged by a rising class of liberal Protestant preachers, such as Henry Ward Beecher and Horace Bushnell, who emphasized the loving, unifying nature of Christ, and who warned against asceticism and attendant forms of cultural isolation.[25] In his 1872 book, *The Life of Jesus, The Christ*, Beecher noted that Jesus himself had not "held himself aloof, wrapped in his own meditations," and, in contrast to "many of the reigning philosophers, who despised pleasure, Christ sought it as a thing essentially good."[26]

Beecher's progressive attitudes toward the representation of Christ in fiction and art, and his advocacy of pleasurable indulgence in the more uplifting distractions of modern culture, pointed the way forward for the major Protestant denominations in the late nineteenth century. Previously strict Congregationalists, Baptists, Methodists, and Presbyterians began to tolerate and even deploy representations of Christ, and, more importantly, began to participate in modern, popular culture.[27] Ben-Hur was released at an ideal moment to capitalize on these rapidly shifting currents of Christian thought, and as the end of the century approached, the novel became a fixture in many Christian households, regardless of their perceived "strictness." For the lax or liberal, the novel crafted an enjoyable adventure based on the tenets of their faith, however vaguely held, while for the pious, it opened a window into a world of spiritually exhilarating entertainment.

The broad appeal of Ben-Hur rested on the way that Wallace merged an essentially frivolous adventure narrative with key events in the life of Christ. This "Tale of Christ" could be understood as a way of making the much more hot-blooded "Tale of Judah Ben-Hur" palatable to readers who might otherwise have dismissed the novel as pure sensationalism. Thus, Paul Gutjahr claims that, "Protestant readers could pick and choose religious elements of the book to rationalise their reading of it, when, in fact, the book may have appealed primarily because of the secular titillation the various episodes provided."[28] In a broader critique of "Biblical fiction," Robert Detweiler argues that Ben-Hur draws "Christ down to the level of trivial entertainment."[29] However, this type of critique assumes that the author used the figure of Christ in a purely cynical and opportunistic fashion—in stark contrast to Wallace's own account of his intentions, and to the ways that many contemporary readers experienced Ben-Hur.

While the literary establishment may have been uncertain about the merits of Ben-Hur, Wallace reportedly received numerous letters from readers who had found it deeply affecting. One such was Samuel Moore, a merchant from Lafayette, Indiana, who wrote to the author claiming that, "I feel I am a better man for having read it."[30] Others included Albert Shelton, who wrote to tell Wallace that he had been inspired to become a missionary after reading Ben-Hur, and Nicholas Smith, who had found "a new home, a new life, and perfect peace of mind," after reading the novel.[31] Recovering alcoholic George Parrish wrote from a YMCA in Illinois to tell Wallace that *Ben-Hur* "had brought Christ home to me as nothing else could."[32] In 1889, *Harper's Weekly* published a lengthy tribute to the novel by an Episcopal Bishop which declared that *Ben-Hur* "is conceived and executed in a spirit of such profound reverence that no-one can become interested in its perusal without its doing him good."[33] In similar fashion, Lord Dufferin, Wallace's superior in the diplomatic service, told him that, "I can quite understand your having received the thanks of those whom you have aided to realize, more acutely than their own feeble imaginations enabled them to do, the heart-breaking incidents of the crucifixion."[34]

As these and other accounts suggest, many readers felt that *Ben-Hur* was imbued with the power to spread the Christian message, to "do" its readers "good." It is, therefore, highly reductive to dismiss *Ben-Hur* as a flip adventure concealed by a loosely worn veil of piety. In many ways, the reverse is true. The great achievement of *Ben-Hur* was the way in which it carefully deployed the "sensationalist" pleasures of fiction in the service of a spiritual agenda. In terms of prose and narrative trajectory, *Ben-Hur* was carefully structured to inspire a personal, almost physiological engagement with the defining story of Christianity, partly by focusing on sensual details within the text, and partly through the broader story of a hero who is himself profoundly affected by his encounter with Christ.

Certainly, a great many readers reported finding *Ben-Hur* affecting at multiple levels. In a letter to Wallace, the poet Paul Hamilton Hayne declared, "Pages in [*Ben-Hur*] have thrilled me through and through while I remark that never on any occasion have you sunk below the dignity of your majestic theme."[35] Many, including Wallace's old nemesis, and then president, Ulysses S. Grant, were also apparently unable to put the book down (Grant reportedly read the entire novel in one, 30-hour sitting).[36] A similar account of the novel's power to thrill appeared in fictional form in L. M. Montgomery's 1909 classic *Anne of Green Gables*, in which the titular heroine is punished for reading *Ben-Hur* during schooltime.[37] *Ben-Hur* may have been a spiritually enriching experience for many, but it was also thrilling and affecting in the manner of sensation fiction, and we might reasonably ask how *Ben-Hur* imbued such thrilling pleasure with Christian intent.

Arguably, the affective power of *Ben-Hur* lies partly in the highly eventful story of its hero, and partly in the physically descriptive prose that Wallace deploys. Certainly, the novel is filled with incident and reversals. Following a prologue which retells the story of the nativity, Wallace shifts attention to the story of Judah Ben-Hur, who only gradually becomes aware of Christ as the narrative progresses. At the start, Ben-Hur is a wealthy Jewish nobleman living in great luxury in Jerusalem. Following a disagreement with an old childhood friend, the Roman Messala, Ben-Hur's relatively privileged life is transformed by a chance accident. As he watches the arrival of the Roman tribune Gratus from his family's balcony, he accidentally dislodges a tile, which falls and injures Gratus, and incurs the full wrath of the Roman colonizers. At Messala's behest, Ben-Hur is sent to die in servitude on the galleys, while his mother and sister are imprisoned.

As Ben-Hur is transported to meet his fate, he is offered some water by a young Jesus Christ, the first of several meetings. He then continues to the galleys, where he serves for three years, before distinguishing himself by rescuing the ship's captain, Quintus Arrius, during a violent sea battle. Arrius adopts Ben-Hur as his son, and the narrative then moves forward several years again, to focus on Ben-Hur's efforts to find his family, and avenge himself on Messala. In Antioch, he encounters his old servant, Simonides, and the last surviving member of the Magi, Balthazar (as well as their respective daughters, the homely Esther and dashing Iras). Ben-Hur is then commissioned by the Arab Sheik Ilderim to race against the now wealthy and powerful Messala, in the arena.

As he prepares for the race, Ben-Hur first hears of Christ's coming from Balthazar, and is tempted by the exotic Iras (who later betrays him for Messala). Eventually, Ben-Hur defeats Messala in the arena, and he makes his way to Jerusalem, where, the reader discovers, his wife and sister are lepers imprisoned deep within the bowels of a Roman fortress. Following a fruitless search, Ben-Hur raises an army to serve the coming Messiah and prepares for what he hopes will be a war to liberate Judea. Eventually, Christ comes to Jerusalem (with Ben-Hur's newly formed legions following in his wake). As he approaches the gates, he encounters and heals Ben-Hur's mother and sister, and the Hur family are reunited. Ben-Hur is then dismayed to witness the crucifixion, where he finds his dreams of a vengeful and righteous leader replaced by a very different, but no less compelling, vision of Christian forgiveness and salvation. The main body of the novel ends with Ben-Hur putting aside his desire for war with Rome and taking on the mantle of the first Christian convert. In a postscript, we discover that Ben-Hur has married Esther and devoted his life to spreading the message of Christ.

At almost every juncture, Wallace uses lengthy and lavish prose to describe both locations and characters, often focusing particularly on sensual physical details. For instance, when Ben-Hur first encounters Iras in the pagan Grove of Diana, the reader is told:

> It was a fair face to see; quite youthful; in form oval; complexion not white . . . but rather the tinting of the sun of the Upper Nile upon a skin of such transparency that the blood shone through it on cheek and brow with nigh the ruddiness of lamplight. The eyes, naturally large, were touched along the lids with the black paint immemorial throughout the East. The lips were slightly parted, disclosing, through their scarlet lake, teeth of glistening whiteness.[38]

By focusing on details of shade, coloring, and texture ("the blood shone through . . . ruddiness of lamplight . . . their scarlet lake,") and by repeatedly using verbs, adverbs, and adjectives which suggest physical touch and sensation ("touched . . . parted . . . glistening"), Wallace literally takes the reader into close physical proximity to Iras. Similar descriptive techniques are used to outline the features of every character, and this obsessive accounting of physical qualities is most notable when Wallace describes the physiological effects of leprosy upon the bodies of Ben-Hur's mother and sister (my italics):

> The disease *spread*, after a while *bleaching* their heads white, *eating* holes in their lips and eyelids, and *covering* their bodies with scales; then it *fell* to their throats, *shrilling* their voices, and to their joints, *hardening* the tissues and cartilages.[39]

In each case, Wallace emphasizes sensory experience in order to inspire some emotive, sensory response from readers—eroticized arousal in his description of Iras and revulsion in his description of leprosy.

Similar tactics are used to situate the reader within the locations of the story. Lengthy description of places occurs throughout the novel, but are most affecting during the sinking of the Roman trireme and the famous chariot race. In each case, the reader is quite clearly positioned within the scene. For instance, the sea battle is described entirely from the point of view of one trapped within the ship's hold:

> There was a mighty blow; the rowers in front of the chief's plat-form reeled, some of them fell. Shrill and high arose the shrieks of men in terror; over the blare of the trumpets, and the grind and crash of the collision, they rose; then, under his feet, under the keel, pounding, rumbling, breaking to pieces, drowning.[40]

Throughout the scene, the reader is situated directly alongside Ben-Hur, hearing rather than seeing the battle. In similar fashion, during the chariot race, Wallace goes so far as to allocate the reader a seat in the arena and poses much of his description as a sensory challenge:

> Let the reader try to fancy it; let him look down on the arena and see it glistening in its frame of dull-grey granite walls; let him then, in this perfect field, see the chariots, light of wheel, very graceful, and as ornate as paint and burnishing can make them . . . Let him see the drivers, erect and statuesque, their limbs naked, and fresh, and ruddy with the healthful polish of the baths.[41]

What follows is one of most renowned scenes of action in popular fiction, and, from the beginning, Wallace carefully locates the reader as a participant in the narrative. Consequently, the lengthy description of Ben-Hur's race with Messala is, we can assume, supposed to feel all the more intimate for our proximity to events as they unfold.

Wallace's highly sensual and physical writing style was rooted in sensationalism, but it was also a key part of his efforts to craft a spiritually meaningful reading experience. Paul Gutjahr has argued that Wallace's descriptions of place encouraged readers to feel that "they were acquiring accurate information about first-century Palestine . . . the obvious historicity of the book's setting [provided] a reason to believe in the historicity of Jesus."[42] A very similar process occurs at the level of character. On almost every page of the novel, Wallace focuses on physical, bodily detail, and seeks to engage the reader with events at an emotional and physiological level. This focus on corporeal, sensuous experience even extends to the figure of Christ himself:

> Looking up, he saw a face he never forgot . . . a face lighted by dark blue eyes, at the time so soft, so appealing, so full of love and holy purpose, that they had all the power of command and will. The spirit of the Jew, hardened as it was by days and nights of suffering, and so embittered by wrong that its dreams of revenge took in all the world, melted under the stranger's look and became as a child.[43]

Later, several more paragraphs are devoted to describing Christ's physical appearance, which concludes by noting that there was

> never a soldier but would have laughed at him in encounter, never a woman who would not have confided in him at sight, never a child that would not, with quick instinct, have given him its hand; nor might anyone have said he was not beautiful.[44]

Perhaps unsurprisingly, Wallace also lingered on Christ's physical state in the moments before the crucifixion:

> He was nearly dead. Every few steps he staggered as if he would fall. A stained gown badly torn hung from his shoulders. His bare feet left red splotches upon the stones . . . A crown of thorns had been crushed down hard upon his head, making cruel wounds from which streams of blood, now dry and blackened, had run over his face and neck. The long hair, tangled in the thorns, was clotted thick. The skin, where it could be seen, was ghastly white.[45]

Not only is intense physical description lavished on the saviour, but Wallace also focuses on the responses of those who observe Christ. When they encounter Jesus, readers were provided with another rich sensual experience, which stressed the corporeality of Christ by seeking to inspire feelings of wonder, revulsion, and outrage. We might say that Wallace's prose sought to establish an intimate, personal connection to Christ as a real person. By doing this, the emotional reality of the Christian message could, in turn, be stressed, and it is unsurprising that many readers found *Ben-Hur* affecting, because so much of the novel is designed to thrill, revolt, or excite.

Furthermore, *Ben-Hur* is structured to ensure that readers understand their responses in religious, rather than frivolous, terms. Wallace provided an ideal, archetypal example of the form that reader responses should take in the form of the central character, Judah Ben-Hur. Over the course of the novel, Ben-Hur experiences a number of profound personal transformations, the most profound of which occurs at the book's climax, when the vengeful Zionist warrior is transformed into a peaceful Christian convert, primarily as a result of his growing knowledge of Christ. Jesus reappears as an active character in the narrative about halfway through *Ben-Hur*, at which point, Ben-Hur sits down for a meal with Sheik Ilderim and Balthazar. The Magi speaks at length of the coming of a King of the Jews, and Wallace notes that:

> Ben-Hur received it as became a man listening to a revelation of deep concern to all humanity . . . in his mind, there was the crystallising of an idea that was to change the course of his life, if not absorb it completely.[46]

Wallace even puts his narrative on hiatus to assure readers that from this point onward, the story of Ben-Hur will "trench close upon the opening of the ministry of the Son of Mary . . . A MAN WHOM THE WORLD COULD NOT DO WITHOUT."[47]

In the chapters that follow, Ben-Hur assumes that Christ will lead the Jews to a military victory, and that Christ's "Kingdom of God," will be a great empire:

> The king implied a kingdom; [Christ] was to be a warrior as glorious as David . . . the kingdom was to be a power against which Rome would dash itself to pieces. There would be colossal war and the agonies of death and birth – then peace, meaning of course, Judean dominion forever.[48]

Ultimately, Ben-Hur's hopes for military glory are rendered null. As he observes the torment suffered by Christ during the crucifixion, Wallace tells us that:

> Ben-Hur was conscious of a change in his feelings. A conception of something better than the best of this life . . . perhaps another life purer than this one – perhaps the spirit life which Balthazar held to so fast, began to dawn on his mind clearer and clearer, bring to him a certain sense that, after all, the mission of the Nazarene was that as a guide across the boundary for such as loved him.[49]

By being present at the crucifixion, by observing and experiencing the defining event of Christianity, Ben-Hur is converted from a man of war to a man of peace, from a Jew to a Christian. His physical presence is a vital element of his conversion, and his personal experiences of Christ lead him to accept Jesus's divinity. In this regard, the character of Ben-Hur provides a very clear responsive model for readers themselves to follow as they make their way through Wallace's book. Repeatedly, Wallace offers his readers an intense physical account of the places and peoples of ancient Judea, culminating in the events of the Crucifixion. The final transformation of Ben-Hur is used to suggest that the correct response to these forms of sensual stimulation is commitment to the cause of Christ. Ben-Hur ends the narrative much like the ideal reader—enlightened, elevated, convinced of Christ's divinity.

Of course, not everyone would or could respond this way, but I have attempted to show that the novel is very carefully structured to provide, if one seeks it, an experience not dissimilar to conversion. Indeed, Wallace repeatedly reaffirmed the efficacy of *Ben-Hur*'s power to connect readers to the origins of Christianity, and even convert them, in his account of *Ben-Hur*'s origins. As we have seen, Wallace was always keen to present the act of writing *Ben-Hur* as a transformative personal experience, much like Ben-Hur's more visceral encounters with Christ. In fact, if one looks for them, there are many parallels between the Wallace's life and that of his hero. Wallace was, or perceived himself to be, a decent man whose life was irrevocably altered by chance and malign intervention—the loose tile and Messala's scheming in the case of Ben-Hur, the Battle of Shiloh and disdain of Ulysses S. Grant in the case of Lew Wallace.

In many ways, Wallace's grievances over Shiloh can be seen reflected in Ben-Hur's boundless desire for vengeance. Both were military men who had sought glory in the service of some greater cause. Both, ultimately, relied on showmanship to defeat their rivals. And, perhaps most significantly, both seem to have been converted to the cause of Christianity by a close study of Christ the man.[50]

The oft-repeated story of the Ben-Hur's origins, and Wallace's subsequent professed belief in Christ's divinity, was a clear attempt to assign the novel some divine power. Wallace confirmed the novel's power to channel the Christian message by presenting himself as its first beneficiary. In all of his public discussion of Ben-Hur, from his account of his inspiration to the letters he reproduced in his autobiography, Wallace provided an accumulated weight of evidence to suggest that, for those who sought it, Ben-Hur was a deeply affecting spiritual experience, imbued with the power to spread the Christian message. In effect, Ben Hur was a novel about conversion, which sought to elicit conversion.

Of course, we can never truly know what ordinary readers made of Ben-Hur, nor can we know for sure what Wallace himself believed. It is reasonable to assume that a significant proportion of readers were affected by the novel in the way that Wallace suggested, and that Wallace too was changed in some way by the writing process. However, we must also view his account of the book's origins as part of what we would now recognize as a marketing exercise, designed to render his book meaningful and palatable to Christians of all kinds. Wallace effectively encouraged Christian readers to believe that the emerging mass media could be a vehicle for the transmission of Christian salvation. This idea would circulate around Ben-Hur for decades to come.

Exhilaration and enlightenment

Ben-Hur leant itself very well to adaptation for stage and screen. Wallace's descriptive prose, and attempts to craft an imaginatively immersive experience, encouraged readers to "see" the events of the narrative in their mind's eye. It was only a matter of time before stage and then screen producers sought to turn this imaginative vision into a reality. Almost from the moment of its publication, the author was contacted by numerous Broadway producers who were seeking to capitalize on the novel's massive readership. Wallace resisted various offers out of a concern that a play would not adopt "the proper spirit of reverence," with regard to Christ.[51] However, in 1899, he sold the rights to respected New York producers Klaw and Erlanger, although he attached numerous provisos to the deal, the most significant of which was that Christ should not appear physically on the stage. The adaptation was written by William Young, and opened on November 29, 1899, to generally positive reviews, and colossal audiences.[52] It may have lacked Christ, but the production included some scenes of great spectacle, including a chariot race run with live horses. The *New York Times* described it as "beautiful beyond expectation," but noted that, "the play appeals for public support chiefly as a spectacle."[53] Excising Christ, (who appeared only very briefly in the form of a blinding flash of light which heals Ben-Hur's mother and sister) was a way of avoiding causing offense to Christians who might have felt that it was acceptable to read about Jesus, but who didn't want to see an actor pretending to be him. It also changed the nature of the narrative. The novel had sought to affect readers by bringing them into close proximity with Christ. The play may have awed its viewers with spectacle, but it provided a notably less spiritual thrill.

Similar strategies were used in the various film adaptations that followed. MGM's 1925 version is replete with spectacle, but the depiction of Christ is fairly confused. During the Nativity, the Last Supper and the Crucifixion, two-strip Technicolor is used to suggest the special, perhaps even divine nature of Jesus.[54] At other points, Christ only appears in the form of a hand, offering Ben-Hur water from off screen, and in one scene, his entire form is blanked out, appearing only as a white blob.[55] Otherwise, the 1925 version sticks fairly closely to Wallace's original. By contrast, numerous changes were made for the 1959 version. Ben-Hur is obviously older, Iras does not feature, and Ben-Hur's mother and sister are healed by Christ's blood at the moment of the crucifixion. However, the film remains equally coy about depicting Christ, whose face is never shown. It is also, as I have argued elsewhere, much more ambiguous about the nature of Ben-Hur's conversion.[56] Both films were colossally successful, and both clearly appealed to Christian viewers. What's more, both versions carried out similar work to Wallace's novel— rendering new forms of commercial entertainment both palatable, and even profound, to those who may previously have dismissed them on moral grounds. For instance, the usually restrained trade newspaper *Variety* claimed that the 1925 film illustrated the power of cinema as a moral and spiritual medium, calling it "the greatest single thing for religion, for the theatre, for the church, for the stage and screen, and for the masses, ever uttered."[57]

The novel has waned in popularity today, but its historical significance to modern Evangelical Christians was illustrated in 2003 when Penguin issued a cheap paperback edition featuring an introduction by Evangelical author Tim LaHaye. LaHaye, who cowrote the bestselling *Left Behind* series, claimed that *Ben-Hur* "was the book that made me realise that fiction could be used to send a message that is even more important to the story."[58] He praised Wallace and applauded the book's power to affect and uplift, commending it to a new generation of Evangelical readers. In making such claims, LaHaye, perhaps unwittingly, reinforced the notion first proposed by Wallace and Harper Brothers over a century before—that *Ben-Hur* would affect and change its readers, that *Ben-Hur* was imbued with the Christian spirit, and that this Biblical bestseller could somehow offer exhilaration and enlightenment in the same breath.

Bibliography

Anon. "A Story of the East," *New York Times* 14 Nov. 1880: unpaginated, obtained via download from www.nytimes.com.

—, "Ben-Hur: Greatest Picture," *Variety*, Jan. 6, 1926.

—, "Dramatic and Musical," *New York Times* 30 Nov. 1899: Unpaginated, obtained via download from www.nytimes.com.

Detweiler, Robert. "Christ in American Religious Fiction," *Journal of the American Academy of Religion* 32, 1 (1964), 8–14.

Finler, Joel W. *The Hollywood Story* 3rd Edn. (London: Wallflower, 2003).

Fox, Richard W. *Jesus in America: Personal Saviour, Cultural Hero, National Obsession* (New York: Harpercollins, 2004).

Gutjahr, Paul. "To the Heart of all Solid Puritans," Historicizing the Popularity of *Ben-Hur*," *Mosaic* 26, 3, 53–67.

Hackett, Alice P. *Fifty Years of Best Sellers 1895–1945* (New York: R. R. Bowker, 1945).

Hanson, Victor D. *Ripples of Battle:How the Wars of the Past Still Determine How We Fight, How We Live, and How We Think* (New York: Anchor, 2003).

Kramer, Peter. "'Want to take a ride?': Reflections on the Blockbuster Experience in *Contact* (1997)," in Julian Stringer, ed., *Hollywood Blockbusters* (London: Routledge, 2003), 128–40.

Lighty, Shaun C. *The Fall and Rise of Lew Wallace: Gaining Legitimacy through Popular Culture*, Unpublished MS (Miami University, Ohio, 2005), 59. Obtained via download from http://www.ohiolink.edu/etd/view.cgi?acc_num5miami1130790468.

Mayer, David. *Playing Out the Empire* (Oxford: Clarendon Press, 2004).

Montgomery, Lucy M. *Anne of Green Gables* (London: Puffin, 1988).

Morsberger, Robert E. and Morsberger, Katherine M. *Lew Wallace: Militant Romantic* (New York: McGraw Hill, 1980).

Russell, James. *The Historical Epic and Contemporary Hollywood: From Dances With Wolves to Gladiator* (New York: Continuum, 2007).

Spiller, Robert L. *A Literary History of the United States* (New York: Macmillan, 1965).

Sutherland, John. *Bestsellers: A Very Short Introduction* (Oxford: Oxford University Press, 2007).

Theisen, Lee S. "'My God, did I set all this in motion,' General Lew Wallace and *Ben-Hur*," *Journal of Popular Culture* 18 (1984), 33–41.

Wallace, Lew. *Ben-Hur, A Tale of the Christ* (1880; New York: Signet, 2003).

—. *Lew Wallace: An Autobiography* (New York: Harper and Brothers, 1906).

—. *The First Christmas* (New York: Harper and Brothers, 1902).

Ward, Henry B. *The Life of Jesus, The Christ* (New York: J. B. Ward, 1872).

Notes

1   John Sutherland, *Bestsellers: A Very Short Introduction* (Oxford: Oxford University Press, 2007), 48.

2   Robert L. Spiller, *A Literary History of the United States* (New York: Macmillan, 1965), 966.

3   In the late 1890s, *Ben-Hur* was technically outsold by another forgotten popular hit, Charles Monroe Shelton's 1896 *In His Steps*. However, Monroe neglected to copyright his work, and as a result, it failed to generate equivalent revenues for the publisher or author. Officially, *Ben-Hur* remained the bestselling novel of the age, but this claim can only be made if one does not take unofficial sales of other novels into account. See Shaun Chandler Lighty, *The Fall and*

Rise of Lew Wallace: Gaining Legitimacy through Popular Culture, Unpublished MS (Miami University, Ohio, 2005), 59. Obtained via download from http://www.ohiolink.edu/etd/view.cgi?acc_num=miami1130790468.

4   For details of Ben-Hur's sales figures into the Twentieth Century, see Alice Payne Hackett, *Fifty Years of Best Sellers 1895–1945* (New York: R. R. Bowker, 1945), 104.

5   See David Mayer, *Playing Out the Empire* (Oxford: Clarendon Press, 2004), 193.

6   Joel W. Finler, *The Hollywood Story* 3rd Edn. (London: Wallflower, 2003), 356.

7   "All time box office statistics, adjusted for inflation." *Box Office Mojo*, http://www.boxofficemojo.com/alltime/adjusted.htm

8   For further details of Wallace's early life, see Lighty, 21.

9   A full account of Wallace's military career can be found in Robert E. Morsberger and Katherine M. Morsberger, *Lew Wallace: Militant Romantic* (New York: McGraw Hill, 1980), 3–78.

10   This account of Wallace's part in the Battle of Shiloh is derived from Victor Davis Hanson, *Ripples of Battle: How the Wars of the Past Still Determine How We Fight, How We Live, and How We Think* (New York: Anchor, 2003), 118–32. Hanson points out that written records "favor Wallace's account" of events, Hanson, 132.

11   For further details, see Morsberger and Morsberger, 195–221.

12   Lighty notes that the period between 1867 and 1876 was not, as some biographers have suggested, a period of idleness for Wallace. Rather it was a moment when his long-suppressed artistic talents were given full reign. See Lighty, 34.

13   Lew Wallace, Preface to *The First Christmas* (New York: Harper and Brothers, 1902), iii.

14   For more on Wallace's dislike of the law, see Lighty, 40.

15   Wallace, *The First Christmas*, v.

16   Ibid., vi.

17   Ibid., vi.

18   Reviews quoted in Lighty, 65.

19   Anon., "A Story of the East," *New York Times* 14 Nov. 1880: unpaginated, obtained via download from www.nytimes.com.

20   Sales figures are derived from Lee Scott Theisen, "'My God, did I set all this in motion,' General Lew Wallace and *Ben-Hur*," *Journal of Popular Culture* 18 (1984), 35.

21 Lighty, 60.

22 Theisen, 60.

23 Robert Detweiler, "Christ in American Religious Fiction," *Journal of the American Academy of Religion* 32, 1 (1964), 8.

24 Theisen, 39.

25 See Richard Wightman Fox, *Jesus in America: Personal Saviour, Cultural Hero, National Obsession* (New York: Harpercollins, 2004), 251–306.

26 Henry Beecher Ward, *The Life of Jesus, The Christ* (New York: J. B. Ward, 1872), 194.

27 Fox, 294–5.

28 Paul Gutjahr, "'To the Heart of all Solid Puritans,' Historicizing the Popularity of *Ben-Hur*," *Mosaic* 26, 3, 65.

29 Detweiler, 14.

30 Lew Wallace, *Lew Wallace: An Autobiography* (New York: Harper and Brothers, 1906), 949.

31 Quoted in Morsberger, *Militant Romantic* 311.

32 Quoted in Theisen, 36.

33 Quoted in Lighty, 62.

34 Wallace, *Autobiography*, 951.

35 Quoted in Ibid., 947.

36 Lighty, 66.

37 L. M. Montgomery, *Anne of Green Gables* (London: Puffin, 1988), 233.

38 Lew Wallace, *Ben-Hur, A Tale of the Christ* (1880; New York: Signet, 2003), 216.

39 Ibid., 406.

40 Ibid., 157.

41 Ibid., 365.

42 Gutjahr, 60.

43 Wallace, *Ben-Hur*, 126.

44 Wallace, *Ben-Hur*, 469.

45 Ibid., 535.

46 Wallace, *Ben-Hur*, 265.

47 Ibid., 265.

48 Ibid., 279.

49 Ibid., 541.

50 Many more parallels have been noted by Victor David Hanson, who has argued that *Ben-Hur* is an allegorical response to the events at Shiloh. See Hanson, 138.

51 Wallace, *Autobiography*, 1000.

52 For a thorough account of the stage production, and the full text of Young's adaptation, see Mayer, 189–290.

53 Anon., "Dramatic and Musical," *New York Times* 30 Nov. 1899: Unpaginated, obtained via download from www.nytimes.com.

54 Hollywood has a tradition of using such special effects to suggest divinity. See Peter Kramer, "'Want to take a ride?': Reflections on the Blockbuster Experience in *Contact* (1997)," in Julian Stringer, ed., *Hollywood Blockbusters* (London: Routledge, 2003), 139.

55 I refer here to the Thames restoration of *Ben-Hur* carried out by Kevin Brownlow. It may be that other versions deal with Christ differently.

56 See James Russell, *The Historical Epic and Contemporary Hollywood: From* Dances With Wolves *to* Gladiator (New York: Continuum, 2007), 32.

57 Anon., "Ben-Hur: Greatest Picture," *Variety*, Jan. 6, 1926, 39.

58 Timothy LeHaye, "Introduction," to Wallace, *Ben-Hur*, x.

8

"Absolutely punk": Queer economies of desire in *Tarzan of the Apes*

J. Michelle Coghlan

"Me Tarzan, You Jane" is undoubtedly the line most synonymous with Edgar Rice Burroughs's *Tarzan of the Apes*, succinctly suggesting the hero's initially limited range of spoken English, even as it simplifies the triangulated love plot between the not-quite Lord, not-quite Ape and his All-American gal, Jane Porter. That the line does not anywhere appear in the novel itself, but rather stems from an early Hollywood incarnation of it, is testament to the reach of *Tarzan*—spawning some three-dozen film adaptations and 23 sequels which sold over 25 million copies in its first three decades alone.[1]

For all that Tarzan's son, Korak, reassures his father in the final pages of *The Son of Tarzan* that "there is but one Tarzan . . . there can never be another,"[2] *Tarzan of the Apes*—and its eponymous hero—has never been altogether singular. Indeed, from the start, Tarzan was phenomenally multiplied and marketed, reconstituted and resold. There was a Tarzan of the pulps before a Tarzan of the novels, soon to be followed by a Tarzan of the films and a Tarzan of the comics. There was even, quite literally, a "Tarzan of the suburbs" (in Catherine Jurca's suggestive phrase)—both in the sense of boys swinging from trees like jungle lords *and* in white families nestled away from racial difference in Edgar Rice Burroughs's planned community of Tarzana, California.[3] Thus, while *Tarzan* is frequently read and most often assigned as a stand-alone text, legible without its entourage of spin-offs, knock-offs, and serialized progeny, it is difficult to altogether separate *Tarzan of the Apes* from Tarzan the American merchandizing extravaganza. For, as literary critic and early pop cultural historian Russel B. Nye once insisted, next to Mickey Mouse, Tarzan may be America's most recognizable fictional character on the planet.[4] Put simply, then, *Tarzan*-the-bestseller comes to us always already prepackaged, most often bearing before it the echo of that other cinematic fiction, the Tarzan yell. Thus, while we will most particularly concern ourselves here with the matter of desire in *Tarzan of the Apes*, the bestseller that engendered Burroughs's Tarzan empire, the trajectory of *Tarzan*'s meteoric rise as novel and stand-alone commodity will most immediately frame our reading of the opening installment of the Tarzan series.

The narrative of *Tarzan*'s rise and eventual critical reception are not as separate as they might seem. For, even as Tarzan's ongoing popularity has encouraged scholars, in the wake of New Historicism, Feminism, Postcolonialism and Cultural Studies, to quite productively revisit and rethink Tarzan, Tarzan's fame—and Johnny Weissmuller's fabled loin cloth—has in turn served to circumscribe many of those very critical readings. Consider again the tagline of "Me, Tarzan, You Jane": as its neat dyad suggests, and the later volumes in the series imply, the union of Tarzan and Jane often functions, for critics and readers alike, as a foregone conclusion to the opening novel despite the resolute failure of *Tarzan of the Apes* to bring them together. While that failed marriage plot might be seen as driving the serial—it did after all keep readers reading—it is nevertheless curious—and not simply because so many books that have gone on to become American bestsellers refuse us the ending we most wanted. In a book that has most often been read as the instantiation of the white male body as "lord of the jungle," why must desire—whether narrative or readerly—be so thwarted? Why must the He-Man here be denied the girl? Reading *Tarzan* through its future volumes—or, rather, reading that future ending back into the opening installment's conclusion—glosses over the ways that desire in *Tarzan of the Apes* is complicated not simply by the fact that another man, the other Lord Greystoke, wins Jane at book's end. For as the replacement of one Greystoke by another already suggests, the economies of desire in the novel are quite literally structured by repetition and exchange—and, as we will see, such exchanges are not exclusively heteronormative.

Put simply, taking desire seriously in *Tarzan of the Apes* means not simply questioning whether Jane is Tarzan's only significant object of affection or attraction, but even more fundamentally whether Jane's affections for the jungle lord are the sole sites of desire for Tarzan in the text. For while Jane has most often been read as the primary attachment and force of domestication in the novel, it is the French Lieutenant D'Arnot who makes a man of Tarzan—and something of a dandy one at that. And what to make, after all, of the fact that Tarzan, upon first encountering another man, desires to eat him? Tracking the novel's economy of exchange, and in particular the trajectory of D'Arnot's relationship to the jungle lord, complicates our reading of *Tarzan*'s end even as it destabilizes our most basic assumptions about the vectors of desire in the novel. More significantly, it suggests that *Tarzan of the Apes'* enactment of and anxieties about interracial desire and intermixings are most often brokered and reinforced by the ongoing threat and possibility of queer exchanges of desire in the text.

From the pulps to Tarzan, Inc

On its road to being an American bestseller, Burroughs's *Tarzan* famously pops up first in the pulps. Story magazines, or more commonly, pulp magazines, were the successor to the popular American story papers and dime novels of the nineteenth century. Printed on cheap paper, they were affordable and highly successful at garnering a wide, cross-class readership among men and boys, but reached substantial numbers of women readers as well. Debuting with Frank Munsey's revamped, all-fiction *Argosy* magazine in 1896, by the turn of the century, the pulps offered readers riveting, full color covers and gripping, formulaic tales of adventure, sci-fi, romance, and later detective fiction that sold in phenomenal numbers straight off the newsstands.

Burroughs got his start writing for the pulps almost by accident. After failing the entrance exam to West Point and later being rejected for service with Teddy Roosevelt's Rough Riders, he first went on to a spectacularly unsuccessful career in commerce—variously peddling candy, light bulbs, pencil sharpeners, and patent medicine before going on to dole out business advice for *System*, "the magazine of efficiency." (Of the latter venture, Burroughs would later recall, "Ethically, it was about two steps below the patent medicine business," for he felt he should be the last to offer advice, having failed at everything.[5]) The idea that he might make a living by writing came at 35, while skimming magazines for ad space during his tenure selling pencil sharpeners: "It was at that time that I made up my mind that if people were paid for writing rot such as I read in some of those magazines that I could write stories just as rotten."[6]

All Story magazine bought Burroughs' first story, "Under the Moons of Mars," published under the pseudonym Norman Bean, in 1911, and went on to publish his *Tarzan of the Apes* the following year. Tarzan's popularity was near instantaneous, and was quickly augmented by the serialization of *Tarzan of the Apes* for an even wider audience in *The New York Evening World*. As historian John Kasson reminds us, long before there was a Tarzan of the novels, "its hero became a cultural icon."[7] Despite the additional success Burroughs enjoyed with two further Tarzan installments in pulp magazines, and letters pouring in from Tarzan fans both within and outside the United States, publishers were initially doubtful about Tarzan's chances in book form. Indeed, the manuscript for *Tarzan of the Apes* was turned down by a number of publishing houses before McClurg and Company finally accepted it two years later. This novel incarnation of *Tarzan* arrived on bookshop shelves in 1914 with illustrations by Fred J. Arting, whose striking cover of Tarzan in his habitat did away with the *All-Story* rendering of a brawny Tarzan mid-battle, leaving in its place a Tarzan in silhouette perched upon a tree branch with "a [Plains Indians'] posture both languid and alert."[8] *Tarzan* had briefly graduated, in other words, from the slightly trashy world of the pulps, to a stint as Literature—enjoying a short-lived favorable book review in the *New York Times*. Yet, this literary Tarzan was no less of a sensation: by 1934, *Tarzan of the Apes* had already sold more than 750,000 copies.[9]

Burroughs was quick to capitalize on America's unabated appetite for Tarzan. Pulp writers were traditionally treated as "piece workers," paid by the story magazines between one and five cents a word[10]—encouraged, in other words, to be veritable fiction factories to make ends meet. But though Burroughs is much remarked upon for his prodigious if increasingly formulaic output, he realized the value of the fictional commodity on his hands, and promptly sought not only serial rights but also the largely unprecedented right to set his own price for his literary product.[11] In turn, he shrewdly kept Tarzan in almost constant circulation, publishing a new installment a year for nearly three decades straight, each volume appearing first in the story magazines and eventually in novel form.[12]

The scale of *Tarzan*'s serial success led to an almost overnight franchising empire. Tarzan's popularity on the page led to his reincarnation on the screen in 1918, and the film, starring Elmo Lincoln, proved to be one of early Hollywood's biggest moneymakers, grossing more than a million dollars.[13] Tarzan on screen in turn fueled fans' desires for further versions in print—not to mention an ever-wider demand for serializations and dozens more film adaptations. Tarzan's continued success in the pulps, and even greater popularity in the films, led to Tarzan as comic book hero: he was solidly serialized from 1929–50. The Lord of the Jungle in turn acquired a second life as "brand," selling everything from ice cream cups to energy bread; by 1939, the market was glutted with "Tarzan candy, masks and costumes, jungle maps, bathing suits, jungle helmets, yoyos, and archery sets."[14] While Tarzan's appeal waned somewhat in the years preceding and following World War II, Tarzan, Inc. experienced an exceptional resurgence in the 1960s: in 1963, one out of every 30 paperbacks published in America was a Tarzan serial. Significantly, it was the fans of *Tarzan*, rather than the publishers or Burroughs's inheritors, who most pressed for the rerelease of out-of-print titles in cheap paperback editions. Tarzan's paperback comeback—and subsequent second turn as an American bestseller—caught the attention of *Life* magazine, and Gore Vidal was quick to posit that the American man of the 60s was once again hungering for an alter ego: Tarzan was, in Vidal's reading, "a fantasy-projection of the man in the pinstripe suit or on the assembly line, caught in a system he had not created and could not control."[15] Decade after decade, then, Tarzan successfully straddled several audiences: adult readers were originally his primary audience, but as Tarzan moved from page to screen, and from pulps to comics, Tarzan as household name achieved an equal following among children. (In 1938, *Time* magazine notably featured *Tarzan of the Apes* not among American bestsellers, but rather alongside

Pollyanna and Little Lord Fauntleroy in its article on the top-selling American "children's classics" of all time.[16]) As the box office success of Disney's 1999 animated (and later Broadway musical) version of *Tarzan* suggests, then and now his story and his bric-a-brac sold well to kids, even as the fantasy of the Anglo-Saxon body faring mysteriously better in the wild than in the city has never lost its purchase for adults.

Early critical readings of *Tarzan*'s popularity focused on its supposedly unequivocal "celebration of primitive masculinity,"[17] rather than the novel's investment in privileging Tarzan's aristocratic origins over his ape-centric upbringing. As attitudes toward bestsellers shifted within the academy, and scholars began to think more critically about the "cultural work" of popular texts, however, a number of critics in the 1990s began to reexamine the endurance of Tarzan and the promise of the "primitive" and "the manly" it seemed to make available to readers. Thanks largely to the groundbreaking work of Marianna Torgovnick in *Gone Primitive: Savage Intellects, Modern Lives* and Eric Cheyfitz in *The Poetics of Imperialism: Translation and Colonization from The Tempest to Tarzan*, and more recently, Gail Bederman, Catherine Jurca, and Dana Seitler, we have come, in Torgovnick's terms, to take Tarzan seriously. In turn, we have come to read his epic popularity as variously a testament to turn-of-the-century obsessions with the white male body and an uneasy equation of white manhood with civilization *tout court*, and the fiction of the Anglo-Saxon aristocrat who is Lord of the African jungle, keeper of private property, and "killer of beasts and many black men" as a cultural outgrowth of the social and racial tensions concomitant with the rise of the suburbs in the United States; as a means of imagining the primitive as a source of possibility and empowerment; as an escape from the confines of both paternity and the feminization of culture; and finally as a fantasy of US imperial designs.[18]

But while critics have compellingly examined the conspicuous racial politics of the novel (the fantasy, in Jeff Bergland's formulation, of "White=Write=Right (Civilization)"[19]), and in turn plumbed the gender and class hierarchies solidified in the text by that very racial equation,[20] sexuality, and more to the point, the economy of desire, has been largely taken for granted in critical accounts of *Tarzan*. Tarzan wants Jane, and the novel takes pains to naturalize his affection for her—of that we may be certain.

(After all, does he not take her into his arms and, in so kissing her, do "what no red-blooded man needs lessons in doing"?[21]) My reading of *Tarzan of the Apes* does not take issue with this fundamental conception of Tarzan's heterosexual identification within the novel. But as Siobhan Somerville has so powerfully argued, sexual identity and sexual desire are by no means necessarily correlative: "One's sexual identity, while at times directly linked to one's sexual activities, more often describes a complex ideological position, into which one is interpellated based partly on one's response to that interpellation. Thus, there is no strict relationship between one's sexual desire or behavior and one's sexual identity, although the two are closely intertwined."[22] For all *Tarzan of the Apes*'s conspicuous positioning of Tarzan's sexual identity, and in turn its move to naturalize or foreclose upon certain possibilities of desire within the narrative, the erotics of exchange remain fluid in the text. Rather than quibbling with Tarzan's attraction for Jane, then, my reading seeks to suggest that our certainty of the way sexuality operates in *Tarzan* obscures not simply latent homoerotic tensions but in fact crucially open-ended sexual dynamics and desires within the novel.

"Brother Men"

Bederman suggests that *Tarzan*'s failure to deliver the goods—that is, the union of Tarzan and Jane—is a sign of the essential effeminacy of civilization, and thus reads the novel as an "elegy for the doomed primal rapist."[23] The Lord of the Apes cannot be at home in civilization, and the Lord of Civilization cannot be the forest god who literally swept Jane off her feet in the first place. At stake in the failed ending is not, however, the resolution of the problematic comingling of civilization and savagery, Ape and Man in a single white aristocratic male body. For, as the novel imagines it, and as many critics have pointed out, the Tarzan who leaves the jungle must indeed be tamed for life as an about-the-town lord—even as readerly interest in the series remains most keen in seeing Tarzan return "home" to the jungle. Consistently, however, Jane surfaces in these readings as the most powerful object of affection and force of restraint on Tarzan's savage masculinity both within the opening volume and across the series. As William Gleason nicely puts it, "Jane curbs Tarzan's wild ways"—and in order to preserve his jungle masculinity, Tarzan must escape Jane's civilizing mission.[24]

The problem with this reading is that Jane is not the only, and in fact is not the primary, civilizing force on the ape man in *Tarzan of the Apes*. Certainly, she restrains Tarzan from exerting his jungle prowess over the villainous cad, Canler: "'I do not wish him to die at your hands, my friend,' she replied. 'I do not wish you to become a murderer'"[25]—at which point "Tarzan remov[es] his hand from Canler's throat."[26] But it is less of Jane's influence and more of Tarzan's reading that most restrains his lust for her when, in proto-Rhett Butler stance, he "took [her] in his arms and carried her into the jungle" earlier in the novel.[27] For, while he certainly *wants* to ask her how a man should behave, the text resolutely denies him the means to do so: Tarzan can read and write in English but lacks the ability to speak it. He, therefore, must rely on the written word—in the form of the English books he found in his father's house—to answer the question: "He would act as he imagined the men in the books would have acted were they in his place."[28] That other men, even in fictional form, should prove singularly formative for Tarzan foreshadows and underscores D'Arnot's later mentorship of the jungle lord. For, it is D'Arnot, rather than Jane, who first restrains Tarzan's violence, and more to the point D'Arnot who most concretely answers Tarzan's unasked question: "You must not, Tarzan!" cried D'Arnot. "White men do not kill wantonly. Mon Dieu! But you have much to learn."[29] That D'Arnot here conflates "civilization" with "whiteness" is in keeping with the text's insistent identification of manliness as a trait of white men rather than African ones. I am less interested, for the moment, in the more obvious racial dynamics underpinning Tarzan's fraternity with D'Arnot, and will focus instead on the latent sexual tensions underwriting the development of their relationship—dynamics that so often remain unaddressed. As we will see, however, sexual and racial anxieties are everywhere intertwined in the novel.

Tarzan does not explicitly figure (or imagine) men desiring other men any more than it can fathom (without immediately disavowing) the possibility of white men feeling attraction for female apes; certainly, it takes pains to show that the vectors of desire cannot work in that direction. And yet we can read, for example, quite charged miscegenation anxieties overlaying D'Arnot's capture by

African cannibals: "And then began for the French officer the most terrifying experience which man can encounter upon earth—the reception of a white prisoner into a village of African cannibals."[30] While it is race rather than gender that is most marked here— D'Arnot, abducted by the cannibals, is reduced to a "white prisoner" rather than a "white man"—it is a moment that nevertheless places the Frenchman in a peril very much like the one Jane faced with Terkoz. For here, erotic desire and racial mixing are literalized in the act of eating, and the cannibals quite literally threaten to consume D'Arnot's white male body, much as Terkoz's abduction of Jane introduces the double threat of violation and miscegenation. (As Torgovnick points out in regard to Jane's kidnapping, "*abduction* always carries the double meaning of kidnapping and rape—and both meanings pertain here."[31]) Although the novel underscores D'Arnot's dignity and manliness—"He was a soldier of France and he would teach these beasts how an officer and a gentleman died"[32]—he must nevertheless be rescued from what the text construes as a fate worse than death, a fate that, like Terkoz's threat to Jane's body, cannot even be spoken aloud. (The French troops, in telling Jane of D'Arnot's supposed fate, fall into circumlocutions to avoid speaking of cannibalism, eventually settling on "We do not know what they did to him *before* they killed him"[33] to which Jane eventually responds, "They are not–? They are not–?" for she could not "frame that awful word."[34]) To further the structural echoes between Jane and D'Arnot's situations, or, rather the ways the plot here replaces Jane with D'Arnot, Tarzan in fact returns Jane—who he just rescued from Terkoz—home to her people before again rushing off to save D'Arnot from this fate that cannot be named: "Without a word Tarzan of the Apes cut the bonds which held the Frenchman. Weak from suffering and loss of blood, he would have fallen but for the strong arm that caught him. He felt himself lifted from the ground. There was a sensation of flying, and then he lost consciousness."[35]

Yet, D'Arnot's capture by the cannibals does not simply repeat the threat of interracial desire and violent interracial mixings first invoked by Jane's kidnapping. For underwriting both these scenes, and most particularly the threat to the French Lieutenant, is Tarzan's earlier encounter with Kulonga. The African warrior is the first man Tarzan meets in the novel, and the jungle lord seeks him out for the slaying of Kala, Tarzan's ape mother; after following him for some time, Tarzan avenges Kala by hanging Kulonga from a tree. As many scholars have pointed out, this act of vengeance on a black body cannot but recall a lynching, with Kala "avenged" not simply because she has died at the African's hands but rather because an arrow from a black body has penetrated her own. But the threats of miscegenation and sexual violation summoned by Kala's death and Kulonga's lynching do not end with the warrior's death. For Tarzan, much as he earlier "looks with wonder" at "this sleek thing of ebony, pulsing with life," now lingers over Kulonga's dead body at some length: "He examined and admired the tattoing on the forehead and breast. He marveled at the sharp filed teeth. He investigated and appropriated the feathered headdress, and then prepared to get down to business for Tarzan of the Apes was hungry, and there was meat: meat of the kill, which jungle ethics permitted him to eat."[36] It is a scene we have come to read as a test of nature over nurture, the epitome, in fact, of the novel's insistence that Tarzan's aristocratic origins win out in the end: Tarzan hungrily considers but does not eat his kill because he instinctively "knows" that men cannot eat other men.

But what would it mean for a white man to consume another man in *Tarzan of the Apes*? On the one hand it would reduce Tarzan, the Ape-Man, to an African cannibal in a novel that most consistently works to code black bodies as savage, primitive and ape-like. On the other hand, however, the scene naturalizes Tarzan's attraction and repulsion to the "sleek thing of ebony"—for while he might gaze with wonder upon it, he cannot eat it. To do so would be to mix black bodies and white bodies in a novel bent on reifying their separation—and to acknowledge the possibility that Tarzan had hungered, however briefly, for another man rather than simply for the body of his "prey." In turn, the jungle must be referenced to justify Tarzan's hunger—even as his essential nobility must be marshaled to naturalize his "hereditary instinct" not to eat. Tarzan's initial, "natural" hunger for Kulonga has elicited some critical attention, and Jurca argues, for example, that the strange repulsion and attraction that Tarzan feels is a classic sign of "racial desire."[37] Yet, this desire is simultaneously racial and sexual. Making sense of this scene requires us, then, to consider that Tarzan's hungering for and revulsion toward Kulonga is as visceral as it is sensuous. Indeed, Kulonga's body, while not eaten, is here anatomized and eroticized (even as it is exoticized), and the taboo of cannibalism invoked and then disavowed by the scene is bound up with the double threat of miscegenation and homoerotic desire repeated in D'Arnot's capture. Moreover, the scene functions to broker the possibility of unspeakable desire in the novel—the possibility of Tarzan's erotic fascination with Kulonga's body—only to forestall it. Yet, as we will see, the queer exchange of desire it briefly imagines later resurfaces in D'Arnot's wonder at Tarzan's own body.

When D'Arnot, shortly after his rescue, wakes in a "bed of soft ferns and grasses," it is exactly like the bed of ferns and grasses Tarzan earlier made for Jane.[38] The similarities have elicited some critical attention; Jurca notes the parallels between Tarzan's caretaking of Jane and D'Arnot, but suggests that both are a sign of Tarzan's noble domesticity. For he is, in her reading, first and foremost a home-maker, and that domestic impulse to house "his own kind" (rather than simply his mate) is what most marks him as civilized.[39] While Jurca's reading shrewdly accounts for the ways in which race discriminates in *Tarzan*, it fails to attend to the ongoing structural parallels between Jane and D'Arnot in the narrative. In particular, its foregone sense that "Tarzan's sexual desire for Jane distinguishes her from all others" forestalls further pursuit of those other parallels and overdetermined desires even in the "Brother Men" chapter under discussion.[40] For much as Jane, lying on the grassy bower, looks up at Tarzan to remark upon "the graceful majesty of his carriage, the perfect symmetry of his magnificent figure and the poise of his well-shaped head upon his broad shoulders,"[41] D'Arnot first sees Tarzan's "broad muscular [white] back" before being struck by the beauty of Tarzan's face: "His face was handsome—the handsomest, thought D'Arnot, that he had ever seen."[42] The chapter on Jane's "bower of bliss" is titled "Heredity" as if to underscore that the passion Tarzan keeps in check therein is directly an outgrowth of his genetic nobility, while the chapter on Tarzan's nursing of D'Arnot in the self-same bower is called "Brother Men." In a sense, the title, like the heredity one before it, underscores Tarzan's whiteness and innate gentility—he and D'Arnot are, instantly, brothers. But the nod to the fraternal here works also to diffuse the homoerotic undertones of their meeting as well as the structural echoes between Jane and D'Arnot's scenes of rescue and desire.

Yet, it is in the "Brother Men" chapter that we see Tarzan at his most extensively maternal and loving mate-like. While Torgovick points to Tarzan's gentleness in the soothing of Jane (stroking her hair much as Kala once stroked his own head), because of the extent of D'Arnot's injuries, for three days "Tarzan sat beside him and bathed his head and hands and washed his wounds."[43] And this intimacy of the body soon becomes an intimacy of words. While the text denies verbal communication between Jane and Tarzan (as such communication would end the misunderstanding that drives the plot), it allows Tarzan to write in front of D'Arnot—thus allowing the Frenchman to realize that the Ape-man can in fact "speak." This recognition leads in turn to D'Arnot's tutelage of Tarzan first in French and then in manners. (In between he will accidentally shoot his "friend and protector" Tarzan and be called upon to nurse Tarzan even as he was once nursed by him—another instance of the economy of exchange in the text.[44]) This communication between the two men seems particularly significant in a novel that so often celebrates the pleasures of the oral—and all the more so for the fact that it is D'Arnot's stamp of civilization (and Frenchness) that is later most legible upon Tarzan.[45] For is it not, after all, the "immaculate Frenchman" D'Arnot has made him to be that Jane cannot finally accept in Wisconsin? The chapter title is all the more suggestive for the ways in which it at once diffuses the latent homoeroticism of the chapter, even as it further invokes the origins of Tarzan's desire for Jane. For, does he not desire her, as Jurca has shrewdly shown us, in part because she is one of *his own kind*—an allegiance of class and race even as it is one of eros? Put differently, the kinship and desire exchanged between D'Arnot and Tarzan across the novel can be sustained even as the possibility that Tarzan might hunger for Kulonga must be immediately foreclosed upon in the text precisely because—rather than in spite of the fact—that Kulonga and Tarzan cannot, finally, be imagined to be brothers.

Kept men, punk endings

When asked by Clayton how he came to be in that "bally jungle," Tarzan replies simply, "'I was born there . . . My mother was an Ape, and of course she couldn't tell me much about it. I never knew who my father was.'"[46] *Tarzan of the Apes* thus closes with a spectacular renunciation: having only moments before received confirmation of his birthright to the title of Greystoke, Tarzan seems immediately poised to return to the bally jungle, ceding in one sensational stroke his lordship and his Jane to his cousin Clayton. And yet precisely as the novel wraps up what one reader famously labeled its "punk" ending, it reopens the possibility of miscegenation in the text. In a novel rife with the possibility of—and anxiety toward—such mixings, this final twist might seem simply more of the same. Yet at no point previously does the novel conceive that the vectors of miscegenation can work in precisely this way. White men, in other words, can be imagined at no other moment in the novel to feel desire for an Ape—while male Apes are consistently figured as the predators of Lady Alice and Jane Porter. This return of the same is then something a little different—a possibility otherwise unimaginable that is now nonchalantly brokered by the text. Yet, the machinery of the narrative forestalls the possibility even as it introduces it: we know Tarzan is a Lord, and it is this knowledge that facilitates the novel's titillating if erroneous disclosure of Tarzan's origins.

The novel's phenomenal success was in no way inhibited by the simple fact that this ending was found even by its earliest readers to be, on the whole, desperately unsatisfying. Indeed, readers immediately wrote in to decry Burroughs's failure to unite Jane and Tarzan, and their ire came to be summed up by one particular letter to *All-Story Magazine*: "The story is a real bean, but, oh, my, the ending is absolutely punk." (Burroughs would later write, "There is so much reference to the 'punk ending' that I am inclined to think that is the very feature of the story that clinched their interest."[47]) Critics, in discussing the punk ending, have long taken its meaning for granted. But while the unhappy reader most likely used the term "punk" to convey a sense of "the nonsensical or foolish" (Merriam-Webster) if not "cowardly or contemptible" in the ending (OED), the meaning of the term was far from settled at the time Burroughs was writing *Tarzan*. As historian Angus McLaren points out, "the term 'punk,' which in the 18th-C was used to refer to rotten wood or something equally worthless, at the end of the 19th-C designated a passive male homosexual."[48] In American slang in particular, the term carried the connotations of a young boy "kept" by a tramp.[49] Reading this sense of the term back into *Tarzan*'s "absolutely punk" ending forces us to reconsider, finally, who gets "bought" and what, finally, gets exchanged in the novel.

It is, of course, Jane who is most obviously purchased in the text. With her family fortune gone, and her father deeply in debt, she is forced near the end of the novel to agree to marry the villainous Canler. Her concession to the marriage is an understandably bitter one, as she is conscious of and later gives voice to the economics of exchange underwriting their prospective union: Canler's money comes with significant strings. The text pointedly gestures to the exchange of bodies for money at work in the marriage proposal, most glaringly in the confrontation it stages between Jane and Canler about her future concubinage:

> 'Do you realize that you are buying me, Mr. Canler?' she said finally, and in a cold, level voice. 'Buying me for a few paltry dollars? Of course you do, Robert Canler," [to which he responds, acidly,] 'You surprise me, Jane. I thought you had more self-control, more pride. Of course you are right. I am buying you, and I knew that you knew it, but I thought you would prefer to pretend that it was otherwise. I should have thought your Porter pride would have shrunk from admitting . . . that you were *a bought woman.*'[50]

The novel's insistence that it is Jane who is bought, and Jane who faces the prospect of being a kept woman, albeit a married one, is further brought into relief by the fact that though Clayton would never treat her as such, by choosing the man with the title rather than the jungle lord, she can't entirely escape this economy of exchange. That Jane might be in danger of being herself an exchangeable commodity in the text is not in itself curious given the timing of *Tarzan of the Apes*: its publication coincides with the height of the American "white slavery" scare epitomized by such films as *Traffic in Souls* (1913). Of more moment, however, is the fact that the text denies her the means and inclination to acquire money of her own— the text cannot, in other words, imagine Jane as a "wage slave." Indeed, the suggestion that Jane could work to help her father make ends meet (if admittedly not to pay back the exorbitant debt owed Canler) is nowhere even hinted at in the novel—despite the fact that middleclass women were going to work in unprecedented numbers at the turn of the twentieth century.

Yet Tarzan, for all his titles, is himself in much the same precarious economic position and the buying of Jane largely functions to deflect our attentions from the echoes in their situation. For while life in the jungle requires work but not money, outside the jungle Tarzan is forced to enter the sordid world of exchange, a workaday world he might ultimately escape only through the title he finally renounces. Early on in his entrance into civilization he seems temporarily saved from the world of work by D'Arnot, who, in moving from tutor to protector and mentor, offers to pay Tarzan's way, no strings attached: "'No, my friend,' returned D'Arnot, 'you need not worry about money, nor need you work for it. I have enough money for two—enough for twenty.'"[51] But as Tarzan negotiates life outside the wild, he comes to see that exchange is at the heart of every financial transaction—that nothing comes from nothing. Much as civilized Tarzan learns the value of table manners and gentlemanly attire, he also gets a lesson in the preeminence of exchange value: "It had become evident to Tarzan that without money one must die. D'Arnot had told him not to worry, since he had more than enough for both, but the ape-man was learning many things and one of them was that people looked down upon one who accepted money from another *without giving something of equal value in exchange.*"[52] Tarzan is then in a double bind: to live off another man's money makes him already a kind of gigolo, but he cannot remain in D'Arnot's debt without offering something in return, or, rather, without exchanging something of equal value.

That Tarzan, like Jane, might be himself the commodity at stake—that, in other words, this exchange *might* be sexual and in turn will structurally presage Jane's relationship to Canler—bears out the text's overarching compulsion to repeat. Reinserting the larger resonances of the term "punk" to the ending suggests then the striking possibility that the Lord of the Jungle faces the sexually ambiguous position of being a "kept man" to his "brother" D'Arnot, and it is in fact the threat of that relationship of exchange which is repeated and displaced onto Jane in a way that seems to rework Tarzan's signature tagline as: See Tarzan, Buy Jane. Simply put, the specter of "white slavery" in the text is thus a doubly determined one: conveniently displacing Tarzan's economic relationship with D'Arnot onto Jane even as it summons the racial subjection of African-American women under slavery so as to reclaim that threat solely for white women. That Tarzan is able, finally, to attain a measure of financial independence from D'Arnot in the novel—not through work but rather through a 10,000 franc bet resting on his jungle prowess—does much to underscore the hierarchy of gender at work in *Tarzan of the Apes*: in Burroughs's plot, Jane literally takes the place of Tarzan so she can take the narrative fall for him. That she might do so resolves the threat of Tarzan as "kept man" and leaves his masculinity, and heterosexuality, unscathed.

Or does it? In my reading, the curious return to origins at the end of the novel similarly functions to uphold the limits of desire in the text: Jane chooses not to marry a title-less Tarzan but cannot, within the logic of the novel, marry that self-same Ape-man if he is, after all, part Ape. But the ending also serves, however briefly, to destabilize those very limits. For the moment that allows for the possibility of racial mixing also makes possible the final closure of Tarzan and Jane's otherwise inevitable union. That it does so suggests, as we have seen already, the ways in which thwarted, tabooed desires—be they interracial or homoerotic—most often serve to haunt and reinforce one another in *Tarzan of the Apes*. Yet, it further allows for the possibility that the ending is "absolutely punk" because it will, however briefly, not entirely foreclose upon the queer exchanges of desire it seeks at once to introduce and disavow. While such possibilities may in some sense be driven from the series with the union of Tarzan and Jane in *The Return of Tarzan*, they nevertheless remain available to Tarzan fans through the campiness of the films and the homoeroticism of the comic book covers,[53] and most recently through "fan fictions"—reader-generated stories that imagine that Tarzan might end up with Conan the Barbarian in the end.[54]

Acknowledgment

I would like to thank William A. Gleason, Diana Fuss, Sarah Churchwell, and Thomas Ruys Smith for their responses to earlier drafts of this essay. I am also grateful for the additional suggestions offered by my Fall 2010 and Spring 2011 Writing Seminar students, most particularly, Daniel Hasler and Sonya Huang: among other things, they reminded me to practice, in my own writing, what I preach in the classroom.

Bibliography

Bederman, Gail. *Manliness and Civilization: A Cultural History of Gender and Race in the United States*. Chicago: University of Chicago Press, 1995.

Berglund, Jeff. *Cannibal Fictions: American Explorations of Colonialism, Race, Gender, and Sexuality.* Madison: University of Wisconsin Press, 2006.

—. "Write, White, Rite: Literacy, Imperialism, and Cannibalism in Edgar Rice Burrough's *Tarzan of the Apes.*" *Studies in American Fiction* 27:1 (1999): 53–76.

"Best Loved Juveniles." *Time*, Aug. 29, 1938, http://www.time.com/time/magazine/article/0,9171,789196,00.html.

Burroughs, Edgar Rice. *Tarzan of the Apes.* 1914. New York: Ballantine Books, 1990.

—. *The Son of Tarzan.* 1917. New York: Ballantine, 1990.

Cheyfitz, Eric. "Tarzan of the Apes: US Foreign Policy in the Twentieth Century." *American Literary History* 1:2 (1989): 339–60.

Gleason, William. "Of Sequels and Sons: *Tarzan* and the Problem of Paternity." *Journal of American and Comparative Cultures* 23:1 (2000): 41–51.

Goulart, Ron. *Cheap Thrills: The Amazing! Thrilling! Astonishing! History of Pulp Fiction.* New Rochelle: Arlington House, 1972.

Jurca, Catherine. "Tarzan, Lord of the Suburbs." *Modern Language Quarterly* 57:23 (1996): 479–504.

Kasson, John F. *Houdini, Tarzan, and the Perfect Man: The White Male Body and the Challenge of Modernity.* New York: Hill and Wang, 2001.

Kidd, Kenneth. "Men Who Run with Wolves and the Women Who Love Them: Child Study and Compulsory Heterosexuality in Feral Child Films." *The Lion and the Unicorn* 20:1 (1996): 91–112.

McLaren, Angus. *The Trials of Masculinity: Policing Sexual Boundaries, 1870–1930.* Chicago: University of Chicago Press, 1997.

Nye, Russel B. *The Unembarrassed Muse: The Popular Arts in America,* New York: Dial Press, 1970.

Porges, Irwin. *Edgar Rice Burroughs: The Man who Created Tarzan.* Provo, UT: Brigham Young University Press, 1975.

Seitler, Dana. *Atavistic Time: The Culture of Science in American Modernity.* Minneapolis: University of Minnesota Press, 2008.

Smith, Erin A. "'The ragtag and bobtail of the fiction parade': Pulp Magazines and the Literary Marketplace." In *Scorned Literature: Essays on the History and Criticism of Popular Mass-Produced Fiction in America,* Edited by Lydia Cushman Schurman and Deidre Johnson, 123–45. Westpoint, CT: Greenwood Press, 2002.

Sommerville, Siobhan. *Queering the Color Line: Race and the Invention of Homosexuality in American Culture.* Durham: Duke University Press, 2000.

"Tarzan Finds a Son." *Life Magazine,* June 26, 1939, 64–7.

Torgovnick, Marianna. *Gone Primitive: Savage Intellects, Modern Lives.* Chicago: University of Chicago Press, 1990.

Notes

1   "Tarzan Finds a Son," 64. In its 1939 piece, *Life Magazine* further noted that the phenomenally bestselling series had been translated into 57 languages.

2   Burroughs, 226.

3   Jurca shrewdly argues that "although few novels are more geographically or narratively remote from the suburb than *Tarzan*, perhaps no other American novel is quite so driven by the very tensions—between savagery and civilization, colonization and home rule—that were conspicuously associated with the nation's urban-suburban conflict in the early twentieth century." See "Tarzan, Lord of the Suburbs," 488.

4   Nye, *The Unembarrassed Muse*, 273.

5   Porges, *Edgar Rice Burroughs*, 111.

6   Kasson, *Houdini, Tarzan and the Perfect Man*, 168.

7   Ibid., 217.

8   Ibid., 217.

9   Bederman, *Manliness and Civilization*, 219.

10   Smith, "'The ragtag and bobtail of the fiction parade,'" 125.

11   Porges, 165.

12   Gleason, "Of Sequels and Sons," 45.

13   Kasson, 218.

14   Porges, 491.

15   Torgovnick, "Taking Tarzan Seriously," 43. Vidal's sense of Tarzan as a fantasy of escape in the 60s echoes later critics, among them Kasson and Gleason, who argue that it functioned in much the same way for its earliest readers.

16   "Best Loved Juveniles."

17   For a brief discussion, see Jurca, 491.

18   For a rich discussion of turn-of-the-century discourses on "manliness" as "whiteness," see Bederman; for a further discussion of turn-of-the-century obsessions with the perfect white male body, see Kasson. As previously noted, Jurca offers an excellent reading of Tarzan as "Lord of the Suburbs." Torgovnick suggests that, at least in the opening volume, the primitive is a source of empowerment and largely functions to destabilize cultural hierarchies in the text. Gleason posits that the series as a whole offered men an escape from the constraints of early twentieth-century fatherhood and a fantasy of the father

revivifying his primitive masculinity through the son's willing cession of virility over to him. Cheyfitz, on the other hand, argues that *Tarzan of the Apes* is finally a fantasy of expansionist foreign policy, allowing "Americans [to] savor, in the act of denying them, their own imperial ventures"; see *Poetics of Imperialism*, 340. Most recently, Dana Seitler has persuasively read Tarzan as "a hybrid figure" who so consistently and ambivalently conjoins "atavistic" primitivism with aristocratic pedigree that he altogether unsettles the narrative of progress undergirding "the prevailing understandings of primitivism in American culture." See *Atavistic Time*, 147.

19 See *Cannibal Fictions*, 84.

20 Torgovnick, for example, reads "Me Tarzan, You Jane" as the solidification of Tarzan's "chest-thumping" masculinity and contends that it is emblematic of the series' later move to naturalize the "man is boss" gender hierarchy (67; 70), while Cheyfitz and Jurca point out the ways that "class is as transparent as race in the text" (Jurca 500), as we see, for example, in the novel's insistent coding of the mutinous working class white sailors as "black."

21 *Tarzan of the Apes*, 175.

22 *Queering the Color Line*, 6.

23 *Manliness and Civilization*, 231.

24 Gleason generally accepts Torgovnick's reading that "Jane curbs Tarzan's wild ways"—though he argues that Burroughs "permanently restores Tarzan's jungle ethic . . . through the simultaneous introduction and expulsion of Korak" rather than through Jane's later hiatus from the series in the 1920s (46). Bederman suggests that "if the perfect man loses his woman to a man like Clayton, masculinity and civilization must be incompatible" (231). Torgovnick points out that in early reviews of Tarzan "much was made of the process by which, under the influence of Jane's love, he 'tries to learn the ways of civilization'"(44).

25 *Tarzan*, 270.

26 Ibid., 270.

27 Bergland offers a rich account of Tarzan's reading, arguing that Tarzan acquires "the instinctive desire for Jane" through "the circuitry of the English book," and in turn learns to act like a "proper man" through the models he finds in his father's library. See *Cannibal Fictions*, 89.

28 *Tarzan*, 185.

29 Ibid., 240.

30 Ibid., 196.

31 *Gone Primitive*, 51.

32 *Tarzan*, 198.

33 Ibid., 206.

34 Ibid., 206.

35 Ibid., 200.

36 Ibid., 81.

37 "Lord of the Suburbs," 498.

38 *Tarzan*, 212 and 186.

39 Writes Jurca, "The domestic impulse in *Tarzan of the Apes* is not directed towards the creation of the nuclear family but is identified with the well-bred white man's instinctive ability to tame the wilderness and with his desire to house and provide community for the extended elite white family." See "Lord of the Suburbs," 502.

40 Ibid., 501.

41 *Tarzan*, 183.

42 Ibid., 213. Seitler shrewdly notes the way that Tarzan's body "entranc[es] both the female and male gaze" in the novel, but argues that this spectacle functions to "emphasize the dramatic effects of Tarzan's body while blurring the kinds of violent actions that he takes against the Africana and Arab populations living in the jungle." See *Atavistic Time*, 143.

43 Ibid., 216.

44 Ibid., 231.

45 In my reading, the kiss between Jane and Tarzan—a kiss that naturalizes their affections even as it marks off *manliness* from *manhood*—underscores the pleasures of the oral in *Tarzan of the Apes*. That pleasure is bound up in the mouth is further signaled in the novel's opening, its insistence on telling its tale, and later in the text's final privileging of spoken rather than written speech. (Reading English by intuition may prove that Tarzan is a white man, but speaking through instruction proves him a gentleman.)

46 *Tarzan*, 276.

47 Porges, 149.

48 See *Trials of Masculinity*, 16.

49 Ibid., 16. See also the online edition of the *Oxford English Dictionary*.

50 *Tarzan*, 257 (emphasis added).

51 Ibid., 235.

52 Ibid., 249 (emphasis added).

53 The blog "Quixotic Quests of Q the Conqueror" devotes a page to "Queeroes! Tarzan of the Apes," offering a queer retelling of the Tarzan comic book covers that imagines Tarzan in love with the apes, for example. http://qtheconqueror.blogspot.com/2007/08/queeroes-tarzan-of-apes.html

54 Kenneth Kidd suggests that Tarzan long functioned as a homoerotic spectacle, and "on page and screen alike inspired homosocial adoration." See "Men Who Run with Wolves and the Women Who Love Them," 91–112.

9

Ornamentalism: Desire, disavowal, and displacement in E. M. Hull's *The Sheik*

Sarah Garland

Luxury imports

Both as a bestselling novel and in its incarnation as the phenomenally successful 1921 movie starring Rudolf Valentino, E. M. Hull's *Sheik* (1919) crystallized erotic fantasies of the Middle East that had been gathering since the nineteenth century around images of the desert, the slave market, the houri and the harem, around Salome and the Lustful Turk, and in the folds of the robes of Lawrence of Arabia and Sir Richard Burton. In 1978, Edward Said's *Orientalism* unpacked the way images of the East are used as a set of signs by the West to legitimize and consolidate colonial power and to articulate the West's disavowed desires, but as early as 1853, the anonymous author of an article in *Knickerbocker Magazine* noted that "strictly speaking, Orientalism is a mode of speech."[1] This use of "the Orient" as a language for the imperial "Occident" to speak its own dreams homogenized the diverse cultures of the Middle East and Asia and brought them together as objects of "the sensuous imagination" of the West to produce a situation where, through the trade routes that created and opened up the market for imported luxury, money can be sexualized and where sexuality can structure both class and conspicuous consumption. The anonymous writer continues: "Orientalism is not merely associated with one country, race or era. It is a complex idea made up of history and scenery, suffused with imagination and irradiated with revelation":

> We frame to ourselves a deep azure sky, alluring atmosphere; associate luxurious ease with the coffee-rooms and flowering gardens of the Seraglio at Constantinople; with the tapering minarets and gold crescents of Cairo; with the fountains within and the kiosks without Damascus—settings of silver in circlets of gold. We see grave and reverend turbans sitting cross legged on Persian carpets in baths and harems, under palm trees or acacias, either quaffing the cool sherbet of roses or the aromatic Mocha coffee . . . and this we call Orientalism. This is Orientalism, not as it is, but as it swims before the sensuous imagination. It is too unreal to be defined.[2]

Even before millions saw the film, Hull's *Sheik* was, in a sense, then, already read. The phenomenal success of the novel—in Britain, it went through 108 editions between 1919 and 1923 and in America, it was the first book to be a top ten bestseller two years in a row—might be, in part, attributed to preexisting middle-brow taste for Orientalism.[3] By the time of *The Sheik's* publication in England in 1919 and in America in 1921, this opulent "Orient" had already been disseminated through objects of mass consumption, in England, through the sale and exhibition of the spoils of Empire, and in America, through the commerce, collectors, and marketplaces of the great cities. As Mari Yoshihara writes, a taste for Asian goods had filtered down from the nineteenth-century world fairs and the aestheticist movement so that by the turn of the century, "stores specializing in 'Asian' goods—variously referred to as 'novelty stores,' 'curio shops,' 'antique stores,' or 'Oriental stores'" had introduced mass-produced Chinese, Japanese, and Persian goods into America's material culture.[4] Billie Melman explains how the profile of women was changing in the early years of the twentieth century to include "that audience which by tradition and social allegiance was a magazine—and not a novel-reading—public, the *petit bourgeoisie* and the better-off working class," and it is this same audience who were targeted by the advertisements for the things found in A. A. Vandine's Broadway Oriental Store, where, Yoshihara writes, "Persian rugs covered the floor, and Chinese porcelains, tapestry, vases, and other pieces of bric-à-brac decorated the walls," "the drapes shed a subdued light through the room, and the Japanese bells jingled softly in the breezes."[5] The effect in *The Sheik* that Sarah Wintle notes where Sheik Ahmed's luxurious tent feels like nothing as much as "an English suburban bedroom," "with its scattered garments, soap and water and glossy magazines and novels" is partly because Empire had spread its versions of cleanliness and of culture abroad, but also because the objects of Empire have already been domesticated in Arabian coffee and spice, in sweets like Turkish Delight, and in Salome, Fatima, and Mogul Cigarettes.[6] When the novel-reading women of England and America chose to take *The Sheik* into their home, it was into a cultural context where a nebulous and fantastic "East" had already become part of domestic style.

For contemporary audiences, *The Sheik's* displacement of passion and illicit sexual relations onto the figure of the Arab needed no explanation, because, as scholars of Orientalism following Said have argued, the East has been so written over with (literally) dis-placed Western fantasies and iconographies of desire that for Western readers, its landscape, figures, art, and traditions act as synonyms for seduction. In American culture of the 20s, the condensation of sex and power into the figure of Sheik Ahmed Ben Hassan as played by Valentino was so clear that the term "sheik" became an easy shorthand for a strong and dashing male lover, as well as, in 1931, a brand of condoms with Valentino's costumed portrait on the tin.[7] Indeed, the novel is itself a kind of screen memory not just of Sir Richard Burton's sexedup version of the *Thousand and One Arabian Nights* (1885) but also for pornographic texts and sex manuals such as *A Night in A Moorish Harem* (1904), Captain Charles Devereaux's *Venus in India* (1889), *The Lustful Turk* (1828), and Burton's translations of The *Kama Sutra* (1883), *The Perfumed Garden* (1886). It was also part of less explicit nascent "desert romance" genre that began with Robert Hitchins' *Garden of Allah* in 1904 and ran through Kathlyn Rhodes' *The Will of Allah* (1908) and *The Lure of the Desert* (1916) before Hull's novel precipitated a deluge of imitations and parodies.[8]

The Sheik starts as a captivity narrative and metamorphoses into a formula romance at the moment of Diana's first encounter with the Sheik's "fierce burning eyes," "passionate stare" and "the handsomest and cruellest face that she had ever seen."[9] This early confirmation that the Sheik is to be desired as well as feared switches the genre of the novel to romance, and from here forth it fits the generic pattern established back as far as Richardson's *Pamela* (1740) and documented in the early eighties by Janice Radway and Tania Modleski. The Sheik's displays of masculinity and repeated erotic domination of the resisting English heiress, Diana Mayo, follow the stock conventions of romance where the heroine's innocence is substituted for sexual awareness and a submission generally couched in terms of "womanliness"—"Why have I brought you here? *Bon Dieu*! Are you not woman enough to know?" (57) the Sheik growls. The threat to the imperial hierarchy represented by the romantic coupling of an Arab and an English aristocrat is signaled loudly by a clanging coda at the end of the book where Sheik Ahmed appears in full tweed and riding breeches to send Diana back to the English and is revealed to be Viscount Glencaryll, the child of a British lord and a Spanish woman with "Moorish blood." Devastated at the prospect of life without her love, Diana tries to shoot herself but is saved by the Sheik's "desert-bred" reflexes in time to live happily ever after. In the final words of the book—Diana's cry of "Ahmed! *Monseigneur*!"—these differences and inversions are righted, as the Sheik's occidental identity finally overwrites his oriental one, and Diana's rebellions are replaced by appropriate humility.[10]

Ornamentalism

Laying aside the ending for a moment, it may seem that there are tentative elements of progressivism in the interracial romance. However, the ways in which Diana reasons with herself about Achmed's "animal strength," "revolting potential," and "brutality" merely suggest that her love for him is both because of and despite traits that mark him as a racist caricature of exaggerated masculinity. Hull writes:

He was a brute, but she loved him, loved him for his very brutality and superb animal strength. And he was an Arab! A man of different race and colour, a native; Aubrey would indiscriminately class him as a "damned nigger." She did not care. It made no difference. A year ago, a few weeks even, she would have shuddered with repulsion at the bare idea, the thought that a native could even touch her had been revolting, but all that was swept away and was nothing in the face of the love that filled her heart so completely.[11]

Despite Diana's enthusiastic reconciliation of her love with his status as Arab, this love of an aristocrat for a "damned nigger" causes considerable problems in terms of the English class system and for the class politics of the romance as a genre, with, as I will argue below, crucial repercussions for the plot and texture of the entire book. *The Sheik's* central exception to the pattern of the romance outlined by Modleski and Radway and developed by Jan Cohn in *Romance and the Erotics of Property* is in the way that Hull's novel is considerably vexed by the relative statuses of its hero and heroine. As all three authors point out, the romantic heroine always marries above herself in order to gain love, status, and security, but within a racist paradigm, the Sheik's own wealth, authority, and leadership does not translate to a social position that is recognized by imperialist powers. The only inquiry Diana "permits herself" to make about Ahmed's lifelong friend, Vicomte Raoul de Saint Hubert, is telling, as is the valet's reply: "The family of Saint Hubert, are they of the old or the new *noblesse*?.," "Of the old, Madame," replied Gaston quickly.[12] Diana's shame at meeting Saint Hubert is the shame of a class affront—"How could she bear to meet one of her own order in the position in which she was? She who had been proud Diana Mayo and now—the mistress of an Arab Sheik?"—and this Saint Hubert recognizes:

> Saint Hubert swung round. "You might have spared her," he cried.
> "What?"
> "What? Good God, man! Me!"[13]

In *Ornamentalism,* David Cannadine points out the social ramifications of being, as the Sheik is, both racially marked by the colonizer culture and of high status in the colonized culture with an anecdote about King Kalakaua of Hawaii's visit to England in 1881. When faced with the problem of where to seat Kalakaua, the Prince of Wales, later to be Edward VII, insisted on the King's precedence over the crown prince of Germany (the future Kaiser Wilhelm II) with the logic that "either the brute is a king or he's a common-or-garden nigger; and if the latter, what's he doing here?"[14] Despite the authority Diana sees Achmed wielding over a tribe who "worship first and foremost their Sheik, then the famous horses for which they are renowned, and then and then only—Allah," the British class system forces the choice that reverses the Sheik's identity at the end of Hull's novel because one cannot be both Arab and aristocrat under Empire, although, like T. E. Lawrence and Sir Richard Burton, it was perfectly possible to be an aristocrat dressed as an Arab.[15]

For an American audience, *The Sheik's* imperial fantasy would offer an English playing-out of old American fears of miscegenation, assuaged to a certain extent by the way that in the film version, the casting of Valentino, an Italian American, whitens the Sheik. For Diana, Ahmed is distinguished from his foil, the robber chief, Sheik Ibraheim Omair, because unlike Ahmed, Ibrahim Omair is identical with "the Arab of her Imaginings," that is, "gross," "unwieldy," and "slovenly," with fat hands, sensual lips, "broken, blackened teeth," and a leer of "bestial evilness."[16]

In contrast, Ahmed's "fastidiously clean" hands and "well-kept" nails, his "spotless" robes, his European manners, and his friendship with the distinguished Vicomte Raoul de Saint Hubert all work toward a rather facile structural irony that tells the reader that because he does not seem like the stereotypical "Arab of their Imaginings," he isn't actually an Arab. Diana asks the question, but it is left for the reader to invoke the stereotypes and to draw the conclusions that pave the way for the book's ending:

> She put the books back with a puzzled frown. She wished, with a feeling that she could not fathom, that they had been rather what she had imagined. The evidence of education and unlooked-for tastes in the man they belonged to troubled her. It was an unexpected glimpse into the personality of the Arab that had captured her was vaguely disquieting, for it suggested possibilities that would not have existed in a raw native, or one only superficially coated with a veneer of civilization. He seemed to become infinitely more sinister, infinitely more horrible.[17]

Ahmed himself plays on the essentialist logic that would unite his absolute autonomy and brutality as with Ibrahim's as part of a merciless "Arab nature"—"What do you expect of a savage? When an Arab sees a woman that he wants, he takes her. I only follow the customs of my people"—but even here, this essentialism is not necessarily undercut by Saint Hubert's knowledge that the Sheik is English "Your people!—which people?"[18] Instead, the qualities that the Sheik takes on as "Arab" could be posited as an exaggerated masculinity, in which case his revealed identity as Englishman need not alter his relish for absolute power and domination. These traits may also (following the argument of Susan Blake in "What 'Race' is the Sheik?") be easily transferred across to his equally essentialist English self where, as she writes, "the 'Arab' qualities approved in the English hero—imperiousness and complete freedom— reflect a romantic-aristocratic orientalist discourse that serves the interests of [an] English aristocracy that claims these privileges for itself."[19] This coalescence between masculine imperiousness and imperialism allow Hull's hero to retain the signifiers of colonialist hierarchy, and even, through a romantic Orientalism of the kind in evidence in Richard Burton and T. E. Lawrence's writing, to evoke a discourse that admires and emulates "'true Arabs' for the very qualities the English aristocracy claimed for itself, 'superiority in point of birth' and 'absolute independence.'"[20] Although the sheik's peerage is hereditary, it would have a historical analogue even if he were an Arab: as David Cannadine points out, the "decoration" of native chiefs with British imperial titles acted as a mechanism for bringing about precisely this kind of union between the two systems.

"Ornamentalism" is the term Cannadine uses to explain how the British imperial society was bound together, comprehended, and imagined "in an essentially ornamental mode," through both these decorations and "unrivalled and interlocking displays of regular ritual and occasional spectacle."[21] As one would expect, the pomp and ritual surrounding colonial power aggrandized native peoples only as far as the social ordering remained useful to the British: "ornamentalism was hierarchy made visible, immanent and actual," as Cannadine writes.[22] This element of blood and breeding is reinforced by the images of haughty but unpredictable thoroughbred Arabian horses in the novel (a commonplace in Orientalist painting, John MacKenzie argues), and, as Blake points out, manages to displace the question of miscegenation in favor of an equally hierarchical discourse on class and nobility.[23]

Desire and disavowal

The Sheik replays the dynamics of racial stereotyping that posits the Other as both attractive and repulsive by reversing the most immediate terms of that representation to present cultural fears as cultural desires, first by including a man of color as the primary object of love and sexual intent, and second by staging the repeated rape of the heroine. The question of how and why Anglo-American bestsellers repeat the trope of rape is the better considered of these questions, possibly, as we see in discussions throughout this collection, because some of the biggest selling novels for women— including Charlotte Temple, Gone With the Wind, Peyton Place, and The Sheik—contain scenes where the heroine is sexually initiated against her will by a man whom she later realizes she loves. This is not to say that the mass consumption of a story of kidnap and rape means that millions of women secretly desire rape, but to suggest that the romantic bestseller repeats a moment of fantasy where desire is transferred from the woman reader or writer to a male figure that symbolizes inexorable and unstoppable desire.

This movement of desire from the woman to the man, and from the white man to the man of color, is especially visible as displacement and disavowal when one considers that most romances, including The Sheik and the three other massive bestsellers listed above, are written by women and for women. It is, therefore, not just the heroine who is the product of the writer's fears and desires; the figure of the sheik, the luxurious orientalist mise en scene and the captivity plot can also be seen as places where patriarchally legitimized forms are rearranged, subverted, reenforced, or sidelined by women. The male sheik is both a representation of the kinds of forces of desire and opposition women face in their lives and a representation of Hull's own agency, just as Diana's plight is a way of writing about both female sexual desire and its difficulties. As Radway points out in Reading the Romance, rape goes on to form a recurrent trope in the plot structure of the mass market romance because it absolves the heroine from the responsibility of discovering and directing her desire. It leaves her free "to enjoy the pleasures of her sexual nature without having to accept the blame and guilt for it," as Radway puts it.[24] Diana's recurrent shame and disdain also means that readers need not question their seduction; the book is sensual enough to bring women to the cinema in their millions prepared to safely swoon, and transgressive enough to allow the reader to live out through Diana fantasies of the New Woman, of the woman adventurer, and of the utterly desired woman. (Diana protests more than enough to make sure that there is no way she can be accused of being lascivious.) The hero's desire translates female erotic agency into a patriarchally acceptable form, while all the other codes of the text signal that both the heroine's and the reader's passionate erotic response are appropriate.

One of the pleasures of the romance is the promise of the inevitable union, and *The Sheik* goes incredibly far in ensuring that Diana's initial reluctance to love or to return the Sheik's desire are given to the reader as mere flotsam in the much more powerful flow of the preordained happy ending. As Jan Cohn argues, the question popular romance poses is not "Will the lovers win?" but "Will the lovers *know*?"[25] Because the heroine is, unlike the reader, not trained in the tropes of her genre, a full structural irony is present until the lover's final, mutually consenting kiss brings the heroine's assured knowledge of her happiness in line with that of the reader's. Unlike real acts of rape—that is, acts that look to violate, degrade, and create pain and suffering in women—the acts of forced intercourse that occur in formula romances and in *The Sheik* are, as Modleski points out, always subject to a positive reinterpretation by the reader and heroine because they are framed by overarching romantic codes that promise a happy ending.[26] Needless to say, this counterintuitive disavowal of violence against women is clearly a very dangerous kind of perspective to naturalize; as Rachel Anderson wryly put it in her 1974 history of the genre, "*The Sheik* is the most immoral of any of the romances, not because of lewd descriptions of sexual intercourse . . . but because of the distorting view Miss Hull presents of the kind of relationship which leads to perfect love, and the totally unprincipled precept that the reward of rapists is a lovely English heiress with a look of misty yearning in her eyes."[27]

Diana and the Sheik are guaranteed to reach the point of passionate lovemaking, because female beauty is figured by the romance as an endless sexual invitation and male sexuality is figured as endless desire. These excessive drives are exaggerated still further by Diana's irresistible beauty and haughty resistance and by the Sheik's "Arab" insatiability. Indeed, Hull's overdetermination of Diana's capitulation, I would argue, is even more overdrawn than that in *Peyton Place*, *Charlotte Temple*, and *Gone With the Wind*:

> It was inevitable; there was no help to be expected, no mercy to be hoped for. She had felt the crushing strength against which she was helpless. She would struggle, but it would be useless; she would fight, but it would make no difference. Within the tent she was alone, ready to his hand like a snared animal; without, the place was swarming with the man's followers. There was nowhere she could turn, there was no one she could turn to. The certainty of the accomplishment of what she dreaded crushed her with its surety. All power of action was gone. She could only wait and suffer in the complete moral collapse that overwhelmed her, and that was rendered greater by her peculiar temperament. Her body was aching with the grip of his powerful arms, her mouth was bruised with his savage kisses.[28]

Diana, it might be said, protests too much because in this situation, displacement and disavowal provide a way for Hull to write a sex scene without having to put her proxy (she used to call herself Diana, Melman tells us) in the socially and culturally risky role of initiator. In the place of the captive and ravished heroine, the woman under patriarchy can commit immodest acts without having to compromise her own modesty and status.

This binary split between active hero and passive heroine reso-nates with the tones of contemporary (and continuing) ideologies of masculinity that posit untrained masculinity as a kind of perpetual and potentially devastating sexual boiling-over and gives Achmed to us as a hyperbolic caricature of manliness, all the while his marked racial identity disavows this connection to a white norm. The way that sexual violence and the realm of erotic fantasy is then displaced and mapped onto a racial Other is well articulated by Frantz Fanon in 1952's *Black Skin, White Masks*: "for the majority of white men the Negro represents the sexual instinct (in its raw state)," "the incarnation of a genital potency beyond all moralities and prohibitions," "the keeper of the impalpable gate that opens into the realm of orgies, of bacchanals, of delirious sexual sensations."[29]

From this perspective, using an Arab rapist as a way to portray the violent eruption of desire constitutes the most immediate and literal translation of racist stereotypes where, as Ella Shohat explains, images of black and Arab men and women in "heat" are habitually juxtaposed with naturally "frigid" white women. By this logic, as she points out, a white woman's sex with an Arab or a black man can only be rape because she cannot possibly desire him, and he cannot possibly *not* desire her.[30] Achmed articulates this "inevitability" with characteristic bluntness: "'Little fool,' he said with a deepening smile. 'Better me than my men.'"[31]

In Hull's novel, Diana's imminent ravishment is given to us as inevitable very early in the narrative when one of her rebuffed suitors tries to tactfully explain why a young white woman should not be traveling alone in the desert: "It isn't safe," protests Arbuthnot, while musing on how Diana "seemed to be totally unaware that it was her youth and beauty that made all the danger of the expedition."[32] Gentlemanly taboo means that Arbuthnot has to fall back on the nonsexual to give what the narration explicitly calls "the easier excuse"—"there seems to be unrest amongst some of the tribes. There have been a lot of rumors lately."[33] The inevitability of sex in the desert is signaled through yet another orientalist trope where the desert becomes a double for a seduced female body "welcoming her softly with the faint rustle of the whispering sand, the mysterious charm of its billowy, shifting surface that seemed beckoning to her to penetrate further and further into its unknown obscurities."[34] Diana's intense longings are given to us as yet another signal that she doesn't know what she *really* wants.

In order to perpetuate Diana Mayo's virtuous frigidity, she is shown not only to be subject to desire despite herself, but an accidental object of desire too—"*Bon Dieu*! Do you know how beautiful you are?"—the Sheik exclaims.[35] Modleski's point that romantic novelists since Richardson's *Pamela* have faced the question of "how to get your heroine from loneliness and penury to romance and riches, without making her appear to have helped herself along or even to have thought about the matter" is equally applicable to the sexual economy of all the romance novels covered in this collection; Diana's irresistibility is figured by Hull as guileless to allow the conciliatory fantasy that if her suitors lose control of themselves, at least they are only usurped by aesthetics or by their own biology—they don't surrender control to the will of a woman.[36] Diana too re-codes desire as aesthetics when she argues with Arbuthnot about what we later know is the Sheik's singing:

> "You say you have no emotion in your nature, and yet that unknown man's singing has stirred you deeply. How do you reconcile the two?" he asked, almost angrily.
>
> "Is an appreciation of the beautiful emotion?" she challenged, with uplifted eyes.
>
> "Surely not. Music, art, nature, everything beautiful appeals to me. But there is nothing emotional in that. It is only that I prefer beautiful things to ugly ones. For that reason even pretty clothes appeal to me," she added, laughing (14).

This disavowal of the conventional pleasures of femininity is revealing; because erotic enslavement is couched in terms of Diana's discovery of "womanliness," there is a powerful sense throughout the novel that being a conventionally feminine woman marks a fall in status, authority, and freedom—'for the first time in her life she was of no account," "for the first time she had been made conscious of the inferiority of her sex," Hull writes.[37] All the way through the novel, the kinds of liberty Diana enjoys in the desert is marked in terms of manliness, and her masquerade in the signifiers of that manliness allow her a tentative appropriation of male freedom. The uninitiated Diana meets men as "a companion with whom I ride or shoot or fish; a pal, a comrade," only to have her position removed by the Sheik:

> It was an order from one who was prepared to compel his commands . . . that made her feel like a slave exposed for sale in a public market. She must take off the boyish clothes that somehow seemed to lend her courage and substitute, to gratify the whim of the savage in the next room.[38]

Although it offers some potential for action within a suppressive patriarchal system, painting female courage as a form of cross-dressing leaves the terms of the initial binary unchallenged. The extent to which the big game expeditions and grand desert tours that train Diana to dress in drag are meant to be read as a class privilege ("that her happiness was due to the wealth that had enabled her to indulge in the sports and constant travel that made up the sum total of her desires never occurred to her") suggests that the terms of Diana's submission should be most strongly felt as a fall in class, rather than as a fall into sexuality.[39] The Sheik keeps asking her whether she hates his kisses so much, but it is her "haughty" character as a daughter of Empire that refuses to allow her to entertain the question until it is too late for her to deny it. Diana sidesteps her own class in eventually wanting to die for love of a man she thinks is an Arab sheik, but even before his exposure as an Englishman the narration makes it clear that this is an exception to the rule: "she, proud Diana Mayo, who had the history of her race at her fingers' ends, who had gloried in the long line of upright men and chaste women, had no thankfulness in her heart that in her degradation she had been spared a crowning shame."[40]

The treatment of physical intimacy in *The Sheik* also implies that a violation of imperial politics is a far worse matter than the violation of sexual ones. Aside from the attention to bodily parts and acts, the greatest differences between *The Sheik* and its pornographic precursor, *The Lustful Turk*, are the *Lustful Turk's* obsession with virginity and the heroine's initial shame at the actual sexual act. Presumably, the cold tom-boy who has never been kissed also lost her virginity to the sheik, but *The Sheik's* modernity is in the fact that this doesn't seem to be an issue. In fact, there is one point where Diana sulks because the sheik doesn't seem to want sex with her any more: "He had never loved her, but now he did not even want her." Hull's novel relocates shame in what Achmed had "dared," that is, assumed the authority, to do:

> Only rage filled her—blind, passionate rage against the man who had dared to touch her, who had dared to lay his hands on her, and those hands the hands of a native. . . . No one had ever dared to touch her before. No one had ever dared to handle her as she was being handled now.[41]

Hull repeats this sense of fury in Sheik Ibrahim Omair's tent to emphasize that rape is an outrage against the racial hierarchy of Empire more than it is against women. Diana is given the authority to respond not by her courage, awareness of sexual threat, or mental strength, but by Empire: "She stared with all the haughtiness she could summon to her aid; she had learned her own power among the natives of India the previous year, and here in the desert there was only one Arab whose eyes did not fall beneath hers."[42]

Hull's best efforts throughout the novel, including, centrally, her extensive use of Orientalist tropes, are to ensure that erotic enslavement under a "native" does not destroy her status and class security in the eyes of the reader, and that sex with the Other is read as risky but not as *déclassé*. By transferring female desire and agency to the stereotype of the Eastern Sheik, Hull circumvents the codes of female modesty, while the reader recognizes that this is sexual fantasy because the Orientalist eroticization of the environment overwrites the heroine's denials and signals seduction, even as Diana protests. Anderson complains of Elinor Glyn's *Three Weeks* (the bestseller that inaugurated the use of the word "it" to mean sex appeal) that one of the novel's greatest immoralities is its "total dependence on luxurious aphrodisiac props to help along their nights of bliss"—"the boudoirs are turned into "bowers of roses," "elaborate meals are eaten, and rare wines drunk"— because love against the odds "seems, on its own, to be not strong enough to ensure sexual contentment."[43] "Eastern" stereotypes and scenery are used in *The Sheik* in a very similar manner, and here too there is no love to ensure any kind of contentment until two-thirds of the way through the novel. The convention of the heroine's naivety in the face of her own happy ending is signaled to the reader through the recurring cameos from exquisite oriental objects that had become objects of desire in their own lives: Persian rugs, silver-embroidered hangings, silk divans, bearskins, cigarettes, and coffee.

These luxuriously overdetermined settings transfer well to film because of their stagy quality, and here too, the *mise-en-scene* is an integral part of the fantasy, in fact, cinemas named The Alhambra and The Oriental suggested that the mythical east represented fantasy itself.[44] The way romances create a space in women's lives in which they can stop work and enjoy sensuous pleasure, seeps into the way that the novels map out sensuous spaces for their readers' imagination based on contemporary objects and scenarios of desire.[45] There is a very strange, almost metatextual, moment when Diana is abducted by Sheik Ibrahim where she becomes aware of the charge of this environment, but also where the distracting and disavowing nature of this setting becomes startlingly apparent. The robber chief has just wantonly killed one of his serving girls for a minor offense, and here, Hull has Diana switch registers:

Her eyes were glued to the still figure on the rug before her
with the gaping wound in the breast, from which the blood was
welling, staining the dark draperies of the woman's clothes, and
creeping slowly down to the rug on which the body lay. She was
dazed, and odd thoughts flitted through her mind. It was a pity,
she thought stupidly, that the blood should spoil the rug. It was
a lovely rug. She wondered what it would have cost in Biskra—
less, probably, than it would in London. Then she forgot the rug
as her eyes travelled upward to the woman's face. The mouth
was open and the streak of blood was drying, but it was the eyes,
protruding, agonised, that brought Diana abruptly to herself.[46]

Diana's earlier confusion between what the romance frames as her
erotic response to the Sheik's singing and what she asserts is pure
aesthetics is fairly understandable given that the slippage between
signals for beauty, otherness, and sexuality is consistent throughout
the book. That this beauty is on imperialist terms is pointed up by
the discourses of cleanliness, and indeed by the paleness of the hands
in the "Kasmiri Song," and also by the fact that the objects of desire
throughout the novel are made rare and expensive by their distance
from the East. In *The Poetics of Spice: Romantic Consumerism
and the Exotic*, Timothy Morton uses kitchen spice to explain how
this Orientalist discourse works to create fetishistic value in the
colonizer cultures. Although Morton's subject is Romanticism in the
canonical sense, his conclusions, I would argue, explain something
of the appeal of the middlebrow ornamentalism *The Sheik* draws so
heavily upon: "spice sensualises certain fantasies about the nature of
money and capital," he writes.[47] Through its sheer insubstantiality
and in the sweep of its movement across global trade routes, spice
"represents not only gem-like texture and erotic perfume, but flow
and liquidity as well"; spice—and Orientalist artefacts in the wider
sense, I would argue—gain their purchase on Western culture as "a
form of sexy money."[48]
The "complex double identification" that Laura Frost writes of,
where the reader is led to "identify with Diana while hoping, like
the sheik himself, for her fall into passion," works in part because
the implied reader or viewer isn't straightforwardly guided to enter
into Diana's naïve consciousness as her shadow and double, but is
instead invited through the signifiers of sexy, spicy money to multiply

her desire and invest emotional energy across the romantic scenario as a whole.[49] Where the content is as challenging to convention as *The Sheik's* story of a lone woman's adventure in the desert and her putatively interracial, premarital, passionate seduction, this splitting and multiplying of desires can be seen as a crucial part of the way these taboos become neutralized enough to become part of culture, while at the same time remaining risqué enough to harness the bestselling momentum of scandal. Racial and sexual stereotypes provide the charge for this scandal, and yet because of their denigration of women and Arab men as lower status characters, the sex isn't enough to hold the narrative to its romantic promise. Instead, the ornament of orientalism prompts us to *The Sheik's* read sexual violence counterintuitively, and the decoration of the Sheik with both a title and an English bloodline ensures that the romance of Arab and Aristocrat is rewritten to provide a happy ending that fits with both the erotics of property under patriarchy and the class logic of imperialism.

Bibliography

Anonymous. *The Lustful Turk*. Ware: Wordsworth, 1997.

Anderson, Rachel. *The Purple Heart Throbs: The Sub-Literature of Love.* London: Hodder and Stoughton, 1974.

Bernstein, Matthew and Gaylyn Studlar. *Visions of the East: Orientalism in Film.* London: I. B. Tauris, 1997.

Blake, Susan L. "What 'Race' is the Sheik?" In *Doubled Plots: Romance and History*, by Susan Strehle and Mary Pannicia Carden, 67–85. Jackson: University of Mississippi, 2003.

Burley, Stephanie. "Homoerotic Reading and Popular Romance" In *Doubled Plots: Romance and History,* Susan Strehle and Mary Paniccia Carden, Jackson: University Press of Mississippi, 2009.

Cannadine, David. *Ornamentalism: How the British saw their Empire.* London: Allen Lane, 2001.

Caton, Steven C. "The Sheik: Instabilities of Race and Gender in Transatlantic Popular Culture of the Early 1920s." In *Noble Dreams, Wicked Pleasures: Orientalism in America, 1870–1930*, by Holly Edwards, 99–119. Princeton: Princeton University Press, 2000.

Cohn, Jan. *Romance and the Erotics of Property: Mass-Market Fiction for Women.* Durham, NC: Duke University Press, 1988.

Edwards, Holly. "A Million and One Nights: Orientalism in America, 1870–1930." In *Noble Dreams, Wicked Pleasures: Orientalism in*

America, 1870–1930, by Holly Edwards, 99–119. Princeton: Princeton University Press, 2000.

Eisele, John C. "The Wild East: Deconstructing the Language of Genre in the Hollywood Eastern." *Cinema Journal* 41, 4 (2002), 68–94.

Fanon, Frantz. *Black Skin, White Masks*. Translated by Charles Lam Markmann. London: Pluto Press, 1986.

Frost, Laura. "The Romance of Cliche: E. M. Hull, D. H. Lawrence, and Interwar Erotic Fiction" In *Bad Modernisms*, ed. Douglas Mao and Rebecca L. Walkowitz. Durham, NC: Duke University Press, 2006.

Gargano, Elizabeth. "English Sheiks and Arab Stereotypes: E. M. Hull, T. E. Lawrence, and the Imperial Masquerade." *Texas Studies in Literature and Language* 48, 2 (Summer 2006), 171–86.

Hull, Edith M. *The Sheik*. Philadelphia: Pine Street Books, 2000.

Lant, Antonia. "The Curse of the Pharoh, or How Cinema Contracted Egyptomania." In *Visions of the East: Orientalism in Film*, by Matthew Bernstein and Gaylyn Studlar, 69–98. London: I.B. Tauris, 1997.

MacKenzie, John MacDonald. *Orientalism: History, Theory and the Arts*. Manchester: Manchester University Press, 1995.

McClintock, Anne. "Soft-Soaping Empire: Commodity Racism and Imperial Advertising." In *Travellers' Tales: Narratives of Home and Displacement*, by George Robertson, Melinda Mash, Lisa Tickner, Jon Bird, Barry Curtis and Tim Putnam, 131–54. New York: Routledge, 1994.

Melman, Billie. *Women and the Popular Imagination in the Twenties: Flappers and Nymphs*. Basingstoke: Macmillan, 1988.

Modleski, Tania. *Loving with a Vengeance: Mass-Produced Fantasies for Women*. London: Routledge, 1990.

Morton, Timothy. *The Poetics of Spice: Romantic Consumerism and the Exotic*. Cambridge: Cambridge University Press, 2000.

Radway, Janet. *Reading the Romance: Women, Patriarchy, and Popular Literature*. Chapel Hill: University of North Carolina Press, 1991.

Raub, Patricia. "Issues of Passion and Power in E. M. Hull's The Sheik." *Women's Studies: An Interdisciplinary Journal* 21, 1 (1992), 119–28.

Shaheen, Jack G. *Reel Bad Arabs: How Hollywood Villifies a People*. Moreton-in-Marsh: Arris Books, 2003.

Sielke, Sabine. *Reading Rape: The Rhetoric of Sexual Violence in American Literature and Culture, 1790–1990*. Princeton: Princeton University Press, 1990.

Wintle, Sarah. "The Sheik: What Can Be made of a Daydream." *Women: A Cultural Review* 7, 3 (1996), 291–302.

Yoshihara, Mari. *Embracing the East: White Women and American Orientalism*. New York: Oxford University Press, 2003.

Notes

1 Holly Edwards, "A Million and One Nights: Orientalism in America, 1870–1930," in *Noble Dreams, Wicked Pleasures: Orientalism in America, 1870–1930* (Princeton: Princeton University Press, 2000) 18.

2 Edwards, *Noble Dreams*, 18.

3 Billie Melman, *Women and the Popular Imagination in the Twenties: Flappers and Nymphs* (Basingstoke: Macmillan, 1988) 46.

4 Mari Yoshihara, *Embracing the East: White Women and American Orientalism* (New York: Oxford University Press, 2003) 30.

5 Melman, *Women and the Popular Imagination*, 47; Yoshihara, *Embracing the East*, 35.

6 Sarah Wintle, "The Sheik: What Can Be made of a Daydream," *Women: A Cultural Review* 7:3 (1996) 294; Edwards, *Noble Dreams*, 204.

7 Jack G. Shaheen, *Reel Bad Arabs: How Hollywood Villifies a People* (Moreton-in-Marsh: Arris Books, 2003) 425.

8 See Melman, *Women and the Popular Imagination*, 91–2.

9 E. M. Hull, *The Sheik* (Philadelphia: Pine Street Books, 2000) 56.

10 Hull, *The Sheik*, 294; 296.

11 Hull, *The Sheik*, 133–4.

12 Hull, *The Sheik*, 158.

13 Hull, *The Sheik*, 159, 171.

14 David Cannadine, *Ornamentalism: How the British saw their Empire* (London: Allen Lane, 2001) 8.

15 Hull, *The Sheik*, 182.

16 Hull, *The Sheik*, 219. Indeed one might see this splitting of Orientalist stereotypes at work in Hosseini's *The Kite Runner* (see Georgiana Banita's chapter in this collection) where Hassan, the absolutely "good" oriental who performs his servant's duties consistently selflessly, is raped by Assef, the "bad," sociopathic, oriental who believes in the savageries of Nazi doctrine. Diana, at least, has moments of rebellion—Hassan, happy in his class-based servitude, has none.

17 Hull, *The Sheik*, 68.

18 Hull, *The Sheik*, 172.

19 Susan L. Blake, "What 'Race' is the Sheik?" In *Doubled Plots: Romance and History*, by Susan Strehle and Mary Pannicia Carden (Jackson: University of Mississippi, 2003) 69.

20 Blake, "What 'Race' is the Sheik?," 74.

21 Cannadine, *Ornamentalism*, 122.

22 Cannadine, *Ornamentalism*, 122.

23 John M. MacKenzie, *Orientalism: History, Theory and the Arts* (Manchester: Manchester University Press, 1995) 55.

24 Radway, Janice, *Reading the Romance: Women, Patriarchy, and Popular Literature* (Chapel Hill: University of North Carolina Press, 1991) 143.

25 Jan Cohn, *Romance and the Erotics of Property: Mass-Market Fiction for Women* (Durham, NC: Duke University Press, 1988) 20.

26 Tania Modleski, *Loving with a Vengeance: Mass-Produced Fantasies for Women* (London: Routledge, 1990) 41.

27 Rachel Anderson, *The Purple Heart Throbs: The Sub-Literature of Love* (London: Hodder and Stoughton, 1974) 189.

28 Hull, *The Sheik*, 59.

29 Frantz Fanon, *Black Skin, White Mask,* translated by Charles Lam Markmann (London: Pluto Press, 1986) 177.

30 Matthew Bernstein and Gaylyn Studlar, *Visions of the East: Orientalism in Film* (London: I.B. Tauris, 1997) 42.

31 Hull, *The Sheik*, 90.

32 Hull, *The Sheik*, 9.

33 Hull, *The Sheik*, 9.

34 Hull, *The Sheik*, 24

35 Hull, *The Sheik*, 80.

36 Modleski, *Loving with a Vengeance*, 49.

37 Hull, *The Sheik*, 91.

38 Hull, *The Sheik*, 11; 81

39 Hull, *The Sheik*, 39.

40 Hull, *The Sheik*, 275

41 Hull, *The Sheik*, 53.

42 Hull, *The Sheik*, 21.

43 Anderson, *The Purple Heart Throbs*, 128.

44 See Antonia Lant, "The Curse of the Pharoh, or How Cinema Contracted Egyptomania," in Bernstein and Studlar, 93.

45 See Stephanie Burley, "Homoerotic Reading and Popular Romance" in Strehle and Carden, *Doubled Plots*, 136.

46 Hull, *The Sheik*, 221.

47 Timothy Morton, *The Poetics of Spice: Romantic Consumerism and the Exotic* (Cambridge: Cambridge University Press, 2000) 36.

48 Morton, *The Poetics of Spice*, 90.

49 Laura Frost, "The Romance of Cliche: E. M. Hull, D. H. Lawrence, and Interwar Erotic Fiction" in *Bad Modernisms*, ed. Douglas Mao and Rebecca L. Walkowitz (Durham, NC: Duke University Press, 2006) 111; 100.

10

Small change? Emily Post's *Etiquette* (1922–2012)

Grace Lees-Maffei

In the contemporary book market, nonfiction genres such as biography and self-help command considerable sales,[1] yet "bestseller" is still a term primarily associated with fiction (the nature of that fiction is explored in this book).[2] This chapter examines a nonfiction text which has been a bestseller for nine decades, and the preeminent example of American advice literature, Emily Post's *Etiquette*. In catering to the social needs and aspirations of its readers, *Etiquette* has *described* as well as *prescribed* US social interaction and is, therefore, a useful tool in calibrating the changing nature of the American dream. Succeeding members of the Post family have renewed the book's content and thereby ensured its continued popularity. By examining these processes of change—of authorship and content—this chapter shows how nonfiction bestsellers maintain and rejuvenate their markets in a manner quite distinct from the majority of bestsellers which are relatively unchanging works of fiction, bound up with their original authors.

Etiquette, self-help, and America

Collectively, the successive editions of *Etiquette*[3] form perhaps the best-known American example of the group of etiquette and manners guides, which can be understood as a small subsection of a larger cultural category, self-help, which is in turn a highly commercially successful strand of the nonfiction market, along with lifestyle genres including cookbooks, biography and reference titles, and textbooks on a range of subjects. Self-help has a long history in the United States, with roots in the chapbooks exchanged by settlers, which combined fairy tales with sermons with a guiding purpose.[4] But while etiquette shares with spiritual literature a concern for doing what is right and good, and the processes of compassion and judgment, it is principally a civil practice concerned with impression management in the social world rather than the next world, the here and now rather than the hereafter.

Etiquette has two basic functions, more and less benign: its codes are intended to regulate social interaction to achieve a smooth and considerate result, and to provide a framework within which to judge others. In pursuing the interpersonal aims of courtesy, hospitality, and ease, etiquette writers have much to say about the things with which we surround ourselves, from the clothes we wear, and the way we decorate our homes, to the accoutrements of home entertaining. Etiquette writers, therefore, share many concerns with the authors of the larger swathe of didactic literature which aims to assist Americans in almost every sphere of life, from the decorating and lifestyle books which invite readers to express their identities through a particular assemblage and use of consumer goods (e.g. Elsie de Wolfe's classic *The House in Good Taste*), to the self-help manuals which suggest ways of managing our personal relationships and love lives (such as Alex Comfort's infamous *The Joy of Sex*), to the guides to home entertaining which encourage us to undertake the social and domestic labor of opening our homes and kitchens to friends and family (for instance, Martha Stewart's launch pad *Entertaining*).[5] All are united in the provision of commodities—books—which can be purchased and read as a way of furthering a sense of self, of who we are and who we *want* to be. Richard Ohmann has made a connection between the discrete areas upon which advice literature has fastened: "Together, manners and material culture partially unveil for our contemplation a style and an ethos well suited to the aspirations of middle class people in growing industrial and commercial cities." The "work in tandem" of the advertising industry and "magazine entrepreneurs" has accelerated the "tight linkage of social identity with the purchase and use of commodities, including cultural products."[6]

As the preeminent etiquette guide and one of the most popular advice books in the United States', and indeed global, publishing history, Post's *Etiquette* has played a key role in the development of specifically American manners.[7] The content and success of *Etiquette* provide evidence of a society that, while theoretically classless—or at least largely homogenized into a self-identified and broadly defined middle class—is practically well-versed in reading subtle delineations of class codes from mien, gesture, expression, and behavior, as well as dress, accessories, and possessions.[8] Post's *Etiquette* has serviced an aspirational need in US society for guidance on integration and upward-mobility. Clearly, aspiration is not a uniquely American quality, but the popularity of commoditized advice within the United States market is symptomatic of an American dream of self-improvement, and *Etiquette* provides a preeminent case study for reading its American form.

Both the self-help genre and its main market, the middle class, have roots in Victorian Britain,[9] yet the self-help genre merits serious scholarly attention as a route to understanding more about specifically *American* aspirations. Sue Currell has critiqued the role of self-help in educating servants of American capitalism, primarily during the Great Depression, both within and beyond the United States,[10] while for Micki McGee, the "self-fulfillment and self-improvement" promised by self-help authors are perceived as "an antidote to economic uncertainty."[11] Sandra K. Dolby observes that, both domestically and overseas, "people do associate the genre with America. Most of the authors are American, and evidently so are most of the readers." However, self-help is not taken seriously: "Many people seem embarrassed by the fact that self-help books are so popular in America."[12]

In recent years, self-help has been the subject of several polemical critiques. Business studies professor Paul Damien has accused self-help authors of misrepresenting research and manipulating buzzwords for profit. For Steve Salerno, the buoyancy of the self-help market exemplifies its inefficacy: if self-help books worked, the afflicted reader would need only one book rather than the succession of titles typically consumed by the self-help addict. Conversely, Dolby argues, readers keep on buying self-help books to "reinforce their optimism," "they allow these books to mediate between the values of the culture . . . and their personal values. Through the process of reading self-help books, readers 'experience' abstract American culture concretely, personally."[13] Both etiquette books and self-help guides, market constantly updated solutions, and also assert their authoritative status and shed light on American ideals. Notwithstanding their shared concerns, recent attempts to better understand the significance of self-help have ignored etiquette.[14] And, while several sociological studies have examined etiquette's underlying significance, it has been overlooked by literary scholars. This is perhaps a result of its perceived low literary value: even Elias called advice "worthless as literature."[15] A contribution of this chapter, therefore, is an examination of the preeminent American etiquette book within the contexts of self-help and the American bestseller.

From Post to Posts

Emily Post's early biography foregrounds the importance of class and gender to the genesis and content of her *Etiquette*. Her conformism to, and deviation from, patterns of upper-class respectability informed the advice she set out in her book. Emily Price was the daughter of architect Bruce Price, who designed the exclusive Tuxedo Park residential area where Post partly grew up.[16] Her early life followed an upper-class pattern, with a private education followed by a season as a debutante and marriage to a banker Edwin Post. However, her divorce from him in 1906 signaled a departure from convention, even as it anticipated the later normality of divorce. In another unusual step for a woman of her social standing, Post made the (questionable) claim that she wrote from financial necessity.[17] Her journalism appeared in national titles such as *McCall's*, *Harper's*, and *Vanity Fair*, and she published five novels between 1904 and 1910.[18] In 1915, Post was again in the vanguard when she "drove" from New York to San Francisco for a series of articles for *Collier's Magazine* (later published as a book, *By Motor to the Golden Gate*) before cars and passable roads had become integral features of American society.[19]

Post's defining book was *Etiquette in Society, in Business, in Politics, and at Home* of 1922. Her account of the book's genesis, disseminated in her son's biography *Truly Emily Post*, was that Frank

Crowninshield, editor of *Vanity Fair* magazine and Richard Duffy, an editor at Funk & Wagnalls, persuaded her to write the book and that only the inadequacy of a competing title convinced her to do so.[20] By 1922, Post was a 51-year-old "society matron"; historian Arthur Schlesinger suggested that her *Etiquette* was motivated by a desire to preserve the social codes in which she had been schooled.[21] However, Post had been writing advice for magazines since 1911 at which point she had proposed an advice book to her agent.[22] In fact, Post's fictionalized version of events better resembles the development of 18-year-old New York advertising copywriter Lillian Eichler's *Book of Etiquette* (1921) which was written at her publisher's suggestion following customer complaints about the outdated nature of Emily Holt's *Everyman's Encyclopedia of Etiquette* of 1901, which Eichler had been marketing.[23]

Eichler's and Post's books were both bestsellers. Post's book reached number one in the 1923 nonfiction bestseller list and number four the following year. Because Eichler's book sold more than a million copies from the first edition of 1921 up to 1945, it was thought to better suit contemporary needs than Post's *Etiquette*, which sold two-thirds of a million copies during the same period.[24] However, in part due to Post's capitulation on the issue of chaperonage and other symptoms of modernity, discussed below, the longevity of her text distinguishes it from competing titles. Amy Vanderbilt's *Complete Book of Etiquette* (1952) sold 900,000 copies in its first half year and enjoyed four editions in the first five years,[25] but along with Frances Benton's *Etiquette*, which reached number 4 in 1956, Post's book was the only etiquette guide in the *Publisher's Weekly* general nonfiction bestseller lists during the twentieth century. Post's book is well represented in contemporary bestselling etiquette lists, as the 75th Anniversary edition (1997) was followed by the 17th edition of 2004 and the 18th edition of 2011.[26] Today, Eichler is best known for her spiritual titles, whereas Post's name has become synonymous with etiquette."[27] Post's *Etiquette* featured in the 1998 Celebrate the Century USPS stamps series, along with Margaret Mitchell's 1936 bestseller *Gone with the Wind*, Dr Seuss's *The Cat in the Hat* and achievements including the first flight, the polio vaccine, and the moon landings.[28] Emily Post's increasing influence is reflected in the occasional changes to the title of her *Etiquette*. The 1922 and 1927 editions had the full title *Etiquette in Society, in Business, in Politics and at Home*. From 1928, the title changed to *Etiquette: "the Blue Book of Social Usage*," with the inverted commas indicating a common moniker for the book; the term "blue book" denoted definitive information, following the output of Automobile Blue Book Company.[29] A later title *Emily Post's Etiquette* referred to the original author even while the work of revising and writing was increasingly distributed among family members.

In addition to overseeing ten editions (in 90 printings) of *Etiquette,* Post wrote the comedic *How to Behave though a Debutante: Opinions by Muriel as Overheard by Emily Post* (1928); *Letters We Write* (1935); *Children are People* (1940); *The Emily Post Cook Book*, with her son Edwin (1949) and a pamphlet, *Motor Manners* (1950). Post's fame was extended from 1931 when she broadcast etiquette advice on the radio and wrote a syndicated daily newspaper column. In 1946, 51 years before Martha Stewart Living Omnimedia was launched, Post founded the Emily Post Institute partly to help answer the extensive correspondence she received from readers and also to train assistants to continue her work. Described on the flyleaf of the 18th edition of *Etiquette* as "one of America's most unique family businesses," the Emily Post Institute represents a model of American enterprise, branding the name, signature, and authority of the late Emily Post in books, TV and radio broadcasts, blogs, films, and live events such as seminars.

Following Post's death in 1960, The Emily Post Institute has extended the production of *Etiquette* and its bestseller status, beyond the life of its original author. From 1965 to 1995, granddaughter-in-law Elizabeth L. Post (1920–2010) oversaw five editions of *Etiquette*, revising Emily's text for the 11th and subsequent editions, and writing the 14th edition, *Emily Post's Etiquette*.[30] The mantle was passed to great-granddaughter-in-law Peggy Post, wife of Allen Post, who wrote the 16th and 17th editions. The 18th edition of *Emily Post's Etiquette* (2011) subtitled "Manners for a New World," is dedicated to "all of our mothers who have made this book possible." This new book was "led" by Peggy Post, and "welcomes a new generation of Posts—Anna Post, Lizzie Post, and Daniel Post Senning—the great-great-grandchildren of Emily Post." Among this fourth generation, Peter Post's daughter Lizzie Post has written a book *How Do You Work This Life Thing?* (2007) aimed at 18–25-year-olds, and Anna Post has written *Emily Post's*

Wedding Parties (2007), and an erstwhile blog, "What Would Emily Post Do?" recalling in name if not in content, the perennial question "What Would Jesus Do?"[31] Additional Emily Post Institute products for business users and men have been overseen by Emily's great-grandson Peter Post, and great-granddaughter Cindy Post Senning (Ed.D) has written books for children and teens with Peggy Post, while at least two films have used Post's writing.[32] *Etiquette* is not only a bestseller, it is also dynastic if not matriarchal. The production of *Etiquette* replicates the passing down of advice through the generations common to most families, a process integral to the generative structuralism developed by historical sociologist and preeminent scholar of manners, Norbert Elias, and later by sociologist Pierre Bourdieu, to understand the mechanics of social change.[33]

Changes of authorship have enabled a single bestseller to grow into a multimedia brand, with many related authors producing a range of products and services for distinct target markets. The Emily Post Institute perpetuates Post as a Betty Crocker-style figurehead[34] for a range of products, both present and not present, authenticating but inauthentic; Betty Crocker products use Crocker's invented "signature" just as the successive editions of *Etiquette* carry Post's signature, a registered trademark of The Emily Post Institute and a personal assurance of quality, integrity, and authority. However, Emily Post's *Etiquette* is now written by a family group of four authors: the 18th edition of 2011 adds to the authority of one woman, earned and reinforced over 90 years, the authority of the committee of collaborating authors each contributing her or his different expertise.

A new *Etiquette* for a new century?

Two of the most influential etiquette books of the American twentieth century, Eichler's and Post's, appeared within a year of one another. In 1946, Historian Arthur M. Schlesinger retrospectively described these titles as "a new etiquette for a new era."[35] More recently, sociologist Jorge Arditi has followed Schlesinger in asserting that Post's and Eichler's books not only brought "a breath of fresh air to a rather suffocating situation" but also restored "the connection between manners and the structures of social life at the time."

Arditi makes the qualification that "it was only in comparison to the turn-of-the-century manuals that Post's and Eichler's seemed to involve a discontinuous transformation. From a longer historical perspective, they involved a continuation of a process that began much earlier."[36] Etiquette manuals of the 1920s responded to World War I, expanded immigration into the United States and—as we can see retrospectively—the conditions which led to the Great Depression and later World War II. Post's and Eichler's books serviced a desire for self-improvement in a shifting social framework and a challenging employment market. They bear comparison, therefore, with Dale Carnegie's 1936 *How to Win Friends and Influence People* of 1936, a manual of how to get ahead in the depression-era workplace.[37] Joan Shelley Rubin has characterized the interwar market as "less deferential and more enamored of business than its nineteenth-century counterpart."[38] For Rubin, "the post-World War I era tended to buttress, rather than to erode, the ideology of culture as it has evolved throughout the nineteenth century," while between 1920 and 1930, a growing book market was supported by prosperity, increased leisure time, the doubling of both college graduates and high school enrollments, and literary and educational radio broadcasting.[39]

In fact, a sense of a new era needing a new etiquette has been a constant feature of advice publishing.[40] The sense of perpetual change expressed in advice literature, on behalf of readers, has sustained a robust publishing industry, in which each new title attempts to respond more effectively to current need. Etiquette discourse in America has shifted in form and content, from the sermons published in seventeenth-century chapbooks to the autodidactic films available on YouTube, and from guidance on how to treat servants to online chat room etiquette. This combination of a constantly changing social and economic context and an oscillation between *describing* and *prescribing* makes advice literature, self-help discourse and, specifically, etiquette books, sensitive tools for the analysis of social ideals and their written expression. Continual reinvention aims to avoid dismissal of etiquette as old-fashioned and irrelevant to contemporary social and business. In his monumental study of magazines, *Selling Culture*, Richard Ohmann acknowledged that: "Granted, etiquette books may be a genre of utopian dreaming more than of ethnography" but their profusion suggests a "preoccupation with gentility among middle class people."[41] Advice books bear no

more relation to lived experience than do magazine articles, radio
broadcasts, and novels, and yet each has much to tell the cultural
historian about past ideals and the development of the American
dream.[42]

Ironically, it was Post's willingness to change her advice in response
to the conditions of modernity which ensured her bestselling book's
definitive status. Historical sociologist Norbert Elias argued that by
reading published advice produced over the long term—the Annales
School's *longue durée*—we perceive broader social changes. We can
infer, argued Elias, that points of advice which were once included
and are now omitted from etiquette books have been internalized
by society and no longer need stating. This runs the risk of
oversimplification; some points of advice which we might regard as
unwritten rules of commonsense occasionally make their way into
published advice. For example, a reviewer of the 18th edition cited
the following point of advice as indicative of a tendency to state
the obvious: "'Use caution going around the corners of buildings
to avoid a collision with someone coming round the other way'.
Roger that." However, numerous changes have been made to the
structure and content of *Etiquette* over its 90 years in print, with
additions, excisions, and omissions each giving the careful reader
pause for thought. Far from being definitive, *Etiquette* is a work
under continual revision. Its historical value is best revealed when
the various editions of *Etiquette* are read retrospectively and
comparatively.[43]

When compared with the starting point of the 1922 edition,
textual changes introduced by 1940 include restaurant etiquette,
"Manners for Motorists"; "Modern Exactions of Courtesy" (on
smoking, radios, punctuality, telephones, and socializing when ill),
which is reduced to "Etiquette for the Smoker" by 1960; "What we
contribute to the beauty of living" (on neighborliness, in-laws and
sending flowers); "American Neighborhood Customs" and "Saying
'No' to Cocktails." These are carried forward largely unchanged
into the 1960 edition, with the further addition of a penultimate
chapter "The Flag of the United States." In the 14th edition of 1984,
Elizabeth L. Post responds to two trends which have "profoundly
affected modern society and our manners": "Your Professional
Life" deals with the increasing numbers of women working outside
the home and "Your Personal Life" examines, among other issues,
the social status of single people.[44] The 2004 edition adopts a

completely different structure organized around nine parts including, in addition to those already mentioned, "Everyday Etiquette," "Communication and Protocol," "Celebrations and Ceremonies," "Weddings," "You and Your Job" and "Travel and Leisure." This leads to a radically different sequence for approximately 50 (sometimes retitled) chapters which appear in earlier editions. For example, part two, "Relationships," juxtaposes topics which were previously compartmentalized within a sequence of chapters that progressed with increasing intimacy from introductions, and social engagements, to dating, engagements, weddings, christenings, funerals, etiquette for children and travel, akin to a theoretical life course. "Relationships" thereby draws connections, unacknowledged in previous editions, between dating, neighborliness, illnesses, and domestic staff, recognizing that appropriate communication is at the heart of ostensibly discrete areas of our lives, however intimate or functional and emphasizing the interpersonal skills which are the stock-in-trade of self-help books. The 2011 edition clusters eight parts into three groups concerning "Etiquette Every Day," "Life in the Workplace," "Life Stages and Special Times" plus a reference section, "Resources." Social networking technologies are foregrounded wherever possible: Part III "Communication and Technology" deals with conversation, letters, titles, telephone manners, personal communication devices and computers, while Part IV has a chapter "Social Networking" and Part VIII, "Weddings" considers the benefits and drawbacks of smartphones and emails, social networking sites, and wedding websites.[45]

The most famous change Post made to her *Etiquette* concerns chaperonage. Post's 1922 chapter "The Chaperon and Other Conventions" was revised in 1936 as "The Vanishing Chaperon and Other Lost Conventions." The 1922 edition states that while the most effective chaperon is a girl's own sense of ethics, accompaniment by an actual chaperon is usually necessary for propriety. By 1940, Post accepts "Today's Reversal of Yesterday's Precepts"; among "Proprieties That Have Been Repealed," are girls and young women acting as hostesses without chaperones.[46] As a successful debutante, Post had herself benefited from chaperonage and her retreat on this issue has been deemed wistful.[47] One reviewer described the second edition as "'putting a kick in etiquette to pacify flaming youth.'"[48] Post admitted that readers' letters informed the revision and the 1940 edition includes "Answers to Readers' Questions" in which she responds directly to changing attitudes and displays her own up-to-date opinions: "I have an enormous sympathy and liking for what I should call the 'typical moderns' of the young generation. I like their honesty of outlook, their complete frankness (if given a chance to be frank)."[49] In the tenth edition of 1960, the questions and answers have been cut and the chapter has been renamed again, as "The Chaperon and Her Modern Counterparts." Post maintains that "there are still a few situations in which a genuine chaperon is required" but "parental *training* has largely taken the place of the chaperon's *protection*."[50] Girls wishing to decline the advances of men who have accompanied them home after a party are, in 1940, told to say "Sorry! It's against rules. Good night" whereas in 1960, the line is "Sorry, another time . . . good night."[51] The 1940 chapter, "The Vanishing Chaperon" is preceded by a chapter "Popularity, Fraternity House Party and Commencement" and followed with "Modern Man and Girl"; in 1960, these have been retitled "At College" and "Dating" with a brevity characteristic of the later text, which addresses largely the same structure of chapters within 671 pages rather than the 893 pages of the 1940 edition. By 2004, the chaperone has neither chapter nor an entry in the index, but in a simplified structure which groups 48 chapters into nine parts, one part is devoted to "Children and Teens" with reader questions and answers reinstated. Chaperones are mentioned here in relation to high school proms and graduation parties and "parents, while they're still chauffeuring for teens, should make sure that these courtesies are observed."[52] In the 18th edition of 2011, the chaperone is absent from the main text and the index, but she is mentioned in the prefatory "note to readers":

Long gone are the 1st edition chaperone and the 12th edition ashtrays at the dinner table and white gloves; they have been replaced by topics that have relevance to the daily lives of most Americans today, such as managing new communications forums and devices, having confidence at work, and navigating new family structures and dynamics.[53]

This sampling above shows a gradual response to a changing social situation, rather than an about-face. Post accommodated social changes attendant upon modernity while also continuing to uphold what she regarded as fundamental etiquette.

Aside from the much-discussed issue of chaperonage, countless other changes to the successive editions of *Etiquette* have responded to broader social change. Post's biographer Laura Claridge notes the difference one word can make, as the 1922 section "One's Position in the Community" became, in 1927 "Making One's Position in the Community."[54] Post's 1922 *Etiquette* infamously assumed a staffed household—even the section "Dinner-Giving with Limited Equipment" presupposed the assistance of cook, waitress, and chambermaid—whereas by 1940, a social shift toward unstaffed households is recognized and by 2004, readers wishing to host a very formal dinner are adviced to hire staff.[55] Both the treatments of chaperonage, and the changing role of the hostess, suggest greater dynamism in the prescribed roles for women than for men, although this impression may be skewed by the extent to which etiquette books, and domestic advice books more generally, dwell on women's roles to the near exclusion of those for men, because women are associated with the home and its labor, whether emotional or physical, and represent the main market for etiquette and self-help books. Post's *Etiquette* has remained a perennial bestseller as much by responding to, and describing, current practice as by anticipating, or prescribing, future practice. Post and her successors have told readers what is *done* as well as what *to do*. Historian of American manners, Gerald Carson, neatly summarized the paradox: "Mrs. Post's text was under constant revision for years, for she was astute enough to follow in order that she might lead."[56]

Changing form

Over the 90 years of *Etiquette*, the book's form has changed along with its content. Post's approach to writing advice drew on her experience as a novelist, as well as her journalism. *Etiquette* is dedicated: "To you my friends whose identity in these pages is veiled in fictional disguise." Those members of Post's social circle who opened the pages of *Etiquette*—it was not intended for them, as they had no need for Post's guidance—would have read the book as much as a *roman à clef* than a manual of manners. Post's 1922 chapter on "Formal Dinners" describes Mrs. Worldly ordering "her secretary to invite the Oldworlds, the Eminents, the Learneds, the Wellborns, the Highbrows, and the Onceweres":

It will not do to ask the Bobo Gildings, not because of the difference in age but because Lucy Gilding smokes like a furnace and is miserable unless she can play bridge for high stakes, and, just as soon as she can bolt through dinner, sit at a card table; while Mrs. Highbrow and Mrs. Oncewere quite possibly disapprove of women's smoking and are surely horrified at "gambling." . . . So she ends by adding her own friends the Kindharts and the Normans, who "go" with everyone. . . . The endeavor of a hostess, when seating her table, is to put those together who are likely to be interesting to each other. Professor Bugge might bore *you* to tears, but Mrs. Entomoid would probably delight in him; just as Mr. Stocksan Bonds and Mrs. Rich would probably have interests in common.[57]

Claridge has suggested that "Emily created vivid fictional characters in her own text" in order to "appear at least among the minor league of the day's novelists" with some success: writer Gertrude Atherton judged that *Etiquette* read "like a fine high-society novel."[58]

Jorge Arditi has written persuasively of a transformation in the discourse of etiquette from narrative treatises to reference books, from discussions of ethics to lists of pointers, as associated with a shift from character to "decentred" personality.[59] In the case of *Emily Post's Etiquette*, we might apply this notion of decentered personality not only to the conduct recommended but also to its authorship, as Emily's original work on the book was subsequently distributed among several of her descendents. But while Arditi recognizes that Post's 1922 *Etiquette* has narrative qualities, the fact that she *continued* to use fictionalized vignettes that were both episodic and intertextual is overlooked. Post's character "Mrs. Three-in-One" was developed for the 1927 edition in response to reader's questions and personal observation and attained a life beyond the pages of *Etiquette*—akin to that of the eponymous Mrs. Grundy—by appearing in an eponymous chapter in later editions, at a dessert bridge party in another chapter and also in *The Personality of the House*. Appropriately, Post herself has enjoyed the same intertextual status as Mrs. Grundy, as exemplified on the pages of other advice books: in 1937, Betty Allen and Mitchell Pirie Briggs cautioned teenagers "Those who gobble and grab are not Emily Posted."[60] She became known for a Bunyanesque tendency to enliven her advice by giving her "characters" allegorical names appropriate to their behavior such as "Mrs. Stranger," "Mrs. Kindhart," and "Mrs. Oldname," and the continuance of this strategy was remarked upon even in 1970, 10 years after Post's death.[61] By using character names, Post imbues her advice with an additional layer of significance and we are able to read more into the situations so briefly sketched.

In maintaining a narrative approach to advice-giving during a period associated by Arditi with a wider shift from treatise to reference work, Post distinguished her work from that of other advice writers. Given this distinctive feature, and her unparalleled success, it is tempting to conclude that Post's narrative approach may have contributed to the bestseller status achieved by her *Etiquette*. In 1950, Funk and Wagnalls made cuts to "a few of the mise-en-scènes" and "Emily's Gilded Age loquaciousness" in spite of the praise earlier editions had garnered from luminaries such as Edmund Wilson and F. Scott Fitzgerald, with an underwhelming effect on sales.[62] The tenth edition of 1960 appeared in the year of Post's death, when her influence over the text was clear and she was still cited as the sole author. In it, we find numerous micronarratives. For example, the contents page offers a wealth of indicative subtitles for each portion of each chapter, as her for Chapter 3, "'How Do You Do?' – Greetings":

> Acknowledging Introductions – The Answer to "How Are You? – A Gentleman and His Hat in an Elevator – A Gentleman and His Hat out of Doors – A Gentleman Lifts His Hat – A Boy Takes Off His Hat – A Gentleman Removes His Glove – Personality of a Handshake – Greetings from Younger to Older – A Gentleman Rises – The Bow of Ceremony – The Informal Bow – The Bow of a Woman of Charm – Greetings in Public – The Intentional "Cut" – Greetings in Church – Taking Leave.[63]

The contents alone have narrative allusions, and the bare bones of a short story. In Chapter 43, "Longer Letters," Post provides an example under the heading "Proper Letters of Love or Affection":

> Instead of "Dear Jim" it perhaps begins "Dearest Jim," but not "Dearest!" Then follows all the news she can think of that might

possibly interest him – about the home team's new players, Betty and Tom's engagement, the political disagreement between two otherwise friendly neighbors, who won the horseshoe-pitching tournament, how many trout Bill Henderson got at Duck Brook . . . Probably she also tells him, "We all missed you at the picnic on Wednesday – Ollie made the flapjacks and they were too awful!" Or . . . *We all hope you'll be home in time for Carol's birthday. She has at last inveigled Mother into letter her have an all-black dress which we suspect was bought with the purpose of impressing you with her advanced age! Mother came in just as I wrote this and says to tell you she has a new recipe for chocolate cake that is even better than her old one. Laura will write you very soon, and we all send love, Affectionately (or Ever devotedly), Ruth.*[64]

When Elizabeth L. Post took up the mantle of revising and eventually rewriting Emily Post's *Etiquette,* she partly retained Emily's narrative approach and even reproduced portions of the 1922 text throughout the book. For example, Post's advice "When a Gentleman Takes off His Hat" is reproduced in facsimile in Elizabeth's 14th edition of 1984 and framed with a decorative border. Elizabeth also retained Post's narrative approach in her sample letters, although she dispensed with characteristic names.[65] By selectively adapting Emily Post's formal techniques, as well as some of her content, Elizabeth L. Post ensured continuity and maintained her audience. Emily Post's narrative approach enjoyed significant longevity before it was gradually abandoned by Peggy Post in accordance with the trend Arditi identified.

While domestic advice writers exercise authority over readers, by virtue of their expertise and pedagogic role, the bestseller status of Post's "Blue Book" means that readers' choices must be considered as significant. Sales figures alone demonstrate that Post's *Etiquette* received the popular vote if not the critical acclaim of readers; it met a need, provided readers with pleasure, or seemed like a good gift to buy for others. By continuing to buy Post's *Etiquette*, and by writing in turn to Emily, Elizabeth and Peggy Post, readers have enabled and contributed to the continual updating of its contents, which has in turn secured a continued market for the book.[66]

The nonfiction bestseller

In addition to USPS's *Celebrate the Century* stamp series, Post's *Etiquette* was included in another centennial celebration, the New York Public Library's 1995 exhibition *Books of the Century* along with other examples of bestselling nonfiction.[67] Like Post's *Etiquette*, Irma S. Rombauer's *The Joy of Cooking* (1931), Dale Carnegie's *How to Win Friends and Influence People* (1936), and Dr Benjamin Spock's *Common Sense Book of Baby and Child Care* (1946) are definitive works in their respective fields, influencing both readers and subsequent titles. Each has been a perpetual bestseller: Post's *Etiquette* is 90 and Rombauer's book is 80 years old, and both have enjoyed 75th anniversary editions and facsimile editions; Carnegie's is in its seventh decade and Spock's is in its sixth decade. Each text has been modified to suit changing social needs over several editions and multiple reprinting and Starker has identified paperback editions as contributing to the bestselling success of Carnegie's and Spock's books.[68] In all cases, the original author has been accompanied or superseded by members of her or his own family and several spin-off titles have been developed from each.[69] Rombauer's daughter Marion illustrated the first edition of *The Joy of Cooking*, and worked with her mother as joint author, taking over the authorship completely from 1955 to 1975 and handing the baton to her son, Ethan Becker, from 1976, while Ethan's son John is now involved in the *Joy* enterprise.[70] *The Joy of Cooking*'s byline is "Best Loved and Brand New," an oxymoron denoting a balance between tradition and novelty, description and prescription, maintained by bestselling advice literature. Dale Carnegie, who had been teaching adult communication course since 1912, and had published on public speaking, developed *How to Win Friends and Influence People* for publication in 1936. By 2008, it had sold 15 million copies.[71] Carnegie's second wife, Dorothy Carnegie, edited a volume of advice containing his writings in 1959 and his daughter, Donna Dale Carnegie, wrote *How to Win Friends and Influence People for Teen Girls*, published in 2005.[72] Authored with his wife Jane, Spock's *Common Sense Book of Baby and Child Care* was published in 1946 and the eighth edition appeared in 2004, by which point it had sold more than 50 million copies.[73] He later collaborated with his second wife, Mary Morgan.

Aside from the common characteristics of changing authorship through collaboration with family members and changing content produced in various new editions, the bestsellers by Rombauer, Carnegie, and Spock also share a publisher: Carnegie has been published by Simon and Schuster and Rombauer and Spock by Simon and Schuster imprints Scribner and Pocket Books, respectively. In addition, each has prompted rejoinders, *The Joy of Not Cooking, How to Lose Friends and Alienate People* and *What Dr. Spock Didn't Tell Us or A Survival Kit for Parents*, respectively.[74] Distinctively, Post produced *How to Behave Though a Debutante*, which was thought by contemporary critics to be a satire on her *Etiquette*.[75]

Like Post's *Etiquette*, these other titles of similar status in related fields—cooking, interpersonal skills, and child care—display the characteristics which distinguish nonfiction bestsellers from their fictional counterparts: distributed authorship and changing content over reeditions. Whereas these nonfiction bestsellers are characterized by changing authorship, fiction bestsellers are usually thought of as the creative output of one author, displaying recurrent thematic preoccupations and/or signature style, woven into her or his *oeuvre* and biography. And while the nonfiction bestsellers discussed here maintained their currency through successive revised editions, for the fiction bestseller, a standard text and veracity to an original manuscript are important. The long-term success of nonfiction bestsellers is not the result of individual genius, or even textual quality, but rather responsiveness, the freedom to change authorship and content as the need arises.

Conclusion

Etiquette books, like self-help books more broadly, and bestsellers in general, loom so large in the popular cultural landscape that they have escaped academic attention. In contributing an original analysis of etiquette, self-help, and bestsellers, this chapter goes some way to addressing their neglect. It adds to the analysis of fiction bestsellers, a nonfiction case study, and helps to overcome a tendency to dismiss bestsellers as merely populist, and unworthy of serious attention, by analyzing one of the bestselling American books of the twentieth century, and the preeminent conduct book, Post's *Etiquette* of 1922 and thereafter. A close reading of 85 years of *Emily Post's Etiquette* as an exemplar of the self-help genre, as family saga and brand, as a barometer of social ideals, reveals how it has successfully negotiated several paradoxes. Etiquette and self-help discourses assist readers in pursuing American values and the American Dream through the commoditization of social interaction and aspiration, albeit subject to continual change as its successive authors have attempted to both reflect and prescribe contemporary manners. *Emily Post's Etiquette* has done this successfully for 90 years by renewing its authorship and its content; perpetual renewal is the promise of the self-help genre, always ready with a new cure. *Etiquette* is, at once, one book and several books, by several authors, a single volume bestseller and a multimedia brand. The constancy of its bestseller status relies on its constantly changing content. During its 90-year history, *Etiquette* has *described* social change—the rejection of chaperonage, the increasing acceptability of divorce—just as it has purported to *prescribe* acceptable manners. It is follower *and* leader. *Etiquette* is *both* an index of class consciousness, as it promulgates an upper middle class norm *and* an egalitarian tool of upward mobility and autodidacticism in a self-declaredly classless society. When read retrospectively, and comparatively, and subjected to contextualized case study analysis, etiquette literature has much . to tell about the mechanics of giving advice and authority, the ingredients for a successful bestseller, and about what a bestseller such as *Etiquette* can tell us of the ideals and aspirations of American society across nearly a century of the nation's history. In introducing the first edition of *Etiquette*, Richard Duffy declared "as a social document, it is without precedent in American literature."[76] Despite this hyperbole, under analysis, Post's *Etiquette* can reveal as much about American society and the enduring American obsession—How to Behave?—as could any classic novel.

Bibliography

Akerman, James R. "Twentieth-Century American Road Maps and the Making of a National Motorized Space," in *Cartographies of Travel and Navigation*, ed. James R. Akerman, 151–206. Chicago: University of Chicago Press, 2006.

Allen, Betty and Mitchell Pirie Briggs. *Behave Yourself!* Philadelphia, Chicago: J. B. Lippincott Company, 1937.

Anon. "Putting a Kick in Etiquette to Pacify Flaming Youth," *Literary Digest*, XCVI. February 4, 1928.

Arditi, Jorge. "Etiquette Books, Discourse and the Deployment of an Order of Things," *Theory, Culture & Society* 16, 4 (1999): 25–48.

—. *A Genealogy of Manners: Transformations of Social Relations in France and England from the Fourteenth to the Eighteenth Century.* Chicago: Chicago University Press, 1998.

Atkinson, Butler M. *What Dr. Spock Didn't Tell Us or A Survival Kit for Parents.* New York: Simon and Schuster, 1959.

Barnes and Noble. "Bestsellers by Subject, Etiquette." Accessed November 29, 2007, October 27, 2011. http://www.barnesandnoble.com/bestsellers/top10everything.asp.

Beecher, Catharine. *A Treatise on Domestic Economy, for the Use of Young Ladies at Home, and at School.* Boston: Marsh, Capen, Lyon, and Webb, 1841.

Beecher, Catharine and Harriet Beecher Stowe. *The American Woman's Home: or, Principles of Domestic Science; Being a Guide to the Formation and Maintenance of Economical, Healthful, Beautiful, and Christian Homes.* New York, J. B. Ford; Boston: H. A. Brown, 1869.

Beeton, Mrs Isabella, ed. *Mrs Beeton's Book of Household Management.* 24 parts. London: S. O. Beeton, 1859–61.

Bell, David and Joanne Hollows, eds. *Ordinary Lifestyles: Popular Media, Consumption and Taste.* Maidenhead: Open University Press, 2005.

Bourdieu, Pierre. *Distinction: a Social Critique of the Judgment of Taste.* Translated by Richard Nice. London: Routledge, 1986 (1979).

Bunyan, John. *The Pilgrim's Progress.* Edited by W. R. Owens. Oxford: Oxford University Press, 2001 (1678).

Caldwell, Mark. *A Short History of Rudeness: Manners, Morals and Misbehavior in Modern America.* New York: Picador USA, 2000.

Carnegie, Dale. *How to Win Friends and Influence People.* New York: Simon and Schuster, 1936.

—. *How to Stop Worrying and Start Living.* New York: Simon and Schuster, 1948.

Carnegie, Dale and associates with Brent Cole. *How To Win Friends And Influence People In The Digital Age.* New York: Simon & Schuster, 2011.

Carnegie, Donna Dale. *How to Win Friends and Influence People for Teen Girls.* New York: Fireside, 2005.

Carnegie, Dorothy, ed. *Dale Carnegie's Scrapbook: A Treasury of the Wisdom of the Ages. Edited, with a selection of Dale Carnegie's own writings, by Dorothy Carnegie.* New York: Simon and Schuster, 1959.

Carson, Gerald. *The Polite Americans: 300 Years of More or Less Good Behaviour.* London, Melbourne: Macmillan, 1967.

Claridge, Laura. *Emily Post: Daughter of the Gilded Age, Mistress of American Manners.* New York: Random House, 2008.

Comfort, Alex, ed. *The Joy of Sex: A Cordon Bleu Guide to Lovemaking.* Illustrated by Charles Raymond and Christopher Foss. New York: Crown, 1972.

Culbertson, Ely. *The Contract Bridge Blue Book.* New York: The Bridge World, 1930.

Currell, Sue. "Depression and Recovery: Self-Help and America in the 1930s," in *Historicizing Lifestyle: Mediating Taste, Consumption and Identity from the 1900s to 1970s*, ed. Joanne Hollows and David Bell, 131–44. London: Ashgate, 2006.

Damien, Paul. *Help! Debunking the Outrageous Claims of Self-Help Gurus.* Austin, TX: Synergy Books, 2008.

de Wolfe, Elsie. *The House in Good Taste.* New York: Century Co., 1913.

Diefendorf, Elizabeth, ed. *The New York Public Library's Books of the Century.* New York: Oxford University Press, 2000 (1996).

Dolby, Sandra K. *Self-Help Books: Why Americans Keep Reading Them.* Urbana and Chicago: University of Illinois Press, 2005.

Draper, Dorothy. *Entertaining is Fun!* New York: Doubleday, Doran & Company, 1941.

Duffy, Richard. "Manners and Morals," introduction to Emily Post, *Etiquette in society, in business, in politics and at home, by Emily Post (Mrs. Price Post) . . . illustrated with private photographs and facsimiles of social forms.* New York, London: Funk & Wagnalls Company, 1922.

Eichler, Lillian. *The Book of Etiquette.* Garden City, NY: Nelson Doubleday, 1921.

Elias, Norbert. *The Civilizing Process.* Vol. I, *The History of Manners.* Oxford: Blackwell, 1994 (1939).

Emily Post Productions. Youtube channel. Accessed October 14, 2011. http://www.youtube.com/user/EmilyPostProductions.

Garner, Dwight. "Classic Advice: Please, Leave Well Enough Alone." Review of *How To Win Friends And Influence People In The Digital Age* by Dale Carnegie and Associates, with Brent Cole and *Emily Post's Etiquette* by Peggy Post, Anna Post, Lizzie Post and Daniel Post Senning. *New York Times*, October 5, 2011.

Gilbert, Dennis L. *The American Class Structure in an Age of Growing Inequality.* 8th edn. Thousand Oaks, CA: Pine Forge Press, 2010.

Goffman, Erving. *The Presentation of Self in Everyday Life.* London: Penguin, 1990 (1959).

Hackett, Alice Payne. *Fifty Years of Bestsellers, 1895–1945.* New York: R. R. Bowker, 1945.

Heinze, Andrew R. "*Schizophrenia Americana*: Aliens, Alienists and the 'Personality Shift' of Twentieth-Century Culture," *American Quarterly* 55, 2 (June 2003): 227–56.

Hemphill, Christina D. *Bowing to Necessities: A History of Manners in America, 1620–1860*. Oxford: Oxford University Press, 1999.

Hodges, Deborah Robertson. *Etiquette: An Annotated Bibliography of Literature Published in English in the United States, 1900 through 1987*. Jefferson, NC and London: McFarland, 1989.

Hoeller, Hildegarde. "Branded from the Start: the Paradox of (the) American (Novel of) Manners," in *Etiquette: Reflections on Contemporary Comportment*, ed. Ron Scapp and Brian Seitz, 135–50. Albany, NY: State University of New York Press, 2007.

Hogan, Robert and Nancy Henley. "Nomotics: The Science of Human Rule Systems," *Law & Society Review* 5, 1 (August 1970): 135–46.

Holt, Emily. *Everyman's Encyclopaedia of Etiquette*. New York: McGlure, Phillips & Co., 1901.

Hutchins, Imar, ed. *Delights of the Garden: Vegetarian Cuisine Prepared without Heat from Delights of the Garden Restaurants*. New York: Main Street Books, 1996.

—. *The Joy of Not Cooking: Delights of the Garden's Guide to Vegetarian Cuisine*. Washington, DC: Delights of the Garden Press, 1994.

Lees-Maffei, Grace. "Accommodating 'Mrs Three in One': Homemaking, Home Entertaining and Domestic Advice Literature in Post-War Britain." *Women's History Review* 16, 5 (2007): 723–54.

—. "From Service to Self-Service: Etiquette Writing as Design Discourse 1920–70." *Journal of Design History* 14, 3 (2001): 187–206.

Lewis, Tania. *Smart Living: Lifestyle Media and Popular Expertise*. New York: Peter Lang Publishing, Inc., 2008.

McGee, Micki. *Self-Help, Inc: Makeover Culture in American Life*. New York: Oxford University Press, 2005.

Nemy, Enid. "In an Age of Finger Food, A New Emily Post." *New York Times*, April 20, 1997.

Neuberg, Victor. "Chapbooks in America: Reconstructing the Popular Reading of Early America." In *Reading in America: Literature and Social History*, ed. Cathy N. Davidson, 81–113. Baltimore, MD: Johns Hopkins University Press 1989.

Ohmann, Richard. *Selling Culture: Magazines, Markets and Class at the Turn of the Century*. London: Verso, 1996.

Post, Anna. "What Would Emily Post Do?" Blog, June 11, 2007 to July 28, 2010. Accessed October 14, 2011. http://annapost.typepad.com/.

Post, Edwin. *Truly Emily Post: a Biography*. New York: Funk & Wagnalls, 1961.

Post, Elizabeth L. *Emily Post's Etiquette*. 14th edn. New York: Harper & Row, 1984.

Post, Emily. "Etiquette an Essentially Elemental Subject." *The National Elementary Principal*, XXIV, 2 (December 1944): 6–7.

—. *By Motor to the Golden Gate*. Edited by Jane Lancaster. Jefferson NC: McFarland & Company, Inc., 2004 (1916).

—. *Etiquette "The Blue Book of Social Usage,"* 10th edn. New York: Funk & Wagnalls Company, Inc., 1960.

—. *Etiquette "The Blue Book of Social Usage,"* 6th edn. New York and London: Funk & Wagnalls Company, 1940.

—. *Etiquette in society, in business, in politics and at home, by Emily Post (Mrs. Price Post) . . . illustrated with private photographs and facsimiles of social forms*. New York, London: Funk & Wagnalls Company, 1922.

—. *Etiquette, "The blue book of social usage."* New York, London: Funk & Wagnalls Company, 1927.

—. *Flight of the Moth*. New York: Dodd, Mead & Company, 1904.

—. *How to Behave Though a Débutante: opinions by Muriel as overheard by Emily Post*. Illustrated by John Held, Jr. Garden City, NY: Doubleday, Doran & Company, 1928.

—. *Parade: a Novel of New York Society*. New York, London: Funk & Wagnalls Company, 1925.

—. *Purple and Fine Linen*. New York: D. Appleton and Company, 1905.

—. *The Feather*. New York: Dodd, Mead and Company, 1910.

—. *The Personality of a House: the Blue Book of Home Design and Decoration*. New York: Funk & Wagnalls Company, 1930.

—. *The Title Market*. New York: Dodd, Mead and Company, 1909.

—. *Woven in the Tapestry*. New York: Moffat, Yard and Company, 1908.

Post, Lizzie. *How Do You Work this Life Thing?* Video. Accessed October 14, 2011. http://www.emilypost.com/home-and-family-life/133-college-and-beyond/432-lizzie-post-discussing-how-do-you-work-this-life-thing-video.

Post, Peggy, Anna Post, Lizzie Post, and Daniel Post Senning. *Emily Post's Etiquette: Manners for a New World*. Illustrated by Janice Richter. New York: William Morrow, 2011.

—. *Emily Post's Etiquette*. 17th edn. New York: HarperCollins, 2004.

Publisher's Weekly Bestselling Hardback Books, aggregated by year. Accessed October 25, 2008. http://www.caderbooks.com/bestintro.html.

Riesman, David, Nathan Glazer, and Reuel Denney. *The Lonely Crowd: A Study of the Changing American Character*. New Haven and London: Yale University Press, 1969 (1950).

Robinson, Dwight E. and Dennis F. Strong. Review of *Etiquette in Society, in Business, in Politics and at Home*, by Emily Post (Mrs. Price Post).

New York: Funk and Wagnells, 1922. Replica Edition, with "A New
  Preface to an Old Edition," 1969 and Elizabeth L. Post, *Emily Post's
  Etiquette*, Twelfth Revised Edition. New York: Funk & Wagnells,
  1969. *Pacific Northwest Quarterly* (July 1970): 173–4.
Rombauer, Irma Starkloff. *The Joy of Cooking*. Illustrated by Marion
  Rombauer. St. Louis, MO: A. C. Clayton, 1931.
—. *The Joy of Cooking: 75th Anniversary Edition*. New York: Scribner,
  2006.
Rubin, Joan Shelley. "Information Please! Culture and Expertise in
  the Interwar Period," *American Quarterly* 35, 5 (Winter 1983):
  499–517.
—. *The Making of Middlebrow Culture*. Chapel Hill, NC and London:
  University of North Carolina Press, 1992.
Salerno, Steve. *Sham: How the Self-Help Movement Made America
  Helpless*. New York: Crown Publishers, 2005.
Scanlon, Jennifer. *Inarticulate Longings: The* Ladies' Home Journal,
  Gender and the Promises of Consumer Culture. London and New
  York: Routledge, 1995.
Schlesinger, Arthur Meier. *Learning How to Behave: a Historical Study of
  American Etiquette Books*. New York: MacMillan, 1946.
Sennett, Richard. *The Fall of Public Man*. New York: W. W. Norton and
  Company, Inc., 1992 (1974).
Senning, Cindy Post. "The Gift of Good Manners: Advice and Tips for
  Parents from The Emily Post Institute." Blog, Accessed October 14,
  2011. http://www.thegiftofgoodmanners.com/
Severson, Kim. "Does the World Need Another 'Joy'? Do You?" *New
  York Times*, November 1, 2006.
Sherwood, M. E. W. *Manners and Social Usages*. New York: Harper &
  Co., 1994.
Simonds, Wendy. *Women and Self-Help Culture: Reading between the
  Lines*. New Brunswick, NJ: Rutgers University Press, 1992.
Smiles, Samuel. *Self-Help: with illustrations of character and conduct*.
  London: John Murray, 1859.
Smith, Caroline J. "Living the Life of a Domestic Goddess: Chick Lit's
  Response to Domestic-Advice Manuals." *Women's Studies* 34 (2005):
  671–99.
Smith, Frank Seymour. *Know-How Books: An Annotated Bibliography
  of Do It Yourself Books for the Handyman and of introductions
  to Science, Art, History and Literature for the Beginner and Home
  Student*. London: Thames and Hudson, 1956.
Smithsonian National Post Museum. *Arago: People, Postage and the Post*,
  USPS 'Celebrate the Century' stamps Accessed October 4, 2011 at
  http://arago.si.edu/flash/?s1=5|sq=%22Emily%20Post%22|sf=0.

Spock, Benjamin Dr. *The Common Sense Book of Baby and Child Care.* New York: Duell, Sloan and Pearce, 1946.

—. *The Pocket Book of Baby and Child Care.* New York: Pocket Books, 1946.

—. *Spock's Baby and Child Care.* 8th edn. New York: Simon and Schuster, 2004.

Starker, Steven. *Oracle at the Supermarket: the American Pre-Occupation with Self-Help Books.* New Brunswick, NJ: Transaction Publishers, 2002 (1989).

Stewart, Martha. *Entertaining.* New York: Clarkson Potter, 1982.

Susman, Warren. "Personality and the Making of Twentieth Century Culture." In *New Directions in American Intellectual History*, edited by John Higham and Paul K. Conklin, 212–26. Baltimore: Johns Hopkins University Press, 1979.

Tressler, Irving Dart. *How to Lose Friends and Alienate People.* New York: Stackpole Sons, 1937.

Walters, Ray. "Paperback Talk." *New York Times*, September 5, 1982.

Warner, Michael, ed. *American Sermons: The Pilgrims to Martin Luther King Jr.* New York: Library of America, 1999.

Watson, Lillian Eichler, ed. *Light from Many Lamps.* New York: Simon and Schuster, 1951.

Weide, Robert B. *How to Lose Friends and Alienate People.* Film. 2008.

Wilson, Edmund. *A Literary Chronicle, 1920–50.* New York: Anchor, 1952.

Winner, Michael. *Behave Yourself.* Film. 1962.

Wouters, Cas. *Informalization: Manners and Emotions since 1890.* London: Sage, 2007.

—. "Etiquette Books and Emotion Management in the 20th Century, Part One: the Integration of the Social Classes," *Journal of Social History* 29, 1, (1995): 107–24.

Young, Toby. *How to Lose Friends and Alienate People.* London: Little, Brown, 2001.

Notes

1   "Self-help book sales rose by 96 per cent in the five years between 1991 and 1996. By 1998 [they reached] some $581million." The self-improvement industry has been valued at $248 billion per annum and "one-third to one-half of Americans have purchased a self-help book in their lifetimes." Micki McGee, *Self-Help, Inc: Makeover Culture in American Life* (New York: Oxford University Press, 2005), 11; also "Bestselling Self-Help Books by Years on Bestseller Lists," in

Wendy Simonds, *Women and Self-Help Culture: Reading between the Lines* (New Brunswick, NJ: Rutgers University Press, 1992), 234–7.

2   On fiction and advice literature, see Hildegarde Hoeller, "Branded from the Start: the Paradox of (the) American (Novel of) Manners," in *Etiquette: Reflections on Contemporary Comportment*, ed. Ron Scapp and Brian Seitz (Albany, NY: State University of New York Press, 2007) and Caroline J. Smith, "Living the Life of a Domestic Goddess: Chick Lit's Response to Domestic-Advice Manuals," *Women's Studies* 34 (2005).

3   The first edition was titled *Etiquette in society, in business, in politics and at home, by Emily Post (Mrs. Price Post) . . . illustrated with private photographs and facsimiles of social forms* (New York, London: Funk & Wagnalls Company, July 1922). Following 17 reprintings, a second edition appeared in 1927 with a revised title, Etiquette, "The blue book of social usage" which name was retained until the 14th edition, Elizabeth L. Post, Emily Post's Etiquette (New York: Harper & Row, 1984).

4   Michael Warner, ed., *American Sermons: The Pilgrims to Martin Luther King Jr.* (New York: Library of America, 1999); Victor Neuberg, "Chapbooks in America: Reconstructing the Popular Reading of Early America," in *Reading in America: Literature and Social History*, ed. Cathy N. Davidson (Baltimore, MD: Johns Hopkins University Press 1989).

5   Elsie de Wolfe, *The House in Good Taste* (New York: Century Co., 1913); Alex Comfort, ed., *The Joy of Sex: a Cordon Bleu Guide to Lovemaking*, illus. Charles Raymond and Christopher Foss (New York: Crown, 1972). In her first book, *Entertaining* (New York: Clarkson Potter, 1982), 12, Martha Stewart placed herself in a tradition of entertaining advice: "When the Emily Post etiquette book was rewritten in 1965, it asserted that a strict code of social behavior was as obsolete as the old social pyramid. I still shudder with a sympathetic case of nerves when I read the pompous little book of entertainment advice written in 1888 by Ward McAllister, Mrs. Aster's famous advisor, or see in Edith Wharton's fiction the severe and detailed instructions for the handling of social habits and rituals . . . But there is no such cause for anxiety today."

6   Richard Ohmann, *Selling Culture: Magazines, Markets and Class at the Turn of the Century* (London: Verso, 1996), 153, 362.

7   On American manners, see, for example, C. Dallett Hemphill, *Bowing to Necessities: A History of Manners in America, 1620–1860* (Oxford: Oxford University Press, 1999); Cas Wouters,

Informalization: Manners and Emotions since 1890 (London: Sage, 2007).

8 Erving Goffman, *The Presentation of Self in Everyday Life* (London: Penguin, 1990 (1959)); Dennis L. Gilbert, *The American Class Structure in an Age of Growing Inequality*, 8th edn. (Thousand Oaks, CA: Pine Forge Press, 2010).

9 For example, Samuel Smiles, *Self-Help: with illustrations of character and conduct* (London: John Murray, 1859); Mrs Isabella Beeton, *Mrs Beeton's Book of Household Management*, 24 parts (London: S. O. Beeton, 1859–61). British publishing on "How-To and Know-How started in real earnest in the 1890s," Frank Seymour Smith, *Know-How Books: An Annotated Bibliography of Do It Yourself Books for the Handyman and of introductions to Science, Art, History and Literature for the Beginner and Home Student* (London: Thames and Hudson, 1956), v.

10 Sue Currell, "Depression and Recovery: Self-Help and America in the 1930s," in *Historicizing Lifestyle: Mediating Taste, Consumption and Identity from the 1900s to 1970s*, ed. Joanne Hollows and David Bell (London: Ashgate, 2006), notes the popularity of American self-help books in developing economies such as India; Steven Starker, *Oracle at the Supermarket: the American Pre-Occupation with Self-Help Books* (New Brunswick, NJ: Transaction Publishers, 2002 (1989)).

11 McGee, *Self-Help, Inc.*, 191.

12 Sandra K. Dolby, *Self-Help Books: Why Americans Keep Reading Them* (Urbana and Chicago: University of Illinois Press, 2005), 56.

13 Paul Damien, *Help! Debunking the Outrageous Claims of Self-Help Gurus* (Austin, TX: Synergy Books, 2008); Steve Salerno, *Sham: How the Self-Help Movement Made America Helpless* (New York: Crown Publishers, 2005); Dolby, *Self-Help Books*, 158–9.

14 For example, David Bell and Joanne Hollows, eds, *Ordinary Lifestyles: Popular Media, Consumption and Taste* (Maidenhead: Open University Press, 2005); Tania Lewis, *Smart Living: Lifestyle Media and Popular Expertise* (New York: Peter Lang Publishing, Inc., 2008).

15 Norbert Elias, *The Civilizing Process*, vol. I *The History of Manners* (Oxford: Blackwell, 1994 (1939)), 67; Jorge Arditi, *A Genealogy of Manners: Transformations of Social Relations in France and England from the Fourteenth to the Eighteenth Century* (Chicago: Chicago University Press, 1998); Wouters, *Informalization*.

16 Interior designer Dorothy Draper also lived in Tuxedo Park. She wrote an advice column for *Good Housekeeping* and books such as *Entertaining is Fun!* (New York: Doubleday, Doran & Company, 1941).

17 Post's first novel was published in 1904 and her divorce decree was issued in 1906. In 1909, Post received a considerable inheritance from her mother. Laura Claridge, *Emily Post: Daughter of the Gilded Age, Mistress of American Manners* (New York: Random House, 2008), 153–4, 178, 196, 202.

18 Post also wrote for *Scribner's*, *Collier's Magazine* and *The Century* and the novels *Flight of the Moth* (New York: Dodd, Mead & Company, 1904), *Purple and Fine Linen* (New York, D. Appleton and company, 1905), *Woven in the Tapestry* (New York: Moffat, Yard and Company, 1908), *The Title Market* (New York: Dodd, Mead and Company, 1909), *The Feather* (New York: Dodd, Mead and Company, 1910) and *Parade: a Novel of New York Society* (New York, London: Funk & Wagnalls Company, 1925).

19 However, "Emily Post's book was part of a dying breed," and while other women had previously completed long road trips, Post traveled with her cousin and son and a chauffeur. Emily Post, *By Motor to the Golden Gate*, ed. Jane Lancaster (Jefferson NC: McFarland & Company, Inc., 2004 (1916)), 12, 4. In 2007, the *Illinois Lincoln Highway Coalition* unveiled a plaque commemorating Post's trip in Rochelle, Illinois, where the rain had stranded her.

20 Edwin Post, *Truly Emily Post: a Biography* (New York: Funk & Wagnalls, 1961), 202–5. This biography was ghost-written by Dorothy Giles, Claridge, *Emily Post*, 443.

21 Enid Nemy, "In an Age of Finger Food, A New Emily Post," *New York Times*, April 20, 1997; Arthur M. Schlesinger, *Learning How to Behave: a Historical Study of American Etiquette Books* (New York: MacMillan, 1946). Claridge, *Emily Post*, 249: "First she reviewed Mrs. John (Mary) Sherwood's etiquette book, which [her mother] had reared her on." This refers to M. E. W. Sherwood, *Manners and Social Usages* (New York: Harper & Co., 1994). Post reflected on different modes of learning etiquette in "Etiquette an Essentially Elemental Subject," *The National Elementary Principal*, XXIV, 2 (December 1944).

22 Claridge, *Emily Post*, 208–9, 246.

23 Lillian Eichler, *The Book of Etiquette* (Garden City, NY: Nelson Doubleday, 1921) and various editions; Emily Holt, *Everyman's Encyclopaedia of Etiquette* (New York: McGlure, Phillips & Co., 1901).

24 Alice P. Hackett, *Fifty Years of Bestsellers, 1895–1945* (New York: R. R. Bowker, 1945), 98, 106. However, sales figures for both Post's and Eichler's books were unreliable, Claridge, *Emily Post*, 343.

25   Claridge, *Emily Post*, 435, 443.

26   *Publisher's Weekly* Bestselling Hardback Books, aggregated by year.
      Accessed October 25, 2008. http://www.caderbooks.com/bestintro.
      html. *Etiquette* (17th edn) was in sixth place in Barnes and Noble's
      etiquette list on November 29, 2007 and the new 18th edn was
      second on October 27, 2011. http://www.barnesandnoble.com/
      bestsellers/top10everything.asp.

27   For example, Lillian Eichler Watson, ed., *Light from Many Lamps*
      (New York: Simon and Schuster, 1951); Mark Caldwell, *A Short
      History of Rudeness: Manners, Morals and Misbehavior in Modern
      America* (New York: Picador USA, 2000), 65. In writing a "science of
      human rule systems," Robert Hogan and Nancy Henley have noted
      that rule systems normally function as codes, prepared by codifiers
      "(God, Emily Post, Congress)"; these codes also have custodians and
      exemplars: "Emily Post was once codifier, custodian, and exemplar."
      Robert Hogan and Nancy Henley, "Nomotics: The Science of Human
      Rule Systems," *Law & Society Review* 5, 1 (August 1970): 138–9.

28   See the stamps at http://arago.si.edu/flash/?s1=5|sq=%22Emily%20
      Post%22|sf=0. Accessed October 4, 2011.

29   Published from 1901, and under the auspices of the AAA from 1906.
      See James R. Akerman, "Twentieth-Century American Road Maps
      and the Making of a National Motorized Space," in *Cartographies of
      Travel and Navigation*, ed. James R. Akerman (Chicago: University
      of Chicago Press, 2006), 169–70, 173. Post mentions the *Automobile
      Blue Books* in *By Motor to the Golden Gate*, 15. In 1930, Post's
      *The Personality of a House: the Blue Book of Home Design and
      Decoration* appeared (New York, Funk & Wagnalls Company,
      1930)—the 1948 edition was subtitled *The Blue Book of Home
      Charm*—and in 1933, Ely Culbertson's *The Contract Bridge Blue
      Book* (New York: The Bridge World, 1930) reached number eight in
      the bestseller lists.

30   Elizabeth L. Post, *Emily Post's Etiquette*, 14th edn.

31   Lizzie Post, video, *How Do You Work this Life Thing?* Accessed
      October 14, 2011. http://www.emilypost.com/home-and-family-
      life/133-college-and-beyond/432-lizzie-post-discussing-how-do-
      you-work-this-life-thing-video; Anna Post, "What Would Emily
      Post Do?" Blog, June 11, 2007 to July 28, 2010. Accessed October
      14, 2011. http://annapost.typepad.com/; Cindy Post Senning, "The
      Gift of Good Manners: Advice and Tips for Parents from The Emily
      Post Institute." Blog, Accessed October 14, 2011. http://www.
      thegiftofgoodmanners.com/; Also, Emily Post Productions, YouTube
      channel. Accessed October 14, 2011. http://www.youtube.com/user/
      EmilyPostProductions.

32 Emily Post is cited as a writer for *Behave Yourself*, dir. Michael
    Winner, 1962 and a film with the working title *Etiquette*, based on
    Post's writing, is in production for 2012.

33 See the discussions of 'sociogenesis' in Elias, *Civilizing Process*, and
    Pierre Bourdieu, *Distinction: a Social Critique of the Judgment of
    Taste*, trans. Richard Nice (London: Routledge, 1986 (1979)), 66.

34 Post appeared on the radio show *Betty Crocker Talk* in 1947.
    Claridge, *Emily Post*, 418.

35 Schlesinger, *Learning How to Behave*, 53.

36 Jorge Arditi echoes Schlesinger in "Etiquette Books, Discourse and
    the Deployment of an Order of Things," *Theory, Culture & Society*
    16, 4 (1999): 32, 33.

37 Dale Carnegie, *How to Win Friends and Influence People* (New York:
    Simon and Schuster, 1936); Currell, "Depression and Recovery."

38 Joan Shelley Rubin, "Information Please! Culture and Expertise in the
    Interwar Period," *American Quarterly* 35, 5 (Winter 1983): 501.

39 Joan Shelley Rubin, *The Making of Middlebrow Culture* (Chapel
    Hill, NC and London: University of North Carolina Press, 1992), 31.

40 Grace Lees-Maffei, "From Service to Self-Service: Etiquette Writing
    as Design Discourse 1920–70," *Journal of Design History* 14, 3
    (2001), 191.

41 Ohmann, *Selling Culture*, 152–3.

42 Cas Wouters, "Etiquette Books and Emotion Management in the 20th
    Century, Part One: the Integration of the Social Classes," *Journal of
    Social History* 29, 1, (1995): 107–24.

43 This chapter is based on five editions of *Etiquette* sampled from
    approximately 20-year intervals (1922, 1940, 1960, 1984, and 2004)
    plus the 2011 edition.

44 Deborah Robertson Hodges mentions some textual changes to Post's
    Etiquette in *Etiquette: An Annotated Bibliography of Literature
    Published in English in the United States, 1900 through 1987*
    (Jefferson, NC and London: McFarland, 1989), 118–21.

45 This emphasis on "manners and technology" is criticized by Dwight
    Garner, "Classic Advice: Please, Leave Well Enough Alone," review
    of Dale Carnegie and Associates, with Brent Cole, *How To Win
    Friends And Influence People In The Digital Age* (New York: Simon
    & Schuster, 2011) and Peggy Post, Anna Post, Lizzie Post and Daniel
    Post Senning, *Emily Post's Etiquette*, 18th edn (New York: William
    Morrow, 2011) *New York Times*, October 5, 2011.

46 Emily Post, *Etiquette 'The Blue Book of Social Usage,'* 6th edn.
    (New York and London: Funk & Wagnalls Company, 1940), 354.

47 Nemy, "Age of Finger Food."

48 Anon., "Putting a Kick in Etiquette to Pacify Flaming Youth," *Literary Digest*, XCVI (February 4, 1928) 56–9, cited in Schlesinger, *Learning*, 52.

49 Post, *Etiquette* (1940), 36.

50 Emily Post, *Etiquette 'The Blue Book of Social Usage,'* 10th edn. (New York: Funk & Wagnalls Company, Inc., 1960), 168.

51 Post, *Etiquette* (1940), 356 and (1960), 171.

52 Peggy Post, *Emily Post's Etiquette*, 17th edn. (New York: HarperCollins, 2004), 217, 219, 212.

53 Peggy Post, Anna Post, Lizzie Post and Daniel Post Senning, *Emily Post's Etiquette: Manners for a New World*, illus. Janice Richter (New York: William Morrow, 2011), x.

54 Claridge, *Emily Post*, 294.

55 Grace Lees-Maffei, "Accommodating 'Mrs Three in One': Homemaking, Home Entertaining and Domestic Advice Literature in Post-War Britain," *Women's History Review* 16, 5 (2007); Lees-Maffei, 2001.

56 Gerald Carson, *The Polite Americans: 300 Years of More or Less Good Behaviour* (London, Melbourne: Macmillan, 1967), 239.

57 Post, *Etiquette* (1922), Chapter 14, Formal Dinners.

58 Claridge, *Emily Post*, 250, 262.

59 Arditi, "Etiquette Books," 25–48. Carnegie's *How to Win* is seen to appeal to personality rather than character; see David Riesman, Nathan Glazer and Reuel Denney, *The Lonely Crowd: A Study of the Changing American Character* (New Haven and London: Yale University Press, 1969 (1950)), 149–50, 73–4. Richard Sennett countered Riesman's ideas, arguing instead that "Western societies are moving from something like an other-directed condition to an inner-directed condition," *The Fall of Public Man* (New York: W. W. Norton and Company, Inc., 1992 (1974)), 5. See also, Warren Susman, "Personality and the Making of Twentieth Century Culture," in *New Directions in American Intellectual History*, ed. John Higham and Paul K. Conklin (Baltimore: Johns Hopkins University Press, 1979), 220–1; Andrew R. Heinze, "*Schizophrenia Americana*: Aliens, Alienists and the 'Personality Shift' of Twentieth-Century Culture," *American Quarterly* 55, 2 (June 2003).

60 Betty Allen and Mitchell Pirie Briggs, *Behave Yourself!* (Philadelphia, Chicago: J. B. Lippincott Company, 1937), 7.

61 Dwight E. Robinson and Dennis F. Strong, Review of *Etiquette in Society, in Business, in Politics and at Home*, by Emily Post (Mrs. Price Post) (New York: Funk and Wagnells, 1922) Replica Edition, with "A New Preface to an Old Edition," 1969 and Elizabeth L. Post, *Emily Post's Etiquette*, Twelfth Revised Edition (New York: Funk & Wagnells, 1969) in *Pacific Northwest Quarterly* (July 1970), 173–4. Reference is made to John Bunyan, *The Pilgrim's Progress*, ed. W. R. Owens (Oxford: Oxford University Press, 2001 (1678)).

62 Claridge, *Emily Post*, 428: "According to Wilson, after finishing [*Etiquette*] Fitzgerald 'became inspired with the idea of a play in which all the motivations should consist of trying to do the right thing.'" Edmund Wilson, "Books," *New Yorker*, July 19, 1947 and reprinted in Edmund Wilson, *A Literary Chronicle, 1920–50* (New York: Anchor, 1952), 380–9.

63 Post, *Emily Post's Etiquette*, 10th edn. (1960), v.

64 Ibid., 534.

65 Elizabeth L. Post, *Emily Post's Etiquette*, 14th edn., 82–3.

66 On readers' contributions to a leading US women's magazine, see Jennifer Scanlon, *Inarticulate Longings: the* Ladies' Home Journal, *Gender and the Promises of Consumer Culture* (London and New York: Routledge, 1995).

67 Elizabeth Diefendorf, ed., *The New York Public Library's Books of the Century* (New York: Oxford University Press, 1996, 2000) records *Books of the Century*, a centenary exhibition of influential texts at The New York Public Library's Center for the Humanities, May 20, 1995–July 13, 1996.

68 Starker, *Oracle*, 59–74; Pocket Books arranged for Spock's book to appear in hardback as *The Common Sense Book of Baby and Child Care* with Duell, Sloan and Pearce (New York, 1946) before publication the same year as *The Pocket Book of Baby and Child Care* (New York: Pocket Books, 1946, 1949). Diefendorf, *Books of the Century*, 95.

69 In an early familial collaboration on a bestselling advice book, Catharine Beecher and Harriet Beecher Stowe (author of the influential antislavery novel *Uncle Tom's Cabin*) adapted *A Treatise on Domestic Economy, for the Use of Young Ladies at Home, and at School* (Boston: Marsh, Capen, Lyon, and Webb, 1841) as *The American Woman's Home: or, Principles of Domestic Science; Being a Guide to the Formation and Maintenance of Economical, Healthful, Beautiful, and Christian Homes* (New York, J. B. Ford; Boston: H. A. Brown, 1869).

70   Irma S. Rombauer, *The Joy of Cooking*, illus. Marion Rombauer
     (St. Louis, MO: A. C. Clayton, 1931) published in facsimile as *The
     Joy of Cooking: 75th Anniversary Edition* (New York: Scribner,
     2006). *Joy* has sold 18 million copies. Kim Severson, "Does the World
     Need Another 'Joy'? Do You?," *New York Times*, November 1, 2006.

71   Carnegie's *How to Win* has never been out of print; by 1954, it
     had sold 1,300,000 copies and in 1980, it was edited for political
     correctness. Ray Walters, "Paperback Talk," *New York Times*,
     September 5, 1982. The cover of the 1998 Pocket Books edition
     boasted of 15 million copies sold, while the current figure is 30
     million and a 2011 edition addresses "the digital age," Garner,
     "Classic Advice." Carnegie also wrote *How to Stop Worrying and
     Start Living* (New York: Simon and Schuster, 1948).

72   *Dale Carnegie's Scrapbook: a Treasury of the Wisdom of the Ages.
     Edited, with a selection of Dale Carnegie's own writings, by Dorothy
     Carnegie* (New York: Simon and Schuster, 1959); Donna Dale
     Carnegie, *How to Win Friends and Influence People for Teen Girls*
     (New York: Fireside, 2005).

73   Spock, *Common Sense Book*; Spock, *Pocket Book*; Dr. Benjamin
     Spock, *Dr. Spock's Baby and Child Care*, 8th edn. (New York: Simon
     and Schuster, 2004).

74   Imar Hutchins, ed., *The Joy of Not Cooking: Delights of the
     Garden's Guide to Vegetarian Cuisine* (Washington, DC: Delights
     of the Garden Press, 1994) reissued as *Delights of the Garden:
     Vegetarian Cuisine Prepared Without Heat from Delights of the
     Garden Restaurants* (New York: Main Street Books, 1996); Irving
     D. Tressler's *How to Lose Friends and Alienate People* (New York:
     Stackpole Sons, 1937) is a faithful parody, unlike Toby Young's
     memoir of the same name (London: Little, Brown, 2001) and the
     associated film (dir. Robert B. Weide, 2008); Butler M. Atkinson,
     What Dr. Spock Didn't Tell Us or A Survival Kit for Parents
     (New York: Simon and Schuster, 1959, 1979).

75   Initially published serially in *Vanity Fair*, Emily Post, *How to Behave
     Though a Débutante: opinions by Muriel as overheard by Emily
     Post*, illus. by John Held, Jr. (Garden City, NY: Doubleday, Doran &
     Company, 1928).

76   Richard Duffy, "Manners and Morals," introduction to Post,
     Etiquette (1922), n. p.

11

Blockbuster feminism: *Peyton Place* and the uses of scandal

Ardis Cameron

She put me on the wrong road early on,
and I am better for it.

JOHN WATERS[1]

In December 1956, a few months after the publication of her novel *Peyton Place*, Grace Metalious was invited to appear on television's hottest new talk show, *Night Beat*. The brainchild of Ted Yates and Mike Wallace, whose irreverent and confrontational interviewing style quickly earned him the nickname "Mike Malice," *Night Beat* pioneered late night programming pulling into televisions' orbit millions of viewers eager to watch the smoldering Wallace interrogate the rich and the famous.[2] "What Yates persuaded me we should do on *Night Beat*," Wallace later recalled, "was to hurl a thunderbolt into that smug and placid world" of television news journalism and, by extension, the tepid topics they covered.[3] That night they hurled Grace Metalious.

Nervous and uneasy, Grace felt especially vulnerable under the *Night Beat* gaze, not only because of its hard-hitting reputation but because the show was recorded live: an unedited hour under tight camera closeups, stark backgrounds, and a one-on-one exchange with Mr. Malice.[4] As she takes her seat, Klieg lights come up almost immediately, wrapping her face in blinding, stark white illumination. Her new boyfriend, T. J. Martin, hides below her chair. Wallace lights a cigarette, slapping the smoke toward his guest like a B movie police interrogation. Already uncomfortable in the requisite panty girdle and skirt that replaced her comfortable dungarees and flannel shirt, Grace wilts under the leering gaze of her host:

"I thought your book was basic and carnal," Wallace sneers, his cigarette stabbing the bluish air.

"You did, huh?" Grace squeaked.

"What gives you the right to pry and hold your neighbors up to ridicule?" Graces' eyes moistened.

Poised off-stage in her Schiffli-embroidered dress, fashion model Jackie Susann watched in fascination and horror as Wallace hammered away at America's most "sexsational" authoress. As Barbara Seaman tells the story, Susann prayed for divine intervention. "Don't let this woman cry in front of millions of people," Jackie pleaded. "Get her through this show, God, and I won't smoke another cigarette tonight."[5] Grace plays with her ponytail, she twitches, pulls at her skirt; but she does not cry. Then, suddenly, she alters course temporarily rattling Wallace by calling him by his hated birth name. "Myron," she taunts, "tell the audience how many times you've been married." Taboo, even on late night television, Wallace is speechless and angry. He refuses to talk about his three divorces.[6]

No longer the orphans of academia, bestselling novels have attracted serious scholarly attention, their popularity no longer suspect but rather a pointed justification for analysis and inquiry. Rich veins of research have suddenly opened up revealing the sentient worlds of lesbian pulps, dime novels, female sleuths, children's series, factory "hacks," and the disparate writing publics they called forth and organized.[7] Historians have been especially adept at pulling print culture into service making legible worlds once lost. As early as the twelfth century, historians have shown how "textual communities" helped promote not only a sense of collectivity but also a collective challenge to repressive traditions. Without "print languages," Benedict Anderson famously points out, individual affiliations to abstract entities such as "the nation" would be difficult to imagine. Nor was reading a practice confined to the salons and parlors of the genteel and influential. Far from an elite habit, vernacular reading played a critical role in shaping popular knowledge, challenging orthodoxy, and fueling working-class radicalism, providing that is, "people with new ways to relate their doings to authority, new and old."[8]

For social historians on the trail of the ordinary and everyday bestsellers provide an especially productive point of entry into the prosaic, calling attention not only to practices of leisure and readerly desire but to the unquiet habits of fans and detractors alike. "Literary texts," the critic Terry Eagleton famously taught us, "do not exist on bookshelves, they are processes of signification materialized only in the practice of reading." And no book is ever read more enthusiastically than the latest bestseller.

Still, texts are more than words on a printed page. Big sellers are also big talk pulling into polite conversation and onto the national imaginary the open secrets of the street, the kitchen, and conversations forged "between you and me." A "literary H-bomb" that scandalized America, more people read *Peyton Place* than any other work of fiction up to that time. One in 29 Americans bought the book, countless others borrowed or stole it and we can only imagine how many flipped through its pages digging out bits of plot, pieces of characters, and quotable lines.[9] Yet, to pick up old copies of *Peyton Place* is to glimpse the other side of print culture, the verbal pentimento that is also and always wedged beneath its dog-eared pages: words fiercely underlined, marginalia fixed with red stars, recognition and disapproval uttered in flaming exclamation points. "Sheila!"—Joanie B. scribbles on page 149, "we need to talk!" Two images emerge from the fan letters and memories of readers. The first is that of a solitary figure reading *Peyton Place* at night, usually with a flashlight under the covers. The second is that of a knot of women or pair of teenagers, huddled together in excited speech.[10]

It is this long-remembered whiff of salaciousness no doubt that keeps *Peyton Place* in the air of public memory, but we forget the extent to which the winds of controversy took shape in the excitable speech that conjoined "dirty" novel with scandalous "New England wife and mother of three," a description that circulated in tandem with the name Grace Metalious. We forget, in other words, that the literary enfranchisement of Metalious was achieved, at least in part, by the seemingly incongruous coupling of a sexually candid book with a respectable housewife—a schoolteachers wife no less—from America's most "puritanical" hinterlands. Today, Grace Metalious is all but forgotten, her remarkable achievement almost erased from the cultural literary landscape, an uncoupling few could have imagined at the time. Between 1956 and 1964, Grace Metalious became a household word, her name and image as famous and controversial a text as the novel she wrote.

This essay is an attempt, therefore, to bring the two back together, to follow "sexsational" bestseller and unnerving "authoress" along the only tracks readers left behind: letters and memories. We need to extend Eagleton's insight, therefore, to include the kinds of excitable speech *Peyton Place* and Grace Metalious authorized as talk of incest, oral sex, divorce, adultery, homosexuality, social inequality, and the bitter unfairness of female desire circulated in the last years of the "long fifties."

There are, as historian Nancy Hewitt aptly put it, "no permanent waves" of feminist struggle, no great surges of liberation superseding one another amidst a sea of inaction and silence.[11] Like all social movements, "second wave" feminism was a mélange of notions, ideas, emotions, needs, aspirations, ambitions, and hopes that were always "in the air" commingling, overlapping, and intersecting, as Hewitt reminds us, with a diverse range of progressive moves and acts. We don't often think of scandalous talk as one of these acts and yet what invites more intensive collective commentary or sets into motion with more force the ordinary affects of life—that sentient realm of expectation and desire that "catch people up in something that feels like something?"[12] Quite suddenly, it seemed, the problem that had no name grew immanent in the nooks and crannies of everyday life, exerting a certain flash of recognition among those on the doleful fringes of public life, came to ground in the utterance of a name, the repetition of a story, the effort to say something.

Certainly, this is part of *Peyton Place*'s legacy as a bestseller and part of Grace Metalious's historical meaning as a writer. In the years before the "revolutionary" 60s, feminism was indeed "in the air," winning for itself a public place in many small acts and unsure moves as readers excitedly spoke of this, that, and the outrageous *Peyton Place*—"can you believe"—written by a mother of three and the wife of a New England school teacher. "Did you hear that she was divorced *again*?"

Peyton place

Peyton Place hit American bookstores on September 24, 1956. New York publishers watched in disbelief as orders raced in and printers frantically sought to keep the ink flowing. In an era when the average first novel sold 2000 copies, *Peyton Place* sold 60,000 copies within the first 10 days of its official release. By year's end, almost one in 29 Americans had shelled out $3.75 to buy the hard-covered edition, putting it on top of the *New York Times* bestseller list where it stayed for 59 weeks. Soon, even these figures were topped as *Peyton Place* rapidly edged out middlebrow's "quality" bestsellers, including *God's Little Acre* and *Gone with the Wind*, to become the century's bestselling novel at the time and the fastest fiction ever printed.

It was Grace Metalious's first novel. Born in the textile manufacturing town of Manchester, New Hampshire, Grace grew up moving from one peeling apartment to the next; her homes, ten in all, in unkempt flats of "dirty, brown-shingled tenement houses" on the fringes of *Petit Canada*. A reflection of the city's general deterioration, they installed in Grace an iron determination to "hack her way" out of poverty. "I don't go along with all the claptrap about poverty being good for the soul and trouble and struggle being great strengtheners of character," Grace wrote in the wake of *Peyton Place*'s financial success. Rather, "it has been my experience that being poor makes people mean and grabby, and trouble makes them tight-lipped and whiny."[13] To escape her surroundings and the "big scale desires" of her grabby and whiny mother Laurette, Grace made the town library a second home and with the help of an "unusually kind librarian," she found solace from "poverty, drunkenness, and violent fights" in the reading of books. Soon, she made up her own stories scribbling down descriptions and tall tales about friends, favorite places, and men who, unlike her vanishing father, would never divorce or desert the family. Her characters,

Grace later confided, "were far more real to me than the humans who surrounded me."[14]

Writing thus entered the life of Grace DeRepentigny less as a specific kind of wage labor leading to self-support, than as a vague creative urge and a doggedly practical way to momentarily escape the world she had been born into. Years later, when a reporter asked her what was the happiest thing she remembered as a child, Grace quietly replied, "I wouldn't say, 'happiest' was the word—more like relieved. And that was when I realized I could leave home."[15] But at the time, neither the personal nor social conditions for literary self-construction existed to provide Grace DeRepentigny with the means to convert her sense of confinement into art that paid. Far more available were culturally sanctioned conceptions of marriage and motherhood and in 1943 they offered Grace, as they did for many women in her generation, a more specific means to escape the past and creatively imagine a different future. This is not to say that Grace stopped writing when she married her childhood friend George Metalious, now a struggling first-year student at the University of New Hampshire. But the route to publication escaped her. George Metalious, a tall, dark complexioned, somewhat passive and insecure young man (Grace called him "gentle and kind" and later, "taciturn and sullen"), encouraged Grace's writing, but the birth of three children and grinding poverty inexorably and discouragingly pushed her work to the margins of their life together.

An indifferent housekeeper, Grace kept her writing a closeted affair, an old typewriter stashed in the corner for when her three children and teacher husband were at school. It was a hardscrabble life in a small New England village where George earned just over $3000.00 a year in his new job as teacher/principal. "I allowed myself $20 a week for food," Metalious later recalled, "because no matter how I figured and fumed, I simply could not feed us for less."[16] A month after publication of her novel, "Mrs. Schoolteacher" signed a movie contract with Twentieth Century Fox, moved into a stately white clapboard Cape house on the edge of town, purchased a used Cadillac, and bought new bathing suits for each of her three kids and for her neighbors' kids too. Then, she bought the largest refrigerator she could find and stuffed it full of food. By the time New Year rang in, *Peyton Place* tolled at number two on the *New York Times* bestseller list, turning the unknown author into a subject of curiosity and escalating controversy. "Wow!" exclaimed

Floyd Major, owner of Charleston, West Virginia's only bookstore. "John O'Hara move over-Grace is coming thru."[17]

Sales moved in rushing waves as soldiers, teenagers, husbands, wives, the old, and middle aged crossed class, ethnic, and regional divides, dog-earing favorite pages and elbowing their opinions into the heart of things. Word seeped into the fabric of the nation. Its story of incest, murder, abortion, class conflict, poverty, female sexual autonomy, and lust in small-town America pushed to the surface of official discourse the hidden talk and secret rebellions of the "silent" generation. "I was living in the Midwest during the 1950's," recalled writer Emily Toth "and I can tell you it was boring. Elvis Presley and *Peyton Place* were the only two things in that decade that gave you hope there was something going on out there."[18] Hidden under beds, behind bookshelves, and in bureau drawers, *Peyton Place* came out during private moments of reading and during confidential chats with friends. "I heard my mother and her best friend whispering in the kitchen. As soon as I entered, they whipped a book into a bag, but they were too slow. I had caught my mother reading *Peyton Place*, a book banned by our own town library." "Everyone and their sister was talking about *Peyton Place*," one 50s reader recalled. "Even if they hadn't read it, they sure had something to say."[19]

The storyline of *Peyton Place* is deceptively simple and like *Uncle Tom's Cabin*, difficult for modern readers to understand what all the fuss was about. The main story follows the lives of three women and their friends, who, in different ways and for different reasons, come to terms with their identity as women and as sexual persons in the repressive and class-bound atmosphere of a small New England mill town. Allison MacKenzie, very much like her youthful author, Grace Metalious, is a restless, insecure girl—"plump in all the wrong places," who was "all thumbs and had a head full of silly dreams." (11) Growing up in a fatherless household and the silence that surrounded his absence, Allison longs to escape, dreaming, like her creator, of becoming a famous author. Her working mother Constance, whom Allison believes to be widowed, lives a lonely and sexually frustrated life, haunted by the fear that her long-ago adulterous relationship with a married man will be revealed and ruin both her life and that of her daughter, the offspring of her passionate relationship with him.

It is Allison's friend Selena, however, who pulls readers back from the brink of melodrama. Sexually abused by her father for years, Selena is the town's diamond-in-the rough and she represents a growing fascination in popular culture with girls outside the confines of white middle-class respectability. In television dramas and hit songs like "Patches," Teen Angel, and Town Without Pity, girls from "the wrong side of the tracks" were increasingly presented as victims of social circumstances and class prejudice, "good girls" wronged by society rather than by character. Like Selena, they find romance on the other side of town with respectable middle-class boys who, unlike their disapproving parents, neighbors, and teachers, reject prejudice and class boundaries as old fashioned and unjust. The narrative arc of the "wrong side of the tracks" story, however, usually ends in suicide or separation, underscoring the difficulties, even naivety, of cross-class, and, at times, interracial, mingling, at least on a permanent basis. For Metalious, on the other hand, the story of Selena becomes a potent vehicle with which to excoriate the indifference of town leaders and churchgoers to the problems of the rural working poor in general and to their daughters in particular. In an era of free education, the narrator of *Peyton Place* explains:

> the woodsmen of northern New England had little or no schooling. "They're all right," the New Englander was apt to say, especially to a tourist from the city. They pay their bills and taxes and they mind their own business." . . . . This attitude was visible too, in the well-meaning social workers who turned away from the misery of the woodsman's family. If a child died of cold or malnutrition, it was considered unfortunate, but certainly nothing to stir up a hornet's nest about. The state was content to let things lie, for it never had been called upon to extend aid of a material nature to the residents of the shacks which sat, like running sores on the body of Northern New England.[20]

Steeped in the custom of a "willful ignorance" or, what historian John Howard calls, the "will-to-not-know," New England reticence was as iconic as the church steeples, autumn colors, and white-washed light houses that dotted its sublime landscape.[21] Far from the "frenzied moralists" decried by H. L. Mencken, New Englanders, especially in the rural northern tiers of Vermont, New Hampshire, and Maine, practiced a carefully balanced casualness toward illicit sexuality that often startled people "from away."[22] What was scorned and pilloried by locals were acts of indiscretion and imprudent revelation. Even incest, long acknowledged along the whispered routes of townspeople, was tolerated if it was kept out of sight. "Mind your own business" was a reminder that the violation was in the asking not in the doing.

If Lucas Cross represented the town's refusal to see the poverty in their midst, Selena exposed their resistance to confrontation; their honed ability to look away, especially from the domestic lives of the rural shack dwellers whose "bestial" habits townspeople suspected with a shrug.[23] Trapped by events, Selena has no words to describe, the "dusky" beauty shields her sexual abuse by dating the "decent, well-brought-up" Ted Carter and by working in the dress shop owned by Allison's mother. Both acts bring a cloak of respectability, although they also raise the stakes should pregnancy force Selena to expose the father of her unborn child. On a snowy night just before Christmas, Selena and her younger brother Joey fight off the drunken father, smash in his head, then bury his body in the family sheep pen.

Based upon a true story of a similarly abused girl in Gilmanton Iron Works, who murdered her father after years of sexual violence, no publisher would touch it. "No one would believe it," Grace's publisher and editor explained to the young author, "no one."[24] Knowing full well that domestic violence and child sexual abuse were as common to the everyday landscape as the running sores of tarred-paper shacks, Metalious was shocked and angry. "I don't know what all the screaming is about," a perplexed Grace later told the beautifully coiffed Joyce Donaldson on Canadian TV. "Why, sex and violence are everywhere." An incredulous Metalious angrily changed the manuscript. Lucas Cross was genetically uncoupled from Selena: he became Selena's stepfather. No one noticed. *Peyton Place* found its mark in untold numbers of the abused putting domestic violence and child sexual abuse back into public conversation where it seeped through the surfaces of official denial and polite disbelief. Letters poured in to newspapers, magazines, producers, and to Grace.

Female fame

Thrust into the public eye as a "literary phenomenon," it was Grace Metalious's gender performance and candor that kept her there. From the time the ink dried on advanced copies of *Peyton Place* to Grace's death from cirrhosis of the liver in 1964, the explosive trajectory of the novel moved in tandem with tales of the authors' turbulent life: the sudden separation from her husband George on the eve of fame; an adulterous affair with a local Disc Jockey named T. J. Martin; a bitter divorce from George in 1958, and then the highly publicized marriage to T. J. three days later. Two years after that, T. J. the D. J. was gone and Grace triumphantly remarried the father of her three children the next day. Selling her story to the syndicated Sunday supplement, *The American Weekly*, Grace explained to 50 million readers, not only why she left Mr. Martin, but "Why I Returned to My Husband."

Like the novel that shot her to fame, Grace's story resonated across America, her participation in "the speaking/appearing conundrum" of televisions visual tract, an opportunity for viewers to see the "real" woman behind the stories. After all, Grace Metalious was on the "Night Beat" stage not only because her novel was rapidly becoming a bestseller but also because the author of *Peyton Place* was widely trumpeted as "a New England housewife and mother whose "dirty" book had cost her husband his job." Representing both a new type of woman and alterative model of female fame, Grace's appearance unsettled viewers in multiple ways. "I expected her to be a seductress," television writer Burton Bernstein confessed. Al Ramrus, a writer for *Night Beat,* imagined the author of *Peyton Place* as "a very flamboyant, outspoken, colorful woman," but found instead an overweight wife and mother who "could just as easily have been sitting behind a drugstore counter."[25] Susann, with her "spiky false lashes, chain smoker's gravelly voice, and glittery dresses," was equally stunned by Metalious's plainness.[26] "How," the future author of *Valley of the Dolls* asked, "could this woman, 'chunky, depressed, and colorless,'" write such a popular book "almost in spite of the author's publicity efforts?"[27]

For audience viewers, however, Grace Metalious was a text that resonated deeply, offering up a sharp tongue, gripping personal story, promise of sudden success, and a down home country style. In her matronly suit, pony tail, and plump, unadorned frame, she offered a stark contrast to both the mass-produced star of Hollywood fame and the glowing television *femcee* who, like Arlene Francis, Betty Furness, Bess Myerson, and Joyce Davidson, charmed audiences by melding beauty and fashion with more accessible traits of "likability, magnetism, and amiability" (Figure 1).[28] In an era when television

FIGURE 1 *One of the era's most famous "femcees," Arlene Francis represented a new type of female fame that was charming, likeable, and fashionable.*

"persisted in displaying woman as feminine spectacle, eroticized or brimming over with emotion" as Martha Cassidy notes, Metalious provided new ground on which "distinctions, differences, and oppositions" could be conceptually played out.[29] "I hate clothes," Grace declared early and often. I'd go naked if I could."[30] On the Ben Hecht show, she almost did. In the middle of the live interview, Grace suddenly began to fidget with her clothes as her mandatory girdle suddenly snapped in a loud "whang." "Clutching her stomach oddly," audiences watched the stricken guest "waddle off towards the ladies room."[31]

Part of the historic reinvention of femininity in the 1950s, the "New Look" of Christian Dior helped turn the female body into a "living sculpture" of cinched waists, padded bras, and stiff girdles that ushered in and helped secure new models of female fame following WWII (Figure 2). After the rationing of wartime, a plethora of new cosmetic products, including eye, cheek, and lip coloring conjoined with ready-mix hair coloring, curling "perms," or chemical straighteners that could be applied at home, inviting housewives to "make up" new bodies, styles, and identities. In this "Rococo decade," the author of Peyton Place chose for her book jacket an image of herself sitting at a typewriter in a kitchen.[32] She wore blue jeans, a flannel skirt, and Keds sneakers. Her very public struggles with the sartorial constraints of era would become part of a sustained unfolding of unconventionality that gave her celebrity a pronounced edginess in the 1950s (Figure 3). "There was nothing like her," a 90-old woman from Ohio recalled.

FIGURE 2 *The sculpted body and glamor of the "New Look" by fashion designer Christian Dior. (January 1952, Photographer Paul Radkai for Harper's Bazaar)*

FIGURE 3 *Grace Metalious rejected the formal studio photograph publishers provided choosing instead, a photo by local New Hampshire photographer Larry Smith for the book jacket of* Peyton Place. *(1956, Larry Smith,* Laconia Evening Citizen)

"When I saw her for the first time, I just stared. I just knew right then and there something in my life had changed. You could see it you know, you could see something out there was happening. So I ran out and bought Peyton Place and my husband thought I had gone mad."

"Not a bad thing to be," she added, "in 1957."[33]

While her novel found praise in several reviews, most notably the *New York Times*, many critics expressed shock that a wife and mother could use such language and tell such a story. Photo magazines on the other hand, especially those geared toward middleclass readers and conventional advertisers, sought to confirm the authors' participation in heteronormative American family life. *Look*, *Life*, and even the Hearst tabloid, *American Weekly*, promoted a visual narrative that emphasized Grace Metalious as an ordinary, average New England housewife, showing her playing games, shopping (always in the same local stores as she did before her fame), "roughhousing" in the snow with her kids and the family St. Bernard, combing the children's hair, and vacationing on the beach.

Yet, the images told others tales as well. Framed by Grace's candid story—her turbulent marriage and endless breakups, excessive drinking and adulterous relationship—the photographs highlighted for readers the twists and turns a woman's life could take until finding true happiness. Images of her smiling children playfully tossing sand at her handsome boyfriend T. J., accentuated as well the benefits for the entire family. "I did not like being Mrs. Schoolteacher," Grace boldly confided to 50 million readers. "I did not like belonging to Friendly Clubs and Bridge Clubs. I did not like being regarded as a freak because I spent time in front of a typewriter instead of a sink. And George did not like my not liking the things I was supposed to like."[34] Her lawyer wrote, warning her against appearing with T. J. in public interviews for fear that she would lose her pending divorce case. "We may be in the soup" he hastily wrote, "I heartily suggest that you do not discuss the situation any further with the newspapers."[35] Her publisher, Kitty Messner, worried that Metalious' future as a serious writer would be ruined by such revelations. The guileless author would not be stopped. "I don't know what all the screaming is about, why, sex and violence are everywhere."

Readers agreed. Thrilled by the boldness of *Peyton Place*, they were riveted by the audacity and courage of its young author. "I read it [Peyton Place] and recognized it for what it really was—a triumph over good and evil, and you, for what you are, a good woman," a reader from New York City explained as he defended her from the charges of critics.[36] He was hardly alone. In the cultural conversations between text and image, readers were invited to imagine domestic upheavals like divorce, alcoholism, and infidelity as part of life in postwar America. When Grace divorced T. J. and remarried George, waves of letters rushed in. Every new revelation about her life was followed by an army of well-wishers describing themselves as "staunch fans" and "kindred spirits" whose lives mirrored her own. "When I read your story in the *American Weekly*," a "plain old housewife" wrote like so many others, "I thought you had used a crystal ball and read my past."[37] "I devoured every word written on your personal life," letter writers typically confessed before defending Grace's choices. Many thanked her for giving them as well "the courage to attempt . . . to tell my own story."[38] *Peyton Place* was risky enough for a woman to write, but to tell of such deep and painful events in so frank a way seemed to require encouragement, gratitude, and a word or two of kindness. "Like a prospector you took leave of one vein of ore and sought another. You are so brave. Keep on writing honey—it is inspiring to people . . . "[39]

Some have argued that *Peyton Place* did not become a scandalous book until well after its publication.[40] But it would be a mistake not to recognize the intense relationship between Grace's unconventional behavior as wife and mother and the controversial trajectory of her novel. From the very beginning, novel and author were stitched together with the ancient threads of a wife's apostasy and a woman's transgressions. "Publishing circles," the gossip columnist Dorothy Kilgallen announced a good month before Grace's "fourth baby" went to press, "are gabbing about a forthcoming novel titled *Peyton Place*—a shocker about life in a small New England town. The author, mother of three, is the wife of a school principal in New Hampshire." [41] In the unquiet act of female nonconformity, Grace Metalious pulled herself in the literary and onto writings new public.

The year was 1956. Could good wives write "bad" books?

Conjoining "dirty" books with housewives and mothers (school teachers wives, no less), Grace Metalious brought into focus the frenzied anxieties of postwar Americans over the dramatic alterations in women's economic and sexual behavior. Intensified by the unleashing of the atom, fears of sexual chaos took on increased symbolic force as the decade unfolded. Unmarried men and "emancipated" women, weak husbands, and frigid wives, overbearing moms and negligent mothers, stray wives and divorced women—all grew suspect, even pathological, as categories of sexual and gender "normalcy" tightened under the widening gaze of postwar experts and the expanded view of popular culture. Widely framed as an antidote to the moral dangers buried within the national fabric, family stability was cast a patriotic duty during a Cold War that was fought with the chilly weapons of perception and appearance. As loving, even erotic wives, women would cement a man's loyalty to the home ensuring, or so the theory went, the rearing of healthy, well-adjusted, "normal" American children. "It was not just nuclear energy that had to be contained," Elaine Tyler May points out, "but the social and sexual fallout of the atomic age itself."[42] Channeled for the good of the country into childrearing and marriage, female sexual energy gained new recognition as normal and healthy, but only if bounded by home and husband.

Because female celebrity embodied the tensions of the era, fame was a serious force in postwar negotiations over gender and the borders of sexual and social "normality." Organized in the 1920s with the advent of mass entertainment and the Hollywood star system, celebrity accrued new power in the 50s, as visual culture increasingly penetrated everyday life both through expanded pictorial coverage in photographic magazines, newspaper supplements, movies, and the dramatic growth of television. When WWII ended, only a small fraction of American households (.02 per cent) contained a television, but by 1955, a new majority did. Five years later, only ten percent of American homes lacked a magic box in front of which they and their fellow countrymen spent five hours a day.[43]

Powerful because they permeated the television networks, the female hostess or femcee, and her guest also mirrored televisions' promise that the personalities they generated were more unguarded and therefore more authentic than screen stars, giving them a familiarity and personality audiences could more easily identify with and recognize as similar to their own.[44] More importantly, recent scholars argue, by putting women on stage in a radically new and widespread public sphere, television "validated femininity's power to be seen and heard."[45] Whether as T.V. hostess or female contestant, women's voices moved center stage and unlike the scripted talk of glamor beauties of stage and film, they constituted a "speaking subject" that emphasized the importance of women's unrehearsed words and the power of female utterance.

Audiences listened in fascination as Grace wove together a halting, almost shy manner with a quick, sharp wit expounding on sex, marriage, divorce, drinking, children, and poverty in America. Like Susann, many found Grace's sudden success dazzling, her journey from an ordinary struggling housewife to a literary celebrity, a tale that seemed to confirm postwar consumerist narratives and the fantasies they enacted. Trumpeted as part of a new class of "Millionaire Writers," her story further confirmed the narrative style and therapeutic messages of popular daytime television shows like *It could be You*, (1956–61), *The Big Payoff* (1951–59), "*Who do You Trust?*" (1957–63), and *Strike it Rich* where the winning confessions of struggling housewives merited rewarding, either through sudden wealth or, like *Queen for a Day* (1956–64), with an array of dazzling consumer products.[46] In newspapers, magazines, Sunday supplements, and television, Grace found fame as a once impoverished New Hampshire housewife who now lived the American Dream. In this sense, Grace's celebrity participated in the optimistic hopes of postwar capitalism holding aloft the promises of consumption and confirming among the nation's worst off workers, their membership in an upwardly mobile middle class society.

Indeed, many hoped to emulate Grace's literary road to fame and fortune. "I'm certain Peyton Place was a gold mine," they wrote. "How do you go about getting material published?" a struggling 64-old widow asked. "Do you have to use a typewriter [sic] or do some accept long hand?" From Massachusetts, a "would-be author" wanted to know if she needed an agent, fame was not her motive, she explained, rather "I just enjoy writing and I want to earn some money, to put it bluntly." Even those who railed against Peyton Place wrote to congratulate her for "pulling a fast one" "The filth nauseated me—I do admit, however, that if I had the talent to write and the opportunity to make so much money, I'd probably would have written as you did."[47]

But as a representational model of female fame, Grace's life story complicated consumerist middle class fictions, bringing into view the hardships of the rural poor and especially, the ordinary housewife, whose discontent and restlessness also ran like sores on the body of America. Fame became in Grace a potent discourse about womanhood in postwar society and about the concomitant boundaries of gender, economic disparity, and sexual normality.[48] Like *Peyton Place*, the name Grace Metalious signified a complex array of emotions and uncertainties that hovered just beneath the surface of official discourse: it named an argument much more than a person. Vilified in the press and pulpit as her unconventional lifestyle publicly unfolded, an outraged few wrote to take their revenge: "I knew that anyone who would write Peyton Place must be a drunken old bag," an Indiana reader gloated.[49] But by definition, fan mail was for fans and their letters cheered Grace on. Part of a cultural battle zone, she continued to open up to debate what polite society sought to shutter away. In broadsheet tabloids, newspaper supplements, photo magazines, and on television talk shows, Grace's story increasingly complicated narratives of domesticity putting divorce, adultery, alcoholism, and female economic independence on display in ways that fascinated, outraged, and unsettled.

Many struggled to understand and explain their motives for writing to a complete stranger usually citing a show, an interview, or a recent article they had read. More often than not, a weary gratitude explained the impulse to take up pen and paper. "I find myself in a similar circumstance and I had to find a way to thank you," a not untypical letter writer explained after following her stories in the *American Weekly*. Finding in Grace's life story a way to reshape her own, she concluded, "So with heart felt thanks, I believe I can find my way."[50] Fans also found in her fame a way to reposition themselves as part of a failed society rather than as failed wives and mothers. "My life was so very much like yours," a woman from Texas wrote Grace. "Nothing has turned out and I find myself turning to drink as you say you did." Now threatened with going to jail for "a theft I did not commit," the writer saw in Grace a way to "put her life in order" asking the "generous" author to read her tale as she too turned to "put her experiences down" and make them count. Grace always complied, dating her letters upon her reply, often sending requests for literary advice to her own literary agent.

Many used the cascading narratives of Grace's life (and at times the fictional characters she created), not simply to reflect upon their experiences but to plot and structure them in ways that gave them meaning. New vocabularies offered new possibilities to understand, even "make up" a life, a past. Again and again, letter writers wrote to tell their stories, explain their acts—using Grace's frankness as way to position themselves as storytellers "in the know," nobodies for whom Grace gave voice. "You gave me courage," they would write, but what she gave them too was agency.

Missteps and poverty moved from shame and victimization to subjects of discussion and evaluation. "You are quite right," a Maine woman gratefully wrote, "that poverty breeds bitterness."[51] With leaky pens and typewriters with chipped keys, the outcast and the outsider, the ordinary and the impoverished wrote to Grace as a friend, often using only her given name. "Dear Grace," they would confide. "I'm buried in self-pity today so I thought I'd write to someone who would understand. . . . Your story [of divorce] jacked me up." Many saw themselves as women life had passed by only to discover in Grace that they were not alone. "I must say you've been a great inspiration to me. Not because I've read any of your books . . . but because I am a nobody like you were." If Grace could speak of such things, then so could they. "I am a 'nobody'" a Belfast, Maine woman wrote, "'an outcast' too who had an abortion, married three times and let me tell you my life would make a book." Narrating their own lives, letter writers took control of their own stories, structuring them in ways that gave an accounting to things once thought out of reach and beyond words.[52]

What seemed shocking and offensive about *Peyton Place* seemed "real" and "human" when spoken about by its author. What seemed "plain" and "colorless" to *Night Beat* staffers, appeared unpretentious and authentic to viewers many of whom used her verbal and visual performances to locate the "real" woman behind the shocking writer. "It is a shame," a housewife from nearby Maine wrote, "that some interviewers cannot bring out the real person that you are and allow you to be sincerely your real self, for your reticence can be felt even over the air waves—and it is only natural for you to be on the defensive."[53] "I had the oddest sensation of kinship with you," another confessed. "I feel I had the pleasure of seeing," another wrote after watching her in T.V., "the inner most recesses of the soul of a real person." Indeed, part of the imaginative labor of *Peyton Place* and Grace's celebrity was to conceptually render authorship "ordinary" and plausible; a domain of social endeavor continuous with, not disengaged from, the lives of women who labored in the distant shadows of the literary, not only as wives and mothers, but as working women whose most salient relationship to working class life was a fervent desire to escape it. "When I read about you it reminds me that it is possible for a Nobody to get up and go forth!" a Detroit wife and mother wrote. "I said to my husband, 'If Grace can write, why can't I?' It used to be fun being a Nobody but I guess I am tired of the role."[54]

Grace was also candid about her "highs and lows" bringing into public conversation the kinds of mood swings we now identify with depression or even bipolar disorders. But it was her frankness as an "ordinary" wife and mother about sexual matters that a hungry public soaked up. "There are very few things which repel me, she quipped to a reporter, such as seeing the kids get a cut finger or pulling their teeth. Far worse to me than any sex act is unattractive food, and I'm no gourmet."[55] Within the conflation of her fiction and life, Grace became a proxy for the dissatisfied and disaffected who felt not only contempt for "the ivory tower types" who claimed control over literary taste and opinion, but also a deep frustration and weariness with the reticence and hypocrisy that seemed to surround them. "You wrote of such complex matters with such sincere simplicity, it is beautiful."[56] Words like "earthy" "real" "human" signaled the distance readers felt themselves from other celebrities, novels, and official fictions. "I have read true books before but none stand up to yours which is fiction," a Vermont teenager wrote.[57] "No one tells the truth, but you," a housewife wrote after hearing Grace on the radio. "You are quite right, facts are facts, and there is much more to be written—long buried facts in the countless country graveyards of New England." In a landscape of social erasure and sexual opacity, Grace's celebrity put the open secrets of an era on display and out to work. "When I read it [Peyton Place] at ten years old," the film maker John Waters recalled, "I knew the world around me was a lie."

Like the discourses of familiarity and "sympathetic identification" shaped by the television "personality," Grace represented for many the quotidian concerns and interests of common folk, her missteps welcomed as a way to navigate and narrate their own. "My life is so like yours," a woman from far off El Cajon, California, wrote after reading Grace's story in the *American Weekly*.[58] "Oh, Mom, she sounds just like you.!," the daughter of another exclaimed as she read Grace's reply to her mother's first letter. Thanking Grace for responding to her "crazy, mixed up letter," the middle-aged wife and mother concluded, "Maybe that's why I had written to you because I felt a closeness—that you are a down-to-earth person and not a snob."[59] In a world where being "nobody" is the norm, fame mattered.[60]

If fame and celebrity culture have most often been explored and held accountable for its hard work in the service of hegemony, particularly as a "consumption ideal," Grace's fame operated in ways that connected those on the other side of American prosperity to a new story about themselves and the world in which they lived. If the extreme lifestyles of mainstream stars—their enormous houses, manicured lawns, fast cars, planes and horses, and healthy, tanned bodies can be thought of as "an extrapolation of a consumer subjectivity," Grace's celebrity aligned fans to an ethos of social critique and the narrative possibilities her infamous differences opened up to public view.[61]

For historians then, this is where celebrity culture turns useful: not because it necessarily reveals anything true about the famous, but because it insists upon the excitable exposure of transgressive behaviors in the form of out-of-control publicity. Like all publicity, *Night Beat* and other shows sold celebrity. It also sold books, and, if given the chance, Ivory soap and Rice Krispies. But, it was the kind of combustible behaviors enacted by and through the celebrity system—from television interviews to newspaper supplements—that outsold any other commodity, opening up to expanding audiences the narrative possibilities of outsider lives lived beyond, often well beyond, the known world. Wrong roads opened up and turned out to be right.

Scandal, in other words, is the very essence of celebrity ferreting out for public consumption the private departures and off-stage escapes from social norms its cry and hue are supposed to regulate and enforce.[62] Audiences took note. Grace's fans took more: hope, courage, a quickening urge to tell. They took as well her autograph, posters, signed photos, even wallpaper from her home—anything to establish a link, a connection and pathway that could lead them perhaps toward alternatives not yet fully imagined, not quite yet worked out. All fame carries with it a certain discursive power that runs, as the following letter writer makes clear, along the sonorous underbrush of the everyday: "SO I GUESSED IT AMUSED ME TO HEAR LOCAL WOMEN CALL YOUR BOOK PEYTON PLACE VULGAR. . . . . HOW BADLY THEY MISSED YOUR POINT," a woman form Davenport, Florida shouted in her letter to Metalious. Continuing more calmly, she sought to describe her neighbors: "Puritanically sex conscious, they never the less gobbled your book . . . so had more to gossip about at their church socials. 'DID YOU READ PEYTON PLACE? WHY WAS IT EVER PUBISHED?' Point is..they read it," she trumpeted.[63]

We can only imagine of course, the deep emotive topography that traverses print and utterance, readers and talkers, viewers and gossipers, but in the letters to Grace Metalious, we can track something of the emotional service rendered by and through the gender and sexual transgressions she so candidly performed. Seven years before Betty Friedan published *The Feminine Mystique*, working class fans of Grace expressed their doubts, uncertainties, and wavering commitment to the postwar fictions of female domesticity and femininity. Their problems had names: poverty, the unfairness of female desire, child sexual abuse, domestic violence, a longing to be a somebody. Grace socialized them, collectivized them, them to female discontent the ring of truth. "I could write pages and pages to you," they wrote, "things I think, feel do . . . But here is a passage from your Peyton Place that I like:

"But it was not the season that weighed heaviest on Allison. She did not know what it was. She seemed to be filled with a restlessness, a vague unrest, which nothing was able to ease . . . " I feel a lot of women now feel this, not only myself, or you, at one time..that feeling of WHAT AM I HERE FOR? Perhaps some women feel only a vague restlessness they can't analyze . . . but it is an unfruitful feeling, and just raising children to maturity doesn't seem the full answer. Perhaps too many modern conveniences have robbed a woman of her own creativeness in the home? Thus that creativeness has no full outlet? . . . I wonder and wonder, and do you, ever, too?" They would plead, "Keep on writing Grace."[64]

Grace Metalious did. She wrote three more novels, each selling over a million copies, was named "outstanding woman in her field" by Women's Editors of Associated Press newspapers in 1957, and made headlines around the nation when she died at the vulnerable age of 39.

To her readers and fans, it was a storied life, and certainly among the many tales that permeate daily life, it is the scandalous that must be counted as the easiest to grasp and in the end, the most unsettling.

Bibliography

Carbine, Patricia. "Peyton Place." *Look Magazine*, March 18, 1958.

Cassidy, Marsha. *What Women Watched: Daytime Television in the 1950s*. Austin: University of Texas Press, 2005.

Davis, Natalie Zemon. "Printing and the People." In *Society and Culture in Early Modern France*, 189–226. Stanford: 1975.

Doane, Mary Ann. *The Desire to Desire: The Women's Film of the 1940s*. Bloomington: Indiana University Press, 1987.

Ewen, Stuart. *All Consuming Images: The Politics of Style in Contemporary Culture.* New York: Basic Books, 1988.

Gourley, Catherine. *Gidgets and Women Warriors: Perceptions of Women in the 1950s and 1960s.* Minneapolis: Twenty-First Books, 2008.

Hammill, Faye. *Women Celebrity and Literary Culture Between the Wars.* Austin: University of Texas Press, 2007.

Hewitt, Nancy, ed. *No Permanent Waves: Recasting Histories of U.S. Feminism.* New Brunswick, New Jersey, and London: Rutgers University Press, 2010.

Howard, John. *Men Like That: A Southern Queer History.* Chicago: University of Chicago Press, 1999.

Kilgallen, Dorothy. *Boston Traveler,* August 7, 1956.

Korda, Michael. "Wasn't She Great?" *New Yorker,* August 14, 1995.

Major, Floyd. "Publishers Advance Reading Copy Card," undated.

Marshall, David. *Celebrity and Power: Fame in Contemporary Culture.* Minneapolis: University of Minnesota Press, 1997.

May, Elaine Tyler. *Homeward Bound: American Families in the Cold War Era.* New York: Basic Books, 1988.

Messner Inc, Julian. Grace Metalious File, *Paul Reynolds Collection,* Columbia University Rare Book and Manuscript Library, New York City, New York.

Metalious Family Collection of Letters.

Metalious, George and June O'Shea. *The Girl From Peyton Place.*

Metalious, Grace. "All About Me and Peyton Place." *The American Weekly,* May 18, 1958.

—. "Me and Peyton Place." *The American Weekly,* June 1, 1958.

—. *Peyton Place.* Boston: Northeastern University Press, Reprint ed. 1999.

Murray, Susan. "Our Man Godfry: Arthur Godfry and the Selling of Stardom in Early Television." *Television and New Media* 2.3 (August 2001): 196.

"Nice Clean Little Town." *Yankee Magazine,* September 1936.

Peiss, Kathy. *Hope in a Jar: The Making of America's Beauty Culture.* New York: Henry Holt and Company, 1998.

Seaman, Barbara. *Lovely Me: The Life of Jacqueline Susann.* New York: William Morrow and Company, 1987.

—. *Lovely Me: The Life of Jacqueline Susann.* New York: William Morrow and Company, 1987.

Spigel, Lynn. *Make Room For TV: Television and Family Ideal in Postwar America.* Chicago and London: University of Chicago Press, 1992.

Stewart, Kathleen. *Ordinary Affects.* Durham & London: Duke University Press, 2007.

Toth, Emily. *Inside Peyton Place: The Life of Grace Metalious.* Garden City, New Jersey: Doubleday, 1981.

Wallace, Mike and Gary Paul Gates. *Between You and Me: A Memoir.* New York: Hyperion, 2005.

—. *Close Encounters: Mike Wallace's Own Story.* New York: William Morrow and Company, Inc., 1984.

Waters, John. Quoted in Laura Lippman. "The Women of Peyton Place." *The Baltimore Sun,* June 14, 1999.

Notes

1   John Waters, quoted in Laura Lippman, "The Women of Peyton Place," *The Baltimore Sun,* 14 June 1999. Sec. SunSpot Features, p. 5.

2   Mike Wallace, with Gary Paul Gates, *Between You and Me: A Memoir* (New York: Hyperion, 2005): 1–4. Wallace and Gates, *Close Encounters: Mike Wallace's Own Story* (New York: William Morrow and Company, Inc. 1984): 22, 40.

3   Ibid. Wallace and Gates, *Close Encounters*, p. 23.

4   While Mike Wallace embraced a more confrontational style, most interviewers developed a confidential approach inviting the subject to speak as Barbara Walters famously put it, "just between you and me," also the title of Wallace's memoir.

5   Barbara Seaman, *Lovely Me: The Life of Jacqueline Susann* (New York: William Morrow and Company, 1987): 239–42.

6   Ibid.

7   The scholarly turn toward popular fiction and the habits of general, working-class, and mass readers is enormous and growing. I list here a few that have been especially important in mapping different kinds of readers and thinking about the kinds of labor reading performs: See Lisa Walker, "Afterword" in Valerie Taylor, *The Girls of 3-B* (New York: The Feminist Press, 2003): 91; Michael Denning, *Mechanic Accents: Dime Novels and Working-Class Culture in America* (London and New York: Verso, 1987); Carolyn Stewart Dyer and Nancy Tillman Romalov, eds., *Rediscovering Nancy Drew* (Iowa City: University of Iowa City Press, 1995); Janice Radway, *A Feeling for Books: The Book-Of –The-Month Club, Literary Taste, and Middle Class Desire* (Chapel Hill and London: University of North Carolina Press, 1997); Richard Brodhead, *Cultures of Writing: Scenes of Reading and Writing in Nineteenth-Century America* (Chicago and London: The University of Chicago Press, 1993); Elizabeth Long, *Book Clubs: Women and the Uses of Reading in Everyday Life* (Chicago and London: The University of Chicago Press, 2003).

8   Natalie Zemon Davis, "Printing and the People," in *Society and Culture in Early Modern France* (Stanford, CA, 1975): 189–226.

9   On sales and popularity of the novel, see Ardis Cameron, "Open Secrets," in Grace Metalious, *Peyton Place* Reprint edition (Boston: Northeastern University Press, 1999): vii–xxx.

10 In fan mail, letters to the editor, remembrances, and in recent correspondence, these two images are pervasive. Letter writers describe how they hid the novel from parents, husbands, and teachers or shared the book with close friends, roommates, and neighbors in soft whispers. Young readers recalled "knots of aunts" in the neighborhood clandestinely taking about *Peyton Place*, church leaders clustered in groups to express their outrage, and friends huddled together sharing "juicy parts." "The best thing you could share with your fellow students," a fan explained to me "was, 'Read page 187!' or whatever." Letter to author, March 15, 2010.

11 Nancy Hewitt, Ed. *No Permanent Waves: Recasting Histories of U.S. Feminism* (New Brunswick, New Jersey, and London: Rutgers University Press, 2010): 8.

12 "Ordinary Affects," the anthropologist Kathleen Stewart, explains "are the varied, surging capacities to affect and to be affected that give everyday life the quality of a continual motion of relations, scenes, contingencies, and emergencies." See Stewart, *Ordinary Affects* (Durham & London: Duke University Press, 2007): 2.

13 Grace Metalious, "All About Me and Peyton Place." *The American Weekly*, May 18, 1958, 10.

14 For a fuller description of Grace Metalious's life, see George Metalious and June O'Shea, *The Girl From Peyton Place* (New York: Dell Publishing, 1965) and Emily Toth, *Inside Peyton Place: The Life of Grace Metalious* (Garden City: Double Day, 1981).

15 George Metalious and June O'Shea, *The Girl From Peyton Place*, p. 38.

16 Grace Metalious, "All About Me," p. 10.

17 Floyd Major, "Publishers Advance Reading Copy Card," undated. Julian Messner Inc. in Grace Metalious File, *Paul Reynolds Collection*, Columbia University Rare Book and Manuscript Library, New York City, New York.

18 Toth, "Inside Peyton Place."

19 Readers, interviewed by author, 1999, 2007. In possession of author.

20 Grace Metalious, *Peyton Place* (Boston: Northeastern University Press, Reprint edition 1999): 29. All quotations are from this edition.

21 John Howard, *Men Like That: A Southern Queer History* (Chicago: University of Chicago Press, 1999).

22 See Anonymous, "Nice Clean Little Town." *Yankee Magazine* September 1936 (pages unknown). My thanks to Joe Conforti for introducing me to this article.

23 A long literary and folk tradition focused on the supposedly sexual depravity of New England's rural and remote poor, continues well into modern times with novels like Carolyn Chute, *The Beans of Egypt Maine*, (New York: Ticknor & Field, 1985); Stephen King, Dolores Claborne, (New York: Signet, 1993). For earlier representations, see Mary Wilkins Freeman, "Old Woman Magoun" in Barbara Solomon, ed. *Short Fiction of Sarah Orne Jewett and Mary Wilkins Freeman* (New York: Signet,): 485–502; Edith Wharton, *Summer.*

24 Interview with Leona Nevler, January, 2002.

25 Quoted in Emily Toth, *Inside Peyton Place: The Life of Grace Metalious* (Garden City, New Jersey: Doubleday, 1981):162–3.

26 The description is from Michael Korda, "Wasn't She Great?" *New Yorker,* 14 August 1995, 66–72.

27 See Toth, *Inside Peyton Place* especially pp. 163–5 for a complete description of the event.

28 Faye Hammill, *Women Celebrity and Literary Culture Between the Wars* (Austin: University of Texas Press, 2007): 1–2; Catherine Gourley, *Gidgets and Women Warriors: Perceptions of Women in the 1950's and 1960's"* (Minneapolis: Twenty-First Books, 2008): 44; Marsha Cassidy, *What Women Watched: Daytime Television in the 1950's* (Austin: University of Texas Press, 2005): 21–2. See also Mary Ellen Brown, "Motley Moments: Soap Operas, Carnival, Gossip, and the Power of the Utterance," in Mary Ellen Brown, ed. *Television and Women's Culture: The Politics of the Popular* (Londo, Sage Publications, 1990).

29 Cassidy, *What Women Watched*, 206.

30 Grace Metalious, quoted in Patricia Carbine, "Peyton Place," *Look Magazine*, 18 March 1958, 110.

31 Barbara Seaman, *Lovely Me: The Life of Jacqueline Susann* (New York: William Morrow and Company, 1987): 241.

32 The term is from Kathy Peiss, *Hope in a Jar: The Making of America's Beauty Culture* (New York: Henry Holt and Company, 1998): 245.

33 Reader interviews. In possession of author.

34 Grace Metalious, "Me and Peyton Place," *The American Weekly* 1 June, 1958, p. 10.

35 "Bernard I. Snierson to Grace Metalious," October 26, 1960. Metalious Family Collection (hereafter MFC).

36 Townend to Metalious, New York City, February 21, 1960. MFC.

37 Korsholm to Metalious, El Cajon, California, May 31, 1961. MFC.

38 Fitchtner to Metalious, San Francisco, Feburary 3, 1961; Jentzen to Metalious, Hobart, Indiana, May 22, 1961. MFC.

39 Mudd Metalious, Washington, DC, Febuarry 7, 1961. MFC.

40 See Evan Brier, "The Accidental Blockbuster: Peyton Place in Literary and Institutional Context," *Women's Studies Quarterly*, Fall/Winter 33. ¾ especially 53–4.

41 Dorothy Kilgallen, *Boston Traveler*, 7 August, 1956.

42 Elaine Tyler May, *Homeward Bound: American Families in the Cold War Era* (New York: Basic Books, 1988): 82.

43 Lynn Spigel, *Make Room For TV: Television and Family Ideal in Postwar America* (Chicago and London: University of Chicago Press, 1992): 1–2.

44 Susan Murray, "Our Man Godfry: Arthur Godfry and the Selling of Stardom in Early Television," *Television and New Media* 2, 3 (August 2001): 196.

45 Mary Ann Doane, *The Desire to Desire: The Women's Film of the 1940's* (Bloomington: Indiana University Press, 1987): 184.

46 Cassidy, *What Women Watched*, pp. 23–4.

47 "Ginny" to Metalious, San Diago, January 21, 1961; Vinal to Metalious, January 29, 1961; Cowley to Metalious, Marblehead, Mass. March 20, 1961; Stevenson to Metalious, Concord, N.H. January 29, 1961. MFC.

48 David Marshall, *Celebrity and Power*: Fame in Contemporary Culture, (Minneapolis: University of Minnesota Press, 1997): 72. Marshall follows Foucaults notion of sexuality as discourse arguing that, "The celebrity, like sexuality, allows for the configuration, positioning, and proliferation of certain discourses about the individual and individuality in contemporary culture." p. 72. See also Terence J. Fitzgerald, ed. *Celebrity Culture in the United States* (New York: H. W. Wilson Co., 2008) and Aaron Jaffe, *Modernism and the Culture of Celebrity* (Cambridge, UK, New York: Cambridge University Press, 2005).

49 Bond to Metalious. Augola, Indiana, January 28, 1961. MFC.

50 Petterson to Metalious. Cubur City, Calf. January 29, 1961. MFC.

51 May to Metalious. Falmouth, Maine, October 28, 1960. MFC.

52 For a brilliant discussion of the uses of pulp fiction in the lives of unmarried mothers, see Regina Kunzel, "Pulp Fictions and Problem Girls: Reading and Rewriting Single Pregnancy in the Postwar United States," *The American Historical Review* 12 100 5 (1995): 1465–87.

53 May to Metalious. Ibid. Oct. 28, 1960. MFC.

54 O'Shay to Metalious,. Detroit, Mich. Feb. 2, 1961. MFC.

55 See Bernard I. Snierson, Letter to Grace Metalious, October 26, 1960 Metalious Family Papers; Patricia Carbine, "Peyton Place." *Look Magazine*, p. 108.

56 Stevenson to Metalious, Concord, N.H. January 29, 1961. MFC.

57 Anoe to Metalious. Rutland, Vt. February 1961. MFC.

58 Korsholm to Metalious, El Cajon, Cal. May 31, 1996. MFC.

59 West to Metalious, Royal Oak, Mich. February 17, 1961. MFC.

60 Stuart Ewen, All Consuming Images: The Politics of Style in Contemporary Culture (New York: Basic Books, 1988): 92–6.

61 Ibid.

62 Moran, pp. 100–1.

63 Johnston to Metalious. Davenport, Florida. February 11, 1961. MFC.

64 Ibid.

12

Crimes and bestsellers: Mario Puzo's path to *The Godfather*

Evan Brier

The Godfather, one of the bestselling novels of the 1970s, is a singular product of a literary marketplace undergoing a complicated transition in the 1960s, and of its author Mario Puzo's simmering frustration with that marketplace. Puzo's frustration was triggered by the poor sales of his well-reviewed previous novel *The Fortunate Pilgrim* and by his publisher's refusal to give him an advance for the novel he wanted to write next. On a broader level, Puzo grappled with two aspects of the book trade that merit more attention than they have received in studies of American literature and of efforts to sell it: first, the inescapable unpredictability of the marketplace for fiction, which has confounded authors, publishers, and media corporations for more than a century, and which confounds scholars' efforts to explain the popularity or lack thereof of individual novels. The second aspect is the publishing business's rapid growth after World War II and subsequent mid-1960s' consolidation, one effect of which was to make it harder for mid-sized publishers to compete with the biggest ones. Conditioned by a literary ideology that held commerce to be the implacable enemy of art, Puzo could not see how these institutional factors were shaping his career. *The Godfather* springs, fortunately, from his misreading of the book trade.

The Godfather is not usually discussed in these terms. Its reputation has been shaped by the towering stature of Francis Ford Coppola's 1972 movie adaptation, which has helped the novel endure and at the same time left it unusually, perhaps uniquely, diminished. This devaluing began before the movie even premiered: in 1971, Coppola told *New York* magazine that the novel was "cheap and sensational" and that he fought with Paramount Pictures to cast Marlon Brando in it in order to give the movie "class."[1] Months later, Pauline Kael, whose film criticism Puzo had admired greatly, started her laudatory *New Yorker* review of the movie *The Godfather* by calling the novel "trash."[2] And film critic Vincent Canby suggested that the novel functioned as merely a "first draft" that Coppola refined and transformed into art.[3] This last notion especially is implicit in much of what limited criticism there is of Puzo's novel, and it falls easily alongside, and is in part responsible for, the related notion that the novel is a specimen of "popular" as opposed to "elite" literature.[4]

This perspective, curiously endorsed by Puzo himself, has produced some brilliant readings of how and why *The Godfather* resonates with readers and moviegoers, but as I will suggest, it also risks reinforcing faulty ideas about the American literary marketplace out of which the novel emerged, masks a complicated story about how the novel came to be written, and ultimately obscures key aspects of the novel itself. In response, this essay shifts the focus away from efforts to account for the novel's popularity and instead examines the complicated circumstances of its production, drawing attention to neglected institutional factors that both constrained and enabled Puzo as a novelist in the late 1960s. Such a perspective does not aim to dispense with the aforementioned popular-elite dichotomy that has long shaped the critical conversation about Puzo's novel; rather it entails showing how that distinction has functioned not just as an enduring, retrospective judgment on *The Godfather* but also as an animating idea, internalized by its author, that helped to produce it.

Sales and unpredictability

The first step is to revisit the commercial failure of *The Fortunate Pilgrim*, Puzo's autobiographical account of growing up poor during the Great Depression, along with Puzo's influential but perhaps distorted interpretation of that failure. On March 5, 1965, the *New York Times* ran a page of book advertisements that featured a revealing juxtaposition. In the center of the page was an advertisement for *Herzog*, Saul Bellow's novel about a letter-writing academic in crisis, which Viking published in September 1964. *Herzog* is nobody's idea of pulp fiction, and it does not typically figure in histories of American bestsellers. But it merits a place in that history: it was, according to *Publishers Weekly*, the third bestselling novel of 1964, and it would become the third bestselling novel of 1965 as well. The week of the advertisement, it topped the *Times* bestseller list for fiction, as it did for several months from November 1964 through the following May (it was eventually replaced by Bel Kaufman's *Up the Down Staircase*). And the advertisement was all about that success: the foreground placed the words "#1 national fiction bestseller" over an image of the book cover, and in the background, the word "Bestseller" repeated throughout the advertisement.[5]

To the left of the *Herzog* advertisement was one for *The Fortunate Pilgrim*. While the Bellow advertisement proclaimed *Herzog*'s extraordinary commercial success, the advertisement for Puzo's recently published novel more modestly announced the novel's literariness, featuring quotes of praise from *Saturday Review*, the *Times* ("A novel of Italian immigrant life which is a small classic"), and from two notable literary figures, both of whom happened to be Puzo's friends: Joseph Heller and Bruce Jay Friedman. This kind of advertisement is the norm for a well-reviewed novel that has yet to catch on commercially; the initial ones for *Herzog* were much the same.[6] But unlike *Herzog*, *The Fortunate Pilgrim* did not become a bestseller, and this was a fateful marketplace failure. According to many accounts, most prominently those of Puzo himself, the novel's modest sales eventually prompted Puzo to abandon what had been purely literary ambitions in favor of crass commercial calculation. He decided, he later said, to "sell out" and write a novel "below [his] gifts" in order to achieve fame and make money.[7] *The Godfather* was the result.

Puzo began telling this tale of capitulation to the marketplace in 1972, in an essay called "The Making of *The Godfather*." The first third of the essay details the circumstances that led Puzo to write *The Godfather*, and the rest discusses the making of the movie. "The Making of *The Godfather*" is an unusual document, which among other things risked making readers who had enjoyed the novel—probably a sizable part of the audience for an essay about how it came to be written—think less of themselves for doing so. To what end? Puzo ostensibly aims to shine a light on the commercial pressures that a corrupt publishing industry imposes on working novelists. "The Making of *The Godfather*" recalls William Faulkner's putdown of his novel *Sanctuary* (1931) in his introduction to the Modern Library's reissue of the novel in 1932. A contemporary model for Puzo is Norman Mailer's "Last Draft of *The Deer Park*" (1959), in which Mailer discusses his struggle to get his novel *The Deer Park* published in the early 1950s. As Chris Messenger notes in his insightful study of the *Godfather* phenomenon, Mailer was a figure of particular fascination for Puzo.[8] The collection of new and previously published pieces in which Puzo's essay appeared, *The Godfather Papers and Other Confessions*, was probably modeled on Mailer's retrospective *Advertisements for Myself*.

Puzo opens the essay in a Mailer-style confessional mode: "I have written three novels. *The Godfather* is not as good as the preceding two; I wrote it to make money."[9] The pursuit of money has literary consequences, as Puzo continues, "I didn't want to write *The Godfather*. There was another novel I wanted to write. (I never did and now I never will. Subject matter rots like everything else)."[10] Puzo explains that he did not write the novel he wanted to write because his publisher, Atheneum, refused to give him an advance for it. And Atheneum refused to give him an advance, he implies, because *The Fortunate Pilgrim* did not sell. The reading public prefers bad books to good ones, Puzo suggests, and publishers, no matter what they say about themselves, are only interested in money, and Puzo was in debt and had a family to support and was working full time writing adventure stories for men's magazines, so he decided to pursue riches—through ostensibly bad, popular fiction—instead of artistry.

Puzo's story affirms and is structured by three persistent but problematic ideas about the literary marketplace and more broadly about the relationship between capitalism and art: first, that there exists a rigid distinction between "elite fiction" (*The Fortunate Pilgrim*; the novel Puzo wanted to write next) and merely popular fare (*The Godfather*, according to Puzo, Coppola, Kael, and others); second, that publishers face a choice between art and integrity on the one hand and profit and "selling out" on the other; and third, that as the twentieth century progressed, publishers became increasingly likely to choose profit over art. As the story of *The Godfather* will make clear, for Puzo these ideas had immense, productive power, and they have remained attached to his novel, partly, perhaps, because of the way in which they affirm long-held truisms about the book trade, partly because they affirm the prevailing view of the novel's relationship with the movie, and partly because Puzo never stopped telling versions of his story. But these ideas do not withstand scrutiny, and if they are treated as facts rather than as ideologically tinged assumptions, they obscure rather than illuminate *The Godfather*.

Before making this point, there is one more reason to consider Puzo's account of how he came to write *The Godfather*. As Messenger suggests, Puzo's narrative of capitulation offers a rather irresistible way to read the novel itself, as a critique of the commercialism and dishonesty of the American literary field: *The Godfather* depicts a corrupt society in which people who strive to achieve success legitimately are not rewarded; it is for this reason that they turn to crime. Analogously, Puzo's artistry—the merit of his novels— was recognized neither by the reading public nor by his publisher, and so Puzo turned to *The Godfather*. Puzo is thus comparable to any number of characters in his novel, including Vito Corleone himself, someone who found the lawful route to success blocked and so forged an illegitimate one.[11] Messenger writes that "in many respects, writing about the Mafia for Puzo was equivalent to joining the Mafia, to doing its business"; the underworld crimes that the novel depicts are analogized to the writing of a popular novel.[12]

It is a persuasive biographical reading. But there are problems with Puzo's account, both in terms of the facts and in terms of its implicit assumptions about the book business, and the great mid-1960s' success of *Herzog* indicates one of them. The literary marketplace of the 1960s did not disdain literariness, and contrary to Puzo's rueful suggestion that "any novel labeled a small classic is automatically labeled noncommercial" by publishers, literariness alone does not suffice as the reason why *The Fortunate Pilgrim* failed to sell.[13] In addition to Bellow, the examples of Puzo's friends Friedman and Heller amplify this point, and the bestseller lists of the 1960s contain numerous other novelists, at various stages of their careers, who were thought to be literary—including John O'Hara, J. D. Salinger, Harper Lee, Henry Miller, Katherine Anne Porter, William Faulkner, Mary McCarthy, John Rechy, Bernard Malamud, and William Styron, all of whom published novels among the bestselling of their respective years during the decade. The bestselling novel of 1969 (*The Godfather* was second) was Philip Roth's scandalous *Portnoy's Complaint*.

The Fortunate Pilgrim might have seemed well positioned for similar commercial success. It was published by a respected house, Atheneum, and as the *Saturday Review* and the *Times* reviews of the novel noted, its subject matter—an immigrant family in New York City during the Great Depression—positioned it to capitalize on the belated popularity of Henry Roth's Depression-era New York novel *Call It Sleep*, which had been reissued several months earlier to great acclaim and surprising sales. The high sales of Luigi Barzini's nonfiction *The Italians* (published in 1964, also by Atheneum) demonstrated a degree of public interest in Italian culture, as did the unlikely popularity of Giuseppe Tomasi di Lampedusa's novel of nineteenth-century Italy *The Leopard*, published by Pantheon Books, a small house devoted ostensibly to noncommercial fare, in 1958.

Why, then, did *The Fortunate Pilgrim* not sell? The best response is probably also the least satisfying one: most novels do not succeed commercially, and searching for reasons for the failure of an individual book in such an unpredictable marketplace is fruitless. The reverse is true as well: it is near impossible to find the reason for a novel's high sales solely within the novel itself. Too many other variables come into play. Lancer Books published a paperback version of *The Fortunate Pilgrim*, which according to Puzo sold more than 2 million copies in the wake of *The Godfather*'s success: there was nothing inherently unsellable about *The Fortunate Pilgrim* when it was first published, and nothing inherently sellable about it several years later. Good fortune had intervened. Unfortunately, Puzo did not benefit: he had sold Lancer the rights for a modest amount before *The Godfather* was published, and when he tells this story in "The Making of *The Godfather*," it is to illustrate the theme of the first part of the essay and much of the rest of *The Godfather Papers*: the rapaciousness of the publishing industry. "Lancer Books," Puzo writes, "makes Hollywood studios look like Diogenes."[14]

Though it is hard to say why *The Fortunate Pilgrim* did not sell in its initial printing, it is a mistake to suggest, in a marketplace featuring a massive bestseller by Saul Bellow (another hard-to-explain phenomenon, as none of Bellow's previous novels sold nearly that well), that the problem is that it was too literary, and it is better to attribute Puzo's modest sales to the luck and contingency that are major features of the American book trade of any era. As Beth Luey recently put it, "Despite advances in market research and management, publishers never have been able to tame an industry of 'infinite variance,' where each title is, in some ways, a completely new product line. That is simply the nature of the business."[15] Luey cites Albert Greco's startling finding that even in the present era of well-capitalized conglomerate-controlled publishers, "7 out of every 10 frontlist hardbound books fail financially . . . 2 books break even, and 1 is a hit."[16] Most books do not sell well and do not make their authors famous, and even the most sophisticated publishers are not able to predict which ones will succeed. It was to this frustrating unpredictability that Puzo unwittingly responded in The Godfather; the novel, I will argue later, enacts a fantasy of hidden forces in control of an unwieldy cultural field.

The changing publishing industry

Poor sales marked only the first step of Puzo's path to The Godfather. He suggests that they were the reason Atheneum rejected his idea for his next novel, and he viewed this rejection as a sign of the marketplace's inhospitality to genuine art. But the story of Atheneum's decision is more complicated than that: while simple bad luck kept The Fortunate Pilgrim off the bestseller list, hard-to-see structural changes then underway in the publishing business precipitated Puzo's divorce from Atheneum. Formed in 1959, Atheneum was a relatively young house, and it was the product of publishing's own family/business drama. The company was co-founded by Alfred (Pat) Knopf, Jr., after he realized that his parents, Alfred A. Knopf, Sr. and Blanche Knopf, had no plans to turn over to him their venerable company, Alfred A. Knopf, Inc. Pat Knopf had little editorial experience, so he recruited two publishing executives to be his partners in the new venture: Simon Michael Bessie, who had been at Harper's, and Hiram Haydn, who had been editor-in-chief at Random House. Atheneum was news: reports of its formation, before the founders planned to announce it, made the front page of the *New York Times* in 1959, and in the article, an unnamed observer explained, "[It is as if] the presidents of General Motors, Chrysler and Ford left their jobs to start an automobile company."[17]

The plan was for each of the founders to bring writers from their old houses to the new one. Haydn, the oldest of the three and the longtime editor of *The American Scholar*, brought Puzo. Puzo had been a student in a fiction-writing class Haydn taught at the New School for Social Research (other students included William Styron, George Mandel, and Kaufman), and when Puzo applied to the Yaddo artist's community in 1957 to work on *The Fortunate Pilgrim*, Haydn wrote a recommendation on his behalf. As his Yaddo application indicates, Puzo had a contract with Random House, which had already published Puzo's first novel *The Dark Arena* (1955), to write *The Fortunate Pilgrim*, but by 1960, Puzo had switched to Haydn's new home.[18] In January of that year, before it had published any books, Atheneum took out a full-page advertisement in the *Times Book Review* and the *Times Literary Supplement* that included a list of 60 authors that it would publish. Puzo was on the list alongside the literary critic Stanley Edgar Hyman, poets Randall Jarrell and W. S. Merwin, and novelists including Paule Marshall, Wright Morris, Andre Schwarz-Bart, and Ignazio Silone. Of its authors, Atheneum's advertisement said, "All of them, we believe, are writers of quality."[19]

As this quote suggests, the company's intentions were high-minded and literary. But Atheneum was relatively small and not well capitalized. It aimed to operate like one of the great houses of the 1950s, if not the modernist 1920s, just as the American publishing industry was beginning, rapidly, to consolidate into a smaller number of larger presses, which would themselves soon be absorbed into still larger media conglomerates. This was the crucial development in the publishing industry during the 1960s and after. Small presses would proliferate in the late twentieth century, but they would have an ever harder time competing with the big ones.[20] Atheneum's initial strategy, in short, was perhaps precisely the wrong one for its time: in an early profile, the *New York Herald Tribune* reported that "they will not publish textbooks, specialized books, technical books, or 'for some time' children's books." Over the succeeding decades, these areas would be the largest growth opportunities in publishing.

The Godfather emerges indirectly from Atheneum's old-school approach. As a small house with no reliable textbook business and a tiny backlist, the company needed bestsellers, and it was not getting enough of them. One result was tension among the founders. After failing to produce marketplace successes and falling out with Pat Knopf, Haydn, who had been brought into the company partly to supply literary prestige, left Atheneum for Harcourt in August 1964, before The Fortunate Pilgrim was even published; according to his memoir, he stopped having a prominent voice in the company's affairs even sooner than that.[21] Haydn's difficult tenure at Atheneum is symptomatic of the institutional pressures faced by a small house trying to compete with larger ones. Random House, Haydn's previous employer, could absorb the modest sales of most of its literary fiction by relatively unknown writers—most novels, after all, do not sell—because it could reliably generate revenues from its backlist and from dictionary and textbook sales. Lacking these sources, Atheneum was less able to withstand losses from low-selling books.

In any event, Haydn's departure, which Puzo does not mention in "The Making of The Godfather," might help to explain Atheneum's decision to reject his follow-up to The Fortunate Pilgrim, but it also suggests what might be missing from his account. In Puzo's narrative, Atheneum shockingly refuses to offer him an advance for the novel he wishes to write next, despite the strong critical reception for The Fortunate Pilgrim and despite the company's avowed commitment to art: "I was a hero, I thought. But my publisher . . . known as a classy publishing house more interested in belle-lettres than money, was not impressed. I asked them for an advance to start on my next book . . . and the editors were cool. They were courteous. They were kind. They showed me the door . . . . I couldn't believe it. I went back and read all the reviews of my first two books . . . . There must be some mistake." He adds,

> The editors didn't like the idea behind my new novel. It sounded like another loser. One editor wistfully remarked that if Fortunate Pilgrim had only had more of that Mafia stuff in it maybe the book would have made money . . . . So I told my editors OK, I'll write a book about the Mafia, just give me some money to get started. They said no money until we see a hundred pages. I compromised, I wrote a ten-page outline. They showed me the door again.[22]

Puzo's timeline suggests that *The Fortunate Pilgrim* had already been published—and thus that Haydn had left the company—when Atheneum rejected his proposed, never-written next novel. It raises a tantalizing question: what if Haydn had remained at Atheneum? Puzo might have received his advance for the novel he had planned, and *The Godfather* might never have been written (thus altering American cultural history and the lives and careers of Puzo and Coppola among many others). But Puzo's story is at odds with Pat Knopf's reminiscence of the company's rejection of *The Godfather*: "Mr. Haydn," Knopf said, "thought it junk."[23] And Al Silverman's recent account of the postwar publishing industry, drawing on an interview with Bessie, corroborates Knopf's version of events: "Puzo gave Haydn the outline of a book he wanted to do about the Mafia. Here was one time at least when all three of the founding partners were on the same page. 'Hiram was very dubious about it,' Mike [Bessie] remembered, 'and so was Pat.'"[24] Finally, Haydn's memoir, published shortly after he died in 1973, mentions Puzo and *The Godfather* favorably and does not mention any role in rejecting it; if he played such a role, it would be a curious omission.[25]

It is hard to reconcile these accounts, but the upshot of each of them is the same. If Puzo's version is accurate, Haydn had left the company by the time Atheneum rejected *The Godfather*, and the departure of Puzo's booster constitutes a reason beyond mere commercial calculation for the company's decision. If Bessie and Knopf's version is the right one, Atheneum would seem to have rejected Puzo's next novel before *The Fortunate Pilgrim* received both strong reviews and poor sales, and thus those sales did not motivate the rejection. Either way, Puzo's narrative of betrayal by his publisher, with all that it implies about the decline of the publishing industry and the relationship between art and commerce in the mid-1960s, appears to be incomplete.

Puzo's hidden success

What is clear amid this uncertainty is that Puzo was stung by the combination of public indifference to *The Fortunate Pilgrim* and Atheneum's refusal to give him an advance for his next novel, regardless of whether the former caused the latter. And this felt betrayal did motivate Puzo to shift literary gears and write a different kind of novel, one which he believed was more likely to earn him an advance, and one which he felt was less true to himself. Puzo's resulting post-*Fortunate Pilgrim* animus toward publishers and the marketplace is evident in the nervy, irreverent book reviews and essays that he wrote between 1965 and 1968, in the *Washington Post* and *New York Times* among other sources. In these reviews, several of which are included in *The Godfather Papers*, Puzo praised and panned literary heavyweights including James Baldwin, Norman Podhoretz, Bellow, and Mailer; as in "The Making of *The Godfather*," the perfidy of publishers is a recurring theme.

The best example is Puzo's assessment of an anthology of *Paris Review* interviews of novelists.[26] *Paris Review* had been founded in 1952; to be interviewed in it quickly became a mark of distinction for younger writers. Puzo criticizes the *Review* for not acknowledging that literature truly is a business, the hard lesson he had learned from his divorce from Atheneum. Written in the form of a mock interview with the *Paris Review* interviewer, he asks, "How come you people never ask writers about money? You ask them if they use a typewriter or a pen, how many pages they write a day, all kinds of personal sex things. How come you never ask them how much they got for their paperback rights?" About reading interviews with esteemed writers, Puzo writes: "Some . . . in this volume made me believe that the finest thing a human being can do is create a work of art. Not that that lasts long once you get mixed up with publishers."

From Puzo's perspective, *Paris Review* epitomizes a literary field that represses what it is really all about: money, profit, and the glory of success. "Next time," he writes, "ask how much money these writers made on their best sellers . . . . How much did they pay Saul Bellow for the *Herzog* paperback? Can Norman Mailer really scrounge a hundred grand advance just by picking up the phone? . . . And . . . don't be so classy . . . interview a guy like Harold Robbins. Then your collections will really sell. And don't forget to ask how much he makes. I hear he gets a million per."[27] Elsewhere, the money denied to writers is the theme. In a satirical essay on the National Book Awards, published in the *Washington Post Book World* in 1968, Puzo mocks the paltriness of the $1000 winner's prize. The piece begins this way, "For years many writers have cited the National Book Awards as proof that book publishers are the dumbest and stingiest business folk in America."[28] Art, Puzo alleges, is a conceit used by business people—publishers—to force all but a few star writers to work for next to nothing, "created by a handful of dangerous men who should expect no quarter; publishing is a business." And the business is a racket in which connections rather than merit determine success: the piece ends by referring to "two literary Mafia gangs: the Southern Gothic symbolized by [Truman] Capote and the New York 'family' as described by [Norman] Podhoretz."[29]

It is impossible not to connect these sentiments to the stories of "Mafia gangs" and "families" that Puzo tells in *The Godfather*. But what Puzo leaves unsaid is equally important. While his reviews and essays exhibit the frustration that underwrites his account of the failure of *The Fortunate Pilgrim*, they are also marks of unacknowledged success. The fact that Puzo had the opportunity to review some of the most prominent US writers for some of its most prominent literary publications suggests that he did have some stature on the American literary scene in the mid-1960s, and that stature is attached to praise he had received for *The Dark Arena* and *The Fortunate Pilgrim*. In the course of trashing the novel in her review of Coppola's adaptation, Kael explained that Puzo "has a reputation as a good writer, so his novel was treated as if it were special."[30] And shortly after Puzo agreed to write *The Godfather* for G. P. Putnam's Sons, he changed agents, replacing the William Morris Agency with Candida Donadio. At a moment when literary agents were gaining in power, Donadio was particularly formidable; her clients included John Cheever, Thomas Pynchon, Puzo's friends Friedman and Heller, and Philip Roth.[31] In 1963, *Esquire* had placed her at the center of what the magazine irreverently called "The Structure of the American Literary Establishment."[32] To be represented by Donadio meant something, and in a sense Puzo's profile had never been higher than it was in the wake of the commercial failure of *The Fortunate Pilgrim*.

All of this suggests that despite poor sales, *The Fortunate Pilgrim* advanced Puzo's career in significant ways that his own "sellout" narrative—with its implications of publishing's decline into a business like any other—obscures. The story of Putnam, his publisher after Atheneum, amplifies the point. Under the leadership of Walter Minton, Putnam after World War II had earned a reputation for making money by courting literary controversy. It had published Mailer's *The Deer Park*, which had been abruptly canceled by Holt after Mailer refused to remove a sexually explicit passage, and it had later published Vladimir Nabokov's *Lolita*. In the 1960s, Putnam continued to generate outrage, acclaim, and sales, publishing Terry Southern and Mason Hoffenburg's *Candy*. The point is not that Putnam chose literature over commerce; the point is that literature, combined with scandal, comprised part of a viable commercial strategy. Capitalizing on the success of that strategy, Putnam became a publicly traded corporation in 1967.

Puzo presented his post-*Fortunate Pilgrim*, pre-*Godfather* years as a failure and a sign that the book business is hostile to art. Understandably so, given that he had made little money from his novels and had been let go by his publisher. But he had accrued other kinds of capital: during that era, Puzo hired a top agent, reviewed esteemed writers for prominent sources, and moved from struggling Atheneum to an older, larger, more successful house with literary and commercial credentials. What had made it possible for him to do so was respect in the field for his previous achievements. William Targ, editor-in-chief at Putnam, signed Puzo without reading a manuscript for *The Godfather* in part because he admired *The Dark Arena* and *The Fortunate Pilgrim*: "They were first-rate books, though commercial failures."[33] Although the failure of *The Fortunate Pilgrim* animates *The Godfather* in intriguing respects, it was at the same time the unacknowledged and hard-to-see success of *The Fortunate Pilgrim* that made *The Godfather* possible.

The Godfather and the marketplace

If Puzo's success put him in a position to write *The Godfather*, it was his deeply felt sense of failure—his sense, more precisely, that a corrupt system had denied him the chance to succeed—that prompted him to write a sensational crime novel rather than one more likely to be celebrated at the time as a great work of art. But does Puzo's sense of an unjust literary world inform the plot and themes of the novel, its critique of capitalism and its romance of outlaws? Is the frustration of his divorce from Atheneum inscribed in *The Godfather*?

Such a reading should be advanced cautiously. *The Fortunate Pilgrim* itself suggests that whatever lessons Puzo claimed to have learned from the failure of the novel, he already believed when he wrote it. The novel tells the story of Lucia Santa Angeluzzi-Corbo and her family—her husband, their three children, and three children from her previous marriage (her first husband died in a work accident)—as they struggle through the Depression. The narrator's description of her son Vincent's first job as an assistant to the baker resembles Puzo's later account of writing *The Godfather*: "He had suffered a common cruelty, a child sent from the warmth of his family to be commanded by strangers to perform their drudgery. It was his first experience of selling part of his being for money."[34] Facing a lifetime of this drudgery, Vincent ultimately commits suicide. After many such misfortunes, the novel ends on a note of ambivalent happiness: Lucia Santa realizes her dream of a house on Long Island. But to get there, she takes money from her oldest son, who is involved in organized crime, and she betrays her second husband, abandoning him to die (another suicide) in an insane asylum. Puzo writes that Lucia Santa "wept for the inevitable crimes she had committed against those she loved."[35] Committing "crimes" in order to escape poverty in an unfair world, she is, as Puzo would later acknowledge, a less sensational version of Don Corleone, and this suggests that both Puzo's account of his divorce from Atheneum and *The Godfather* itself were shaped by a preexisting worldview, rather than, as Puzo suggested, that Puzo's worldview was shaped by his divorce from Atheneum.[36] Crucially, such a worldview does not leave much room for art. Lucia Santa laments that her children "read books, they go to movies, they think they can act like rich people."[37] Books and movies convince the children of immigrants that there is something more to life than the brute struggle to survive—that there are higher and grander abstractions such as art or ethics or heroism—but Lucia Santa, like Puzo in his book reviews and "The Making of *The Godfather*," is dubious.

The Godfather is surprisingly more sanguine about the possibility of art in a capitalist society. It does not suggest that one needs to sell out or commit crimes or betray one's principles in order to succeed in the cultural world, and it allows for the possibility of artistry within the context of the marketplace. This is an implication of the novel's extended subplot about the celebrity singer and actor Johnny Fontane. Johnny is a star corrupted by the trappings of fame, but the novel offers no reason to doubt his self-assessment: "Even aside from the special voice . . . he was good. He had been a real artist."[38] Johnny's success, of course, is not entirely based on merit. Don Corleone helped him rise at the start of his career, and the Don helps again later: first getting Johnny a key role in a movie and then helping him win an Academy Award. It is not a fair system for anyone who lacks connections, but nowhere does the novel suggest that Johnny needs to compromise the integrity of his art, the way Puzo said *he* did in writing *The Godfather*, in order to find an audience and earn a living worthy of his talent.

Two aspects of this subplot are particularly notable in light of Puzo's experiences in the book trade. The first is the novel's depiction of the Oscar itself. Johnny explains, "An Academy Award can make an actor . . . He can get his pick of roles. The public goes to see him . . . . for an actor it's the most important thing in the business."[39] The Academy's recognition is presented, with a surprising absence of cynicism, as an enabler of art, part of the complex cultural economy that marries prestige both to the opportunity to create and to popularity; it contrasts with Puzo's own rather blinkered essay about the National Book Awards, written while he was writing *The Godfather*, which treats the cultural prize solely in terms of its stingy cash payment to the winners.[40]

More curious, because more out of step with the rest of the novel, is the limit Puzo places on the Don's power in the cultural realm: the Don can ensure Johnny the award only if Johnny is nominated, and the nomination depends solely on the quality of his performance. "Of course you have to be good," Tom explains, "you have to be in contention on your own merits."[41] It is a surprising qualification; elsewhere, the Don's powers are close to limitless, so much so that, in a morbidly comic early scene, the Don's dying friend Genco asks if he can make a deal for Genco to ward off damnation. Puzo's depiction of the Oscar nomination process is one of the novel's rare hints of a level playing field in the world outside of the Cosa Nostra. And it is all the more strange because Hollywood otherwise is presented as morally bereft, a place where the decadent ills of the United States are amplified, with both actors and directors vividly, despicably sleazy. In recognizing the possibility of the convergence of fame and artistry, *The Godfather* offers a more plausible and at least slightly less pitiless depiction of that field than Puzo presents in his account of the failure of *The Fortunate Pilgrim*. And the Don serves as Puzo's stand-in for the marketplace's actual, invisible unpredictability—a hidden, possibly capricious force with the power to determine who among the worthy (as Puzo and Bellow were both worthy in 1964) receives the highest rewards. The Don becomes an imagined way to make sense of the otherwise maddening randomness of the cultural field, or he becomes yet another way to deny that randomness.

But the story of *The Godfather* in American cultural history, as I have tried to suggest, is a kind of monument to randomness, and it tells us much more about the contingency of the American cultural field than it does about any supposed relationship between the popular and the elite. Born out of circumstances specific to the 1960s' literary marketplace, the novel might not have been written at all if *The Fortunate Pilgrim* had caught on, or if Haydn had stayed at Atheneum or had never left Random House in the first place. It would be remembered differently, if at all, had Coppola not directed the movie version and insisted, against the studio's wishes, on doing it his way. In a preface for a reissue of *The Fortunate Pilgrim* published in 1996, Puzo explained, again, that *The Fortunate Pilgrim* was a bid for immortality, and that when the bid failed, he gave up on those dreams and tried instead to write "a bestseller."[42] His notion of the kind of book that could be "immortal" is conventional; the fact that it is his popular novel that seems likely to endure might be grounds for rethinking it. Had Puzo recognized the cultural world as it was in 1965, or had he been able to afford to recognize it, he might have written the literary novel he had planned. In that case, it is likely that neither that novel nor *The Fortunate Pilgrim* would be well remembered today. We have benefited from his misreading.

Bibliography

Barzini, Luigi. *The Italians*. New York: Atheneum, 1964.

Bellow, Saul. *Herzog*. New York: Viking, 1964.

"Books: The Agents: Writing With a $ Sign." *Time*, March 8, 1968.

Canby, Vincent. "Bravo, Brando's Godfather," *New York Times*, March 12, 1972.

Conley, Robert. "3 Book Executives Forming Own Firm," *New York Times*, March 15, 1959.

Eller, Jonathan R. "Catching a Market: The Publishing History of *Catch-22*," *Prospects*, 17, 1992, 475–525.

English, James. *The Economy of Prestige: Prizes, Awards, and the Circulation of Cultural Value*. Cambridge: Harvard University Press, 2005.

Faulkner, William. Introduction to *Sanctuary*, by William Faulkner. New York: Modern Library, 1932.

Ferraro, Thomas. *Ethnic Passages: Literary Immigrants in Twentieth-Century America*. Chicago: University of Chicago Press, 1993.

—. "'My Way' in 'Our America': Art, Ethnicity, Profession," *American Literary History*, 12 (Autumn 2000), 499–522.

Gelmis, Joseph. "Merciful Heavens, Is This the End of Don Corleone?" *New York Magazine*, August 23, 1971.

Greco, Albert N., Clara E. Rodriguez, and Robert M. Wharton. *The Culture and Commerce of Publishing in the 21st Century*. Stanford: Stanford University Press, 2007.

Haydn, Hiram. *Words and Faces*. New York: Harcourt Brace Jovanovich, 1974.

Hills, L. R. "The Structure of the American Literary Establishment, with Shaded Heraldic Tree" *Esquire*, July 1963.

Kael, Pauline. "Alchemy." Review of *The Godfather* (Paramount Movie). *New Yorker*, March 18, 1972.

Kaufman, Bel. *Up the Down Staircase*. New York: Avon Books, 1964.

di Lampedusa, Giuseppe Tomasi. *The Leopard*. Translated by Archibald Colquhoun. New York: Pantheon Books, 1959.

Lehmann-Haupt, Christopher. "Alfred A. Knopf, Jr., Influential Publisher, Dies at 90." *New York Times*, February 16, 2009.

Luey, Beth. "The Organization of the Book Publishing Industry," in *A History of the Book in America, Volume 5: The Enduring Book*. Edited by David Paul Nord, Joan Shelley Rubin, and Michael Schudson. Chapel Hill: University of North Carolina Press, 2009.

Mailer, Norman. *Advertisements for Myself*. New York: GP Putnam's Sons, 1959.

—. *The Deer Park*. New York: GP Putnam's Sons, 1955.

McGee, Micki. *Yaddo: Making American Culture*. New York: Columbia University Press, 2008.

Messenger, Christopher. *The Godfather and American Culture: How the Corleones Became 'Our Gang'*. Albany: State University of New York Press, 2002.

Nabokov, Vladimir. *Lolita*. New York: GP Putnam's Sons, 1958.

Puzo, Mario. *The Dark Arena*. New York: Random House, 1955.

—. *The Fortunate Pilgrim*. New York: Ballantine, 1997.

—. *The Godfather Papers and Other Confessions*. New York: GP Putnam's Sons, 1972.

—. *The Godfather*. New York: New American Library, 2002.

Roth, Henry. *Call It Sleep*. New York: Avon Books, 1964.
Roth, Philip. *Portnoy's Complaint*. New York: Random House, 1969.
Silverman, Al. *The Times of Their Lives: The Golden Age of Great American Book Publishers, Their Editors and Authors*. New York: Truman Talley Books, 2008.
Southern, Terry and Mason Hoffenburg. *Candy*. New York: GP Putnam's Sons, 1964.
Sutherland, John. *Bestsellers: Popular Fiction of the 1970s*. London: Routledge & Kegan Paul, 1981.
Targ, William. *Indecent Pleasures: The Life and Colorful Times of William Targ*. New York: Macmillan, 1975.
Thompson, John B. *Merchants of Culture: The Publishing Business in the Twenty-First Century*. Cambridge: Polity Press, 2010.
Writers at Work: The Paris Review Interviews, Third Series. New York: Viking, 1967.

Notes

1 Joseph Gelmis, "Merciful Heavens, Is This the End of Don Corleone?" *New York Magazine*, August 23, 1971, 52.

2 Pauline Kael, "Alchemy," review of *The Godfather* (Paramount Movie), *New Yorker*, March 18, 1972, 132.

3 Canby, "Brando's 'Godfather,'" D25.

4 Canby, "Brando's 'Godfather,'" D25. Thomas Ferraro makes a compelling case for the novel's literary significance, but few others have followed his example. See Thomas Ferraro, "'My Way' in 'Our America': Art, Ethnicity, Profession," *American Literary History*, 12, Autumn 2000, 499–522. The most thorough look at *The Godfather* as novel and movie is Chris Messenger's *The Godfather and American Culture: How the Corleones Became 'Our Gang'* (Albany: State University of New York Press, 2002); Messenger treats the novel specifically as an example of "popular fiction." See also Thomas Ferraro, *Ethnic Passages* (Chicago: University of Chicago Press, 1993); John Sutherland, *Bestsellers: Popular Fiction of the 1970s* (London: Routledge & Kegan Paul, 1981).

5 The advertisements appeared on page 31 of the March 5, 1965 *New York Times*.

6 See, for example, the advertisement placed on page 13 of the *New York Times Book Review* on September 27, 1964, which featured Alfred Kazin's praise for Bellow's novel.

7   Mario Puzo, *The Godfather Papers and Other Confessions* (New York: GP Putnam's Sons, 1972), 25, 33.

8   Messenger, *The Godfather and American Culture*, 71–3.

9   Puzo, *The Godfather Papers and Other Confessions*, 24.

10 Puzo, *Godfather Papers*, 24–5.

11 Puzo, *The Godfather*, 388.

12 Messenger, *The Godfather and American Culture*, 53.

13 Puzo, *Godfather Papers*, 201.

14 Puzo, *Godfather Papers*, 37.

15 Beth Luey, "The Organization of the Book Publishing Industry," in *A History of the Book in America, Volume 5: The Enduring Book*, ed. David Paul Nord et al. (Chapel Hill: University of North Carolina Press, 2009), 42.

16 Albert N. Greco, Clara E. Rodriguez, and Robert M. Wharton., *The Culture and Commerce of Publishing in the 21st Century* (Stanford: Stanford University Press, 2007), 30.

17 Robert Conley, "3 Book Executives Forming Own Firm," *New York Times*, March 15, 1959, 46.

18 Micki McGee, *Yaddo: Making American Culture* (New York: Columbia University Press, 2008), 110–15.

19 The ad appeared on page 9 of the January 31, 1960 *New York Times Book Review*.

20 See John B. Thompson, *Merchants of Culture: The Publishing Business in the Twenty-First Century* (Cambridge: Polity Press, 2010).

21 Hiram Haydn, *Words and Faces* (New York: Harcourt Brace Jovanovich, 1974), 123, 131.

22 Puzo, *Godfather Papers*, 24–5.

23 Christopher Lehmann-Haupt, "Alfred A. Knopf, Jr., Influential Publisher, Dies at 90," *New York Times*, February 16, 2009, A16.

24 Al Silverman, *The Times of Their Lives: The Golden Age of Great American Book Publishers, Their Editors and Authors* (New York: Truman Talley Books, 2008): 295.

25 Haydn, *Words and Faces*, 240.

26 *Writers at Work: The Paris Review Interviews, Third Series* (New York: Viking, 1967).

27 Puzo, *Godfather Papers*, 78–84.

28 Puzo, *Godfather Papers*, 175.

29 Puzo, *Godfather Papers*, 178, 179.

30 Kael, "Alchemy," 132.

31 See Jonathan R. Eller, "Catching a Market: The Publishing History of *Catch-22*," *Prospects*, 17, 1992, 475–525. See also "Books: The Agents: Writing With a $ Sign," *Time*, March 8, 1968, 96.

32 L. R. Hills, "The Structure of the American Literary Establishment, with Shaded Heraldic Tree" *Esquire*, July 1963, 41–3.

33 William Targ, *Indecent Pleasures: The Life and Colorful Times of William Targ* (New York: Macmillan, 1975), 112.

34 Mario Puzo, *The Fortunate Pilgrim* (New York: Ballantine, 1997), 60.

35 Puzo, *The Fortunate Pilgrim*, 274.

36 Mario Puzo, Preface to *The Fortunate Pilgrim*, x.

37 Puzo, *The Fortunate Pilgrim*, 85.

38 Puzo, *The Godfather*, 179.

39 Puzo, *The Godfather*, 158.

40 On cultural prizes generally, see James English, *The Economy of Prestige: Prizes, Awards, and the Circulation of Cultural Value* (Cambridge: Harvard University Press, 2005).

41 Puzo, *The Godfather*, 160.

42 Mario Puzo, Preface, ix.

13

Master of sentiment: The romances of Nicholas Sparks

Sarah Churchwell

She had seemed to be such a normal and healthy young woman. How was it that she bled to death next to an empty cradle?

VLADIMIR NABOKOV, *THE REAL LIFE OF SEBASTIAN KNIGHT*

Return to paradise

If narrative nostalgia is, as Michael Wood once said, a compulsive plunge back into the past, this essay considers its obverse, the relentless attempt to wrest the past back into the present, a regression represented as progress, and retreatism as correction. This regressiveness takes many forms across many discourses, but my focus here is on the recent resurgence of Victorian models of sentimental domestic fiction in mainstream popular romance. One trope, in particular, has recurred in domestic fictions in the early twenty-first century: the cognitive dissonance surrounding the question of "choice," which has been recoded from a second-wave feminist discourse asserting reproductive rights, into a postfeminist disavowal of choice *as* a choice. These romances are propelled by difficulties in reconciling a "new belief" (or at least a newly espoused belief) in female agency, popularly couched as "women's right to choose," with the maintenance of traditional gender roles. The revival of the nineteenth century novel of sentiment, complete with its exaltation of feminine morbidity, and sublimation of erotic desire into religious ecstasy, has enabled evangelical writers to smuggle a covert but explicitly Christian agenda into ostensibly secular fiction via the rhetoric of "choice." It isn't merely the case that even death can't stop romantic fantasy in the twenty-first century, any more than it could in the nineteenth century: instead, death enables it.

For exactly two decades, between 1980 and 2000, blockbuster epic romances written by Danielle Steel, Judith Krantz, Sidney Sheldon, Jackie Collins, and Jean M. Auel dominated the US bestseller lists, accounting for between four and six of the top ten bestselling novels in each of those 20 years without exception, according to *Publishers Weekly*'s annual lists. But between 1999 and 2000, these metropolitan fantasies of cupidity fell precipitously from grace, and "women's fiction," as it had for so long synecdochally been understood, virtually disappeared from the annual bestseller list overnight; with it went sex. There is no space here to delineate carefully the formulas and cultural implications of what the "romance novel" meant between 1980 and 2000, but in his brilliant and justly famous *New Yorker* essay on the bestselling novels of the week of May 15, 1994, Anthony Lane summed up both the reality and the culturally current assumptions about what a Judith Krantz novel *signified* in a way that should serve synecdochally to suggest what was understood by the generic label "romance novel" during is this era, and how clearly fixed its formulas were:

> This was my first visit to Krantzland, and I relished the occasion . . . The astonishing thing is that, with seven breakneck novels already behind her, this woman should still be in such a *hurry*. Characters are tumbled in and out of bed without a qualm, of course, yet the haste goes beyond that; no other writer could leave the plot on hold for two complete chapters, take a detour through the erotic history of a minor character, then swing back into line as if nothing had happened. But Krantz gets

away with it. She takes us to the heart of trash appeal: she gives people space, and credit, for their preposterous dreams. She is perfectly at ease with the manner in which her heroine chooses to live, and this in turn allows readers a clear, conscience-free view of their own cravings in action . . . I thought [Krantz] would be partial to soft-core euphemisms like 'manhood' and 'moistness' but [she] never hesitates to call a fuck a fuck.[1]

Lane's representative expectations are signaled by phrases such as "of course" and "I thought," while the formulaic nature of Krantz's books are indicated by his notion of "Krantzland," a place whose topography Lane assumed he knew. Most important, for my purposes here, is Krantz's (and Lane's) emphasis upon an unapologetically explicit female-centered eroticism. After two decades of a romance genre dominated by similar interests, suddenly, around the year 2000, the frantic, urban, erotic modernity of those late twentieth-century romances disappeared. Blockbuster romance was transformed virtually overnight into a genre defined by the nostalgic, decorous, slow return to a chaste, domestic arena emblematized by symbolic conservative locales, from sleepy small Southern towns all the way to Amish farming communities.[2] The reasons for this are myriad, and complicated, and include the rise of the Christian right in the United States (greatly facilitated by the popularity in these years of Fox News), as well as the social and cultural conservatism, and insularity, that characterized much of the nation's response to the September 11 attacks in 2001. My purpose here is not to explain America's recent cultural shift toward the conservative, but rather to consider the implications of some of the ways it has played out in bestselling romance novels in the twenty-first century.

In 2000, Jodi Picoult wrote a bestselling novel called *Plain Truth,* in which an unmarried Amish girl hides her pregnancy from her family, and then her newborn baby is found dead. She claims innocence, but all evidence suggests that she has killed her child. Meanwhile—in the big bad city—a successful female attorney, according to one review, "has had it with her fast-paced life and dead end relationship, and escapes to the quiet comforts of Paradise, PA, where she spent her childhood, in search of the answers she needs."[3] By no coincidence, she finds those answers among the Amish.[4] In Picoult's *Plain Truth*, Ellie is returning to the "Paradise" of childhood: the infantilism of these fantasies is also implicitly religious. When Ellie returns to Paradise, she discovers a neo-Victorian community (the Amish) whose conflicts revolve around the question of reproductive rights. Women's "choices" in these stories will continually invoke childbirth and then death, especially death in childbirth, as an image of involuntary choices, of the suspension of agency in the name of choice. Happy endings, conversely, are envisioned not just as marriage, but as pregnancy and the decision to repudiate urban careerism for rural domesticity: Ellie reunites with her high-school boyfriend (in yet another image of regression) and becomes pregnant, deciding to make her home in regenerative Paradise, where she belongs.

Picoult was among the vanguard, if it can be called that, of a new wave of Amish romances that in the last few years have begun to break out as bestsellers in the United States. These so-called bonnet rippers, as a review in *New York* magazine noted, also known as

> 'Bonnet books,' or Amish-starring romance novels, are doing swift business at dry-goods stores all over the country. 'It's almost like you put a person with a bonnet or an Amish field in the background and it automatically starts to sell well,' exclaims a buyer for Barnes & Noble, where the top 100 'religious fiction' releases currently include fifteen bonnet novels. Mostly focused on female Amish characters swept away by handsome, non-Amish paramours, the books are strictly G-rated, sometimes with one or two chaste kissing scenes, and millions have already been sold to both Mennonites and electricity-enjoying readers alike (some titles are even available for the Kindle, hilariously).[5]

The fact that these novels are available for the Kindle is less "hilarious" than it is revealing: bonnet-rippers are not being marketed to the Amish at all. They are selling a nostalgic fantasy about rural domesticity and reproductive choice (or lack thereof) to the non-Amish, to the evangelical and adolescent mainstream reader.

Some commentators have tried to make sense of this sudden popularity of the Amish—and of the abstinent vampires of the *Twilight* series, written by Mormon Stephenie Meyer—by arguing that conservatism is on the rise during a global recession. But the trend toward popular romances affirming chastity before marriage and motherhood after it, instead of more or less "liberated," often professional women engaged in sexual exploration in the metropolitan late twentieth-century romance of Krantz, Collins et al., is not a post-2007 trend: it began around 2000, at just the same time, by no coincidence, as the evangelical Left Behind books (also known as "The Rapture" series), by Tim LaHaye and Jerry Jenkins, became a publishing sensation. The popularity of these stories has been remarked upon, if not well understood, but their gender politics, based on a revision of the narrative of "choice" into a story about female passivity and morbidity, has been neglected, as has their elision of evangelism with romance.

One of the most popular romance writers on the US annual bestseller list in the twenty-first century has also been one of the most critically overlooked, and his evangelism gone even more unnoticed than his influence: Nicholas Sparks. Despite the fact that Sparks has had a novel finish in the top 10 every year since 2000 and was the bestselling American author in hardcover in 2005 (outselling both John Grisham and Dan Brown in aggregate by some half a million copies), his novels have received no academic consideration to date. This despite the increasingly intermedial ubiquity of his stories, whose film adaptations, including especially *The Notebook* (2004) but also *A Walk to Remember* (2002), proved surprise hits with teenaged filmgoers, and the film adaptations of his novels ever since have continued to prove commercial successes: so much so that for the first time in 2009, Sparks wrote the screenplay of *The Last Song* first, and subsequently "novelized" it in 2010.

In the first decade of the twenty-first century, Sparks published a new book like clockwork in October each year; each title debuted at number one on the *New York Times* and the *Publishers Weekly* bestseller lists, including his 2007 number-four bestseller, tellingly titled *The Choice*. In 2008 and 2009, *The Lucky One* and *The Last Song* both ended their respective years at number five; in 2010, *The Last Song* and *Dear John* were numbers one and two on *Publisher's Weekly* list of top-selling mass market paperbacks. Sparks's popularity is noteworthy not only because of its relative stealth. He recast the face of romance fiction with what he prefers to call "love stories"—a point to which I'll return—that are targeted at women but are largely male-focalized and almost entirely chaste. His novels clearly encode Sparks's evangelical agenda, an agenda he makes explicit outside the margins of his fiction but camouflages within it.

Conversion narratives

Nicholas Sparks is at the leading edge of a wave of evangelical fiction flooding the American literary landscape. In his revisionist romances, Sparks has helped replace the old prurience with a new prudishness: the 'liberated' sexuality, ecstatic materialism and exaltation of modernity that were such a prominent feature of the urban romances of Krantz, Sheldon and Collins have disappeared. Instead, Sparks has correctively installed their conservative obverse values: traditional gender roles, ecstatic religiosity and nostalgic exaltation of the past. I don't have space to linger over demographic questions, so I'll just offer one emblematic instance from Sparks's 2003 novel *The Wedding,* in which a middle-aged wife explains to her husband of 30 years why she married him:

> She hesitated for a moment. 'But it wasn't just about my feelings. The more I got to know you, the more I was certain that you'd do whatever it took to provide for your family. That was important to me. You have to understand that back then, a lot of people our age wanted to change the world. Even though it's a noble idea, I knew I wanted something more traditional. I wanted a family like my parents had, and I wanted to concentrate on my little corner of the world. I wanted someone who wanted to marry a wife and mother, and someone who would respect my choice.' (145–6)

This passage's clumsy exposition is self-evidently for an audience supposed not to remember the 1960s: as a putative speech to a man to whom the speaker has been married for three decades, who would also presumably remember what it was like "back then," it is absurd. The speech explicitly rejects the liberal, feminist ideals of the 1960s, transforming second-wave feminist discourse into a contemporary postfeminist notion of "choice," in which women voluntarily choose traditional domesticity, and voluntarism is elided with feminism. Sparks is writing not just for an adolescent audience who needs modern history explained to it, but also to transform the rhetoric of choice into a mandate that all women make an identical choice—namely, to repudiate a career in favor of marriage. It is not a choice at all, but a prescription, a cultural commandment, rewriting the fight for reproductive choice into a disavowal of making any choices at all.

Instead of "rapture," Sparks offers romance, but his "romance" doesn't amount to a euphemism for safe eroticism, as it did in the genre novels of the 1980s and 1990s; instead, Sparks has returned to an older, more theological model of romance for his submerged religiosity: the typological. His tendency to allegorize human love as divine love creates problems on the level of diagesis, however: the "unconditional love" of God and Jesus, which Sparks reiterates cannot be questioned and which allegorically appears in his novels in the shape of idealized, all-forgiving lovers, forecloses the desire and conflict which drive any plot. If desire is contingent upon absence, Sparks keep reconstituting desire by taking away what he gives his characters. Hence, the emphasis upon narratives of renunciation: they keep desire perpetual and resist entropy. The majority of Sparks's novels rely on an even simpler solution than renunciation: more often than not he kills off one of his lovers, usually the woman. (Needless to say, Sparks's romances are resolutely heteronormative.)

A reductive definition of "tragedy" helps resolve several conflicting impulses in Sparks's stories: their subcultural religious discourse of conversion, faith, and assumption (exemplified by titles such as *True Believer*), which can be disguised by the convention of troping heterosexual romance in religious terms; the emotional pornography demanded by the reader of mainstream romance; and the cultural politics of commercial success and masculine authority. How does a male writer of godly romance dominate the market place? By mastering sentiment. For example, *The Wedding* opens with what reads like a Freudian slip, as the middle-aged male narrator introduces himself with an apparent *non sequitur*:

> I've never considered myself a sentimental man, and if you asked my wife, I'm sure she would agree. I do not lose myself in films or plays, I've never been a dreamer, and if I aspire to any form of mastery at all, it is one defined by rules of the Internal Revenue Service and codified by law. (1)

The passage sets up an opposition between the sentimental and the masterful, a slippage between feminized audiences whose self-effacement through spectacular identification (i.e. losing oneself in films or plays) is how the passage defines the "sentimental," and the highly masculinized, commercialized, and institutionalized "mastery" that Sparks's narrator disavows. Sparks's success lies in his ability to repackage feminized sentimental fiction *as* male mastery. His reliance upon primarily male protagonists and his predilection for killing off his female protagonists keep his regressive stories firmly in line with the postfeminist backlash, reestablishing an old sentimental orthodoxy while explicitly protecting the "youth" of today from the more dangerous temptations of contemporary fiction.

The Sparks romance becomes the newest version of America's most constitutive narrative form, the redemption tale—or conversion narrative—and repentance, regret, and reorientation of one's way of life. But in Sparks, conversion is reimagined as reversion. Sparks's conversion narratives have proved so powerful that they have helped convert the formula of American romance, in both literature and film, to serve an explicitly articulated Christian agenda. Take, for example, the following excerpts from an interview Sparks gave to *Christianity Today* in 2004:

Q: Does faith inform your writing?

Sparks: Absolutely. Without a doubt. I do not use profanity in my novels. My characters all go to church. My characters have drawn great strength from church. For instance, in my last novel, *The Wedding*, he credits his wife with showing him that Christ is his Savior. And he says, "This is the greatest gift." I try and work these elements into my novels, some more so than others. . . . *A Walk To Remember* was very strong in that, and *The Wedding* was strong in that.

Q: How does faith play out in *The Notebook?*

Sparks: It's a metaphor of God's love for us all. The theme is ever-lasting, unconditional love. It also goes into the sanctity of marriage and the beauty you can find in a loving relationship.

Q: Is it obvious in the film that it's a metaphor for God's uncon-ditional love?

Sparks: It's very subtle. Spreading the news is your duty as a Christian, and there are many ways to do this. There are those who are so wonderful from the pulpit and so telegenic— your Billy Grahams and your Robert Schullers. Others do it through literature, very God-based literature—like Rick Warren. Others do it through the examples that they lead—like Mother Teresa. Others do it more subtle, and that's where I would go.[6]

The ungrammatical phrase "others do it more subtle" is not so subtly a Southernism, a folksy populist locution of the type regularly employed by George W. Bush and Sarah Palin to speak to a conservative American audience. This "subtlety" (which Sparks uses to mean both "fiction" and "euphemism") is used to disguise Sparks's evangelicalism—the folksiness is not itself actively proselytizing, but it is invoking a recognizable evangelical code, reaffirming small-town Southern family values as a covert way of promising to "keep the [conservative Christian] faith" even with a mainstream secular audience.

If the thriller is a mode dominated by paranoia, then sentimental fiction has always offered metanoia, or spiritual conversion: specifically as penitence, repentance, a reorientation of one's way of life.[7] Sparks's metanoia is not just regressive, but retrotelic, responding to a compulsive urgent need to return to a past imagined as the only possible future. Metanoia has dominated recent American cultural mythologies: in fact we've seen something of a discursive exchange between politics and religion in American culture. Politics, once the realm of the paranoid, as in Richard Hofstadter's famous formulation, is now metanoid, characterized by repentance and public shame, whereas religion as a public discourse is today increasingly characterized by paranoia.

Sparks's tales offer variations on the theme of conversion narratives, in which a skeptical protagonist must take the leap of faith and become a "true believer" (as in the title of his 2005 bestseller) in the ideology of heterosexual domesticity: he (less frequently she) must recant former beliefs (in science, careerism, in solitude, in intellectual or political pursuits, or indeed in any other secular ideology), apostates one and all, and lay themselves on the altar before the trinity of love of God, home, and family. The archetypal structure of the conversion narrative is a revelation that facilitates an alienated individual's move into communion with a higher authority, a communion that also enabled a (re)integration into a community of the righteous, of other true believers. By no coincidence, all of Sparks's heroes are skeptics, either romantic skeptics or religious skeptics (or both), and faith is the fulcrum between romance and religion in his tales.

Thus, in *True Believer*, a scientific journalist and professional debunker of supernatural stories, a professional skeptic, comes to a Southern town called "Boone Creek" to disprove a supernatural ghost sighting. Jeremy falls in love with a local librarian who forces him to rethink his urban ways and repudiate his decadent cosmopolitan life. He wants to marry her but is ambivalent about moving to Boone Creek ("the boonies" is derogatory US slang for rural areas), and also anxious because he has been told that he can't have children. At the end of the novel, he decides to move to Boone Creek, at which point he discovers that Lexie is pregnant. The child is a miracle: our hero was only infertile while living in—if not eating from—the Big Apple. Once he falls in love with a small-town girl and agrees to move into a big old-fashioned house in the South, Jeremy's masculine mastery and potency are magically reaffirmed. The urban space is troped as exhausted, arid, and sterile; the rural space is regenerative, productive, and fertile.

Daughters of God

The metanoia that sentimental fiction achieves is traditionally by means of the death of a woman, often a daughter, whose death effects reunion or reconciliation. The prototype of this converting dead daughter in American fiction is Little Eva in *Uncle Tom's Cabin*, whose death makes her slaveholder father repent his casual acceptance of the conveniences of slavery, and even unites white hand in black, as St Clare unconsciously clasps the hand of devoted Uncle Tom in his grief at Eva's deathbed.[8] Pity easily extends into piety: this model for sentimental reconciliation and spiritual conversion did not die with Little Eva—she was merely its apotheosis. The clearest example of metanoia in Sparks's fiction comes in *A Walk To Remember*. Rather than provide my own plot summary, let me offer the paperback cover's marketing blurb:

> *There was a time when the world was sweeter. . . when the women in Beaufort, North Carolina, wore dresses, and the men donned hats. . . when something happened to a seventeen-year-old boy that would change his life forever.*

It was 1958, and Landon Carter had already dated a girl or two. He even swore that he had once been in love. Certainly the last person in town he thought he'd fall for was Jamie Sullivan, the daughter of the town's Baptist minister. A quiet girl who always carried a Bible with her schoolbooks, Jamie seemed content living in a world apart from the other teens. She took care of her widowed father, rescued hurt animals, and helped out at the local orphanage. No boy had ever asked her out. Landon would never have dreamed of it. Then a twist of fate made Jamie his partner for the homecoming dance, and Landon Carter's life would never be the same. Being with Jamie would show him the depths of the human heart and lead him to a decision so stunning it would send him irrevocably on the road to manhood . . .

The world was "sweeter" in 1958 because women wore dresses and men wore hats: the novel's nostalgia is specifically for a neo-Victorian era defined by traditional gender roles. Quiet and pious Jamie has been forbidden to date by her evangelical preacher father; the plot twist is that after Landon falls in love with Jamie (which instantly makes him a better person who starts volunteering for charities and reading the Bible), Jamie reveals that she's dying of leukemia, thus redeeming her father, and his religiosity. The minister was protective from the purest of motives, safeguarding not only his daughter, but anyone she might date from falling in love with her: he understands that anyone who dates her will instantly and irrevocably love her. Conveniently, this paternal protectiveness also defended her chastity.

Seventeen-year-old Jamie has only one ambition in life: to marry. When Landon realizes this, he also understands that it is God's will that he marry her: "In my mind it was the first time God had ever spoken directly to me, and I knew with certainty that I wasn't going to disobey" (209–10). Jamie has no other desires, and implicitly is happy to drop dead once she's said "I do," which is exactly what happens, in a conclusion that hyper-literalizes to the point of parody the traditional romance narrative's supposed disinterest in women after they are married. As the back cover of *A Walk to Remember* makes clear, what is at stake in this story is not Jamie, but Landon's sentimental education, his journey toward "manhood." His nostalgic subjectivity dominates the tale, and Jamie's impending death serves merely as a vehicle to enact the conversion of those around her: Landon begins reading the Bible with Jamie, and eventually finds

God with her help. Similarly, when they learn that Jamie is dying, Eric, the stock-character high-school athlete who takes nothing seriously, and his equally stereotyped popular, promiscuous girlfriend Margaret, both make speeches declaring that Jamie has "the biggest heart of anyone I've ever known . . . you're the best person I'll probably ever know":

> When Eric had finished, Jamie wiped tears from her cheeks, stood slowly, and smiled, opening her arms in what could only be called a gesture of forgiveness. Eric went to her willingly, finally beginning to cry openly as she gently caressed his hair, murmuring to him. The two of them held each other for a long time as Eric sobbed until he was too exhausted to cry anymore. // Then it was Margaret's turn, and she and Jamie did exactly the same thing. (190–1)

Even Sparks is bored by this point: he can't be bothered to write a different speech for Margaret. It doesn't matter: Jamie's perfect forgiveness is as pure as the repentance of the two "bad" teenagers, whose immorality is marked by their secular values. The 1950s comes to represent the prelapsarian, a "sweeter world": there is no original sin here. Jamie doesn't merely forgive: she mothers, embracing Eric and Margaret like small penitent children. Her secret smile is part of the trope: the women in these novels spend a lot of time smiling knowingly.

We might also note the access of weeping in the scene—it could be a nineteenth- or even an eighteenth-century sentimental novel, in which true character is revealed through emotional outpouring: modern sentimental fiction is nearly as fascinated as late eighteenth-century texts with the involuntary, and especially with involuntary displays of emotion, such as fainting, weeping, sighing, and blushing. Jamie similarly embodies emotions: she incarnates the hackneyed passage from Corinthians she wanted read at her wedding, which Sparks helpfully modernizes for a presumptively culturally illiterate audience:

> 'Love is always patient and kind. It is never jealous. Love is never boastful or conceited. It is never rude or selfish. It does not take offense and is not resentful. Love takes no pleasure in

other people's sins, but delights in the truth. It is always ready to excuse, to trust, to hope, and to endure whatever comes.' Jamie was the truest essence of that very description. (193)

Jamie is the truest essence of that description because she's not a human being, she's the Holy Spirit. All those things may be true of love, because it's a metaphysical concept. It is not true of people, who are all of the things love isn't: they are impatient, unkind, jealous, boastful, conceited, resentful, ungenerous. The fact that Jamie is never any of those things simply demonstrates that she's not really human, and not really meant to be. She is love incarnate; a daughter of God who will return to Him very shortly because there is no place for her in this corrupt world.

A Walk to Remember is an especially transparent example, but Sparks's fiction consistently spins variations on the theme of the redemptive death, usually a dead wife, occasionally a dead daughter, one dead father (The Last Song) and one dead husband—which happens, tellingly, in the only quasithriller Sparks has written, The Guardian. Genre is not an accident: dead husbands belong to the paranoid, not the metanoid form. The heroine of The Guardian is the victim of a deranged stalker: that's the paranoid model, and it relies on absent guardians and victimized women. The metanoid romance formula, however—which is by far Sparks's favorite—kills off its women.[9] The core pattern derives from the Christian faith in the death of the redemptive individual—in the end, Sparks's evangelism trumps his gender politics.

Rejecting romance

The metanoid romance is actually male-centered (hence the high female mortality rate; they're not really about women) and is one of the causes of taxonomic debates among Sparks's audience (and himself) over whether his books are generic romances. The mortality rate in Sparks's fiction is too high to admit of his writing "romance" according to contemporary definitions, which equate romance with "happy endings" (i.e. with weddings). If modern romance is understood to be defined by the formula "boy meets girl-boy loses girl-boy weds girl," Sparks's readers insist that he is not a romance writer because he departs from this formula. But in point of fact, his books are less a departure than a reversal: Sparks has returned romance to mythic archetype by inverting the second and third elements of the formula. In most of Sparks's novels, boy meets girl, boy weds girl, boy loses girl—to God. She never leaves the boy voluntarily, of course, because for all of his endearing foibles, she loves him as devotedly, uncritically, and unconditionally as any mother (or Father, a Christian likeness that Sparks likes to draw). She leaves the hero, reluctantly, because she is a heroine in a sentimental novel, in which chastity and religiosity have taken the place of sex.

Sparks hotly disputes anyone who claims he writes romance novels, maintaining in interview after interview the crucial distinction between "romances," which he doesn't write, and "love stories," which he does:

> They are different genres. Love stories are Greek tragedies. I wrote modern day Greek tragedies. Look at literature, Shakespeare wrote *Romeo & Juliet*, Hemingway wrote *A Farewell to Arms*, that's a love story. *Casablanca* in film is essentially a love story. Moving to more modern literature, *Love Story* by Erich Segal, *The Bridges of Madison County* by Robert James Waller, and *The Horse Whisperer* by Nicholas Evans are all love stories. I write in that genre, and if I submitted one of my stories as a romance novel it would be rejected. The differences between the two genres are numerous. Romance has to have a certain structure to it.[10]

Sparks does not delineate what that structure is, or what the differences are, but we might note how many of the titles he names end with the death of the woman (*A Farewell to Arms, Love Story*), or with renunciation (*Casablanca, The Horse Whisperer, Bridges of Madison County*). Only in Shakespeare do both protagonists die, a plot device that Sparks has not yet employed. In another interview, he insisted on the same associations of his books with high art ("modern literature") and repudiation of romance as a genre. His genre, he says, is exemplified by

> 'Aeschylus, Sophocles, and Euripides. They were called the Greek tragedies. . . . A romance novel is supposed to make you escape

into a fantasy of romance. What is the purpose of what I do? These are love stories. They went from (Greek tragedies), to Shakespeare's *Romeo and Juliet*, then Jane Austen did it, put a new human twist on it. Hemingway did it with *A Farewell to Arms*.' That's one of his favorites, and he points it out as he walks the aisles of the bookstore. 'Hemingway. See, they're recommending *The Garden of Eden*, and I read that. It was published after he was dead. It's a weird story about this honeymoon couple, and a third woman gets involved. Uh, it's not my cup of tea.' Sparks pulls the one beside it off the shelf. '*A Farewell to Arms*, by Hemingway. Good stuff. That's what I write,' he said, putting it back. 'That's what I write.' . . . Asked what he likes in his own genre, Sparks replies: 'There are no authors in my genre. No one is doing what I do.'[11]

Another interviewer noted that Sparks "bristles when compared to Barbara Taylor Bradford—'she writes romance novels', and Danielle Steele [*sic*]—'women's fiction' . . . 'And I have more men readers than what you would consider a traditionally female author to have,'" he adds.[12] Finally, Sparks concludes that "love stories" entail "basically universal characters in a universal situation . . . It's very different and distinct from, let's say, a romance novel."[13]

The masculine panic and anxieties about originality and literary authority on display throughout these interviews are manifest, as are the presumptions about the "universality" and "literariness" of male writers ("modern literature") versus the particularity of "women's fiction"—a universality measured by how many "men readers" Sparks can claim. The "modern literature" and modern-day "Greek tragedies"—*Love Story, The Horse Whisperer, The Bridges of Madison County*—with which Sparks associates himself share two defining characteristics: they were all bestsellers, and they were all written by men. Anxiety about generic categories themselves is clear in the appropriation of the universal perspective, used to shed the diminishing trappings of gender and genre. Women write women's fiction, which means romance; men write universal love stories ("a completely different genre"). The gender hierarchies quickly and "naturally" give way to cultural ones: men write literature and women write trash.

Sparks also continually insists that he is less formulaic than romance writers, despite his reliance upon the formula of the "love story" in which the story ends with the death of one of the lovers, preferably the heroine, and even more preferably in childbirth— presumably the reason why he returns again and again to *A Farewell to Arms* as his favorite (and why he rejects *The Garden of Eden*, with its gender-bending fantasies of bisexuality and role play, as "weird"). The clear implication is that being less formulaic makes him more "artistic" in the Romantic conception of artistic (male) originality. And this is why, I take it, there is the wonderful moment when, to dissociate himself from romance writers, and insist upon his place in a genealogy of writers of classical tragedy, Sparks invokes Jane Austen, that well-known tragedian, and talks about the "new human twist," she put on Greek tragedy, although he neglects to tell us whether that new human twist on tragedy was comedy, happy endings, or her happening to be a woman.

The resistance is partly to the banality of formula itself, defended against by means of the cult of originality, which Sparks tries to reclaim even as he profits off of his mastery of sentiment. In the nineteenth century, emotion was a mark of moral and aesthetic value, and in particular, signaled one's godliness, the open Christian heart. The modernist twentieth century, by contrast, valorized the aristocratic masculine virtues of sophistication, discipline, and restraint over the middle-class feminine excess of sentimentality. Instead of being an ethical and religious imperative, sentiment came to characterize a deeply suspicious space in which wallowed the untutored, the uncultured, and the unwashed. Sentimentality is understood to be automatic, unthinking, unsophisticated, and easy. That said, if Sparks repudiates romance as a genre, it is not quite the case that there is no sex in Sparks (although it is certainly true that there is no spark in his sex). Halfway through *The Notebook*, his breakout hit, Sparks's hero Noah feels his "loins stir"—a smoking gun of a phrase proving beyond reasonable doubt that Sparks is, indeed, a writer of genre romance.

More seriously, Sparks is demonstrably a genre romance writer, but not in the sense he hopes. Sparks's romance is of the type famously distinguished by Northrop Frye from tragedy, comedy, and irony/satire (and there is certainly precious little of the latter two in Sparks). Frye defined romance as a "perennially child-like" formula marked by an extraordinarily persistent nostalgia for a golden age, with virtuous heroes and heroines who represent cultural ideals. "At its most naive it is an endless form in which a central character who never develops or ages goes through one adventure after an other until the author himself collapses."[14] Sparks' form can certainly seem endless, not to say formulaic: love at or near first sight; conflict arising not from external forces but from internal struggles to resist temptation and lead an exemplary life; reconciliation with a community of believers; a "miracle" of love, fertility, and/or redemption; and the exalting death of the heroine. This sentimental formula is typified by *True Believer* and its sequel *At First Sight*, in which Jeremy, the recovering skeptic, has married pregnant Lexie and moved to Boone Creek. He starts hankering after a bachelor life, wanting a sports car instead of a family car, and other familiar symbols of masculine identity crisis. To resolve this crisis of faith, Sparks kills Lexie off in childbirth.

Myth, said Northrop Frye, is "the imitation of actions near or at the conceivable limits of desire."[15] By this definition, *At First Sight* is most certainly a myth. In 2000, according to the HRSA, the maternal mortality rate (MMR) in the United States was 9.8 in 100,000 live births. This means that what happens to Lexie at story's end had a .0098 per cent probability in real life: for once it is possible to measure precisely the plausibility of a particular fictional plot turn. Sparks's *diabolus ex machina* seems even more egregious if we factor in Lexie's race and class: the 2000 MMR for black women was at 22.0 per 100,000 live births, almost three times the rate for white women, which was just 7.5. As a white middle-class woman, that is, in real life, Lexie would in fact have had just a .0075 per cent chance of dying in childbirth—which surely means that the probability of her death is "near or at the conceivable limits of desire." But if we read *At First Sight* as a nineteenth-century sentimental novel, Sparks's plot device becomes considerably more realistic. At the beginning of the twentieth century, maternal death rates were around 1 in 100 for live births. So in 1900, instead of in 2000, Lexie's death would have been credible, even likely. And going back 100 years—or at least 50—seems to be where we go when we read a Sparks novel, marked as they are by "extraordinarily persistent nostalgia, [a] search for some kind of imaginative golden age" (Frye, 186).

Sparks conforms quite neatly to the formula of the eighteent- and nineteenth-century novel of sentiment. Consider for instance the repudiation of "fashionable" urban life and reconciliations with domesticity in Maria Cummins's hugely popular 1854 novel *The Lamplighter*. Its hero, tired of the empty, frivolous, "wearisome and foolish" life he has had seeing the world, returns home to the woman he has always loved and declares his feelings in terms of domesticity, communion, and eternity:

> What is there, in the wearisome and foolish walks of Fashion, the glitter and show of wealth, the homage of an idle crowd, that could so fill my heart, elevate my spirit, and inspire my exertions, as the thought of a peaceful, happy home, blessed by a presiding spirit so formed for confidence, love, and a communion that time can never dissolve, and eternity can but render more serene and unbroken?

The sentimental education of the hero across *True Believer* and *At First Sight* is identical. First, at the end of *True Believer,* Jeremy must repudiate New York and move to the South to be with Lexie, because, of course, just holding her means that "he was home," although they are in a cemetery at the time—which will soon become her home, not his. Kissing her, he knows that "he would never leave her again." Jeremy has to learn this lesson all over again in *At First Sight,* during which he must reconcile himself to the loss of his selfish, superficial desires: although he is paying for their family's car entirely by himself—Lexie no longer works, of course—Jeremy can't have the convertible he wants, but must instead buy a sensible family car, and resents it. Eventually, however, his writer's block is resolved when he realizes that he is happiest in Boone Creek:

> He imagined the energy of the city, the lights of Times Square, the illuminated outline of the Manhattan skyline at night. He thought of his daily runs in Central Park and his favorite diner, the endless possibilities of new restaurants, plays, stores, and people . . . [sic]
> But only for an instant. As he glanced through the window and saw the whitewashed bark of cypress trees standing on the banks of Boone Creek, with the water so still that it reflected the sky, he knew he wouldn't leave. Nor, he realized with an intensity that surprised him, did he want to. . . .
> He wanted to celebrate by taking Lexie in his arms and holding her forever. He was looking forward to raising his daughter in a

place where they could catch fireflies in the summer and watch the storms roll in from the shelter of their porch. This was home now, their home . . . (229–30)

This passage is, in sentiment, identical to the 1854 epiphany of Cummins's hero at the end of *The Lamplighter*. No mere longing backward glance, these stories recoil so hard from present-day domestic sexual realities and economic struggles that they aren't just part of a backlash, they have whiplash: they can only look in one direction. Sparks's stories transform the ingenuousness of nostalgia to the disingenuousness of doublethink. Not reconciliation, but rationalization; not regret but disavowal on a cultural scale.

In 2007, Sparks's *The Choice* literalizes the cognitive dissonance and disavowal created by his formula of suspended agency, voluntarism and passivity, love and morbidity, by having its heroine not quite die—but rather spend the entire book in a vegetative state. The titular choice is now the hero's—whether to respect his wife's "choice," which was to die (she has left a living will in case of accident). So, the woman's choice is death, the voluntary relinquishment of life, power, and indeed choice itself, in a perfectly literal manifestation of his covert ideological agenda. Nearly all of Sparks's stories recode women's choices in exactly those terms: as the choice not to make a choice, the suspension or repudiation of agency or even life itself. It is the man who makes the active choices, in this case, a choice whether to kill off his wife or save her, in what can only be a particularly accurate and perverse image of authorial agency, the degree to which female passivity and morbidity remains wish fulfillment, "at or near the conceivable limits of desire," the murderous wish that dare not speak its name.

Bibliography

Armstrong, Nancy. "Why Daughters Die: The Racial Logic of American Sentimentalism," *Yale Journal of Criticism* 7.2 (1994): 1–24.

Cummins, Maria. *The Lamplighter,* ed. Nina Baym (New Brunswick, NJ: Rutgers University Press, 1988, 1995. First published Boston, 1854): 359.

Frye, Northrop. *Anatomy of Criticism: Four Essays* (Princeton University Press, 1950).

Hindmarsh, D. B. *The Evangelical Conversion Narrative: Spiritual Autobiography in Early Modern England* (Oxford University Press, 2005).

Lane, Anthony. *Nobody's Perfect* (NY: Knopf, 2002).

Nabokov, Vladimir. *The Real Life of Sebastian Knight.* (London: Penguin Books, 1941, 1995).

Picoult, Jodi. *Plain Truth.* (NY: Washington Square Press, 2001).

Sparks, Nicholas. *At First Sight.* (NY: Grand Central Publishing, 2006).

—. *The Choice.* (NY: Grand Central Publishing, 2007).

—. *True Believer.* (NY: Grand Central Publishing, 2005).

—. *The Wedding.* (NY: Grand Central Publishing, 2003).

—. *A Walk to Remember.* (NY: Grand Central Publishing, 1999).

Wilson, Rob. *Be Always Converted, Be Always Converting: An American Poetics.* (Harvard University Press, 2009).

Notes

1   Anthony Lane, *Nobody's Perfect* (NY: Knopf, 2002): 366–9. Emphasis in the original.

2   It is, naturally, not coincidental that during this decade, the publishing market was also going through several transformative changes itself, including the introduction of ebooks, and the accelerated fracturing of popular markets into niche demographic audiences, enabled by online publishing. I am certainly not claiming that the erotic romance disappeared or ceased to be popular; simply that such romances no longer defined what constituted "blockbuster" popular romances at the top of the mass market fiction lists: Danielle Steel and Judith Krantz continued to publish well into the twenty-first century, but both authors slipped precipitously from the top 10 and as of this writing have not recovered their positions.

3   http://www.suite101.com/article.cfm/romance_through_the_ages/39141

4   Recent successful romantic comedy films replicate the trope: a career woman fed up with her career decides to return to childhood, symbolized as traditional domestic paradise. Films such as *Sweet Home Alabama, The Devil Wears Prada, New in Town, Kate & Leopold,* all feature women voluntarily repudiating modernity, figured as a sterile, unfulfilling, exhausting career, in favor of the restful, comforting ease of life in domestic tranquility, symbolized by small-town, rural America (or, in the case of *Kate & Leopold,* time-traveling to become an Edwardian duchess).

5   http://nymag.com/daily/entertainment/2009/09/which_amish_
    romance_novel_shou.html

6   http://www.christianitytoday.com/ct/movies/interviews/2004/
    nicholassparks.html

7   See, for example, Rob Wilson, *Be Always Converted, Be Always
    Converting: An American Poetics* (Harvard University Press, 2009,
    p. 9), who notes: "Conversion, in the more Catholic sense elaborated
    through two centuries of catechesis, remains close to the Greek verb
    metanoia, meaning a grace-drenched change of mind and thought
    turning the subject away from wrong living and sinfulness toward a
    pursuit of godliness and the vocation to beatitude that William James
    (stressing the consequences of lived belief) called, in various modern
    contexts, "saintliness." Conversion is most commonly translated into
    English as the verb "repent," as in the mandate from John the Baptist
    (Mark 1:15), "The time is fulfilled, and the kingdom of God is at
    hand: repent ye, and believe the gospel." Such a conversion "turn"
    implies a three-stage pattern of turning around, from sinfulness
    (conversion), as a conviction of wrongdoing and wrong living
    (repentance), toward regenerating acts of sacrifice and transformation
    (penance)." D. B. Hindmarsh notes the link between metanoia and
    the Christian "good news" that Sparks invokes: "The gospel and
    conversion are closely linked in the pages of the New Testament in
    terms of divine call and human response. In the synoptic Gospels, the
    good news (*evangelion*) of Jesus commences with John the Baptist's
    call for conversion (*metanoia*) as preparation for the kingdom
    (Mark 1:1–4). . . . Again, at the beginning of Jesus' preaching, the
    announcement of good news is followed by a call to conversion: 'The
    kingdom of God is near. Repent (*metanoeite*) and believe the good
    news (*evangelio*)!" *The Evangelical Conversion Narrative: Spiritual
    Autobiography in Early Modern England* (Oxford University Press,
    2005): 13.

8   See, for example, Nancy Armstrong, "Why Daughters Die: The Racial
    Logic of American Sentimentalism," *Yale Journal of Criticism* 7.2
    (1994): 1–24.

9   The only time the male lover dies in Sparks is at the end of *Nights
    in Rodanthe* (2007), a book whose plot Sparks has said he drew
    from life, when his own father died after falling in love again after
    the sudden death of his wife, Sparks's mother. When reality writes
    the plot, male protagonists can die; when Sparks writes the plot, the
    victim is usually the woman.

10 http://www.newyorkbestsellerlist.org/archives/71

11 http://www.usatoday.com/life/movies/news/2010–03-11-lastsong11_ CV_N.htm

12 http://living.scotsman.com/features/Food-for-thought.2631255.jp

13 http://www.teenreads.com/authors/au-sparks-nicholas.asp

14 See Northrop Frye, "The Mythos of Summer: Romance" in his *Anatomy of Criticism: Four Essays* (Princeton University Press, 1950).

15 Ibid., 136.

14

The Kite Runner's transnational allegory: Anatomy of an Afghan-American bestseller

Georgiana Banita

America was a river, roaring along, unmindful of the
past. I could wade into this river, let my sins drown to the
bottom, let the waters carry me someplace far. Someplace
with no ghosts, no memories, and no sins. If for nothing
else, for that, I embraced America

THE KITE RUNNER, 144.

When the Afghan-American writer Khaled Hosseini showed up for a book signing at a California store shortly after the publication of his novel, *The Kite Runner*, in 2003, he greeted exactly one reader expecting an autograph. Since that disappointing event, over two million copies of *The Kite Runner* have been sold, a figure that kept the novel on the *New York Times* bestseller list for over a year. In 2005, the book was outsold only by *Harry Potter and the Half-Blood Prince* and James Frey's controversial memoir *A Million Little*

Pieces. Also in 2005, US libraries reported the book as number eight on *Library Journal*'s list of the most borrowed fiction books.[1] Early signed copies of *The Kite Runner* are now expensive collectible editions, with asking prices up to $2,500. Undoubtedly, more than literary merit and effective marketing account for the runaway success of this California physician's debut novel, driven by word-of-mouth at a moment when fiction sales were beginning to dip. Truly, the first novel to be written by an Afghan-born American, *The Kite Runner* singlehandedly forced into visibility a hitherto obscured segment of ethnic America and was praised by reviewers for representing the culture of Afghanistan, a country permanently on the cusp of political upheaval.[2] Yet, it also garnered accolades for its transcendence of history and place to reveal universal questions of guilt and redemption of the sort that countless book clubs have debated over the past years.[3] Scores of municipalities have selected the novel for their Community Reads programs—which also sponsor lectures on Afghanistan and even kite-flying days—citing its "universal" themes and Laura Bush's words of praise—"really great" (Nelson 2004). This combination alone may not have sufficed to propel the book to the rank of a bestseller had it not been assisted by Hosseini's sophisticated engagement with the rhetoric of ethics and justice that informs the so-called war on terror. Disguised by a heavy-handed parable is a subtle critique of exceptionalist discourses of justice—a critique only partly intended and significantly sharpened by the political context of the novel's publication. Specifically, it is no accident that an Afghan-American novel should touch a chord with American readers precisely at a time when, in the aftermath of the 9/11 attacks, Afghanistan once again attracted the attention of American geopolitical strategists. The nexus of political and cultural forces that define this conjecture is, however, more complicated than it may seem.[4] To the extent that the novel's representation of Afghanistan is both eye-opening and palatable to American audiences, Hosseini steers clear of contrarian views on the Afghan-American conflict, opting instead for a version of history that hails America as the uncontested "brash savior" (132) and liberator in ways that superficially endorse the rhetoric of the war on terror yet occasionally verge on mockery and criticism of moralistic historiography and cultural imperialism.

Accounting for the role of plot, ideology, and allegory in Hosseini's novel enables, I argue, a clarification of its success as a piece of transnational metafiction. Underlying this argument is the suggestion that Hosseini's particular ideological location is geared toward a mass readership—and the other way around: that his status as a widely read celebrity author inflects the ideological makeup of his writing and reflects indirectly on products of the larger cultural brand his novel initiated, including the film adaptation of *The Kite Runner* (dir. Marc Forster 2007), Hosseini's second bestselling book, *A Thousand Splendid Suns* (2007), as well as the graphic novel *The Kite Runner* (2011). The Hosseini aesthetic—an eminently recognizable blend of epic storytelling, sentimentality, and morality tale—is a symptom of the broader turn to the transnational after 9/11, especially through narratives that recount the "untold stories" of the regions in which the United States is taking a distinct strategic interest. Hosseini himself did not initiate this deterritorialization of post-9/11 fiction, although his was, next to William Gibson's *Pattern Recognition* (also 2003), one of the first post-9/11 narratives to engage with the politics of the war on terror. Yet, by virtue of its popular success, *The Kite Runner* has rightly been taken as a key manifestation of this new transnational aesthetic. Whether the novel indeed reflects a post-American outlook or merely disguises its deeply American convictions beneath a cosmopolitan façade of traveling identities and fates is the question that will guide my analysis of the narrative and its reception. *The Kite Runner*, I would contend, is a novel with significant ethical purchase because it mobilizes moral truths in a climate that would be better served by the lack of certitude and the rash condemnations that certainty engenders. It is precisely this conspicuously assertive moralism that shores up the novel's cultural and political force, making it an urgent vehicle for thinking about the productive interplay between literary and political narratives, to the extent that they may be fully disentangled as separate avenues of discourse. Through the disorienting smoke thrown up by the 9/11 attacks, Hosseini clearly invites or at least allows the appropriation of Afghan native and immigrant culture(s) by large publics interested less in history lessons than in ways to assuage a guilt-ridden national conscience in the aftermath of the 2001 invasion of Afghanistan by the United States and its allies. To that extent the novel illustrates the assumption that the success of bestselling fiction has as much to do with timing as with content or literary quality. To elucidate these contextual causalities, I will focus not only on the entwinement of the novel with the ideological climate of its emergence and reception, but also on what this relationship entails for its success as a post-9/11 transnational allegory.[5]

The clash of civilizations

Although the thread that ties *The Kite Runner* together is a personal plot of friendship and estrangement (from others and from oneself), the dramatic political backdrop is the main source of the fierce cruelty that characters encounter and of the love with which they respond. Amir, the novel's young narrator, comes of age during the last peaceful days of the Afghan monarchy, just before the onset of the revolution and the invasion by Russian forces, "bringing the death of the Afghanistan [he] knew and marking the start of a still ongoing era of bloodletting" (39). The political fragility of the nation is encoded in the tenuousness of human relationships, symbolized here by Amir's close friendship with Hassan, the son of his father's servant and a child of preternatural goodness. "That was the thing with Hassan. He was so goddamn pure, you always felt like a phony around him" (62), Hosseini writes, although the "phony" element on display is clearly Hassan's unlikely purity as an early symptom of the novel's hyperbolic tenor. The friendship reaches a breaking point during a kite-flying tournament: Amir fails to defend his friend against a brutal attack by racist bullies, a gesture of cowardly restraint that will haunt him for the rest of his life, most of which is then spent in Californian exile. Assef, the leader of the group that assaults Hassan, is described as a Nazi sympathizer convinced that defeating Hitler was a miscarriage of history: "Now, there was a leader. A great leader. A man with vision. . . . if they had let Hitler finish what he had started, the world would be a better place now" (43). In the aftermath of the rape, Assef attends Amir's birthday party and offers the latter a biography of Hitler as a birthday gift (104). The recruitment of Hitler as a moral and ideological shorthand helps mediate Amir's own racialized identity for a US audience, normalizing this identity by casting Amir as the opponent of a Nazi in ways that draw unequivocal sympathy.

Yet Amir isn't entirely free of preconceptions, and his own prejudices reveal the key structural discrepancy that is constitutive of the novel as a whole: Even as one set of moral transgressions is exposed, another is retained and reinforced. The friendship and subsequent estrangement between boys of different social castes ultimately encapsulate the antagonisms and rivalries that divide Afghan society. As Amir himself admits, "The curious thing was, I never thought of Hassan and me as friends either. Not in the usual sense anyhow. . . . Because history isn't easy to overcome. Neither is religion. In the end, I was a Pashtun and he was a Hazara, I was Sunni and he was Shi'a, and nothing was ever going to change that. Nothing" (27). The differences between Pashtuns (Amir's group) and Hazaras (Hassan's lower caste) as belonging to the two separate religious denominations Sunni and Shi'a are permanently interrogated in the novel. One of Hazaras' alleged negative traits is that of always "passing themselves as martyrs" (10), a typical accusation from the superior group toward the one it victimizes. In the case of Hassan, his religious and cultural affiliation is further marked by his harelip, described as the result of a blunted act of genesis: "I can still see his tiny low-set ears and that pointed stub of a chin, a meaty appendage that looked like it was added as a mere afterthought. And the cleft lip, just left of midline, where the Chinese doll maker's instrument may have slipped, or perhaps he had simply grown tired and careless." (3)

While the description of prerevolutionary Afghanistan cannot circumvent the friction among ethnic groups, the novel turns especially dark when Hosseini describes the tyranny of the Taliban after Amir returns to the sniper-infested environment of Kabul to help Hassan and his family and thus make amends for his mistakes as a child. The impulse to return, an inevitable and typical trope of diasporic narrative, is prompted by the phone call of an old friend, now on his death bed, who promises Amir that "there is a way to be good again" (2)—a sentence that comes to haunt the novel from beginning to end. On a secondary level, by returning to Kabul, Amir also seeks to disprove his father's statement—inspired by the boy's "mean streak" (25) as a form of passive aggressiveness—that "a boy who won't stand up for himself becomes a man who can't stand up to anything" (24). The novel replicates Amir's mission in that it aims to be "good" while "standing up" for a rigid set of ready-made moral convictions, whose barefaced incorporation into the narrative suggests a certain degree of self-conscious ambivalence.

As soon as Amir meets his old nemesis Assef, now a powerful Taliban official, the novel descends into a vortex of mannerisms that blends fantasies of evil retrieved from the dustbin of history, turning the Taliban into reprehensible cartoon villains while occluding the political and social conditions that fostered their ascent. Aryan and heartless, Assef engages in what the narrator calls "ethnic cleansing" (298), a phrase borrowed from the official nomenclature of the Bosnian War. With epiphanic enthusiasm, Amir uses Western sociological idiom to give a recognizable face to the evil he knew as a child, thereby defacing the specific cultural environment in which it was embedded: "Years later, I learned an English word for the creature that Assef was, a word for which a good Farsi equivalent does not exist: 'sociopath'" (41). Seen in this light, the inability of the Afghan people to eradicate the evil of the Taliban may be traced back to a linguistic insufficiency or a form of conceptual ignorance. While the novel's message of resistance to violence may be genuine and heartfelt, the evil that the characters set out to oppose is clearly the result of ethical discoloration: the reader is tempted to compare the American intervention in Afghanistan to NATO's military actions against genocidal governments in World War II and the Bosnian conflict on the chessboard of a Manichean global politics impervious to cultural distinctions and debate.

Once Amir finds Hassan's son Sohrab (under unlikely circumstances), he decides to adopt the boy, as he and his wife Soraya cannot have children. Yet, the international adoption system proves hostile to his morally irreproachable intentions. America, once part of the solution to Afghan woes, now becomes part of a new transnational problem. It is, in fact, debatable whether America was a solution to anything at all: In the United States, Amir's father manages a gas station while selling second-hand goods (such as black velvet portraits of Elvis) at weekend swap-meets to augment his paltry income, so that Amir can study writing at a community college. Making the rounds of weekend garage sales hardly conforms to Amir's American Dream; nor is Fremont, California, the hub of cosmopolitanism he had expected. The only significant advantage gained from moving to the United States is an emotional rapprochement between Amir and his father, both of whom suddenly find themselves marginalized by poverty. Their relationship comes to resemble the initial bond between Baba and his illegitimate son, Hassan: "Maybe that was why Baba and I had been on such better terms in the US," Amir muses. "Selling junk for petty cash, our menial jobs, our grimy apartment—the American version of a hut; maybe in America, when Baba looked at me, he saw a little bit of Hassan" (317). Yet, this transfer of the social caste system from the external environment in Afghanistan to the personal father-son relationship in the United States only sharpens the father's need for social and cultural segregation. Despite the difficulties he encounters in the United States and his dislike of the American culture of mistrust (135), Amir's father (*Baba* in the novel) may be seen to embody aspects of America in ways that cast him as the metaphorical love child of America's Afghan affair. His understanding of morality brooks no ambivalence or restraint, and he fervently embraces a brand of Republicanism that allows him to assume a national identity to supplant the Afghan past: "My father molded the world around him to his liking. The problem, of course, was that Baba saw the world in black and white. And he got to decide what was black and what was white" (16). He adopts a worldview deeply inflected by the moralism of the war on terror, his early idealism retooled in the service of an equally idealized notion of America: "Baba loved the *idea* of America. It was living in America that gave him an ulcer" (132).

The ideological makeup of this unusual diasporic narrative impinges on its literary style in interesting ways. In its "plot twists better suited to a folk tale than a modern novel" (Hower 2003), *The Kite Runner* remains untroubled by the narrative complexity and linguistic playfulness that characterize much diasporic writing in English. The text does translate key Afghan words and phrases—also cited in their original form but romanized spelling, yet linguistic difference and otherness are not prominent in the novel or otherwise thematized, serving the purpose of local color rather than cultural critique. Reviewers have remarked upon the novel's informative but sentimental style, its utilitarian prose and sturdy but modest storytelling skills. Although it certainly "fleshes out the cartoonish picture many Americans have of Afghanistan as a culture of warlords and cave hideouts" (O'Rourke 2005), offering a pointed rebuke to prevailing accounts of that country as nothing but a terrorist haven, *The Kite Runner* remains a moralizing tale of simplistic convictions. The question I want to ask is whether this reductive vision may harbor the potential for critique precisely because of its streamlined narrative, whose lack of ambivalence provokes reflections on the ethics of ambiguity as a necessary tool in unpacking the mechanisms and transgressions of the war on terror.[6] Put differently, what I am interested in is the indirect challenge the novel poses to simplified ideological narrativization through a cautionary, caricatured tale that dramatizes the pitfalls of caricature. Essential to this challenge is the metafictional function assigned to writing as a profession—in America, Amir becomes a moderately celebrated writer—and a means of bridging the textual fractures arising from the novel's transnational drama. Kite-fighting itself, of course, also embodies on a smaller scale the violence of war and displacement. In fact, it is in the layering of highly dichotomized conflicts that the secondary, more complex structure of the novel's intercultural and intertextual transfers becomes apparent.

Afghanistan, made in America

Interest in Afghan history and culture has surged since 2001 as the United States grappled with the aftermath of the 9/11 attacks. The instability of the region and the questionable success of the war on terror have consistently preoccupied the international community. As Amir sarcastically observes, "now Dan Rather, Tom Brokaw, and people sipping lattes at Starbucks were talking about the battle for Kunduz, the Taliban's last stronghold in the north" (382). Kabul becomes the focus of global attention and concern rather than "the heading of an AP story on page 15 of the *San Francisco Chronicle*" (253). In making Afghan culture accessible to a Western readership, Hosseini not only satisfies this curiosity about Afghanistan, but also immerses a personal struggle into a motley mix of ideas and buzzwords meant to remove all traces of ambiguity and self-doubt obstructing the path of American empathy with the Afghan characters. One means of achieving empathetic shortcuts resides in Amir's enlightened relationship with his wife, Soraya, a "fallen" woman in Afghan society but a perfectly reasonable partner to Amir, who explains his disinterest in Soraya's past by invoking his own share of grief, guilt, and remorse: "I think a big part of the reason I didn't care about Soraya's past was that I had one of my own. I knew all about regret" (190). Above all, however, Amir is portrayed as a champion of female emancipation: "I cringed a little at the position of power I'd been granted, and all because I had won at the genetic lottery that had determined my sex" (157). We may add this to the list of devices used to Americanize Amir and ensure that his progressive tolerance is sympathetically distinct from the Nazified Taliban and its oppression of women.[7]

Another source of easy empathy can be found in Amir's decision to become a writer, a decision that resonates with a particularly American pathos of self-expression yet goes unexplained in the context of Amir's immigrant condition or his memories of poverty and persecution in Afghanistan. Even more startling (though no less successful) is the way in which Hosseini recruits American popular culture as a friendly and familiar looking glass meant to magnify the commonalities between the United States and far-flung cultures otherwise inimical to the insidious imperialism of US cultural capital. On his return to Kabul, the Nazified Taliban leader wearing dark round sunglasses suddenly strikes Amir as resembling John Lennon (284); "Arnold Whatsanegger" (330) is as popular in Afghanistan as anywhere else. In ways that the screen adaptation has confirmed, the narrative reproduces classic Hollywood tropes—in addition to plot points from Victor Hugo's classic *Les Misérables* (344)— especially elements of the Clint Eastwood canon. Westerns are particularly prominent during the protagonist's childhood years, the films' swashbuckling rhetoric completely at home among the harsh climates of Afghanistan. After having watched dubbed Westerns for years, Amir and Hassan are shocked to find out that John Wayne is not Iranian (28); a hat similar to Clint Eastwood's in *The Good, the Bad, and the Ugly* also makes a brief appearance: "Hassan and I took turns wearing the hat, and belted out the film's famous music as we climbed mounds of snow and shot each other dead" (48). The symbolic significance of the Western in the novel is similar to the role played by Vladimir Nabokov's *Lolita* in Azar Nafisi's *Reading Lolita in Tehran*: that of a transitional object facilitating readerly identification while casting Middle Eastern and South Asian cultures as avid audiences and followers of Western culture and mores. *The Kite Runner*'s pat emotional semantics plays a similar role: Amir's return to the Nazi hornet's nest is couched in redemptive language intelligible to all Americans irrespective of their faith. It is not by chance that Judy Slayden Hayes' introductory study *In Search of the Kite Runner* (2006), a book written from an explicitly Christian perspective, includes an overview of Islamic culture and faith as well as comprehensive comparisons of the novel's plot elements with biblical narratives.

Yet, the novel's widest window into its Afghan subject is opened by its alignment of narrative and ideology to examine how political norms are encoded in fiction and vice versa. *The Kite Runner*, I would argue, provides an allegory of Afghan national policy, reflecting— under the guise of a trite coming-of-age story—on the turmoil that plagues a country under constant regime change, as well as on the responsibility of the United States to be "good again," that is, redress global wrongs through diplomatic or military intervention. Amir's cowardice as he bolts from the scene that severs his friendship with Hassan may be taken to symbolize the consequences and the price of ethical inaction. Seen in this light, America's interventionist practices are redeemed on a Shakespearean scale. The pathology of guilt at the heart of the story can only be assuaged by the reader's projection of redeeming forces onto the nation: Like Amir, the United States return to Afghanistan to make amends for its earlier involvement in the country and its contribution to the rise of the Taliban. The novel, thereby, correlates the currently popular trope of sin and reparation—witness for instance the success of another global bestseller, Ian McEwan's *Atonement*, both in book form and as an award-winning motion picture—with the climate of guilty responsibility that partly accounts for the military and humanitarian involvement in Afghanistan. The redeeming spirit of this intervention is set against the defeatist, nostalgic morale of the Afghan people. Some negative character traits of Afghan characters are even elevated to the status of national flaws, such as *laaf*, "that Afghan tendency to exaggerate—sadly, almost a national affliction" (13), coupled with a general pessimism about the country's ability to recover: "Maybe what people said about Afghanistan was true. Maybe it *was* a hopeless place" (280, emphasis in original). By contrast, America lures Amir as a bastion of virtue and positive thinking; as one of his friends bitterly remarks after the young man's return to Afghanistan: "America has infused you with the optimism that has made her so great. That's very good. We're a melancholic people, we Afghans, aren't we? Often, we wallow too much in *ghamkhori* and self-pity. We give in to loss, to suffering, accept it as a fact of life, even see it as necessary" (212). The medium that channels the projection of self-pitying melancholia from the individual to the nation is that of storytelling.

The link between narrative and international policy is supplied by casting Amir as a fiction writer straddling two cultural spaces and idioms. Hosseini in fact dramatizes the possibilities of storytelling as political allegory by weaving authorship and reading as integral plot elements into the story of Amir's childhood and youth. Among the shared pleasures that bond Amir and Hassan during their idle childhood is the reading of Afghan folk tales, especially that of Rostam and Sohrab (32)—Hassan, in fond remembrance, will name his only son Sohrab. Some of the book's storytelling patterns are, however, not articulated in the narrative itself. The young Amir hones his narrative skills by deceiving Hassan and improvising new stories for him. Finally, Hassan makes a prescient pronouncement about Amir's gift as a storyteller and implicitly about the success of Hosseini's novel as an international bestseller: "Some day, Inshallah, you will be a great writer, Hassan said. And people all over the world will read your stories" (36). Fiction writing and reading provide the link between personal and national allegory. Reading in particular is what allows the extrapolation that *The Kite Runner* undertakes from an intimate story of ethical redemption to a larger paradigm of political and cultural alliance between strikingly unequal forces on opposite sides of the war on terror. "Reading" also entails here the ability to peer through masks of pretension, as if to unveil legible cores of human drama underneath—a gesture on which the novel may be said to turn. Hassan is capable of such clairvoyance despite his lack of formal education: "I was the one who went to school, the one who could read, write. I was the smart one. Hassan couldn't read a first-grade textbook but he'd read me plenty. That was a little unsettling, but also sort of comfortable to have someone who always knew what you needed" (66). The unbalanced relationship between the two friends is emphasized by Amir's final takeover of the plot, after Hassan's death. The sentimental plot finale is a continuation of the tales Amir would spin as a child: satisfying, unlikely, modeled on Clint Eastwood-style bombast, ultimately bound to enter the realm of legend.

Indeed, *The Kite Runner*'s symmetrical plot enlists hackneyed fictional formulae that require little creative energy to construct and even less interpretive finesse to understand. The hand that planted money under a mattress in order to accuse someone of a faked theft will later plant money under another mattress to help out a family in need; the rapists are either raped or brutally injured; the wound Amir incurs as he attempts to liberate Hassan's son perfectly resembles Hassan's own facial disfigurement—and the list could go on. The narrator's attempt to justify his reliance on well-worn formulae does little to dispel their triteness: "A creative writing teacher at San Jose State used to say about clichés: 'Avoid them like the plague.' Then he'd laugh at his own joke. The class laughed along with him, but I always thought clichés got a bum rap. Because, often, they're dead-on. But the aptness of the clichéd saying is overshadowed by the nature of the saying as a cliché" (207). Sohrab's posttraumatic silence after his humiliation and abuse at the hands of Assef is a rare instance of both subtle and realistic representation of a story that might have benefited from a more serious engagement with the violence of its plot. A deeper foray into the effects of these physical assaults against the boy would, however, have entailed forms of narrative disequilibrium and rupture otherwise alien to Hosseini's writing style, features that his reductive humanism emphatically strive to curtail. Paradoxically, it is precisely such destabilizing experiences—inherently resistant to linguistic representation—that move a work of fiction toward the realm of ethical activism, an aim that Hosseini, then, does not seem to follow very consistently. Instead, a tidy trajectory of spiritual recovery animates the narrative, resulting in a facilely moralistic view of Afghanistan that promotes the exportability of Western values and the universality of human tragedy.

Selective reading and the erasure of difference

In a studiously balanced fashion, then, the novel wishes to remind us that we are all human, fighting very similar battles in different circumstances. Yet, these circumstances are radically at odds in some cases (as with the United States and Afghanistan), and sometimes the very differences between them determine the battles we are fighting. Hosseini's effort to make the novel accessible to his American readership seeks to erase all differences between "us" and "them," only to unwittingly reinforce the friction between two nations that may well be human in themselves, but become inhumane in their relations to each other. The novel's simplicity ultimately occludes the clear-cut stakes of the conflict it describes, complicating it through oversimplification. One example of this effect is the narrative's therapeutic trajectory—derived from the vocabulary of psychoanalytic spiritual recovery. The universal idiom of therapy is meant to gloss over the messy predicament of a nation ravaged by war. Western values of redemption and healing turn out to be not only exportable, but perfectly in tune with the society on which they are being imposed. The resulting "perfect" fit reads like the misguided Western remake of a melodrama, intimate and fleeting motivations trampled under the trail of desert dust and hooves.

While an authentic exploration of conflict should illuminate the underlying assumptions and preconceptions that do divide people, *The Kite Runner* suggests that shared values outweigh conflicting principles. This simplification may also originate in a deeply ingrained readerly impulse to downplay the inaccessible (or puzzling) aspects of the text and play up what seems easier to grasp: some problematic aspects of Afghan and American culture do crop up, yet they remain in the shadow of what seems comforting and familiar. In a striking aside, former Secretary of State Henry Kissinger is described watching the brutal Afghan national sport called *buzkashi*, in which galloping horsemen bloody one another as they compete to spear the carcass of a goat—perhaps an allusion to the gory tug-of-war between Russia and the United States over the "carcass" of Afghanistan (22). Amir's conversion from a secular Muslim to a practicing one—which could be taken as a sign of radicalization in a less saccharine context—passes almost unnoticed, while his epiphanic experience at the close of the novel is made to conform to a generic kind of spirituality in a further instance of religious and cultural discoloration.

Nor does the novel take the time to probe the immigrant experience, made especially difficult by the family's diminished social status postemigration. Amir never truly "arrives" in America, settling instead within a Californian community of Afghan expatriates whose perfectly conserved habits and morals he has to navigate as if he had never left Afghanistan at all. For this reason, *The Kite Runner* might be expected to attract primarily Afghan audiences. Yet, to become a bestseller, a book needs to exceed its specific target audience, cross over, and transcend industry norms.[8] *The Kite Runner* achieves this partly by tapping into the idiom of psychotherapy. Amir is the proponent of an ethics based less on the Other than on what Anthony Giddens calls "a revisable narrative of self-identity"

(Giddens 1991: 81), encouraging revisions of the narrative self much the same way that therapy trains psychological remaking, pointing at the same time toward the political and strategic uses of such narratives in reshaping international relations and the periodical makeovers they entail. The novel juggles homogenizing aspects of US global culture (from Mark Twain to Reagan and Carter, and from John Wayne and Steven McQueen to Elvis and Jim Morrison) on the one hand and heterogeneous elements of transnational circuits and patterns of violence, including war, fundamentalism, and terror. The essential gesture of this novel—and the key to its success—lies in what Arjun Appadurai calls "repatriation of difference" (307), by which aspects of global and diasporic culture are absorbed into the novel, only to be repatriated, through mass international readership, as an easily decoded discourse on US hegemonic morality.

The novel's screen adaptation, released in 2007, continues this work of repatriation. The film removes even the last traces of potentially problematic material, offering an episodic, coincidence-heavy plot that frequently shift gears and generally fails to deliver on the novel's visual promises. In many ways, the simplicity of the adaptation might be commended as a means to steer clear of unnecessary controversy and highlight the storyline itself. Yet, even though the lack of cinematic gloss distinguishes the film as a serious, thoughtful story at a vast remove from the thriller and adventure genre dominating Middle Eastern and South Asian-themed Hollywood productions, the film leaves out all nuance and historical accuracy. Merely by force of elision, it appears less accessible than the novel, diverting attention from the plot to the mechanics of Hollywood casting and the politics of post-9/11 cinema. The lead actor playing the part of Amir was previously seen as one of the 9/11 hijackers in Paul Greengrass' *United 93*. Homayoun Ershadi, the protagonist of Iranian director Abbas Kiarostami's 1997 film *Taste of Cherry*, plays Amir's father, in a further twist on cultural homogenization and repatriation. Despite these casting overlaps, the adaptation goes to great lengths to keep Afghan politics off its map and to prevent post-9/11 international events from interfering with its story of redemption and healing. While historical authenticity has clearly been compromised, the film's fidelity to the novel is also partial at best. On the face of it, Forster never strays from the novel, yet at the same time, he deploys CGI sequences of kite-fighting to mark key moments in the narrative. Nor is Hassan's humiliation scene a particularly realistic representation of child rape. Sohrab's graphic suicide attempt (360–1) does not feature at all in the film. As a result of this selective retooling of the story to create a compassionate storyline incapable of perturbing any viewer, the film manages to disrupt the symmetrical narrative landmarks and oppositions that the novel took pains to establish. In trying to telegraph the plot even further, the screen adaptation thus reaches the tipping point where its narrative becomes culturally and politically unintelligible.

Allegories of (mass) reading

In explaining the peculiar ideological location of this novel and its adaptation, Fredric Jameson's key theory of national allegories is particularly instructive. Jameson famously associates Western literature with a radical division between the public and the private, whereas in the Third World, "the story of the private individual destiny is always an allegory of the embattled situation of the public third-world culture and society" (Jameson 1986: 69). Jameson's assumption that unallegorical communication is virtually impossible, in that speaking practices and positions cannot stand outside of inherited notions of history, is an intensely vilified perspective that has recently been undergoing some revivification.[9] Julie McGonegal, for instance, seeks to recover its significance as an interpretive strategy that "brings into focus the trajectories of cultural mediation" (256). *The Kite Runner* provides a fine example of mediating allegorical discourse. The novel is consistent with the concept of allegory as a discursive force that whittles reality down to one-dimensional patterns by imposing closure and teleology on a complex ideological landscape that is lacking in both. Thus, the perfectly tidy denouement stands in stark contrast to the bankruptcy of Afghanistan's political projects. Allegory is largely constituted by the accretions of previous and now reified cultural forms. In this sense, Hosseini's sustained metaphor of the inescapability of the past can be taken as a heuristic for the allegory of cultural entrapment: "It's wrong what they say about the past, I've learned, about how you can bury it. Because the past claws its way out" (1). In other words, despite the "discovery" of America as a makeshift *tabula rasa*, there is no circuitous route by which the characters can bypass the past, no method that will separate the life they live today from the lives that preceded them.

This imbrication of past and present sustains the embeddedness of *The Kite Runner* within its historical and ideological context as an instantiation of Third World national allegory, repurposed to satisfy and enthrall a Western audience accustomed to a wider separation of the public and private spheres. On the surface, Hosseini refutes Jameson's theory by suggesting that America and the Third World share allegorical forms of ideological mediation, and that the public and private realms have not undergone a complete division in the First World. What the novel ultimately dramatizes, however, is another form of ideological repatriation: the allegorical aesthetic of the Third World plot is redeployed to shore up the project of First World narrative capital on a global literary market. What Hosseini has written is less a national than a *"trans*national allegory," one that resists political polarization and cuts against Jameson's theories of the allegorical as a system of political and social coding, yet recuperating its ideological sharpness in its afterlife as an international bestseller.

Hosseini also enlists the ethical project of the novel as a means of colluding First and Third World allegorical discourse. In taking up the private, self-oriented moral idiom of the First-World self-help ethos, *The Kite Runner* holds the promise of an ultimate consensus through self-realization, which is of course no consensus at all once the alterity of its different worlds has been abolished. The reader and the protagonist of this novel should, in theory, adhere to different moral paradigms, yet their convictions are reconciled in the image of a nation—the United States—plagued by remorse and aching to be good again. The novel thus takes the form of a First World national allegory by emplotting the moral consciousness of a nation in the personal trajectory of an individual that moves between worlds in search of a safe and stable ethical terrain. By blending allegorical discourses to forge a transnational allegory, *The Kite Runner* moves beyond the question of where cultural difference lies to interrogate what happens when differences have been eradicated yet the tension they engender linger on. Because the narrative inflections and shadings of moral discourse remain "open-textured and essentially contestable," Anthony Appiah explains, "even people who share a moral vocabulary have plenty to fight about" (59–60).

Hosseini's own status as a cultural commuter between the United States and Afghanistan corresponds to that group of minority elites to whom Richard Werbner attributes a form of "cosmopolitan ethnicity" (Werbner 2002). In September 2007, after an absence of three decades, Hosseini returned to Afghanistan as an envoy for the UNHCR (the United Nations refugee agency), visiting villages in northern Afghanistan and observing firsthand the humanitarian assistance provided by Western aid organizations. His impressions of this journey—mainly that Afghanistan is still hopelessly dependent on the support of the international community—reinforced his hope that wealthy Western nations will continue their rebuilding efforts in Afghanistan.[10] Clearly then, Hosseini's cosmopolitanism is a "rooted" (Appiah 1998) or "vernacular" (Bhabha 1996) one, grounded by membership in a morally and emotionally significant community (his family and, by extension, his ethnic group) while espousing notions of tolerance and openness to the world, the transcendence of ethnic and class differences, as well as a moral responsibility for the other. Implied in the novel's partly autobiographical plot is Hosseini's own evolution from a representative of what Pnina Werbner calls "working-class cosmopolitanism" (Werbner 1999) toward the odd mixture of transnational elitism, humanitarian chic, and popular accessibility epitomized in his UNHCR work and bestselling success. Hosseini thus joins the ranks of other ethnic writers of middlebrow fiction and nonfiction (including Azar Nafisi, feminist and political advisor; or even Jhumpa Lahiri, a widely read literary celebrity in her own right) whose works often remain alienated from their working- and middle-class backgrounds despite the authors' vocal celebrations of cultural hybridity.

To sum up the results of this reading—a reading that locates the first Afghan-American, and perhaps most prominent, bestseller of the post-9/11 era within an ideological context both in terms of its production and its reception—*The Kite Runner* is the unique product of a varied set of circumstances that elucidates for us the workings of transnational allegory in ways that revise Jameson's still-useful conceptualization of national allegory for an international reading public in need of a new heuristic to decode fictional allegories whose "national" subtext is significant only to the extent that it reflects on a transnational geostrategic paradigm. Hosseini's Afghan narrative is relevant in a post-9/11 cultural climate in ways that would have seemed unimaginable just over a decade ago. Overall, the plot only partly uncovers the ambivalent dynamic of immigration and religion in a world still reeling from the effects of 9/11; rather, it remains premised on a bifurcation of good and evil rooted in Western (popular) culture. Large-scale societal differences between Afghanistan and the United States are obliterated in the process, as the novel assembles national stereotypes into a simple narrative code and idealized eth(n)ic community. At its core, *The Kite Runner* remains a deeply American fable disguised as a transnational text, yet the apparent fraudulence of this gesture is counterweighed by its use of the transnational paradigm to shed light on Afghanistan's national project and humanitarian crises. Against some critics' "disenchantment with allegory as an arguably appropriative and ultimately hegemonic process of signification" (McGonegal 254), Hosseini uses allegory in ways that both illustrate and condemn its pitfalls. Ultimately, the novel's bestselling success cannot be understood without recourse to its transnational allegoric patterns, the parallels between Afghanistan's struggles for political and cultural autonomy and a shaken US national consciousness after 9/11, the ethical questions raised by the invasion of Afghanistan, and the ways in which the voices of this country, keyed into the simple tones of melodrama, achieve both a national cohesiveness and international esteem.

Bibliography

Ahmad, Aijaz. "Jameson's Rhetoric of Otherness and the 'National Allegory.'" In *In Theory: Classes, Nations, Literatures*. London: Verso, 1992. 95–122.

Appadurai, Arjun. "Disjuncture and Difference in the Global Culture Economy." *Theory, Culture and Society* 7 (1990): 295–310.

Appiah, Kwame Anthony. "Cosmopolitan Patriots." In *Cosmopolitics. Thinking and Feeling Beyond the Nation*. Ed. Pheng Cheah and Bruce Robbins. Minneapolis, MN: University of Minnesota Press, 1998. 91–116.

—. *Cosmopolitanism: Ethics in a World of Strangers*. New York: W. W. Norton, 2006.

Aubry, Timothy. "Afghanistan Meets the Amazon: Reading *The Kite Runner* in America." *PMLA* 124.1 (2009): 25–43.

Bahramitash, Roksana. "The War on Terror, Feminist Orientalism and Orientalist Feminism: Case Studies of Two North American Bestsellers." *Critique: Critical Middle Eastern Studies* 14.2 (Summer 2005): 221–35.

Banita, Georgiana. "Affect, Kitsch and Transnational Literature: Azar Nafisi's Portable Worlds." In Sarah Säckel, Walter Göbel, and Noha Hamdy (eds.) *Semiotic Encounters: Text, Image and Trans-nation.* Amsterdam: Rodopi, 2009. 87–102.

—. *Plotting Justice: Narrative Ethics and Literary Culture after 9/11.* Lincoln, NE: University of Nebraska Press, 2012.

Bhabha, Homi. "Unsatisfied: Notes on Vernacular Cosmopolitanism." In *Text and Nation.* Ed. Laura Garcia-Morena and Peter C. Pfeifer. London: Camden House, 1996. 191–207.

Forster, Marc (dir.). *The Kite Runner.* Hollywood, CA: Paramount Home Entertainment, 2008.

Gibson, William. *Pattern Recognition.* New York: G. P. Putnam's Sons, 2003.

Giddens, Anthony. *Modernity and Self-Identity: Self and Society in the Late Modern Age.* Oxford: Oxford University Press, 1991.

Hayes, Judi Slayden. *In Search of the Kite Runner.* St. Louis, MO: Chalice Press, 2006.

Hirsch, M. E. *Kabul.* New York: Atheneum, 1986.

Hosseini, Khaled. *The Kite Runner.* New York: Random House, 2003.

—. *A Thousand Splendid Suns.* New York: Riverhead Books, 2007.

Hower, Edward. "The Servant" [Review of *The Kite Runner*] *New York Times*, August 3, 2003.

Jameson, Fredric. "Third World Literature in the Era of Multinational Capitalism." *Social Text* 15 (Autumn 1986): 65–88.

Jefferess, David. "To Be Good (Again): *The Kite Runner* as Allegory of Global Ethics." *Journal of Postcolonial Writing* 45.4 (2009): 389–400.

Khadra, Yasmina. *The Swallows of Kabul.* New York: Nan A. Talese/ Doubleday, 2004.

Kiarostami, Abbas (dir.). *Taste of Cherry.* Irvington, N.Y.: Criterion Collection, 1999.

McGonegal, Julie. "Postcolonial Metacritique: Jameson, Allegory and the Always-Already-Read Third World Text." *Interventions: International Journal of Postcolonial Studies* 7.2 (2005): 251–65.

Michener, James A. *Caravans.* New York: Random House, 1963.

Minden, Michael. "Bestseller Lists and Literary Value in the Twentieth Century." In *Literarische Wertung und Kanonbildung.* Ed. Nicholas Saul and Ricarda Schmidt. Würzburg: Königshausen & Neumann. 2007. 163–72.

Mitchell, Margaret. *Gone with the Wind.* New York: Macmillan Company, 1936.

Nafisi, Azar. *Reading Lolita in Tehran: A Memoir in Books*. New York: Random House, 2003.

Nelson, Martha. "A Winning Season." *People* 62.26 (December 27, 2004): n. pag. Web. 15 October 2011. http://www.people.com/people/archive/article/0,,20146422,00.html.

O'Rourke, Meghan. "*The Kite Runner*: Do I Really Have to Read It?" *Slate*, July 25, 2005.

Reich, Christopher. *Rules of Betrayal*. New York: Doubleday, 2010.

Seierstad, Asne. *The Bookseller of Kabul*. London, N.Y.: Little, Brown, 2003.

Shamsie, Kamila. *Burnt Shadows*. London: Bloomsbury, 2009.

Werbner, Pnina. "Global Pathways: Working Class Cosmopolitans and the Creation of Transnational Ethnic Worlds." *Social Anthropology* 7.1 (1999): 17–35.

Werbner, Richard. "Cosmopolitan Ethnicity, Entrepreneurship and the Nation: Minority Elites in Botswana." *Journal of Southern African Studies* 28.4 (2002): 731–53.

Wilson, Steven E. *Winter in Kandahar*. Shakey Heights, OH: H-G Books, 2003.

Notes

1   In 2008, Hosseini's second novel *A Thousand Splendid Suns*, ranked at number four on the same list.

2   Other fictions about the history and people of Afghanistan have been written by American-born, European, or Asian authors: Asne Seierstad, *The Bookseller of Kabul* (2003), Yasmina Khadra, *The Swallows of Kabul* (2004), *Burnt Shadows* (2009) by Pakistani novelist Kamila Shamsie, and M. E. Hirsch's 1986 saga *Kabul*. The prolific American novelist James A. Michener, a writer of tremendous thematic range, published *Caravans* in 1963. Since the publication of *The Kite Runner*, several popular fiction narratives of Afghanistan have been published, including Christopher Reich's espionage thriller *Rules of Betrayal* (2010). Within months of *The Kite Runner*, 2003 also witnessed the publication of *Winter in Kandahar*, a 9/11-themed Afghanistan thriller by Steven E. Wilson, a debut novelist and—much like Hosseini himself—a practicing physician.

3   Reviews of the novel have been predominantly positive, despite the occasional caveats regarding the modest aesthetic standards of the book and its failure to provide more than a feel-good story of spiritual renewal. Yet, most critics commend the timeliness

of the plot and its undeniable virtue of putting a human face to the recent events in Afghanistan. The combination of personal struggle and historical devastation has even prompted from *People* magazine a comparison with Margaret Mitchell's equally bestselling novel *Gone with the Wind* (1936): Both novels locate "the personal struggles of everyday people in the terrible sweep of history" (website endorsement, http://www.khaledhosseini.com/hosseini-books -kiterunner-praise-text.html).

4   In his fascinating analysis of reviews of the novel on Amazon, Timothy Aubry remarks that the novel's largely apolitical stance in fact pleased many readers already exhausted by the monstrous stigmatizations and ideological fantasies of the war on terror: "Their appreciation of the ostensibly nonpolitical aspects of the book suggests an unspoken frustration with, perhaps even repudiation of, the polarizing rhetoric that posits a conflict between Islam and the West and may reflect a desire to transcend ideological and ethnic divisions through an affective experience that underscores our shared, though culturally differentiated, humanity" (36).

5   I have applied a similar reading strategy to Azar Nafisi's equally controversial transnational narrative *Reading Lolita in Tehran*. See Banita 2009. For a reading of *The Kite Runner* as an "allegory of global ethics" (390) in the tradition of humanitarian projects, drawing especially on Anthony Appiah and Judith Butler, see Jefferess.

6   For a comprehensive ethical reading of narrative ambiguity after 9/11, see Banita 2012.

7   On the use of women's rights discourse as justification for a Western politics of interventionism and regime change, see also Bahramitash 2005.

8   See also Minden, who argues that "the bestseller genre is defined by convergences and spillovers" (170).

9   For a virulent critique of national allegory, see Ahmad 1992.

10   *The Kite Runner* is also dedicated "to the children of Afghanistan"— a phrase that anticipates the author's humanitarian interests and activities as a result of the novel's success.

15

The fiction of history: *The Da Vinci Code* and the virtual public sphere

Stephen J. Mexal

It is the romance of history which attracts the half educated and secures the publisher.

THE PERILS OF HISTORICAL NARRATIVE, 1890

[B]ooks can't possibly compete with centuries of established history.

THE DA VINCI CODE, 2003

Fables of history

In March 2005, Cardinal Tarcisio Bertone, Archbishop of Genoa, took time from his schedule to offer a short bit of literary criticism. Speaking on Vatican Radio, Bertone offered an emphatic and pithy denunciation of a popular novel. His informal edict was blunt: "don't buy," he said, "and don't read that novel." Later, Bertone elaborated on his remarks. This particular novel, he said, "aims to discredit the church and its history through gross and absurd manipulations." The book's chief danger, it seems, lay in its massive popularity. "The book is everywhere," he said. "You can't be a modern youth without having read it." It appears the novel warranted the Vatican's attention for two reasons: first, because of its ubiquity, and second, because of its potential to shake the edifice of the conventional historical narrative. "There is a very real risk," Bertone concluded, "that many people who read it will believe that the fables it contains are true." In short, the Catholic church felt that a novel—a cultural repository for "fables"—somehow held the possibility of convincing its readers that its narrative fictions were, in fact, nonfictional, and that those narratives could influence history itself.[1]

Bertone was, of course, referring to *The Da Vinci Code*, Dan Brown's 2003 novel that effortlessly wed a paranoiac's obsession with secret societies and the Roman Catholic church to the action-movie adventures of Brown's protagonist, Harvard "symbologist" Robert Langdon. On the surface, Bertone's condemnation of Brown's novels seems peculiar, and even a little absurd. How does one confuse the novelistic for the factually true? In the popular imagination, the two are binary opposites. The entire premise of the novel is that it is *not* factually true.

In the seventeenth and eighteenth centuries, when the novel was developing into its modern form, the word "novel" was often contrasted with "romance," with "novel" denoting a more recognizably realistic type of fiction, as opposed to the more romantic or fantastical qualities of the romance. Both forms denoted something not historically true, but "novel" referred to a literary form that more closely *resembled* the historically true. And yet for a brief moment in the eighteenth century, the word "novel" could also be used as a rough synonym for "lie" or "untruth." If novels are fictions offering historical verisimilitude, they are nevertheless still *fictions*, and the eighteenth-century slippage between fictional literary representation and deceptive nonfictional *mis*representation is instructive.

Regardless, the word "novel"—at least as used in reference to long-form narrative—has never been precisely synonymous with the direct and factual representation of historical actuality. Cardinal Bertone took the time to clarify what most people, presumably, already knew. Indeed, as *The Da Vinci Code* began to sell many millions of copies, a virtual cottage industry of books, articles, and television programs appeared, all dedicated to making the same, and ultimately very simple, point that Bertone made in 2005: *This book is a novel. If something is a "novel," that means it's "not true."* Had Brown's novel been about, say, swamp monsters, one would be hard pressed to imagine the Vatican taking the time to express concern that an overcredulous lay public might inadvertently believe that "fables" expressed about swamp monsters "are true." Yet, the fact that Bertone felt compelled to disavow the novel tells us a few things about the cultural capital accorded to historical narratives in the twenty-first century, about the relationship between bestsellerdom and historicity, and about the way in which bright-line divisions between true and not-true, between histories and novels, are easily blurred.

Dan Brown himself has sought to present *The Da Vinci Code* as a new cultural form. On the title page of the novel reads the standard disclaimer, "All of the characters and events in this book are fictitious, and any resemblance to actual persons" or events is "purely coincidental." Not five pages later, though, appears the apparently contradictory claim—clearly announced in large, bold typeface as "FACT"—that the "Priory of Sion" (a secret society figuring in the novel) "is a real organization," and that all descriptions of "documents, and secret rituals in this novel are accurate" (1). Before the reader even begins the narrative proper, *The Da Vinci Code* announces itself as a strange new hybrid: not historical fiction, but fictional history. That is, it is fiction that makes claims on, and purports to affect, the reader's status as a historical subject. And Brown took pains to underscore this fusion of fictional and historical narratives in interviews to promote the book. Appearing on the *Today* show in 2003, Brown was asked, "How much of this is based on reality in terms of things that actually occurred?" Brown responded, "Absolutely all of it. . . . Robert Langdon is fictional, but all of the art, architecture, secret rituals, secret societies, all of that is historical fact." Along similar lines, in an interview with *Good Morning America*, Brown was asked to imagine writing *The Da Vinci Code* "as a nonfiction book" rather than "a novel." "How would it have been different?" host Charlie Gibson asked. Dan Brown responded, "I don't think it would have." I contend that the significance of *The Da Vinci Code*, and the reason for its bestseller status, lies in this interplay between narrative history and fiction. The novel has provided a cultural site in which the nonacademic public can come together and critically debate what constitutes the "fictional," and how narrative fiction has shaped what we typically recognize as historical. This is a topic resonant with global public, for as the economic borders of the nation-state have eroded in recent decades, so also has the solidity of the conventional historical narrative. The public debate created by *The Da Vinci Code* in the press and in online forums such as Amazon.com's "Customer Reviews" reveals a deep and persistent ambivalence about the relationship between fictional narrative and historical subjectivity. This debate has largely occurred in online discussion forums and user-generated book reviews, examples of what literary critic Stanley Fish calls "interpretive communities": social matrices in which literary or historical meaning is produced. In these global public spaces, the public is able to debate the degree to which history and fiction are intertwined narrative discourses, all the while upholding *The Da Vinci Code* as the text uniting those discourses in the public imagination.

Stories of history

The Da Vinci Code is the highest selling American novel ever. It is, literally, the bestselling bestseller. As of 2009, it has sold over 80 million copies worldwide and been translated into more than 40 languages. It has also spawned a school of related books seeking to participate in the novel's representations of myth and history, books like *Truth and Fiction in The Da Vinci Code*, *The Da Vinci Hoax*, *The Da Vinci Fraud*, *The Real History Behind The Da Vinci Code*, and *Breaking The Da Vinci Code*. There are a number of ways to explain why the novel speaks to a global public: it's a ripping good yarn, of course, with its thrilling chase scenes, secret societies, and touristic whirl through the Louvre and other French landmarks. It also congratulates readers on their familiarity with the signifiers of high culture. (Although in practice, the only real familiarity required seems to be the knowledge that the Mona Lisa is a painting, and that France is a country in Europe.) And although the novel fuses twin narrative discourses, historical and fictional, it is important to remember that bestseller status and a novel's *topoi* are mutually informing entities. *The Da Vinci Code* is a bestseller because it has provided a site for public debate about the relationship between fictional and historical narrative, and then again, it has provided that site because it is a bestseller.[2]

If a bestselling book is a phenomenon that is indivisible from the existence of a particular public, *The Da Vinci Code* has sold so many copies as to render any traditional conception of its "public" virtually meaningless. The text is a global spectacle in a way that no novel has been previously.[3] This at least in part because the novel has positioned itself as being able to make claims upon, and indeed affect, historical actuality. But it is also because the relationship between historical narrative and fictional narrative is complicated stuff.

Conventionally, there is a sharp distinction between historical stories and fictional stories. To this way of thinking, both history and fiction events must employ the coherency of narrative in order to be accepted, but historical stories are distinguished by their use of real, rather than imaginary, events. Historian Hayden White, though, argues that those conventional distinctions are actually quite problematic. He writes that the fact that narrative "predominates in both mythic and fictional discourse makes it suspect as a manner of speaking about 'real' events" (57). After all, one can "produce an imaginary discourse about real events that may not be less 'true' for being imaginary" (ibid.). A recent example of this phenomenon is Edmund Morris's authorized biography of Ronald Reagan, *Dutch*, which was, famously, narrated by a wholly imagined contemporary of the president. The narrative discourse of *Dutch* is imaginary—there was no "Edmund Morris," lifelong friend of Reagan, only the historian Edmund Morris inventing that character—but the real events of Reagan's life, as well as, arguably, the insight into Reagan's personal tendency toward invention and fantasy, are nonetheless true. History and fiction, then, draw on a shared confluence of meaning. As White concludes, the "affiliation of narrative historiography with literature and myth should provide no reason for embarrassment," because the "systems of meaning production shared by all three are distillates of the historical experience of a people" (44–5). The coherency of narrative *is* the content of both historiography and literature. Narratives themselves are necessarily imagined, even if the events contained in those narratives are real. Conversely, (imagined) narratives about imaginary events still contain an organic connection to the (nonimagined) historical experiences of a public.

Although academic historiography had by the late nineteenth century come to affirm the rigidity of the binary opposition between fiction and history, under the classical model of historiography, fiction was included as an integral part of historical writing. Nancy F. Partner writes that the classical *historia* often incorporated small fictions into the narrative fabric of the larger nonfictional historical project. Fictional stories were seen as fulfilling crucial functions in the historical narrative. Fiction, in short, was not the opposite of history; fiction *explained* history:

> Fiction, as deployed by Herodotus and Thucydides, raised history from a mere descriptive record of events in sequence to a level nearer philosophy, nearer to those permanently apt generalizations about human character, politics and the causes of war so prized in Greek intellectual life. To be serious, valuable, elevated in classical culture, was to move beyond the particular. The fictions allowed history to be *about something*. (Partner 27)

Narrative fiction provided a context and meaning to lived historical experience. In the classical imagination, history and fiction were fused into a single discourse with the larger goal of creating a single, coherent, and "permanently apt" truth.

Even at the end of the nineteenth century, history was perceived by both academic historians and the public alike to be a singular and monolithic entity that was gradually written over time. As Allan Megill notes, "intelligent men believed that the then relatively new academic discipline was poised to produce a unified account of the history of humanity, or at least of that part of humanity whose doings were worth recording" (189). Today, of course, mainstream academic historiography has embraced a complex multiplicity and abandoned any pretense of constructing—or rather *re*constructing— a coherent master historical narrative.

But the historical model presented in *The Da Vinci Code* is a single, sweeping narrative—the sort of thing that can be hidden and discovered, like an artifact or secret plot. It is the stuff of conspiracy buffs and paranoiacs, not actual historians. But what is most interesting about Brown's novel is not whether it does or does not hew to the dominant academic model of historicity, but rather that it reveals a deep longing, in a global, transnational public, for a coherent master historical narrative. And in so doing it also reveals, by contrast, the senses of ache and fragmentation that result from the complexity of contemporary historical multiplicity.

Realism and *The Da Vinci Code*

The plot of *The Da Vinci Code* is literally a grail quest. Brown's holy grail, though, is not the chalice of Christ, but rather the suppressed history of Christianity. This idea—which Brown drew largely from Baigent, Leigh, and Lincoln's 1982 book *Holy Blood, Holy Grail*—in practice means that the novel's two main "historical" revelations are these: that "*The Holy Grail is a woman*" (242, ital. in original), and that Mary Magdalene was married to Jesus Christ (244). Interestingly, the revelation of this secret history is never fully resolved in the narrative. The novel ends with an ambiguous epilogue in which Langdon kneels outside the Louvre pyramid, seeming to make the decision to *not* subvert established "official" history by revealing the "real," but hidden, history.

Before moving on, it is perhaps worth dispensing with the obvious: all claims about the historicity of Christ's martial status, or lack thereof, are necessarily speculative to some degree.[4] There are no marriage records or photographs from that time, and so while different forms of knowledge are applicable—such as educated guesses given the best available historical evidence, or appeals to the religious authority of the Bible—all of those forms of knowledge necessarily involve a sort of speculative fiction, an act of imagination. And this act of imagination, in turn, is similar to what Brown attempts in his novel. But the cultural use value of Brown's imagining lies not in its ability to reveal historical actuality of 2000 years ago, but rather the historical actuality of *right now*.

Brown uses a three-tiered system of geographic and historical signifiers to create the effect of historical realism. The first word of the novel, immediately preceding the prologue, is "FACT." And it is the foundation of facts, or at least the appearance of facts, upon which Brown builds the first tier of his realist edifice. There is nothing unusual or insidious about this; this has been common novelistic practice since the emergence of literary realism in America in the nineteenth century.[5] Brown is careful to inject into his opening pages a surfeit of tangible objects and places, things that actually exist in the world: the Opus Dei building on "Lexington Avenue in New York City" (1); "Harvard University" (7); the "Pavillon Dauphine" in Paris (8); "*Boston Magazine*" (9); and the "Direction Centrale Police Judiciaire" (10). The presence of these material geographic signifiers serves as a narrative bridge for readers into the imaginative world of the novel. Those objects provide a reassurance that the fictive story world is—as Brown claims on the first page of the novel—indeed intertwined with the material reality of the nonstory, or real, world. The presence of those details creates a link between fictional and historical narratives both inside and outside the novel, providing an assurance that *The Da Vinci Code* is, as Hayden White suggests about imaginative narratives, no "less 'true' for being imaginary" (57). By including tangible items that exist in contemporary historical reality, Brown works to confirm the essential realism of his fiction.

The second tier of Brown's realist aesthetic involves what I call proprietary realism. This approach achieves the sheen of realism through specificity. Brown's narrator, in this narrative scheme, is privy to the same level of details for any given object as the proprietor of that object. Unlike the first tier, the information in this tier is often not easily verifiable. But because the first tier has already established the narrator's general reliability, the second tier confirms it. For example, Langdon knows that the Louvre pyramid "had been constructed of exactly 666 panes of glass" (21). Or that there are "65,300 pieces of art" in the museum (18). The fact that neither of these things is empirically true is irrelevant.[6] Their very specificity bespeaks accuracy, and so the reader, already having cognitively verified the essential realism of the fiction in the first tier—or perhaps literally verified it, by finding the Pavillon Dauphine on a map, or buying an issue of *Boston* magazine—further confirms for him- or herself the sense of being-in-history that is put into narrative by *The Da Vinci Code*.

In the third tier of Brown's system of historical and geographic signifiers, the narrative discourse shifts almost completely from realist-historicist to imaginative-conjectural. This shift, though, is near imperceptible, because it draws on the narrative authority established in the first and second tiers to imaginatively reassemble historical actuality. This is best illustrated by the revelatory climax of the book, in which protagonist Sophie Neveu is informed of the secret, hidden history of Christianity and Mary Magdalene's "marriage to Jesus Christ" (244).

"It's a matter of historical record," Teabing said, "and Da Vinci was certainly aware of that fact. *The Last Supper* practically shouts at the viewer that Jesus and Magdalene were a pair." [Here Teabing identifies the figure traditionally to the left of Jesus, conventionally identified as the apostle John, as Mary Magdalene.] "Notice that Jesus and Magdalene are clothed as mirror images of one another." Teabing pointed to the two individuals in the center of the fresco. . . . "Venturing into the more bizarre," Teabing said, "note that Jesus and His bride appear to be joined at the hip and are leaning away from one another as if to create this clearly delineated negative space between them." Even before Teabing traced the contour for her, Sophie saw it— the indisputable V shape at the focal point of the painting. It was the same symbol Langdon had drawn earlier for the Grail, the chalice, and the female womb. (244)

Here, Brown fuses fanciful hermeneutics with history. Symbols are not, for Brown and his characters, complex, multivalent things, subject to the vagaries of interpretation and the historical moment. Instead, they are singular, static entities. They mean *one* thing. In this tier, Brown takes things that exist in history and, through a singular and hermeneutically uncomplicated symbol, reassembles them into imaginative narrative.

Brown conjoins disparate, nonimaginative historical phenomena to create symbolic, imaginative associations unsupported by historical data. This is somewhat akin to the phenomenon of pareidolia, in which random data are perceived as possessing coherence and significance. One might, for instance, "find" an image of Richard Nixon in a tortilla. The fact that Richard Nixon was historically real and the tortilla is historically real does not necessarily mean that there is a historically real explanation for the apparent presence of Nixon in the tortilla. Or, to put it more directly: Leonardo was a historical being. The tempera "The Last Supper" was painted at some point in history. Jesus and Mary Magdalene were beings who existed in history. The materiality of these people and objects all hew to accepted norms of historical veracity—they were *real*. But simply because Leonardo, the tempera, and the figures in the painting all possess a historical actuality does not mean that the V shape made by those figures necessarily translates into a particular symbol that *itself* possesses a historical actuality. And that imagined symbol, in turn, does not necessarily reflect a secret historical actuality that has been suppressed for hundreds of years.

Of course it doesn't. But why would anyone think it would? How does Brown's literary realism become linked to his claims to historicity in the public imagination, and, more significantly, how does the public respond to that model of history? The answer to those questions in part involves the notion of coherency in historical narrative. Allan Megill writes that a century ago,

> the basis for history's coherence was held to lie in the possibility of eventually constructing a single, authoritative narrative of human history. When this hope failed, the basis for coherence was held to reside in a shared method. Among [certain historians . . .] the commitment was not to a distinctive method of history but rather to an investigative process . . . that would yield authoritative, although possibly provisional knowledge. What is striking now is the degree to which [. . . this] version of coherence has become passé. (202)

The historiographic model of *The Da Vinci Code* is, in brief, the reemergence of this narratological view of historical coherence: the allure of a single and "authoritative narrative of human history." The vision of historical actuality offered by Brown is one in which all events and narratives are part of a singular and satisfying whole. Jesus, Leonardo, and "The Last Supper" are not discrete historical entities, but rather integral parts of a single, coherent historical narrative.

The authority of history and the virtual public sphere

There is comfort in the coherency of a historical master narrative. And the widespread longing for this sort of comfort is revealed not only in the text of *The Da Vinci Code* itself, but also in online forums and bulletin boards, in public-generated texts such as

Amazon.com's "Customer Reviews" that stand as examples of a virtual global public sphere.

In *The Structural Transformation of the Public Sphere*, philosopher Jürgen Habermas charts the emergence of this sphere in eighteenth-century Europe, based in part on historical accounts of public conversations occurring in English coffeehouses. In Habermas's view, the bourgeois public sphere was formed when private individuals drew together and, through rational debate, formed a "consensus about what was practically necessary in the interest of all" (83). The press, for Habermas, was crucial to the production of public identity. Beginning with the daily political journals appearing in the middle of the seventeenth century, public information was dependent on private correspondence for its material. But by the first half of the eighteenth century, "in the guise of the so-called learned article, critical reasoning made its way into the daily press" (25). The press, he suggests, not only provides a discursive framework that structures the public, it also creates the critical reasoning skills that allow for public opinion. As a result, the popular press is foundationally connected with the emergence of the public sphere.

In its traditional role, the press acts as a mediator between the state and the public. One of the by-products of the pervasiveness of the internet, though, is that it has diffused some of the conventional responsibilities and functions of journalism. New digital media—forms of so-called citizen journalism such as blogs; virtual meetinghouses like online discussion forums; or "wikis," where knowledge is produced democratically—have offered opportunities for reconceptualizing the public sphere, recapturing some of the immediacy and vitality of the eighteenth-century coffeehouse. Constituents of any given micropublic can come together directly, without the impediments of geographic or national boundaries, to form a new, macro-level community: a global, virtual public sphere.

The public that has revealed itself though discussions of *The Da Vinci Code* is one that is obsessed with historical narrative. Perhaps more to the point, it is a public obsessed with the existence and the veracity of a singular narrative historical edifice. In virtual public spaces such as Amazon.com's Customer Reviews, the public is able to debate the degree to which history and fiction are intertwined narrative discourses, all the while upholding *The Da Vinci Code* as the text uniting those discourses in the public imagination.

As of this writing, *The Da Vinci Code* has garnered over 4,000 individual reviews at Amazon.com, from readers around the globe.[7] Predictably, the tenor of the reviews is wide-ranging. There are attempts to situate Brown within a contemporary, popular literary canon by comparing him—unfavorably—to Umberto Eco or Arturo Pérez-Reverte. There are also numerous attempts to correct, or at least counterbalance, the novel's ideas about Biblical historicity with claims of divine infallibility or personal revelation (User "E. Hughes," for example, dismisses the text as "historically a joke" because "[i]n a period of 9 months Jesus Christ revealed Himself to me in a variety of ways, both natural and supernatural"). More notably, many of the reviewers cite one another, creating a sort of lay scholarship of the novel.[8] The reviews, then, serve as a site of critical public debate centered on a popular text. The fact that the novel seems to have created a virtual public sphere, inviting deliberative analysis from users around the globe, has clearly influenced, if not outright produced, its bestseller status.

Within this virtual community of readers and lay critics, much of the discussion of the novel tends to indulge the assumption that any particular knowledge system is coherent and monolithic, and to debunk one part of the system is to destroy the entire edifice. More to the point, the authority of the singular historical master narrative is most often the subject of debate in this virtual public sphere. *The Da Vinci Code*, for these readers, is an assault on the solidity and surety of history itself, and to dismantle one mechanism of Brown's text is, within the logic of these reviews, to restore the coherency of the historical master narrative.

For example, "J. Creamer," from Perpignan, France, argues that the text is "anything but" history; it is, instead, a "slur against Catholicism." For this assertion, the author offers the seemingly unrelated evidence that "[h]aving lived in Paris, I can vouch that the [geographical] descriptions of that city bear no relation to reality." Another anonymous reviewer dismisses Brown's claims to history as mere "heresies and conspiracies" by arguing that "it's not physically possible to drive into the Tuileries Gardens from the direction the hero, Langdon, did in Chapter 4," because the gardens are "ringed by a twelve-foot wall on that side." While criticisms such as these are logically suspect—after all, geographical accuracy would seem to have little bearing on the veracity of Brown's historical claims—they do suggest quite a bit about how the public *perceives* history to be produced.

For many reviewers, time and space are conflated. Readers refute the novel's geography (an element from the first tier of the novel's realist aesthetic), in their attempts to refute the novel's imagined history (in the third tier of Brown's aesthetic). Anonymous user "A Customer" argues that Brown's "credibility" as an "historian" is marred by his geographic errors: "the Louvre," he notes, "is east of the Tuileries, not 'west' as Brown has it." Along similar lines, "Sam Kay" makes a telling slip in his confusion of Brown and Langdon: "[f]or all of Dan Brown's 'remarkable research and detail' I was lost at Chapter 3 when he [i.e., Langdon] 'skimmed south past the Opera House and entered the Place Vendome' on his way to the Louvre." Furthermore, Brown's imagined history is "spoiled," Kay writes, by the novel's geographic departures from historical actuality: "The last time I looked, the Hotel Ritz was in the Place Vendome and the Opera House was several blocks north in the wrong direction from the Louvre." The implied historical narrative here is one that is singular and cohesive. Otherwise, these are two separate and nonoverlapping issues: Brown's "credibility" as an imaginative "historian" in matters Biblical should be distinct from his credibility as a cartographer. Yet for these readers, the production of history is a distinctly coherent enterprise, one inseparable from geographic actuality or religious truth.

This tendency appears time and again. Reader "BigJake" dismisses the novel's narrative as a "quasi-religious chase," in part because "the author [writes that] Charles and Diana [got] married at Westminster Abbey," when in fact, "[t]hey got married at St. Paul's." "Liloo," from Paris, France, rejects the novel's "theories about the Holy Grail" as "singularly lack[ing] research." For this reader, too, it seems that Brown's Grail narrative is a historical failure *because of* its geographic failures:

> [Y]ou cannot hope to go to Lille from Gare Saint-Lazare [as the protagonists do in Chapter 35]; you would have to leave from Gare du Nord. [. . . In addition, to] go from Tuileries to the American Embassy, you would not need to go up rue des Champs Elysees, since the embassy is exactly at the beginning of that street.

For Liloo, the novel suffers in its claims to historicity as a result of its flaws in representing geographic actuality: "If that is all the extent of his research on Paris, I refuse to believe he has done serious work on the other aspects of the book." Given all this, it is important to underscore that the tendency to conflate historical actuality with geographic actuality is fundamentally epistemological. It does not reflect a category error, but rather a particular ideology about coherency and the historical narrative.

That is to say, common to all these critiques of Brown's novel is an implicit worldview with two key tenets. The first concerns the firm distinction between "real" and "imaginary" events, and the second concerns the coherency and authority of history. This ideology holds that history is a single, coherent narrative that concerns itself solely with "real" events. Because of this, to critique or disprove any one part of this narrative is necessarily to imperil the authority of the narrative as a whole. This, in sum, is why Brown's novel is perceived as a social or political threat in so many quarters, as well as why some readers felt they could combat that threat by disproving the coherency of Brown's (imaginary) historical narrative in a global public forum.

Bestselling history

The gap between academic historiography and public perceptions of that historiography is apparently a wide one. Though academic historians long ago abandoned the pretense of discovering a single, authoritative historical master narrative, the lay public has not relinquished that romantic view of history. Because the debate over *The Da Vinci Code* has concerned not only literary quality and Christianity, but also the production of history itself, that debate has revealed a deep and persistent alienation among vast swaths of the public. The desire for the comfort and security of a historical master narrative—and not a thousand wisps of disconnected information masquerading as small, fragmented histories—is, I think, one rooted in a certain postmodern melancholy. As user "Brown" writes in his Amazon.com review of *The Da Vinci Code*, "[w]orld history is being blurred and revised and erased. With it goes our hopes of finding real solutions for our current problems." By "world history," the author clearly means a single, coherent historical narrative, one grandly detached from any postmodern slippage between "real" and "imaginary" events. And the subversive work of "blurr[ing]" and "revis[ing]" is implied to be the fault of Brown and his novel. But the indignation at Brown's imaginary history masks a real sadness over the loss of historical certainty. Seen in this light, *The Da Vinci Code* is the locus of a global public sphere, a space where persons can come together, offer narratives of historical coherency and, in so doing, mourn the loss of the authority of a historical master narrative.

Because of its bestseller status and its claims to historical truth, Dan Brown's novel has become a public document that tells us much about the status of historical narrative in the age of globalization. The user-generated criticisms of Brown's novel reveal a longing for a historical narrative that is singular, cohesive, and uncontested. But the text itself reveals that historical cohesion to be impossible. Due in part to Brown's three-tiered realist aesthetic, one cannot easily equate the fictional with "the imaginary" and the historical with "the real" in *The Da Vinci Code*. Indeed, to the apparent dismay of many readers, the novel reveals the fictional and the historical to be interrelated narrative discourses. Because it claims to weave a complex blanket of fictive and historical narrative threads, *The Da Vinci Code* reveals to a global public the degree to which history is always contested and constructed. Yet in so doing, it also encourages the reader to enter into an active dialogue not only with the text, but also with a broader public. By participating in this virtual public sphere, and debating the nature and coherency of narratives fictional and historical, the reader ultimately imagines him- or herself as an agent of a new postnational history.

Acknowledgment

A version of this chapter originally appeared in *The Journal of Popular Culture* 44.5 (2011): 1085–101. The editors are grateful to Wiley-Blackwell for permission to republish.

Bibliography

Baigent, Michael, Richard Leigh, and Henry Lincoln. *Holy Blood, Holy Grail*. New York: Dell, 1982.

Bell, Michael Davitt. *The Problem of American Realism: Studies in the Cultural History of a Literary Idea*. Chicago: University of Chicago Press, 1993.

Bock, Darrell L. *Breaking The Da Vinci Code*. Nashville, TN: Thomas Nelson, 2004.

Brown, Dan. *The Da Vinci Code*. New York: Doubleday, 2003.

Ehrman, Bart D. *Truth and Fiction in* The Da Vinci Code*: A Historian Reveals What We Really Know about Jesus, Mary Magdalene, and Constantine*. New York: Oxford University Press, 2004.

Fish, Stanley. *Is There a Text in This Class? The Authority of Interpretive Communities*. Cambridge: Harvard University Press, 1982.

Habermas, Jürgen. *The Structural Transformation of the Public Sphere: An Inquiry into a Category of Bourgeois Society*. 1961. Trans. Thomas Burger. Cambridge: MIT Press, 1991.

"Interview with Dan Brown." *Good Morning America*. ABC. 3 Nov. 2003. <http://www.danbrown.com/media/multimedia/final/smaller/gma_cbds.html>.

"Interview with Dan Brown." *Today*. NBC. 9 Jun. 2003. <http://www.danbrown.com/media/multimedia/final/larger/today_show2.mov>.

Kaplan, Amy. *The Social Construction of American Realism*. University of Chicago Press, 1988.

Louvre.fr. 2008. 4 Apr. 2008 <http://www.louvre.fr>.

Megill, Allan. *Historical Knowledge, Historical Error: A Contemporary Guide to Practice*. Chicago: University of Chicago Press, 2007.

Miller, Laura J. "The Best-Seller List as Marketing Tool and Historical Fiction." *Book History* 3 (2000): 286–304.

Morris, Edmund. *Dutch: A Memoir of Ronald Reagan*. New York: Random House, 1999.

Newman, Sharan. *The Real History Behind* The Da Vinci Code. New York: Berkley Publishing, 2005.

Ohmann, Richard. *Selling Culture: Magazines, Markets, and Class at the Turn of the Century*. London: Verso, 1996.

Olson, Carl E. and Sandra Miesel. *The Da Vinci Hoax: Exposing the Errors in* The Da Vinci Code. San Francisco, CA: Ignatius Press, 2004.

Orvell, Miles. *The Real Thing: Imitation and Authenticity in American Culture, 1880–1940*. Chapel Hill: University of North Carolina Press, 1989.

Partner, Nancy F. "Historicity in an Age of Reality-Fictions." *A New Philosophy of History*. Ed. Frank Ankersmit and Hans Kellner. Chicago: University of Chicago Press, 1995: 21–39.

Price, Robert M. *The Da Vinci Fraud: Why the Truth Is Stranger Than Fiction*. Amherst, NY: Prometheus, 2005.

White, Hayden. *The Content of the Form: Narrative Discourse and Historical Representation*. Baltimore, MD: The Johns Hopkins University Press, 1987.

Williams, Daniel. "Top Italian Cardinal Is Out to Break 'Code.'" *The Washington Post*. 17 March 2005: C01.

Winsor, Justin. "The Perils of Historical Narrative." *The Atlantic Monthly*. 66.395 (1890): 289–97.

Notes

1 The quotations from Bertone are transcribed as they originally appeared in Williams C01.

2 As Laura J. Miller notes, "the best-seller list is actively participating in the doings of the book world rather than just passively recording it" (289).

3 Take, as an example of the novel's global spectacularization, this brief sampling of books from the international *Da Vinci Code* industry: *Code Da Vinci: l'enquête*, by Marie-France Etchegoin and Frédéric Lenoir, *Le Da Vinci Code expliqué à ses lecteurs*, by Bernard Sesboüé, *Das Sakrileg und die Heiligen Frauen: Die Wahrheit über den Da Vinci-Code*, by Walter Jörg Langbein, and *Las Claves del Código Da Vinci: La estirpe secreta de Jesús y otros misterios*, by Lorenzo Fernández Bueno and Mariano Fernández Urresti.

4 As Bart D. Ehrman points out, the scholarly consensus is that Jesus was *not* married. He writes that "in *none* of our early Christian sources is there any reference to Jesus' marriage or his wife" (153). While I defer to the relevant scholarship, I would point out that an absence of evidence *for* marriage is not precisely the same thing as evidence of being *un*married. To put it another way of saying that imaginative speculation, even if educated imaginative speculation, is necessary in historiography.

5 Of course, the idea that particular novels are able to claim historical factuality predates the nineteenth-century emergence of literary realism. Susanna Rowson's late-eighteenth-century novel *Charlotte Temple*, for instance, was subtitled "A Tale of Truth," and Hannah Webster Foster's 1797 novel *The Coquette* was subtitled "The History of Eliza Wharton . . . Founded on Fact." For more on realism and the novel, see Orvell 193–137, Bell, and Kaplan.

6 According to the museum's own website, there are actually 673 panes of glass and 35,000 works of art, not 666 and 65,300.

7 Although the "Customer Reviews" section features comments from a global readership, note that I confine my analysis to the US American Amazon.com, and do not take account of the text's (ample, to judge from the volume of user reviews) popularity at Amazon.com's international sites in Austria, Canada, France, Germany, China, Japan, England, and Hispanophone countries like Spain and Mexico.

8   User "Parity" from Canada, along with at least three other users, cites
    an anonymous user from Evergreen, CO as writing a particularly
    influential review. Similarly, "Eric W. Hulbert," from New York, cites
    the work of "Maria Russo," from Italy, whose critique of one of the
    novel's many historical fallacies observes that Brown seems to think
    Constantine spoke English.

16

Contributor biographies

Editors

Sarah Churchwell

Sarah Churchwell is Professor of American literature and Public Understanding of the Humanities at the University of East Anglia. She is the author of *The Many Lives of Marilyn Monroe* (Granta: 2004 [UK]; Henry Holt: 2005 [US]). She has also published scholarly articles, book chapters, and introductions on subjects including Sylvia Plath and Ted Hughes, F. Scott Fitzgerald and Ernest Hemingway, Anita Loos's *Gentlemen Prefer Blondes*, Janis Joplin and biography, and the short fiction of Scott Fitzgerald and of Katherine Anne Porter. She writes regularly for newspapers and magazines including the *Guardian*, the *Independent*, the *TLS*, the *Times*, the *Telegraph*, the *New Statesman*, and the *New York Times Book Review*, and frequently appears on television and radio. Her new book, *Careless People: The Great Gatsby and the Undoing of F. Scott Fitzgerald*, will be published by Virago (UK) and Penguin (US) in early 2013.

Thomas Ruys Smith

Thomas Ruys Smith is Senior Lecturer in American Literature and Culture in the School of American Studies at the University of East Anglia. He is the author of *Southern Queen: New Orleans in the Nineteenth Century* (Continuum, 2011), *River of Dreams: Imagining the Mississippi Before Mark Twain* (Louisiana State University Press,

2007) and the editor of *Blacklegs, Card Sharps and Confidence Men: Nineteenth-Century Mississippi River Gambling Stories* (Louisiana State University Press, 2010). He is currently at work on an exploration of Mark Twain's relationship with the Mississippi River.

Contributors

Sarah Garland

Sarah Garland is a lecturer in American literature and culture at the University of East Anglia with a background as an interdisciplinary scholar of literature, film, and visual studies. Her work concerns intersections between style, form, and literary aesthetics and she has published on twentieth-century literature and the baroque, on aestheticism, modernism, and the apocalyptic, and on the language of food writing. Her research interests include transatlantic modernism and postmodernism; avant-garde style, and the role of the reader; taste, consumption, and the material; gender, sexuality, and writing; canonical and noncanonical American literature of the 1920s and the 1930s (particularly expatriate writing); and American visual cultures. She is currently working on a book-length critical study of Henry Miller's novels and a monograph on the function of excess in American experimental prose.

Gideon Mailer

Gideon Mailer is a Title A fellow at St John's College, University of Cambridge. He lectures and supervises in American and Atlantic history. His research focuses on the literary, social, intellectual, constitutional, and religious history of America from 1600 to 1865. He has been interested in the contested role of the enlightenment and religious reasoning of the British Atlantic world, and in early-national America. He has published several journal articles on this matter, including: "Anglo-Scottish union and John Witherspoon's American Revolution," *William & Mary Quarterly* 67.4 (October 2010), and "Nehemias (Scotus) Americanus: Enlightenment and Religion between Scotland and America," *Historical Journal* 54.2 (February 2011). Other contributions to books and edited collections include: "The ambiguous legacy of American civil rights theology, 1776 to 2007" in Charles McKinney (ed.), *Looking Back: Legacies and Lessons From the Civil Rights Movement*, (forthcoming), "Seduced by the self: moral philosophy, and evangelicalism" (with K. Collis) in Tita Chico and Toni Bowers (eds.), Atlantic Worlds in the Long Eighteenth Century *Seduction and Sentiment* (Palgrave Press, 2012), "Europe, the American Crisis, and Scottish Evangelicalism: the Primacy of Foreign Policy in the Kirk?" in William Mulligan (ed.), *The Primacy of Foreign Policy in British History*, (Palgrave Macmillan Press, 2010), "Daily life and the family routine in colonial America," in Rodney Carlisle (ed.), *Daily Life in America: the Colonial and Revolutionary Era*, (Golson Books: 2008); "Syllogism in the Declaration of Independence," in Geoff Golsen (ed.), *July 4 1776: One Day in History* (HarperCollins and Smithsonian Books, 2006).

Rachel Ihara

Rachel Ihara is Assistant Professor of English at Kingsborough Community College, CUNY, in Brooklyn, NY. Recent publications include "'Rather Rude Jolts': Henry James, Serial Publication, and the Art of Fiction," in the *Henry James Review* (2010); "'The Stimulus of Books and Tales': Pauline Hopkins's Serial Novels for the *Colored American Magazine*," in *Transnationalism and American Serial Fiction*, edited by Patricia Okker (2011); and (with Jaime Cleland) "Ethnic Authorship and the Autobiographical Act: Zitkala-Ša, Sui Sin Far, and the Crafting of Authorial Identity," in *Selves in* Dialog, edited by Bego Simal (2011).

William Gleason

William Gleason is Professor of English at Princeton University, where he also teaches in the Program in American Studies and is Associate Faculty in the Center for African American Studies. He is the author of *The Leisure Ethic: Work and Play in American Literature, 1840–1940* (Stanford University Press, 1999), *Sites Unseen: Architecture, Race, and American Literature* (New York University Press, 2011), as well as essays on such writers as Henry David Thoreau, Frederick Douglass, Charles Chesnutt, Edgar Rice Burroughs, and Edith Wharton.

Hsuan L. Hsu

Hsuan L. Hsu is associate professor of English at the University of California, Davis. His publications include *Geography and the Production of Space in Nineteenth-Century American Literature* (Cambridge, 2010), an edited special forum of the *Journal of Transnational American Studies* entitled *Circa 1898* (forthcoming), an edition of Sui Sin Far/Edith Eaton's *Mrs. Spring Fragrance* (Broadview, forthcoming), and articles in *American Literature*, *American Literary History*, *Camera Obscura*, and other journals.

James Russell

James Russell is Senior Lecturer in Film Studies at De Montfort University. He specializes in the history of popular films and popular culture more generally in the United States, and is the author of *The Historical Epic and Contemporary Hollywood* (2007).

J. Michelle Coghlan

J. Michelle Coghlan holds a postdoctoral lectureship at the Princeton Writing Program, where she teaches courses on cityscapes in American literature and culture. Her current project, *Revolution's Afterlife*, recovers the Paris Commune's spectacular second life in nineteenth-century American literary, visual, and performance culture. Recent essays have appeared or are forthcoming in *Arizona Quarterly* and the *Henry James Review*.

Grace Lees-Maffei

Dr Grace Lees-Maffei is Reader in Design History at the University of Hertfordshire where she coordinates the TVAD Research Group, working on relationships between text, narrative, and image. She is Managing Editor of the *Journal of Design History* (OUP) and Advisory Board member for the *Poster* (Intellect). Her research centers upon design historiography, design historical methodology, and the mediation of design through channels including domestic advice literature, corporate literature, and advertising. Publications include the edited book *Writing Design: Words and Objects* (Berg, 2011), and *The Design History Reader* coedited with Rebecca Houze (Berg, 2010), chapters in *Performance, Fashion and the Modern Interior* and *Autopia*, and articles in *Modern Italy*, *Women's History Review* and the *Journal of Design History*. Lees-Maffei was an Editor of the *Journal of Design History* (2002–8) and an executive committee member of the Design History Society (1998–2002).

Ardis Cameron

Ardis Cameron is the Director and a Professor of American and New England Studies University of Southern Maine (Ph.D., Boston College). She was named a Fellow by the John Simon Guggenheim Memorial Fellowships in 2002 and received a National Endowment for the Humanities Senior Research Fellowship in 2001. Both were for her project "Tales of Peyton Place: The Biography of a Big Book." She is the author of *Radicals of the Worst Sort: The Laboring Women of Lawrence Massachusetts, 1880–1912* (University of Illinois Press, 1994) and *Looking For America: The Visual Production of People and Nation* (Blackwell Publications, 2004). Professor Cameron is also the author of numerous articles about women, cultural politics, and working class history.

Evan Brier

Evan Brier teaches English at University of Minnesota Duluth. He is the author of *A Novel Marketplace: Mass Culture, the Book Trade, and Postwar American Fiction* (University of Pennsylvania Press, 2010), and he has published articles on American fiction in *Women's Studies Quarterly*, *PMLA*, and *Lit: Literature Interpretation Theory*.

Georgiana Banita

Georgiana Banita is Assistant Professor of Literature and Media Studies at the University of Bamberg in Germany, currently on leave as Postdoctoral Fellow at the United States Studies Centre, University of Sydney. Her book manuscript *Narrative, Ethics, and Post-9/11 Literary Culture*, under contract with University of Nebraska Press, proposes an ethical approach to post-9/11 literature, linking narrative ethics with literary portrayals of racial profiling, psychoanalysis, and globalization. She is now at work on a cultural history of the American oil industry. Her work has appeared or is forthcoming in *Textual Practice*, *LIT: Literature Interpretation Theory*, *Biography: An Interdisciplinary Quarterly*, *Critique: Studies in Contemporary Fiction*, *Parallax*, and *Peace Review: A Journal of Social Justice*, in addition to chapters for several edited volumes.

Stephen J. Mexal

Stephen J. Mexal is Assistant Professor of English, Comparative Literature, and Linguistics at California State University, Fullerton. He has been published in *The Chronicle Review*, *The Journal of Popular Culture*, *MELUS*, *Studies in the Novel*, *English Language Notes*, the anthologies *Eco-Man: New Perspectives on Masculinity and Nature* and *The Philosophy of the Western*. His book, *Reading for Liberalism: The Overland Monthly and the Writing of the Modern American West*, is forthcoming from the University of Nebraska Press.

INDEX